A BALTIC ODYSSEY:
WAR AND SURVIVAL

A Baltic Odyssey

War and Survival

Martha von Rosen
Jürgen von Rosen

Edited by Elvi Whittaker

University of Calgary Press

© 1995 Elvi Whittaker. All rights reserved.

Canadian Cataloguing in Publication Data

Von Rosen Jürgen, 1907-1954.
A Baltic odyssey

   Includes bibliographical references and index.
   ISBN 1-895176-24-7

   1. Von Rosen, Jürgen, 1907-1954. 2.Von Rosen, Martha, 1904-
3. World War, 1939-1945—Personal narratives, German.
4. Immigrants—Canada—Biography. I. Von Rosen, Martha, 1904-
II. Whittaker, Elvi W. III. Title.
D811.5.V66 1995   940.54'8243   C95-911162-X

COMMITTED TO THE DEVELOPMENT OF CULTURE AND THE ARTS

Financial support provided in part by the Alberta Foundation for the Arts, the Canada Council, and the Baltic Aid Society of British Columbia.

All rights reserved. No part of this work covered by the copyrights hereon may be reproduced or used in any form or by any means – graphic, electronic or mechanical – without the prior permission of the publisher. Any request for photocopying, recording, taping or reproducing in information storage and retrieval systems of any part of this book shall be directed in writing to the Canadian Reprography Collective, 379 Adelaide Street West, Suite M1, Toronto, Ontario M5V 1S5.

Printed and bound in Canada by DWFriesen.

∞ This book is printed on acid-free paper.

To the memory of Else, friend and daughter

CONTENTS

Preface ix
Introduction by Elvi Whittaker xv

The Reminiscences of Martha von Rosen

1 From Geppertsfeld to the Oder 3
2 From the Oder to the Elbe 25
3 An End to Flight 45
4 Life Under Soviet Occupation 63
5 Marking Time 79
6 New Surprises 91
7 Reconnaissance 103
8 Reunion 113
9 The Last Return 125

The Diary of Jürgen von Rosen

Introduction by Elvi Whittaker 133

1 Bellaria, Camp 14 139
2 From Bellaria to Ile-de-France 193
3 Forced Labour Camps in France 209
4 Ried, Upper Bavaria 247

Life in Canada: The Open World, by Martha von Rosen 271

Editor's Afterword: Some Anthropological Reflections on
Ethnography, War, Ethnicity and Other Matters 281

Index 310

Illustrations

1. Wedding of Jürgen von Rosen and Martha von Kügelgen 4
2. Martha von Rosen with children, 1941 4
3. Ernst and Anna von Kügelgen, Geppertsfeld, 1944 6
4. Geppertsfeld, a birthday celebration, 1944 6
5. Conveyances used on journey 11
6. Certificate with Iron Cross to Jürgen von Rosen 134
7. Baron Jürgen von Rosen, 1942 136
8. Fragment of Jürgen von Rosen's diary 137
9. Chess figures carved by Jürgen von Rosen, 1945 174
10. Game carved by Jürgen von Rosen, 1945 174
11. Three-ton truck used on journey to British Columbia 274
12. Picker's cabin, Okanagan Valley, 1952 276
13. Baltic German exiles in Siberia, 1915 300

Maps

1. Europe (journeys of the von Rosens) 12
2. The flight of Martha von Rosen (Poland-Germany) 13
3. The capture of Jürgen von Rosen (Piave River Valley, Italy) 160
4. The map carried by Jürgen von Rosen on his escape 248
5. The escape from prison (Lothringen-Saar district, France) 249

PREFACE

by

Elvi Whittaker

This book is about two people, a wife and husband, separated by the Second World War. In their struggles to be reunited, they found themselves embarked on two extraordinary journeys. Their individual recountings of these journeys, in all their vivid details, dominate this book. In one sense, the book is about war and survival, in another it is a family love story.

When Martha von Rosen and I first talked about putting the two narratives, hers and her husband's, between the same set of covers, the notion of a book dealing with such an important time in world history from two separate perspectives was a heady idea. For her, it was the culmination of a dream of many years that these precious documents should be made public. That they could actually be published together fulfilled the sense of legacy she attached to them.

How does an anthropologist become involved in such a project? In my case, the von Rosens had been friends for some decades, and I recognized that there was much in their past – and in how they retold it – that would appeal to many audiences – the public at large, other survivors of the war, academics, and students of history and anthropology. While anthropology has long appreciated life history and oral history, it has had little access to the events and cultures about which the von Rosens have written. The knowledge conventionally circulated in English about the Second World War excludes detailed descriptions of the daily life of those we thought of as the enemy, of women and children in war, and of life in forced labour camps run by the Allies. It is the personally experienced, the individually written, script, that makes these particular histories of the war come alive.

For an anthropologist, the writings also present a rare example of the social organization of knowledge. Not only do they provide undeniably authentic accounts of events, but they are unique in their unplanned and parallel recording of the same historical time, written by two people intimately connected to each other, in different geographical locations and under opposing political circumstances. The documents are a forum to display the familiar notion that knowledge comes in both ideological and cultural packages and in parallel and competing versions. The reader is exposed to these rare writings in all their richness. Other perspectives, such as those of history, ethnicity, war, migration and displacement, are too often buried in esoteric writings unfamiliar to many readers, and it is documents such as the von Rosens' that permit entry into these other generalized experiences. By their vividness, they make the discourses of academic specialists come alive. The Afterword to these stories engages some of these other sub-texts.

As the stories reveal much more than could be found in the sterility of conventional histories of the Second World War, they reflect what Walt Whitman is believed to have noted, that *real* wars never get into books. This particular book, therefore, is meant to redress that criticism. These narratives are truly both history itself and anthropology. Such disciplines, in essence, are created by individuals in their daily existence, as much as ever they are at the level of formal, conceptual discourse. The scales of relevance have tipped. It is now clear that those who lived through those times that we later call "events," view them significantly differently than those who construct them formally and from a distance. Each has his or her own agenda. Anthropologists have long conceded that original experiences have claims to truths that cannot be challenged. Thus, they have felt it appropriate to relegate themselves to the position of commentators and writers of critique. This approach was a comfortable allocation of rights and responsibilities in this particular enterprise as well. Many readers will be content with the simple eloquence of the stories as they stand and will create their own private analysis. Others may wish to transform the stories into other packages of knowledge. The Afterword, the privilege I have claimed as editor, is designed to encourage this excursion.

One obvious scenario was to place the narratives in a biographical, familial history frame, which would connect the stories of the von Rosens to those of other journeying ancestors and family members. The titular "Odyssey" suggests classic themes. Indeed, their wanderings do have mythic proportions.

Some decades ago, along with others of my generation, I listened with unwavering interest to the stories told by Martha von Rosen. She told them as the odyssey of her family, people connected by birth and marriage moving through space and time. She narrated tales of war, of lost family, of flight, of refugees, and most of all stories about faith and courage. I became engaged with the wider story of the von Rosen family and with Martha's family, the von Kügelgens. When the book finally became a possibility, I interviewed Martha von Rosen in depth and a rich family history emerged. The reminiscences and diary should not go to press and stand as solitary capsules in time, without the reader also knowing that these writings extended the context of the ongoing odyssey of many ancestors caught, like the von Rosens, in turmoil and survival, migration and statelessness. The oral history that Martha von Rosen told took the listener from Germany and from Sweden to Estonia, which was to become home. From there, her history took them to Russia, to Japan and eventually back to Estonia. The present stories take them elsewhere in Europe and finally to Canada. Behind this particular history is a family and cultural narrative writ large.

Martha von Rosen is a gifted storyteller. In listening, one could not escape the power of the human story itself, its lucidity over other forms in engaging the imagination. Stories have functioned over the ages, after all, to make the world understandable. The themes of the von Rosen stories have universal appeal. Within their denouements and conclusions are fragments of classic stories embedded in our cultural memories as known truths. They carry a moral message about war, survival, ethnicity. They continue to be powerful ethnographies about cultural experiences.

What the von Rosens' writings afford is a detailed exploration of the lives of those we called "the enemy" in the Second World War. Quite recently, our comfortable view of ourselves and the enemy has been shaken by the knowledge that the prisoners of war taken by the Americans, the French and the British led harsh and deprived lives. This was a revelation to those inured by visions of the Allies fighting for universal decency and the moral good. Indeed, the very fact that the Allies actually ran huge camps, filled to overflowing with prisoners of war, was probably surprising enough. The book draws attention to the plight of these "captured enemy soldiers," a category of person whose fate was largely unknown to the English-speaking world. In juxtaposition, Martha von Rosen portrays the plight of an enormous mass of homeless refugees, mostly women, children and the aged, living in temporary shelters and, indeed, often no shelters at all, positioned in undefended isolation before the oncoming Allied offensive. Utterly vulnerable, totally on their own, they seek to avoid capture and death as best they can.

In addition, the reader is afforded a glimpse of the fate of the many categories of persons, created by combatants in the war or by post-war analysts. It is immediately obvious that these are the histories of many immigrants who eventually found their way to Canada. Given the contemporary interest in the politics of identity, there is much to be learned about class and ethnicity. There can be little doubt that the upheavals of the twentieth century contributed to changes in the lives of aristocratic families and ended in a redistribution of territory and privilege. The ethnic designation of Baltic Germans, which the von Rosens recognize as their own, has altered by virtue of enforced migrations, the passing of generations and the post-colonial world generally. Today, in respecting the position and moral prerogatives of indigenous people everywhere, colonization is receding into history. These emerging conditions, now changing the world drastically, add a further poignancy to the von Rosen writings.

Specifically, this volume brings together two disparate discourses – of those who live and recall the events and those who analyze them. To have one without the other is to commit an oversight about the importance of the nature of knowledge and its construction. Each illustrates the other, enters into a natural dialogue with the other and, in so doing, enhances it. To this end, the Afterword asks the reader to consider a kind of stage-craft which transforms the everyday realities of the stories into the abstractions created by other analyses.

It is now half a century since the events of this book occurred. Enemies have become friends and, sometimes, enemies again – such are the ironic paradoxes of history. The book is a testimonial to the immigrant experience – an experience that inevitably separates individuals not only from their roots but also from past historic arrangements. Before the war the paths of the authors and editor, brought together between the covers of this book, would not have crossed. It is unlikely that we would have been acquainted, given the ethnic, linguistic and privileged divisions of pre-Second World War Estonian society. We would have been unequal antagonists in a struggle over land and culture, over nationalism and commitments. Being from different cultural backgrounds, however, did not preoccupy me as did the daunting problem of turning friends into text. It meant subordinating them to analysis, to anthropological conceptualizing and to transformation in an abstract landscape – a difficult process. They have born this objectification with generosity and understanding.

In the multiple tasks that bring a book to print, some assistance was of the irreplaceable kind. I acknowledge the contributions and collegial generosity of Jean Barman, Julie Cruikshank, Bill McKellin and Jean Wilson of the University of British Columbia and Karla Poewe of the University of Calgary. There were also those who made the text readable at various stages of the work. Peter Colenbrander was an important player in the early production of the two narratives and is thanked for lending me support in my efforts to have both manuscripts published as one book. Gerhard von Rosen, in particular, has researched maps, helped trace the authors' complicated movements during the final year of the war, contributed his computer skills, and has been an indispensable member of the production team. The maps were produced by Marilyn Croot. Patricia Kachuk uncomplainingly acted as my research assistant even during the time of her doctoral defence, and Joanne Richardson gave priority to some editing. Neil Eaton is to be acknowledged for help in editing and in giving invaluable suggestions. In its earliest stages, Martha von Rosen produced her text with the important assistance of her mother, Anna von Kügelgen, and her friend Martha von Borch. The earlier versions of the manuscript also benefited from help in translation and typing by Myra von Riedeman and in word processing by Wendy Edelson, Aly Carridan, and Kate Hawthorne. The support of the British Columbia Baltic Aid Society is appreciated. Linda Cameron of the University of Calgary Press adopted the project enthusiastically, recognized it as a manageable affair, and later passed it on to Shirley Onn, the present director of the press. Both are appreciated for their encouragement and their continued support of the book. Production editor John King is thanked for his ongoing careful shepherding of the manuscript.

We, Martha von Rosen and I, dedicate the work to Else von Rosen, her daughter and my good friend of many years, and a major player in the drama that enfolded about fifty years ago. She did not live to see her parents' words become print.

INTRODUCTION

by

Elvi Whittaker

Over fifty years have elapsed since the events depicted in this volume. *A Baltic Odyssey: War and Survival* arrives at a time when the Second World War is departing from the realm of individual experience into the legends and texts by which it will be remembered. What was known first hand has become the imagery, the formal history, the lore and the symbolism by which that period is understood. These transformations will have forgotten their own origins in ordinary everyday human existence.

The origins of this work were two documents in German, one by Jürgen von Rosen, the other by Martha von Rosen. They were unprecedented in the published literature. Focussing on the last year of the Second World War, they were written by a woman and a man, who, in the smoke of conflict and in the endless columns of the moving dispossessed, were seeking each other.

One document is the diary of Baron Jürgen von Rosen, a prisoner of war of the Allies, written to make sense of his seemingly meaningless life. How else can one explain why he wrote under conditions which made such undertaking both difficult and very dangerous? To occupy his mind? To escape boredom? To make something human out of an essentially inhuman situation? To divert his attention from hunger, thievery, and the cries of other prisoners? To try to look at his fate objectively, as a scientist might? To acknowledge that momentous events were occurring and that he was, very intimately, a part of them? To pay witness to history? To distance himself from his own distress and the distress surrounding him? To talk to his wife and family? The original diary was written in secret during a year of imprisonment and uncertainty. Under conditions where pencil and paper were forbidden and unavailable, he had carried on his person the smallest of pencil stubs and, with ingenuity, had acquired various scraps of paper – cardboard, bureaucratic forms, rough grey toilet paper. This coarse stationery, itself a testimonial to a life in a prison camp, became the vehicle for the story in his volume. On these ungainly surfaces, he wrote in the finest of scripts. Somehow, and no one knows just how, he carried the growing bulky document from one prison camp to another and, finally, on his escape. In Bavaria after his liberation, he transcribed the coarse sheets into exercise books. These sheets and transcriptions, humble in appearance, remain as museum artifacts that testify to human ingenuity and determination. Translated into English, they become the second part of this volume.

The other document is written by the woman he seems to be addressing – Baroness Martha von Rosen. The conditions of her existence were markedly different from those of her husband. While he had meaningless time on his hands, she was faced with endless tasks. At first, it was the work of the farm, the care of two young children and two aging parents. Later, it was the resourcefulness required to confront the terrors of war and the planning and cunning needed to orchestrate a complicated flight, an odyssey to safety from a situation forced upon her by the uncaring turn of events in the conflict. Some years after these events, using scratched notes, relying on memory, recruiting the memories of others, she began the reconstruction of her story. Working together and focussing on a shared past, they recalled dates, names and the nuances of events. These vignettes of memory and fragments of notes formed the skeleton of the narrative and ultimately a constructed history, the one that she had not had the time to write in the mid-1940s. Her preoccupation then had been with organizing the flight by which she hoped to escape the advancing military forces which she believed would separate her forever from reunion with her husband, as well as from the world she had known.

Placed together, back to back, however, the two documents are unique. They constitute a female and a male account of events endured by two people, brought together by marriage and separated by war. As separate odysseys, they have an unplanned symmetry. They speak to events in recent European history, not as they have been passed on to us by historians, but as they were actually lived and remembered. They tell parallel stories of a year of inconceivable hardship, 1945 to 1946. In doing so, they also speak for the countless others who will always remain unheard.

For the English-speaking world, the documents are particularly valuable. They do not depict the more familiar record of experiences of Allied fighting forces and their families in various homelands, nor the reminiscences of great generals, Allied or German. Rather, they permit us to understand the experiences of Germans, ostensibly the enemy – a prisoner of war held by the Allies and a woman escaping from the advancing Allied military. While the political circumstances are obviously strange to us, the fear and anxiety are strikingly familiar. The von Rosens, however, were not counted among those Germans commonly seen as the enemy, but rather they were members of a genre of historically migrated and displaced Germans whose plight was little understood by the major powers at the time. While these Germans were acutely aware of their German identity, continued to speak German and marry their own kind, they were born in, and had become affiliated with, other European countries. Reluctantly and ambivalently, they had become incorporated into the war that engulfed their adopted countries. The nature of their fate was made clear many decades later when the conflicts between ethnicity and nationality became better understood. The von Rosens were Baltic Germans and their fate was similar to that of other ethnic communities that find themselves isolated in the land where they live when that land is at war with the country of their ethnic origin.

Martha and Jürgen von Rosen were Germans whose ancestors had settled in the Baltic countries of Estonia, Latvia, and Lithuania. The von Rosen journeys, like the journeys taken by Baltic Germans through the centuries, contribute to the notion of odyssey which frames this book. The forced journeys brought them from Estonia to Poland, to Germany and Italy, and finally to Canada. During this time, they experienced all the horrors of war – dispossession, homelessness, fear, anxiety about family, loss of identity and deprivation. Added to this were the trials of daily existence, food, shelter and safety. In Martha von Rosen's case, the experiences are those of a woman in a war, not of her own making, nor directed towards ends that she would have valued. As mother and daughter, and as the adult in command of a small group of refugees, she symbolizes the particular hardships of those who were on what is often romantically referred to as "the home front." In Jürgen von Rosen's case, the trials lie in deprivation and uncertainty, conditions which became the expected and the everyday.

The notion of a grand odyssey is also central to the whole Baltic German experience. Germans had spread into the Baltic area during the medieval period as crusading Teutonic Knights, with intentions to missionize, and as merchants of the Hanseatic League. For centuries they maintained a political and economic stronghold in the Baltic where they constituted a close-knit and privileged national minority. This privileged land-owning existence remained essentially unchallenged until the Second World War. It began to crumble with the rise of Baltic nationalism, with the threats to aristocracy brought about by the First World War and with the serious political upheavals that came to the Baltic region. In addition, the Bolshevik Revolution and the ascendancy of the Communists did not promise a continuance of the privilege previously enjoyed. Being born in these countries or having citizenship in these countries and calling them home, Baltic Germans inevitably became part of the general fate that befell these regions in war. More specifically, however, their fate was not the same as that of Estonian nationals conquered in war but rather it was a special fate reserved for them as Germans in appropriated countries.

Their situation was especially problematic politically. Both Germany and the Soviet Union had interests in the Baltic. In August 1939, in a move to accommodate each other, these powers signed the Molotov-Ribbentrop Pact that essentially paved the way for the Russians to fulfill their strategic needs by annexing the Baltic states. Before this occurred, however, the German community in the Baltic states was summoned by Hitler to Germany, or so it was believed. The von Rosens were part of this summons, abandoning their farm and possessions and, with Martha von Rosen's parents, embarking for the German mainland. Their journey ended, however, not in Germany where they had hoped to join relatives but rather on a farm confiscated from Polish farmers in central west Poland near Posen. Both the von Rosens had agricultural experience, having worked their own farm, and Jürgen had had training as an agriculturist. Thus they were well-prepared for the work of farm management. Martha's parents, the von Kügelgens settled nearby. Ernst von Kügelgen had been abruptly forced to terminate his position as the medical director of the Estonian psychiatric institute at Seewald.

It was here, two years later, that a long-dreaded event happened. Jürgen von Rosen was drafted, assigned to the anti-aircraft arm of the *Afrika Korps* and stationed in Italy. This placement took advantage of the skills he had learnt in anti-aircraft defence while in the Estonian army in the 1930s. Martha von Rosen soon thereafter arranged for another position in estate management at a location in Geppertsfeld near Jarotschin in western Poland. It is at the Geppertsfeld estate where we find her with her family at the beginning of her story. The previous exodus from Estonia, the displacement from traditional property and employment, from a preferred identity, and the experience of statelessness were quickly to lead to a more serious homelessness. A new threat now awaited them.

Meanwhile the most catastrophic war the world had known had come to what was to be its final year. The struggle that had occupied Europe since 1939 had escalated beyond all expectations. Much of Europe had fallen to the Germans. By the end of 1944, however, two events, which have since been historicized as heralding the beginning of the end of the war, had occurred. The first of these was D-day, June 6, 1944, now widely memorialized and honoured by the Allies for both the boldness of its strategy and the enormity of the human sacrifices made. The second event was the liberation of Paris at the end of August in the same year. These events are iconized as marking the beginning of Allied victories and the ultimate end of the war.

When the von Rosen stories begin at Christmas in 1944, fighting was continuing on the Western Front. The Allies, accompanied by heavy aerial bombardments, were battling in major campaigns in France, Belgium and Germany, as well as in Italy, clinging desperately to ground already won, and taking the offensive to push eastward whenever possible. On the Eastern Front, the Russian armies were moving their own offensive from the Baltic Sea to the Carpathians, pushing ever westward. Byelorussia, Rumania, Bulgaria, Hungary, Czechoslovakia and Poland were falling to the Russians. By September, Warsaw was threatened, and after shattering the German defences, the city was claimed in mid-January of the new year.

On the eve of December 25, 1944, the von Rosen family celebrated a modest Christmas with other Baltic Germans. They had heard little about the state of the war, or the closeness of the conflict in Poland, and what they did know was carried by word of mouth. They were innocent of the details and of the actual proximity of the conflict to their location in Poland. There had been, however, continual and imminent threats during their whole stay in that country. A constant anxiety revolved around the larger issues about the turn of events in the war, about ongoing military strategies, about the nature of manoeuvres undertaken and the meaning of their outcomes. And always, there were rumours. The underlying dread of what the advances on the Eastern Front would mean never left them. It was an unquestioned imperative that they should do their utmost to escape the Russian advance, to flee from any possible incorporation into the Russian sphere of influence. This possibility was far more serious, and potentially more threatening, than the war itself. Being captured forever behind Soviet lines had long been dreaded as the worst of fates. As Jürgen von Rosen was in Italy, it could only mean a possible life-long separation from each other and from the world they knew. Many other unsolved issues dimmed in comparison. How would the war turn out? Who would claim final victory? What would be the outcome for refugees, displaced persons, Baltic Germans? While uncertainty was merciless, there had been a lull in their odyssey since 1939 and several years had passed in relative calm. At this point, we join the von Rosens at Geppertsfeld at their Christmas festivities. Little did they know what was to befall them.

THE REMINISCENCES OF
MARTHA VON ROSEN

✳ 1 ✳

FROM GEPPERTSFELD TO THE ODER

―▶•◀―

It was Christmas Eve 1944 in Geppertsfeld. We all had assembled in an unusually warm, festive living room. It was generously decorated, especially for this occasion, to the point where the linen-covered tables were nearly breaking under the weight of the many offerings. There was a profusion of presents, as everyone in the house had tried to give something, even though hard times prevented extravagance. Although financial circumstances were strained, for these were war-torn times, it was important to create a feeling of happiness during this season of celebration. If it had not been Christmas Eve, we would never had thought of sitting in so spacious a room, as the winter was bitterly cold and there was a desperate shortage of coal.

Mrs. von Stritzky played Christmas carols on the large piano. These were the familiar songs from our childhood. The adorned tree was lit up with a few candles. It was Christmas.

After the prayers were said, the various families scattered to their different corners of the festive room. The largest family was that of Irmgard von Stritzky, which consisted of three grown-ups and three children. Included was the baby, who was seeing her first Christmas candles, and Irmgard's older sister, Freda, with her two, old aunts – the von Horns. Everyone was aware of a sadness as the father of this little group was missing. The news from the front lines was sparse, but at least there was news.

Irmgard's sister-in-law, Benita von Stritzky, with her little daughter Verena, was less fortunate. She knew, all too well, that she could never expect any news of her husband again. He had given his life to this senseless war.

Wedding of Jürgen von Rosen and Martha von Kügelgen in St. Nikolas Church, Tallinn, Estonia, 22 April 1934.

Martha von Rosen with Else and Gerhard in Posen, Poland, 1941.

As ever, Count and Countess von der Borch brought a special brand of *Gemütlichkeit* with them. Gräfchen, as we called her, was my son Gerhard's favourite storyteller. He would sit uncommonly still, listening contentedly whenever she read to him. Aunt Elizabeth and Frau Baumann also belonged to our own family corner, for they were both related to the von Rosens. And lastly, Jan took part in our gift-giving.[1] He had been with us since 1927, sharing joys and pains with us in his position of handyman. "The last loyal servant of the twentieth century," my father liked to call him. Despite his being deaf and dumb, he was still a real handyman, strong and skillful. We had to learn his language, consisting of the few sounds and grunts he made, however, as he could never hope to learn ours. We had invited the Polish manager of the estate, Herr Sczyfter, as well. Although this was a natural thing for us to do, it had to be kept a secret for the safety of all, as personal contact with Polish people was strictly forbidden.

My husband Jürgen (Jörn, as I called him,) was with us, only in spirit, as he had already left for the front in Italy, after a short leave away from the war.

Immediately after New Year, I took my nine-year-old daughter Else to visit very close friends of mine, the von Rosenstiels, who lived on their estate, Lipie, located about a hundred kilometres to the north of us, near the town of Hohensalza. It was like a second home to Else, as she had lived in their house for a year and a half, and had gone to school with their daughter who was the same age. Previously we had been neighbouring land-managers for two and a half years.[2] The trip was awkward, for we had to change trains in Posen. We visited my parents who had been settled here. A wonderful opportunity, as Else was my father's special pet.

---

1 Jan Grünbaum was a former patient of Seewald, the only psychiatric institute in Estonia, which had been headed by Ernst von Kügelgen, Martha von Rosen's father. He was "deaf and mute." Jan presumably had no known name when he arrived at the institute, but was given one when he left Seewald to work on the von Rosen farm. The von Rosens created a system of communication with him.

2 After the *Umsiedlung* (resettlement) from the Baltic states in the fall of 1939, the von Rosen family were resettled on the farm of Buchenbusch in Poland, thereby becoming neighbours of the von Rosenstiels. After von Rosen went to the front in Italy in 1941, Martha von Rosen took her children to Posen (Poznań), to her parents. They lived there between 1942 and 1943. In 1944, she found another country estate to manage, Geppertsfeld, located in the Warthegau area of Poland.

Ernst and Anna von Kügelgen visiting their daughter Martha and her children at Geppertsfeld, Warthegau, Poland. In the background to the left is their grandson Gerhard.

*Martha von Rosen's birthday at Geppertsfeld in 1944.
The coachmen cracked their horsewhips to honour the event
as Martha and others watched from the verandah.
Gerhard is on the right, and Else peeks out of an usptairs window.*

My beloved mother, always prepared for all eventualities, gave me 3,000 marks. "You never know," she said, "keep it!" This foresight saved me later, as I had no chance to go to the bank once I decided to flee.

Also, at this time, we agreed on a meeting place. We did this because I would not be able to pick up my parents in Posen, in case I had to flee. We agreed upon the town of Sprottau, in Silesia, which would be our location for reunification. This would be a perfect place, as the widow of my father's brother lived there.

In Lipie we drank delicious coffee (a rare luxury in these times), and talked with Buja, a name given our hostess by her children. We spoke of the plans we might have to make, in case, on some distant day, we were forced to flee from the Russians.[3] It was a vague possibility, but we were all accustomed to thinking ahead. "Where to?" was the most important question.

"We are going to Gorgast, our property on the Eastern railway line, near Küstrin (Kostezyn), but if the Russians should go there too, then we will flee without a goal, just like you," said Buja.

There we were, perhaps luckier than she was, because, God willing, we would still have an address to go to, that of my sister's home in Munich, Bavaria. Bavaria certainly seemed a safe haven, away from the Russian front. Such matters as transportation, horses, things to wear and supplies to eat, we decided to worry about later. But why worry at all? These eventualities were obviously entirely remote.

And so, after a few wonderful days spent in this manner, I went home alone, and with a light heart, leaving Else with my friends. "*Auf Wiedersehen, Mutti*," she said, proud to be allowed to stay there without me. How could we have foreseen the threat, looming before us – the fact that this had been my last visit to Lipie? I planned to fetch Else after two or three weeks. Everything seemed so safe.

On the 14th of January we celebrated Aunt Elizabeth Baroness von Rosen's eightieth birthday. Her niece, Baroness Lucy von Schilling, came from Posen to join us. Our cook, Stanislawa, baked the traditional *Butterkringel*, a veritable masterpiece in pastry, which surprised and thrilled our

---

3 During December 1944 and the early days of January, the Russians planned a concerted offensive against the Germans, positioning an enormous force along a line leading southerly from Memel, on the Baltic Sea, to eastern Czechoslovakia. This front was driving westward along the main Warsaw-Berlin axis. As of 12 January, however, most of the action was still occurring east of Warsaw.

dear aunt immensely. We chatted of old times and again touched, though almost as an aside, the subject of the future, as well as the terrible question of "what if we should have to flee?" But no, it would never come to that. The German troops were much too strong, and they had held off the Russians near Warsaw since August.

That birthday comprised our last party. Barely five days later we joined the great trek, the mass of people, heading west as fast as possible, seeking refuge from the advancing Russians.

On Tuesday, the 16th of January, I paid a short visit to my parents. My mother did not feel at all well, and this worried me. On the following Saturday she was to go to hospital for an operation. Buja also came for a brief visit, and again we discussed the vital questions:

"What if we had to flee? – When should I pick up Else?" No, there was no apparent danger. We reasoned that Herr von Rosenstiel, as a prominent, knowledgeable man, would be aware of any changes.

Quite reassured in the belief that I had such reliable and well-informed friends, I drove back to Geppertsfeld, deeply engrossed in pondering these questions.

Irmgard von Stritzky's oldest child, who was four years old, had a gastric condition and since the tenth of January had been in the hospital in Jarotschin (Jarocin), a town located about twenty kilometres west of Geppertsfeld. On Wednesday, the 17th, however, the matron telephoned, requesting that we come to fetch the child, as she could keep her there no longer. As Irmgard needed to care for her baby, I went there myself on Thursday. The matron told me in confidence that they had to begin packing immediately, as the whole hospital was secretly being evacuated. All the patients, who could be sent home, were being discharged that day. Then she whispered to me that if I wished to, I could give her a box or a case full of valuables because, as a hospital, they would surely be given plenty of military protection.

"But where will I find my things again?"

"Oh, they will be easy enough to find. Everyone in Germany will be able to tell you where the Jarotschin Hospital is!"

What a hopeless mistake!

At this time, one was allowed to send things to western Germany only by parcel post. However, there was a team of horses, leaving the next morning for Jarotschin to fetch a rare and greatly needed load of coal. I took advantage of this vehicle, sending our trunk with all our silver, some bed linen, and so on, to be combined with the shipments made by the hospital toward the west. As an extra precaution, I had also taken the matron's home address. I laid this on top of the things inside the suitcase, together with the address of my brother's wife Fritzi, who lived at Leitzkau, a town located near the city of Magdeburg.

As early as August, at my mother's insistence, I had sent two big steamer trunks of linen and my husband's clothing with Fritzi, when she left for Leitzkau. She, together with her three little boys and their nurse, had been staying with me in Geppertsfeld. They had left us in August 1944, when Russian troops came too close for her comfort. Her goal was the large Leitzkau estate, which lay on the right hand side of the Elbe River, and belonged to a friend, Baron Münchhausen. At that time, I still firmly believed that it was quite senseless to send things away, and had done so simply because of my mother's earnest pleadings. However now, Leitzkau became my own goal as well.

The estate of Geppertsfeld lay quiet and alone. There were no neighbouring friends, with whom I could discuss the political situation. Furthermore, as we also had been without a radio for quite some time, we were completely cut off from the outside world. In the past, our Polish manager used to receive news broadcasts in Polish from England on my radio. Our German broadcasts were hopelessly vague, though by now we could all guess that something was very wrong indeed. On the evening of Thursday the 18th, the sky in the east glowed red. What could that mean? From our manager we heard that the town of Litzmannstadt (Lódź) was burning.[4] This meant that the Russians had succeeded in crossing the Vistula River, where they had been since August! Now we all started worrying about what would happen next.

The telephone rang that very evening. It was my mother calling from Posen. She had heard from Buja, who had tried in vain to telephone me. She had asked my mother to let me know that her own children would leave on Friday morning (19th) for Gorgast. They would be accompanied by Kohli, the nurse, and Frau von Rosenstiel, senior, the grandmother. They would take Else with

---

[4] As can be expected the version of the war broadcasted by the Germans was for public consumption and obviously different from what was recorded into history. The von Rosens did not realize that the Soviet offensive, having amassed much strength, was at this very moment victoriously crossing the Vistula River. Lódź, called Litzmannstadt by the Germans, located west of Warsaw and about 140 kilometres east of Geppertsfeld, had been reached by the advancing Soviets from the south. Russian forces had also encircled Warsaw. On capturing Poland in 1939, the Germans instituted their own names for Polish cities and towns.

them as there was no longer any possibility of sending her back to us. She had asked me to send clothing by mail, as Else had not enough with her. I still refused to believe that I would have to leave Geppertsfeld. All these stories that we kept hearing were surely just security precautions to prepare us for matters becoming more serious. I found out none too soon that our general situation already had become extremely precarious.

It was Friday the 19th, with loving thoughts, I put together a parcel for my little Else. In it I packed her nicest doll, her coral necklace, along with her favourite books, and took the package to the post office, where, to my surprise, it was accepted. While I was at the post office, I saw the village school teacher, together with some other women, making coffee and distributing it to the refugees. One could see the endless columns of big wagons on the main highway – people were fleeing, and they came from the east. We had simply been living too far away from the main course of traffic to have realized the truth.

Our estate was bordered by the Prosna River, which was, at the same time, the border of eastern Poland. There was no bridge across the river at Geppertsfeld. Everything had looked so peaceful and quiet to us, even pleasant, if it were not for the wintry icy cold. Reflectively, I drove home in my carriage, brooding over our situation at hand. What fate lay ahead of me, of us?

That was the morning of the Friday the 19th of January 1945.[5] A bitterly cold wind blew over the frozen fields. My manager, Herr Sczyfter, with great excitement, came out to meet me, informing me, in secret, that the Polish workers, who had been sent east to dig trenches for the troops, were returning in hordes. Some of those, who had been taken from our farm, were also back. They told of great chaos and disorder in the German army. This was not a mere retreat, but simple flight! I had better get the wagons ready quickly. I thought that my neighbours were surely not thinking of leaving, but I discovered that they had all left that very morning. Even the much-hated SS general had fled with all his flashing badges of bravery and honour, along with his golden *Ritterkreuz*.[6] We too began to get ready.

Our last meal at home was grimly silent. I asked each person to pack one good suitcase and to be ready on time, as we were leaving the next morning. In the stable yard, I picked out the horses and the wagons myself. I

---

5 The Soviet troops, having advanced west past Litzmannstadt (Lódź), were now probably less than fifty kilometres away.

6 A medal given for bravery, the golden version of it being the highest citation.

The journey of the von Rosens, showing various types of conveyances used: open hay wagons, closed coaches (the Buda), and horseback. (Sketch by Dora Arronet.)

found that almost all our horses were sick. Muckel, our little horse from Estonia, was even too ill to come out of his stall. They had all been fed frozen sugar beets. Only too late did I realize the cunning of some of the Polish people. Apparently they wished to inherit the horses after I left.

I chose six team-horses and had my own Trakehner mare saddled.[7] I took plenty of feed, for that would certainly be scarce along the way. However, without a doubt, we would not have to travel for long! Count Borch figured three days. So the blankets, with which I had originally thought to cover the wagons, were left behind. We took the *Buda* (a horse-drawn coach) for the very young and the very old passengers. Arras, my Arabian stallion, had to let his harness-partner pull alone, for his hind foot was swollen to dangerous proportions. It was a colourful collection of horses, sharp-shod at the very last minute, for the roads were frighteningly icy. I had neglected to pick out the harnesses personally, however, believing that the workers would naturally select out the usual sets. Too late I noticed my mistake. It was pitch dark when we left, and only Jan's talents with needle and thread saved us from being stuck with broken harnesses. Old relics and rotten tack

---

7 "Trakehner" refers to a breed of horses that originated in a stud estate near Trakehnen, a village in East Prussia.

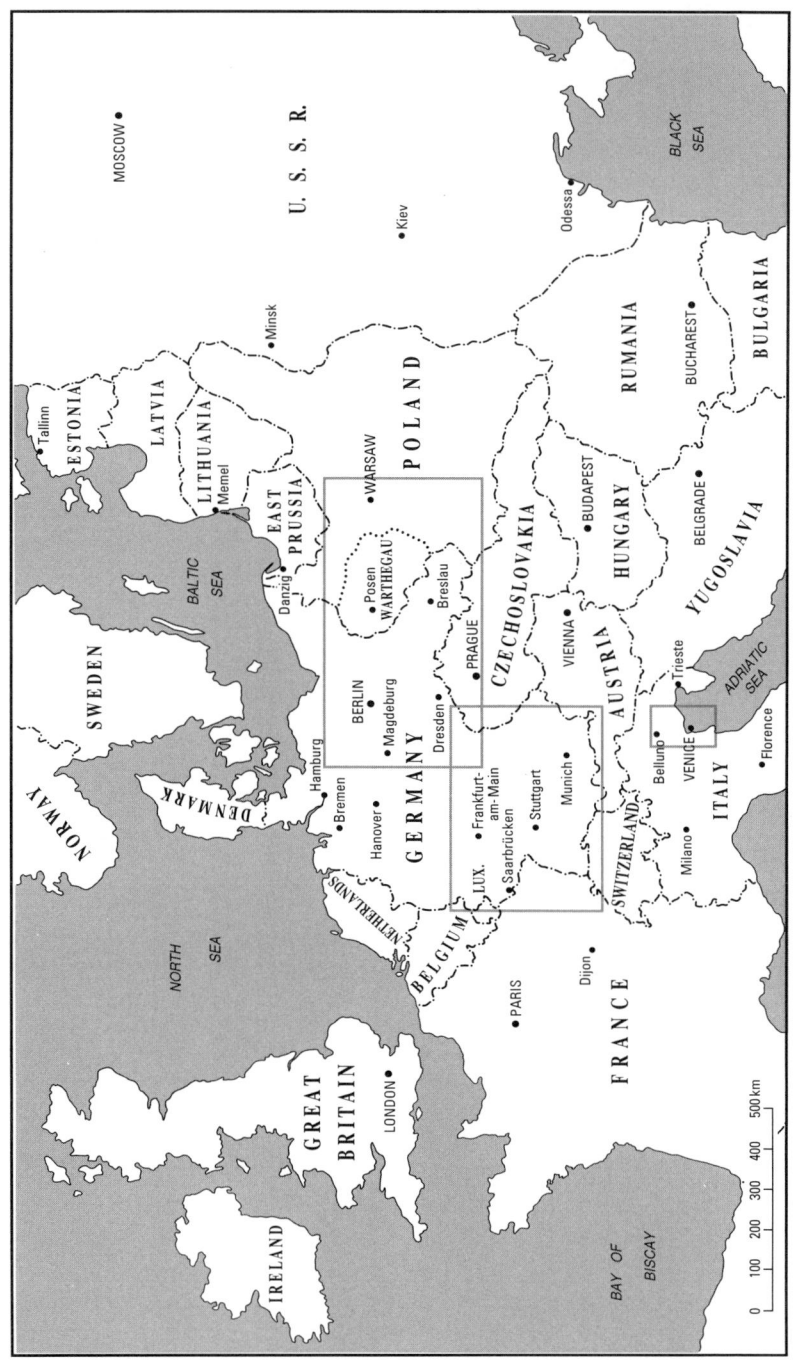

Map 1. Europe (journeys of the von Rosens)

MARTHA VON ROSEN: *From Geppertsfeld to the Oder* 13

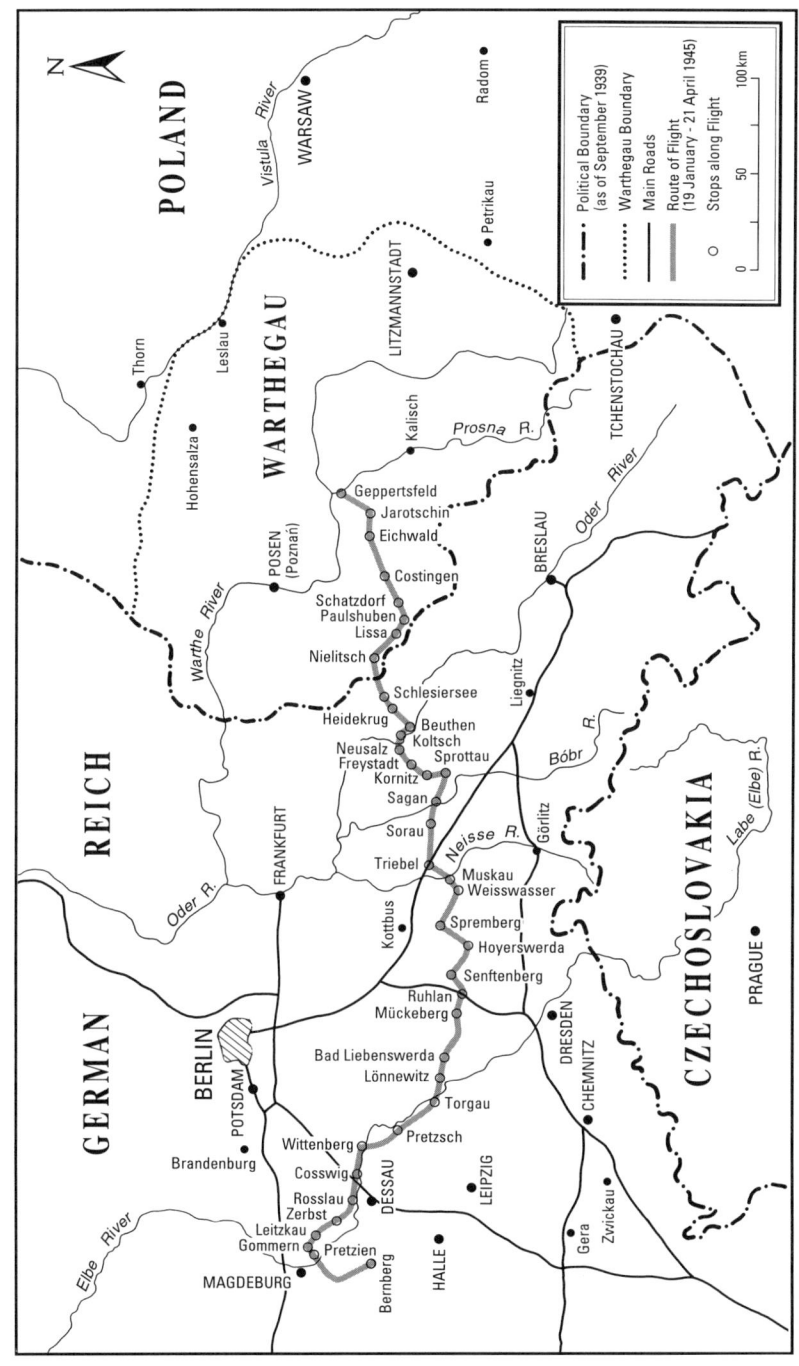

Map 2. *The flight of Martha von Rosen (Poland-Germany)*

had been insidiously ordered for us by our Polish manager. He had helped me a great deal before, but now for his own safety, he had to show that he was not helping German people.

I raced between the stable and the house. It grew darker and the rumours about the approaching Russians became more alarming. No one could provide details of their actual position. It was stated, however, that they were steadily advancing from Ostrowo through Pleschen and Jarotschin to Posen.[8] All who found themselves behind this advancing line, it was said, were completely cut off from the outside world forever. In the house, there was frenzied packing. The plan for "tomorrow sometime" became "tomorrow very early," and then was further amended to "as soon as we can get ready." We all knew that we had to leave right away. Herr Sczyfter warned me, with great sincerity: "I know what awaits all Germans, Baroness, I don't want this to happen to you."

What does one pack when one has a house full of things, each carrying a heartfelt meaning, and one can take only one suitcase? Photographs of grandparents, parents, my husband, and his parents. I weighed Jürgen's letters in my hand – those many long, vivid descriptions. No, that would not work, we had to have some changes of clothes for Gerhard, and myself. And a few pictures from the walls. At least a few, chosen from among so many. It is no use accusing oneself now – it is much too late.

"If only I had … If only I had … If only I had…."

No, it is of no use, for nothing is gained by it. I could waste little time in packing anyway. Like an idiot, I even gave further instructions to my manager about running the farm. I gave him the 1,500 marks remaining in the till, so that he could pay off the hired hands. It was no longer possible for me to visit the bank to get my own money for the trip. But I did have the 3,000 marks my parents had given me in August. "Just in case …" How their foresight had saved me!

Frau Baumann and Aunt Elizabeth packed, displaying great care and intelligence. Count and Countess Borch, with great determination, lit every kerosene lantern they could find. We should at least enjoy all the bright

---

8   The highway, heading northwest from Ostrowo (Ostrów) through Pleschen (Pleszew) and Jarotschin (Jarocin), leading directly to the strategically important city of Posen (see Map 2), was obviously an important thoroughfare for the advancing forces. Martha von Rosen, however, who was still on the estate, located *east* of this highway, must have felt enormous apprehension about being cut off from the western world.

lights, no longer denying ourselves the pleasure we were forced to forgo, due to kerosene rationing! Poor Irmgard von Stritzky had her hands full with her three little ones, the youngest of whom had been born as recently as August. Her sister was not the very best of helpers, although she was sweet and very kind. To make up for this, she had two conscientious, darling, old aunts, both of them in their seventies. The packing continued seemingly without end, but at last, at 1:30 that morning, we were ready.

Jan, our good 'Nani,' as Gerhard called him, drove the work wagon. As none of the Polish workers, normally employed on the estate, agreed to drive with us, I had to drag our maid Anja's brother out of his bed to help me. In addition, the old tubercular night watchman Borowiak, freely offered his services.

I believed that I could be of most help on horseback, but this mistake became evident by disastrous consequences!

Riding in the minus twenty degree winter night, became an excruciating experience. To add to all the troubles, my plan to have the Trakehner mare, Delight, a fine riding horse, stay ahead of the three vehicles, scouting out the best way to go, turned out to be a miserable fiasco. It was impossible to pry her away from the work horses. Delight became stubborn, frightened and refused to leave the wagon.

On these roads, glazed with ice, I had to ride back and forth managing the six horses hitched to the three vehicles – the Buda, a two-door covered coach, and two work wagons. Jan, driving one of the wagons, was of little use, as I could not communicate to him the reason for this strange midnight odyssey. We had long ago created a language of grunts useful for normal farming operations; however, we had no vocabulary for these emergencies. Borowiak was of little help. He did, however, drive the Buda well. The second work wagon was driven by a young worker.

The kerosene lantern was hung in front of the house. All the Polish workers from the nearby village that I employed on the estate, Valerie, Anja, Stanislawa, Sophia and Herr Sczyfter, helped with the packing and departure. I saw the weight of fear on all their faces – what is coming next? Five-year-old Gerhard, wrapped in my brother's old sheepskin, was the eldest of the children, and Aunt Elizabeth, the oldest of the adults. Count Borch was close to eighty. Despite his fragile age, he sat bravely on the big open hay wagon, along with the two aunts von Horn, Frau Baumann, and Countess Borch. He had his shot-gun between his knees. Everyone was covered with blankets, which the servants, with great care, had tucked around them.

At the very last minute, Valerie brought my old hand-operated sewing machine, and stuck it under Frau Baumann's feet.

So our little company started to move out into the unknown, away from our home of more than two years, and away from the menacing Russians. The lantern was put out and the icy January darkness surrounded us. I had simply one thought in mind: "Would we reach Jarotschin before the Russians took over the train station?" And further, "Could we still get through the railway underpass?"

The horses, still fresh, trotted gamely on, in spite of the heavy wagons. The rattle of their shoes on the frozen ground resounded with a hollowness that rang loudly in the quiet of the wintry night.

Shortly after four o'clock in the morning, we reached Jarotschin, illuminated in a blaze of lights. Noise, excitement, loud cries, frightened people rushing to and fro, clattering wagons, all in spite of the very early hour of the cold winter's night. My heart pounded. Were these Russians? Would I need to use my husband's revolver, which I had strapped around my waist? How ridiculous those thoughts seem to me now, but how could I know then how it would all turn out?

The people milling around were like us, poor hunted refugees.

The train was still running. Perhaps I could let Aunt Elizabeth and the Count and Countess Borch carry on by train? Thousands, however, already stood on the station platform, and there was no train to be seen. So we drove on, and the relief in my heart at that moment is unforgettable. What joy I felt when we had left the railroad underpass behind us! I threw my revolver into the snow, and Count Borch, with an aching heart, did the same with his shot-gun. It was just too dangerous to hold onto them, as the Bolsheviks would have no mercy with armed refugees. The fear of their overtaking us was all too apparent.

In great haste, before leaving, I had torn out the pages of Andree's *World Atlas* which dealt with Silesia. How would I ever find my way otherwise? Our four children slept sitting up. Every now and then Gerhard would ask: "Are we there already?" The question troubling me continued to be: "Where was 'there'?"

Our first stop was located west of Jarotschin, on the estate of Schalkau.

We warmed ourselves and stretched our legs. Understandably, the horses also deserved a rest and feeding. We hurried on as we wanted to keep on traveling until nightfall. That night we were taken in at the big house on the Eichwald estate, quite near the highway. A lieutenant, a *Kriegsverlängerungsrat* (professional warmonger), and another military man were already there. The real owner, Baron Alexis Hahn, had gone, leaving behind two big, beautiful, German shepherd dogs, howling in their misery.

We dragged straw into a big room. A tiny stove sparingly gave out a little heat. Gerhard whimpered, yearning for his warm bed and his beloved huge stuffed poodle, a fantastic invention of fur and a present from his father. In the barn, where our horses, to my great satisfaction, were fed and stabled, stood an excellent herd of cattle. Without hesitation, I had a twenty-litre can full of milk loaded onto our wagon. How lucky that I thought of it, for we had no chance for another refill for a long time after that.

We were all tired and sank, with deep gratitude, onto our straw beds. But I was restless and could not sleep. Overloaded wagons, rattling along the highway, clattered endlessly past the house, a grim and endless chain of refugees to which we now belonged. At that time, I did not have the slightest idea of the dimensions which that succession of distraught people would ultimately reach. No one could really visualize what it meant to go into that unknown. Were we all wandering into complete nothingness? How far behind us were the Russians?

Suddenly the clashing, grinding noises stopped. What followed was almost worse – the absolute deathly quiet of the night. I heard, to the exclusion of all else, the uneven breathing of those people who were my sole responsibility. Where should I take them?

I went out into the night. It was cold and very dark, and the suddenly quiet and empty street was full of overwhelming menace. From far away, I saw huge beams of light drawing closer, and I heard a distant rattling roar that almost made the blood curdle in my veins. Were those tanks?

Shaking, I cowered in the bushes to see, and yet not be seen. Yes, they were. One and then another, and more followed. I fled into the house and pounded on the lieutenant's door. We had decided that each was to warn the other of anything suspicious. We hurried outside, spying from my hiding place.

"Those are German Panzer," he told me, "nothing to worry about." Yes, nothing to worry about, but why would he then immediately give orders to make his own wagons ready? Without any explanation, he disappeared into the night. I did not dare to wait any longer and woke my poor, sleepy companions. It was four o'clock in the morning, and before we were eventually ready to get under way, it was six. The first refugees were already on the road, pushing steadily and wearily westwards. The rolling countryside was slightly hilly and the road, because of the many wagons on it, had become mirror-smooth. Thus we could only travel very slowly. A horse had slipped far, far ahead of us, and had fallen, blocking the road. We caught up with its frozen remains. Most horses were not sharp-shod like ours.

We saw this one, but how many others had experienced a similar fate, and we had passed without noticing? How many more such hold-ups would we encounter on the road?

The sun shone brightly, but there was a constant merciless wind. There were always new vehicles, incessantly pushing their way into the thick, congested line of traffic. The rich man was crowded next to the destitute one. In the town of Gostingen, I met my dear friend Baron Herman Ungern-Sternberg. What a pleasure it was to see a face I knew among those of countless strangers! As I wanted to buy some supplies, we planned to meet again on our way out of town.

This naive kind of thinking was only possible between two people who were as clueless about the situation as we were. For at the exit gate of Gostingen, there was such a rush that it was quite impossible to find a curbstone to sit on! I never saw Baron Ungern-Sternberg again.

Amongst the crowd we did, however, see Baron Werner Hahn, from Haus Memelhof. He was in uniform. We also caught a glimpse of Baroness Elisabeth Koskull. She was driving in a wagon with Uncle and Aunt Alexander Baron Koskull-Adsirn. But we soon lost sight of them too. We still had time to enjoy the scenery, however, and driving by, saw the estate of Gostingen with its beautiful parks, lying against a mountain. At noon, it was impossible to leave the road. At long last, nevertheless, we pulled off to one side near the state-owned farm called Gola. This was also the location of an air-force base. Its layout was pleasing, situated by a lake, but there was nowhere to enter, not even to brew a cup of tea. So we drank cold milk, making do with bread and cold cooked potatoes.

The sun was shining already low over the horizon, and we could feel the bitter cold again. Alas, I had nothing with which to warm my poor, half-frozen, little group. The refugee column crawled along at a snail's pace. When we came to a small country road, I turned off, and we soon arrived at an estate called Schatzdorf. The owner, a man without family, was preparing to leave. He was Dr. Schubert, a leading agriculturist, well respected throughout the country. At first he told us to go to the manager's house, but after hearing that we were friends of the von Rosenstiels, he became most congenial. When he was told of Else being in flight with the von Rosenstiel children, he gave me an address of people related to the family. He realized that the whole situation was a very serious one for Germany, but saw it as not altogether hopeless for all of us. He told us that one had simply to be sufficiently well prepared. When he found our provisions quite inadequate, he sold me a freshly slaughtered young pig, a few potatoes, peas, and some wheat, possibly the last that I would see for a long time.

We continued onward that same afternoon, quite reassured that we now had plenty of supplies. The milk can was recently refilled, and all of us were content after a warm meal of milk-soup and bread. Our goal was Lissa. The highway was now completely congested and our pace was nerve-wrackingly slow. Wagon followed wagon. Occasionally, we saw a creaking, grating sleigh dragged behind a tired horse, half asleep and hopelessly unprepared for the task. There were children, crying from hunger and cold, whining and complaining mothers, frightened men trying in vain to keep their horses at a trot, before they too died like so many others whose remains were evident on the side of the road. No, this was madness. We could not stay on this route much longer.

Before we set out that morning, we discovered that Anja's brother had disappeared without a sound, taking with him our sheepskin. So I drove the Buda myself. It hardly seemed as if we were moving at all any more, but we finally reached the outskirts of Lissa. We passed two graveyards situated alongside the road. Beside the low stone walls, lay many little, cold bundles, now unsuffering. The ground was frozen to an impenetrable depth, and no one had the time to dig graves. Someone counted thirty-five bodies. These unfortunate people had not been prepared, having taken neither the warm clothing nor the provisions needed for survival. The agonies and miseries of those who found no shelter were indescribable, and I thought of the countless children who had already frozen and starved to death.

It was quite late when we gratefully took the first opportunity to leave the main highway. We took a country road through Paulshuben. I attempted to obtain rooms at the estate, but everything was already full. An army captain stood at the entrance of the village. I stopped and asked him for advice. "The best advice I can give you is that you come and stay with me," and he kindly took us in at the deaconry, which the German army was occupying.

A larger, as well as a smaller room, were put at our disposal. There was enough room at the neighbouring farm for our seven horses. Jan and Borowiak stood guard, as horses were becoming rare and were frequently stolen. While on the road, I constantly kept my eye on my reserve horse, as my teams would undoubtedly have collapsed without the needed rest that the constant changing gave them.

We were lucky to have found this opportunity to stay, for everyone in that endless chain was looking for a place to spend the night. The deacon had left the day before, and the captain assured us that he would certainly hear of any advancing Russian troops in plenty of time for us to make a getaway. He suggested that we could quite safely stay there. Apparently all the roads leading to Lissa were blocked and impassable. With a sigh of relief, I decided to stay. Aunt Elisabeth was at the end of her strength. It was hard for her, sitting on the narrow seat in the covered wagon with the three small children, who were not able to sit still and be quiet. Gerhard sat with me in the coachman's seat, which luckily had a small canopy to shelter our heads.

The captain helped us with all kinds of supplies such as eggs, butter, preserves, and other things, which were packed into our wagon. He even took a letter that I had written to Jörn and saw that it was sent. It could not have gone without his help, for by now all mail routes were disrupted. We benefited greatly from the rest, and it was a blessing not to have to be on the road again right away. As Aunt Elisabeth could no longer travel on the wagon, we gratefully accepted the captain's offer to send her to Lissa on the following day in a military car. From there she could continue by train to Berlin, where she would be accompanied by Frau Baumann. I gave her my polar fox fur coat, originally brought from Siberia, which had kept her warm in the wagon. There was little enough that I could do for this pitiful and helpless person.

We decided that we would also get under way the following morning, skirting Lissa on a southerly route, as suggested by the captain. With all his advice and protection we felt secure - a wonderful feeling. Beef was slaughtered just for us, and the best pieces were salted in a wooden tub to make it simpler to take along. We would now have more room in the wagon, a lighter load, and two fewer mouths to feed. In the evening, as we were all sitting together enjoying a rare cup of tea, our new protector entered, clad in full battle uniform, and said in a carefully controlled voice, barely concealing his alarm:

> "My friends, I ask you to be quiet and not to turn on any lights, even if there is shooting. Furthermore, on no account should you venture out onto the road. The Russian tanks are coming and are merely a few kilometres away!"

We sat petrified on the floor. The children slept in beds. The fear and tension of waiting in the dark was almost unbearable. In order to turn our thoughts elsewhere, I told stories of my experiences in Siberia, of the long journey my family had made in 1918, through Bolshevik Russia, travelling from Japan, back home to Estonia.[9] We whispered. Minutes went by, then hours, but nothing happened. It was deathly quiet outside. One could no longer hear the constant coming and going of refugees. Late in the night, the captain came to tell us that all immediate danger had been averted. The Russians had taken a side road, just outside the village, and had been caught by the German troops as they tried to push westward. The battle was still under way, he said. A prayer of thanks went through my heart. That was the route we had planned to travel the next day!

So, once again, we changed our plans. We would now bypass Lissa the following day, using paved logging tracks to the north. My only map was of the wrong scale to show the little bush trails, so the captain drew us a new one. First we had to cross the big highway, on which a steady stream of wagons pressed slowly forward. The insurmountable question facing us was: "How could we possibly hope to stop or interrupt this endlessly tight colonnade of terrified people travelling on this main thouroughfare?"

Again we were saved by pure chance. The evening before, I had helped two reserve policemen from Litzmannstadt find lodgings. These two young men set out at the same time as we did, and as uniforms had an immediate effect everywhere, they temporarily stopped this train of refugees, making a passage for us through the traffic. Like a heavy curtain, the procession of humanity closed behind us!

We soon lost sight of our new friends, forgetting them in the face of a new threat. The icy road had become as smooth as the back of a wet seal. The least swing off the crown of the road, made the whole wagon slide, agonizingly nearing the brink of deep road ditches. To the left and right lay the dreadful evidence. The fleeing owners had continued without their wagons. How, I don't know. Here and there one could witness the sad spectre of a completely exhausted horse. Quite worn out from the constant skidding and sliding, it simply had given up the fight, refusing to advance one step further.

At one point, our wagon slipped, swerving with great acceleration, against one curbstone and then another. I had trouble holding my fighting, shying team. We nearly tipped over; however, I ultimately managed to get the wagon back to the centre of the road. To our right on the edge of the ditch, overturned in the snow, lay a box of books. On the very top of the pathetic

---

9 For details of this earlier odyssey, see pp. 298–302.

heap lay *Struwwelpeter*, a children's story book. It was so difficult to keep our children occupied and how that book would help. I could not let go of my horses, so I called to Freda von Horn on the last wagon. Before the words were even out of my mouth, someone else was swifter, jumping from his wagon. We had missed our chance.

Slowly we lost sight of the other refugees. There were fewer smashed and abandoned wagons on the roadside. We crossed other roads, driving through endless forests and dense woods. It was fantastically beautiful, but it was so hard to stay oriented! Had I gone the wrong way? I tried to follow the hand-drawn map as well as I could. At around three o'clock, we would have to look for shelter. Later, there would be no room available anywhere, as everyone would be looking for a protective roof. We drove along the secluded and dark road, searching for the exit from this endless forest. At long last, the trees thinned, and the woods opened to the right onto Nielitsch, the very place I had been trying to reach. A quick race for shelter, first come, first served, the unwritten law. There were many contenders, apparently congregating from other roads. Nearly all the original owners had already left. This time 'our' house was a decrepit little hut, but it had a roof, and offered shelter and warmth from its little stove. I allowed the horses to roam loose in the barn, where they picked out the food they wanted from the unthrashed wheat lying there.

By now, we were very well organized. Each member of our group had his or her job to perform. The old people helped as much as they could, but they were usually hopelessly stiff from sitting long and motionlessly in the cold. There was always a great deal to carry in. Irmgard von Stritzky kept herself and her sister at a constant trot. I always looked for a stable first, saw that the two men unharnessed the teams, and then started worrying about warmth, food, and bedding. Beds were always rare and often filthy. To make up for this, there was usually plenty of straw, and our good fortune was that we carried all our bedding in the wagons. In the daytime, we tucked it around us, and sat on our pillows.

Whenever possible, I cooked potatoes after supper. These could be fried immediately at our next stopping place, or, in an emergency, they could be eaten cold. We had simple food, yet always enough. We were endlessly grateful for having brought our own provisions, as there were no longer any stores nor places where one could buy anything. Frequently we found cows left behind, and I was able to fill, and refill, our big milk can.

The night passed quietly. After a good rest, we continued through beautiful forests. Our strength and health were still good, but fear weighed heavily on us all. We knew that we had to cross the Oder River before all the bridges were dynamited. There were always accounts of bridges being destroyed by our own troops in an effort to impede the advances of the enemy. If this should happen at the Oder, we would be helplessly cut off. So we never stopped longer than to rest for the night and then went on, always at a fast walk of about six kilometres an hour. When walking alongside, one had to really stretch one's legs to keep up with the horses.

We reached our next goal in daylight. It was the little town of Schlesiersee, where we found a place in the convent of the Grey Sisters. There were only a few old nuns left. They had remained behind to care for the few patients who had not been well enough to be moved. That night, we slept in beds, not all crowded together in one room, but with a separate one for each family. A wash basin, and even a chamber pot, were provided! How I missed these things for the children, for I had not taken a potty along in spite of my maid Valerie's good advice. I was, however, given this one to keep, and this practical souvenir later emigrated with us even as far as Canada! We all found that we had almost forgotten what it felt like to spend a night in so fine a fashion!

The next morning we had a little time to look around the small town, and I took this opportunity to go to the pharmacy to purchase a few vital medicines. I had taken the most important items with me, but this was the first place since we left home that was not completely abandoned and empty. As I entered the door, I saw a tall figure standing to the right of the counter. It was Count Borch. He turned and started to speak something, but at that very moment he crumpled and fell heavily to the floor. The druggist and I both rushed to his side. There was plenty of heart medicine available, but not a single hypodermic! I rushed to look for his wife, but he recovered without help. The strain had simply been too much for his old heart. How helpless I was; how little I could do.

We could not risk waiting for even one day, however, as we always kept in mind the possible demolition of the Oder River bridge. Count Borch bravely sat down amongst the others in the big hay wagon. I can still see his big frame, his calm aristocratic face, the coat with the fur side turned in, with only the karakul sheepskin collar showing, and the big winter cap, of the type worn so much in the Baltic. He was then seventy-nine years old, and lived another ten years thereafter.

We left Schlesiersee at noon. Again it was Friday, only one week since our flight had begun. Hard to believe. It seemed like an eternity. We drove through wooded and slightly rolling country. We, the endless human migration. At the estate of Heidekrug we settled in for the night. The owner was frantically packing, for he too was eager to cross the Oder River bridge in time.

And on we went next morning, walking as fast as we could, towards the Oder River. We crossed the river at Beuthen, on a lovely stone bridge with a coat of arms boldly emblazoned on it. Not many more people would cross it after us. We were at last on the western side and the heavy load on my heart stayed behind.

✳ 2 ✳

FROM THE ODER TO THE ELBE

My first instinct always was to stay away from the main roads as the danger of not finding shelter was terrifying. People appeared to become progressively more bewildered and disoriented. Helplessly, they pressed closer and closer together in their nameless, homeless fear.

The last road I had chosen was terrible, so leaving it, I felt that I would certainly be able to find a place to stay in Költsch, the next village north, directly on the banks of the Oder River. My instincts had served me well, for in that little hamlet there was no wild, hasty hunting for shelter. The military personnel, already stationed there, had found a house to which they invited us. Provisions were also distributed for the horses. Everything was well organized, and there was plenty to eat. Our lodgings were comfortable, even though our beds were merely of straw.

We were in great need of rest as the little five-month-old baby had pneumonia. We had neither penicillin nor a doctor, so the vital requirements were warmth and recuperation. A little store was situated here, but the only real pharmacy existed in Neusalz, fifteen kilometres north. I drove there with the Count Borchs. They were, at this point, especially intent on trying to continue by train. I took them as far as the high school where military personnel and army trench-diggers were quartered. They wanted to get further advice there. I got the necessary medications, and fortunately the condition of the baby improved swiftly. In spite of this success, I did not want to risk going on.

On Tuesday, I received a message that the Count Borchs wanted me to pick them up again of Neusalz. They had been warned by a corporal of the First Lancers not to try to go by train, as there was active fighting in Grünberg, a mere twenty-eight kilometres north-west from Neusalz. I drove to fetch them that evening. Although we had already spent four nights in Költsch, I did not want to move our little patient yet, so we lingered on another day in this rapidly emptying village. We could not wait any longer. On the 1st of February, we packed again and left, although our children were still far from well. We had advanced only a short distance when the wheel broke on our Buda. We had no choice but to turn back, for without the closed wagon it was impossible to travel with sick children.

Though there was a blacksmith in Költsch, he was of little help. He complained that being overworked, he did not wish to stay there longer. I bribed him with the most valuable and rare commodities I could think of – chocolate and cigarettes. At last, the Buda was fixed, but as it was now too late to continue, we returned to our quarters. The next day Gerhard had a high fever.

I went to the local military chief but was shattered when he instantly became almost rude: "What are you still doing here," he said, "you should be gone long ago! Leave this place, right now!"

Yes, he was right. As there were no longer any women and children to be seen anywhere, it was plain to understand that we were actually the last ones remaining in the village. I wrapped up Gerhard and we hastily broke camp for the second time. It was Friday, the second of February. The baby fortunately was much better and no longer in any real danger.

No sooner had we left, than the cannonade started. The shots came from left, right, and above. I could not tell precisely where they came from. It was like hell. The well-rested horses reared and kicked with each percussion. I had a terrible time controlling them. We galloped, without control, over bouncing roads, until, at last, I succeeded in mastering the stampeding, panic-stricken animals. We felt safer when we ultimately reached the big road, the very same one we had left five days ago – now lying empty and abandoned. Later we discovered that on the following day the Russians had driven a spearhead across the Oder River into Költsch, the village we had just left.

We passed through Freystadt ... lifeless and abandoned. Beautiful silent land of Silesia through which we were driving that day, what will happen to you? Very soon you will not look so lovingly tended. A majestic Gothic church greeted us with its high, pointed steeple, and from a mountain, a peaceful Catholic monastery looked down on us.

Our next destination was Sprottau, an important goal, causing great turmoil in my hopeful heart. Would my parents be there? Or had they failed in their flight from Posen? Sprottau had been the meeting place we had agreed upon because Kasi, my uncle's widow, lived there. Her house lay approximately three kilometres east of Sprottau. This would be right on our route, if we continued this way. Yes, if.... But merely one hour before our destination we encountered a detour. The direct road was open only to German fighting forces, so once again we started off on an unknown, unpaved road. It was an endless detour. The evening was dark, wet, and cold. To make matters actually unbearable, a wheel on Jan's wagon broke. He tied a pole underneath, and the horses continued dragging the crippled wagon over the soft, miry road. Very late that night, filthy and tired, we reached Kortnitz. We were still an hour's drive away from Sprottau.

I banged on the door of the first lighted house. "Could we have shelter, there are eleven people?" "Yes, gladly," was the answer, "but we have scarlet fever here."

That was too dangerous. The people inside were baking cakes in preparation for their departure and insisted on giving me some before we went on. The next houses were all overflowing. There was no room for us anywhere. It seemed a very long way from one house to the next. Someone suggested that we should continue further, trying to find a place in the dining-room or lounge of a closed-down inn, not very far away. The room was almost empty, and we laid ourselves down on the straw partially covering the dirty floor. Some sleeping soldiers were lying there already. We were tired and hungry. We had snatched a quick meal at noon on the wagons, and now we ate nothing more than dry bread. I held Gerhard close to me. We had slept like this since the flight began. We did not risk undressing.

What was that crawling on my neck? I lit my little candle, and a cold shiver ran through my veins. A louse, the dangerous bearer of typhus! I spent the remainder of that night watching over the little sleeping treasure next to me. As soon as he became restless, I checked him all over carefully in case I found another one of those dreaded carriers of disease. What a relief when I saw the first grey glimmer of the morning.

While Count and Countess Borch drove with a baker to Sprottau to inquire about trains, I returned to the house with the scarlet fever. I had noticed that they had a bicycle. I had left our ruined and broken-down wagon in their yard, and our horses were standing in their barn. They lent me the bicycle readily, whereupon I started out alone towards the house of my uncle's widow where I hoped my parents would be. It lay right beside a military airport, and that created yet another unexpected difficulty for me. I was stopped abruptly by an unfriendly guard who would not allow me to pass. He accused me of having stolen an army bicycle! I said that it certainly did not belong to me, but that it had been lent to me by some friendly people so that I might carry out this trip. He grew more cheeky and rude, and in the end took the bicycle away from me. What a predicament! I demanded a receipt from him, for I felt that without it I could never face the kind souls who had lent it to me.

I had to continue on foot. It was at least three kilometres to the house. The suspense was indescribable. Would they be there? With throbbing heart I stood on the steps and rang the bell. The door opened, and I fell into my father's arms. He still had a dressing gown on, for it was early in the morning. Then I rushed to mother. We had been given this one great blessing, to find each other again, amidst the terrible turmoil in those trying times.

My parents had escaped from Posen with only a rucksack, and just in time. They faced and overcame many difficulties, and had been here fourteen days already. Kasi, my aunt, generously invited us to come and live with her. There would be room in the living-room for Gerhard and me. We should come and stay, for where else was there for us to go? However I still had other people to consider. There was the large von Stritzky family. But Kasi found space for them as well in an empty room upstairs. I did not hesitate long, and hurried back. This time I had to walk the whole way, but my heart sang and I scarcely noticed the distance. With an awful feeling, however, I returned the receipt instead of the bicycle. The woman admitted that it was an army bicycle, but not a stolen one. A passing soldier had broken his, so they had given him their own in exchange. Thank God, the woman had her own returned to her later after it was found in a big warehouse of requisitioned bicycles.

Count Borch found a place to stay in the county government building, where he and his wife waited for a chance to travel on. A week later, a special refugee train took them to Leipzig. We settled in with Kasi for the time being, and waited for further developments. We put the horses up at a farm, less than a quarter of a kilometre to the east. The night watchman and Jan slept quite serenely with the seven animals. I bought our food, for even here ration cards were being distributed. This seemed quite amazing to us, after having come through huge areas of unwanted surplus.

Actually the only item impossible to procure was hay. There did not even exist any coupons for it. It could only be obtained further east. I was told of a likely source of supply and how to get there, so I decided to risk the drive back east against the stream of refugees. I took Jan with me in the little wagon. It was a full day's journey away, against the traffic, but there were so many roads that I missed the correct one. Nevertheless, I obtained hay, but from a totally different location. How relieved my parents were to see us back that evening. They had heard over the radio on the same day that Russian tanks had entered the very place where I was supposed to have gone! Apparently, there had been a small skirmish in which the Russians had been defeated. What a merciful hand had led me on to that different road!

Now it was obvious that, sooner or later, we would have to continue our travel west. We had many children and old people, and only the one covered wagon in which my parents would also have to ride. We were saved by a stroke of luck, for the N.S.V.[1] took over the care of the families von Horn and von Stritzky, sending them on by train. Kasi had definitely made up her mind to stay on in her house. She wanted to give us some things to take with us as in his will, her husband had left all his family treasures to my brother, Werner. On Saturday, I drove with my father to Sprottau to redeem our oat coupons to feed the horses. I harnessed Delight and Udine, the two exceptionally well-bred horses, which my father had given me from the stables of Count Stollberg. What a pleasure it was to drive these spirited animals.

We bought potatoes and then went on to the warehouse to obtain the oats. It was afternoon, and the civil servant on duty had decided to stop work for the day. "Come on Monday, then you'll get them." For me, the oats were like gasoline for my horses' motors. He never thought that I might have to journey on right away. Stunned at this insensitivity and selfishness, I retorted: "On Monday, the Russians will get it, if you'd rather have it that way!" I never guessed how close my words were to the truth.

We went home, however, with nothing more than our small load of potatoes. The road was disturbingly empty in comparison to the former ceaseless stream of people. On arriving home, I gave the horses to Jan to unharness and went indoors to drink a refreshing cup of tea, while I recovered from my furious frustration at the civil servant.

My father quickly wrote a short letter. We had decided to walk together to the farm to find out if anything new had transpired in our absence, and to mail his letter in the mailbox right behind the farm. It was a mild February afternoon. It was already growing dark.

---

1 N.S.V. = *National Sozialistische Volkswohlfahrt* (National Socialist Peoples' Welfare).

Again I noticed how strangely still and empty the road was. Where had all the wagons vanished? The farm remained lifeless. Slowly we began to get worried. The manager had promised to tell us immediately if anything suspicious happened. The officers who were quartered there had agreed to this plan, and now where were they all? I saw a wagon moving out on the opposite side of the yard. I hurried over. To my startled question as to what was the matter, the driver answered shortly: "Don't you know? The Russians are coming." All further queries remained unanswered. Why ask questions at all?

Now we had to act. There was no Jan to be seen anywhere, no Borowiak. I fought desperately with the harnesses and the horses. Stupefied in my frightened frenzy, I no longer knew what belonged to which animal. They did not understand this sudden rush at all! They stood hitched up to the newly repaired little wagon, with my saddle horse tied in the lead. Finally, Jan appeared. Two wagons were parked near the house, but we chose a big work wagon that had been left behind by refugees. It had big arched metal bands, over which one could easily stretch a canvas, providing cover against the weather. At last, Borowiak also presented himself. He turned out to be quite tipsy. He had discovered an abandoned alcohol factory where he had systematically filled himself with everything he could find in the distillery. As well as himself, he had filled a huge milk can with the valuable liquid, and now appeared in front of the little wagon with his trophy, begging me to promise to take special care of it!

My father took Borowiak with the big wagon to fetch oats. We obtained grain from the granary, where coupons were no longer needed. I drove my wagon over to the house, and Jan followed with the third team. A little dachshund, belonging to the farm, sat alone howling on the road. I stopped and, without hesitation, took the forlorn little animal along. Suddenly, the moment I reached the house, the heavens flamed with a furious light, like a flash of lightning. A fearsome detonation followed. I grabbed the horses' reins, crouching down in the wagon. That must be the Russians shooting, but why ahead of us, in the west? I barely had time to think before the flash flamed up again, followed by that terrible noise. The panicking horses leaped and shied. Window panes fell crashing out of their frames. Gerhard, who had stayed in the house with my mother, could be heard crying furiously. At the first bang, the little dachshund leaped from the wagon. At the second, I did too. Fear simply drove me out and flung me onto the ground, but I continued holding onto the reins. How I managed to hold the horses, I do not know.

Out of the night, soldiers appeared – our own soldiers. They dug ugly deep trenches in the gateway and around the house, as well as along the road. A guard was stationed at the gate. I asked him to watch the horses for a minute, while I rushed into the house and tried to calm my terrified child. Everyone was feeling their way around in the dark. The electricity had gone out. My extraordinarily far-sighted mother had a small candle, and watched the soldiers filling their pockets with whatever was tempting. My father's razor? No, she stopped the looter in time. I grabbed a suitcase and hurried back to the wagon, renewing my appeal to the guard to watch my horses. "You'd better stop packing, and leave immediately," he answered. "Yes, yes, right away, but we still have a few more things to put in…."

Jan hitched the big horses to the fully loaded wagon parked under the roof. He merely drove it through the gate and onto the road, for luckily the track was not yet dug up by the soldiers (preparing their trenches). Whether the wagon was too heavy or the ground too soft, I could not tell, but the horses pulled their load to the end of the driveway and not one step further. Being too busy with my packing to investigate, I only heard Jan's bewildered shouting, but could do little to help. As I went into the house for another load, there was that ear-splitting noise again. The sudden light cut through the night, blinding all our eyes completely to the darkness. By now, however, I had found out what the noise was. The airplane hangars were being dynamited to make them useless for the enemy.

I raced outside again. Was I really blinded, or had my well-tied horses vanished? My heart was pounding. There, before me, was a soldier. I did not even know whether he was the same one whom I had asked to watch the team, or not. To my distracted pleadings for information, he simply replied unconcernedly: "Oh, yes, they've gone." "But where?" "I think, down there." And he gave a careless wave of his hand into the night.

At least I had a small indication of the direction in which I should search. My father was nowhere to be seen. Only Jan fought on helplessly – his wagon still solidly stuck. I raced away into the darkness. My eyes got accustomed to the night and indeed there were the hoof prints leading downwards into a meadow, located at the edge of a river. In this dim light, I noticed a shadow. It moved! There they were, my beautiful, much needed horses! The wagon had tipped over during their wild stampede. They had turned too sharply on abruptly reaching the river, and now stood trembling, nervously trampling the tangled harnesses under their restless hooves.

Never ask me how I untangled that mess! I made no attempt to take anything back other than the horses with their harnesses. I left the wagon and all that was on it, including Borowiak's precious alcohol. I knew we still had the Buda, which we had originally planned to tie on behind. Leading the trotting horses. I ran back to the yard as fast as my legs could carry me and stood them next to the other team, which was still incapacitated, heaving helplessly. I failed in trying to turn the Buda around in the yard. The driveway was just too narrow. The space was diminished by the soldiers' trenches and my strength did not suffice. Being seriously worried, because my father had not yet returned, I screamed at the soldiers to assist me. Real *soldateskas* (unruly soldiers), I thought in frustration!

At last the Buda was turned around, and thankfully my father also appeared. What a relief! He had been shoveling oats and wheat out of the loft into the wagon box. As it had been pitch dark up there, he had only been able to find the grain by feeling his way.

My observant father noticed right away why my usually reliable horses refused to pull. One wheel had been solidly wedged behind one of the gateposts. In the darkness with all the excitement, Jan had not seen the post. It was hopeless to back up now. The only option left was to saw off the offending stump, but with what? We were in a completely strange place, it was pitch dark, and we had neither a saw nor a sharp axe. Jan did his best, but to no avail. The post was too good, it was set well. He almost managed to lift it out, but had to drop it, swearing dejectedly.

Suddenly a German officer appeared. He asked whether he could hitch a ride with us on our journey. "Certainly," said my father, "but it will take us at least half an hour before we can start." Our grandmother's portrait by Timoleon Neff,[2] and the priceless big Persian carpet simply had to be taken along. The latter we could stretch over the new wagon as a roof. "No, that is too risky," said the soldier, "the Russians overtook me hardly three kilometres from here. I was shot in the arm, but just managed to escape them." My father gave him some wine, and he disappeared into the night.

---

2 Timoleon Neff (1804-1876), Estonian-born foster son of Wilhelm von Kügelgen's uncle, Heinrich Zoege von Manteuffel. He was a painter appointed to the court of the Tsar, and a professor at the *Akademie* and Director of the Hermitage in St. Petersburg. The Zoege von Manteuffels were a wealthy Baltic German family in Livonia (later part of Estonia). Zoege von Manteuffel was the personal physician and friend of the mother of Tsar Nicholas II. Further references to Wilhelm von Kügelgen and the Zoege von Manteuffels can be found on p. 296n.

Were the Russians really so near? Sudden fear gave me a fantastic new energy. Desperately I shook the post, and with almost inhuman strength I lifted it out of the ground! Jan looked very sheepish, but we had no time for tact. The picture and the carpet were loaded, and then, in the last minute, Kasi gave in and decided to come along. I looked around for my coat, but I had left it in the overturned wagon. It was only later that I realized that I had also left in the pocket the piece of paper, with the valuable address to reach the von Rosenstiels. They would have helped me in my search for Else.

The roads were darkly dead. There were no fleeing people left to fill them. The heavens behind us were blazing red. I drove the Buda again. How fast the rested horses moved! The Bolsheviks burned everything down, but we drove on. The horses shied as lonesome figures appeared along the roadside. We crossed the bridge over an arm of the Bober River even as the engineers were laying the dynamite to demolish it. We drove without stopping to think, for wasn't that fire? And weren't those cannon blasts behind us?

Without forewarning, a brilliant beam of light shone straight at us. The road followed the ridge of a high dyke. Below, far below us, flowed the Bober River. I drove as far to the side of the road as I could and stopped my wagon. An apparition, something huge, with a high glaring light, rattled by, pressing us down almost into the abyss. I shook in every weary limb. This is what living war looked like! No one here bothered about us tiny, meaningless mites. For them, there were bigger, more brutal jobs to do. I drove about one quarter kilometre further, before I turned to look, as I frequently did, for the other wagons. They were no longer there! Nothing! They had simply vanished – disappeared into the night!

We stopped. My father held the team while I started back on foot. It was all so terrifyingly eerie with that unnatural glow of the fires in the east, and constant growling in the air. How ghostly the woods, the trees, and the fields next to the road. To the right and the left of the road, there were flares in the sky, but everything behind them was sunk into the deepest darkness. Out of pure physical fear, my feet simply refused to move any further. Then my overwhelming anxiety took over again. When, really, had I seen the wagons last? Jan had been driving the last one, Borowiak in the middle. Yes, I had seen them for the last time just before that huge spectre had passed us. I hurried on again, my heart beating so loudly that undoubtedly it could be heard.

There! Again there was another one of those flares beside the road, and in this light I saw something in the distance. Something moved on the very edge of the opposite side of the road, but we were traveling along a high and precipitous dam, and the threatening valley of the Bober lay terribly deep beside it!

I ran onward and arrived just in time to prevent an even greater mishap. Borowiak, blinded by the strong lights, had lost all sense of direction. Having driven too far to the left, he had mired his wagon in the wet shoulder of the road. At that point, he was trying to get back onto the firmer ground, but the wheels, sinking in deeply under the heavy load, caused the wagon, after each heave of the team to slip further into the abyss! One more misguided jerk and gravity would have pulled the whole load into the chasm, horses as well.

There was nothing to do but to unload. Jan was so excited and overwrought that he was unwilling to do anything. Borowiak was also quite put out and unhelpful, due to his being rather tipsy still. He was very offended at my having lost his precious milk can filled with alcohol. So I had to set an example and began unloading things much too heavy for me. First I threw down sacks of horse feed, then the heavy carpet that we had not had time enough to span over the top of the wagon. When over half the contents of the wagon lay on the road, I hitched the other two horses in front of the team, and we all lurched heavily up the bank, shouting encouragement to the four-in-hand. Once again, we were on firm ground.

If it had been difficult to get Jan to unload, it was now even harder to get him to load up again. How happy I was that, in the hurry, we had left the huge barrel of salt-meat in Sprottau! It is incredible how in a crisis and with great physical fear, one's strength increases. I tugged and yanked at things. There were about three wagon-lengths between the heap of possessions and the wagon. The huge carpet was the heaviest, but even that, in the long run, lay on top. The whole operation was enacted in the blinking play of light from the flares – continuous, irregular, near, and then far away. My fears had been allayed, and we were all relieved, when, at last, we set out as one unit again. From then on, I looked back often, but we continued without stopping.

That night we drove through Sagan. A young man was out in the dark street. We asked him the way. Would it be possible for us to find any place for ourselves and the horses to rest? But when he heard that the Russians had been outside Sprottau the previous night, a mere seventeen kilometres away, he ran off without answering. The town must be warned, for as yet they had heard nothing.

It was early in the morning. We stopped at Massdorf. The horses received their well-earned feed, and likewise, we ate something ourselves. Exhausted, I sat with half-closed eyes, seeing repeated pictures of the past terrible night.

We went further and always further, but never faster than at a walk's pace. Sorau was in upheaval, for it had been rumoured that sixty Russian tanks were less than four kilometres away from Sagan. Alarmed people ran excitedly, here and there, aimless and planless. An officer in his long coat passed us. He was pushing a baby carriage, with his little child lying inside. His bewildered wife hurried next to him. Two trembling old women stood in the road, fumbling with their broken umbrellas.

At noon, we stopped for a short rest. It seemed to me that for an aching eternity I had been sitting on my driver's seat. My eyes burned, and the horses' sides heaved. While they ate their feed, I watched the tightly packed, endless train of people as they pushed on past us. A desperate middle-aged woman staggered by, pushing a wheelbarrow. Pitifully, on top of it, sat her old mother. I hoped for her sake that she was only going as far as the train station, but I did not know.

No one had any definite plans any more. There was simply the instinctive urge to get away, away from the blood-red flood that could at any moment break over us all. We allowed ourselves a very short rest, and then continued.

Our next goal was to get to Leitzkau, where my brother's wife was. It was the fear of being overtaken, however, that drove us on, for the Russians obviously were motorized, while we merely had our tired string of horses. My chestnut, the weakest of them, fell from pure fatigue. Thus my reserve horse saved us again. I allowed the chestnut to run loose behind. We still hoped to cross the Autobahn, the direct route from Breslau to Berlin, the same day. Once that was taken by the Russians, we would be cut off from the western world forever. Having crossed it, we drove on, without stopping, until five-thirty that evening. At last, we left this heavily barricaded road to Berlin behind us.[3]

In the village of Krohla some very kind peasants gave us a place to spend the night. They realized that they would soon be as homeless as we were. Almost devoid of life, we fell onto the bedding to sleep. On Sunday, the eleventh of February, we were happy to leave the freeway behind us. We now had new difficulties to overcome. In Sprottau, Anmuth, one of our horses, needed to be reshod, and my three-year-old half-breed, Udine, also needed shoeing. She had gone unshod since Geppertsfeld. Since the long trek of the previous Sunday,

---

3 The Autobahn was barricaded to vehicular traffic by the Germans in order to hinder the advance of the Russians.

the horses were very tender-footed, but it had simply not been possible to do anything about it until now. All the thousands of trekking refugees needed help of some sort – either horses shod, or axles fixed. Understandably the blacksmiths en route could not keep up with the work.[4]

Ultimately, I was successful in a little town called Sörchen. I held Udine's rear feet myself, and she got her first shoes. I was very pleased at how obedient and calm she was, for in Geppertsfeld she had been quite unmanageable. We were also well taken care of, and received free macaroni soup from a travelling army soup kitchen. In Muskau, we were told to go further south, as the direct roads to Kottbus and Spremberg were closed.

We reached only as far as Krauschwitz on that day. The daughter of the house where we spent the night showed me to the remains of a bookstore operated by her friends and here I found *Knorrherz und Ermelinde* by Bonsels. How happy Gerhard was with my purchase, for at home he had been used to having stories read to him every day.

It was already Tuesday, the 13th of February, and still more of our horses needed to be shod, and, in addition, our wagons needed greasing. Axle grease was difficult to find, and lifting the big, heavily loaded wagons was hard work. We managed to get the job done, however, in Weisswasser. After this hold up, we managed to put only a mere seven kilometres behind us, spending the night in a little town called Schleife. Here again, as so often before, my father was able to repay the generosity of our hosts with his professional help. As a doctor, he could always be counted on to give his advice, and even write out prescriptions, if necessary. These poor, friendly people told us that, although the Russians had captured Görlitz (about 55 km south), they were making no preparations to flee. Why should they? They had no place to go.

We had no luck with our detour of Spremberg, for I had been told that it was also blocked. So, eventually, we found ourselves on a barely passable

---

4 The von Rosen wagons were only one or two days ahead of the Russian advance. At this very time, Marshal Zhukov's First Byelorussian Front was holding its fire, building up strength for the final push to Berlin. To their south, Marshal Konev's First Ukrainians were across the Oder and driving for the line of the Neisse, which for the most part followed the Neisse River. Six Soviet armies burst from their bridgeheads on the morning of 8 February, ignoring, for the moment, the strong German concentrations in Glogau and Breslau. On 11 February, the rest of the Neisse-Oder line now held their positions up to the Küstrin bridgehead. Küstrin fell to Marshal Zhukov on 12 March, 1945.

road leading towards Hoyerswerda. As this was evidently too strenuous for our horses, we reluctantly changed onto a harder road leading toward Spreewitz. It had suddenly become hard to reach a chosen destination by following a road shown on the map, as we were continuously being forced to make enormous detours. We drove right on through Spremberg, for it was an unpleasant place, over-filled and unfriendly. We had found a good road again, and as expected, all the houses were crowded. There was no room to be found anywhere. No amount of begging or persuading helped – no one took us in.

Similarly in Heideberg. As I was standing in front of an inn, asking for advice, we heard a distant rumbling in the air, and the ground heaved heavily under our feet. Above me the shingle, advertising the name of the inn, swung on its black iron chains. At first, I could not understand what it meant, but the townspeople had experienced this before. Twenty-two kilometres away, the town of Kottbus was being bombed heavily. This was an air-raid attack! What a blessing that the road we had planned to travel on had been blocked!

That night, for the first time, we slept out in the open. To the left of the road was a little meadow, bordered by a grove of trees. It lay somewhat higher than the road, and looked ideal for camping. A wagon road passing underneath big, old trees, branched off the highway. I tied up my fettlesome team, letting the other horses range free to graze on the frozen meadow grass. We had oats with us, and water was available in a low spot in the meadow. As there was nothing available for making a camp fire, we ate our supper cold. My father lay down to sleep in the covered wagon, protected from the cold by the big Persian rug. My mother and Kasi slept sitting up in the Buda. Jan and Borowiak settled down in the other big wagon, while Gerhard and I lay on the only mattress, under the large oak tree. How wonderfully the starry sky twinkled, with the shining moon in its first quarter! I thought how glorious it is to be outside, listening to the silence of the night, broken only by the sound of a child's breathing, for my son had fallen asleep instantly. Every now and then, one of the horses snorted gently, or blew the oats or dry grass out of its nostrils.

But the peace did not last long. This time I recognized the deep, distant rumbling. Again the heavens were lit up by the so-called 'Christmas trees.' What a spectacle! Awful, and yet strangely beautiful to watch. The bombs growled, and the earth heaved grimly beneath us. It was a heavy attack on

Dresden, fifty kilometres away in a southwesterly direction.[5] In spite of the distance, I seemed to live through it all, as if I was right there. How much better protection we had there, in God's open countryside, than those unfortunate, walled-in people in their big cities. The lights had scarcely died down when the sky grew cloudy and dark and heavy raindrops started to fall. First singly, then more, and more. Taking Gerhard and the mattress, proud of my bright idea, I crawled under the big wagon. It made a wonderful roof over us. No sooner had I arranged our bed, when the deep rumbling began again and, in spite of the poor visibility, the sky became distinctly red in the south. I could not even guess how many of our friends, fleeing as we were, met their deaths that night. Our beloved aunt had been spared miraculously as her train had left Dresden station fifteen minutes before the attack began. That very station was one of the hardest hit. Thousands of refugees died, sitting in the trains, or waiting for them.

Sleep was now an impossibility for all of us. We lay thinking, wondering, listening, as the rain pattered down more and more incessantly. At last, this too had its beneficial effect on our tense and over-tired minds, and slowly the longed-for, healing sleep came.

A rushing sound, steadily increasing, was heard. How strange. Where was I, really? Surely not in a ditch? Yes, for the track on which my wagons stood had turned into a veritable stream. My mattress, although sheltered from above, was inundated from below! How could I have been so unobservant? Wet, cold, and tired, I crowded into the Buda, which was airless, and very cramped, with my mother, who was celebrating her seventieth birthday, and Kasi, who had developed a heavy chronic cough. At last, dawn arrived. A welcome change from the horrible night! This is one of the eventful nights that will always remain sharp and pointedly clear in my inner book of memories.

On the road to Senftenberg, we continually saw strange wanderers – soldiers, marching home without their companies. Going home was foremost in their minds. Sporadically and unexpectedly, interception posts had been set up for the apprehension of these lonely, forlorn people. Their cer-

---

5 Dresden was heavily bombed, between February 13 and 15. For the first time in the war, there was a massive night attack on Dresden by 773 British (Royal Air Force) Lancaster bombers, followed in daylight by about 600 planes of the United States Eighth Army Air Force. The city was devastated by the firestorm. By some estimates, up to 200,000 were killed. This, of course, included many refugees from the Eastern Front. This bombing has come to be considered a controversial move as Dresden was not a major military target.

tain fate was the ruthless return to their ranks in the armed forces. Earlier we had seen a Saxon (judging by his dialect), walking towards freedom, pulling a side of bacon behind him on a string. The next passerby was a pitiful, footsore, little man in battle fatigues, with his gun and a small bundle. On that day, Kasi was in the big wagon, Gerhard was in the covered wagon, and so I had room for him beside me on the driver's seat. He took up my offer of a lift so eagerly that he swung his gun around wildly while scrambling in and smashed the wagon window that divided the driver's seat from the interior. Against the window, on the inside, was the precious oil painting of my father's grandmother by Timoleon Neff, depicting her when she was a young woman. Luckily, neither the gun nor the glass went through the canvas. My ancestor, covering up the gaping hole, became the protector from the icy February winds, and she was faithful to this task right to the end in Leitzkau. The little soldier travelled with us no further than Senftenberg, where he disappeared, grey-clad, into the grey fog.

For the first time, since we had left Sprottau, we were supplied bread. The National Safety Service, in conjunction with the army, handed out free soup to the refugees – a wonderful, tasty and nourishing soup. Added to the soup was a special offer of army bread, and we got eleven loaves. This addition to our food was very welcome as, due to the freezing temperatures, we had not been able to take potatoes with us. My bread supply from Geppertsfeld had come to an end. It had lasted a long time, and we had eaten the last of it, sparingly, like precious cake. Jan and Borowiak were both hearty consumers.

The first thing, we now heard, was that the women and children from Kottbus and Dresden, were expected to arrive here, and, furthermore, that Senftenberg itself was to be evacuated, for the people feared an imminent air attack.[6] In spite of this, Kasi wished to remain here in Senftenberg, for she was tired of the endless, tedious journey. My father rented a room for her with a Frau Busch, the friendly woman with whom we had spent the previous night. After all had been taken care of, and we had unloaded her things, we had lost half a day. Thus, it was afternoon when we started out.

Jan and Borowiak were proving to be increasingly careless and inattentive with the horses. I had to be constantly on the watch to verify that our four-legged helpers really got the good care that they needed and deserved.

---

6 On 22 February, there were more heavy air attacks by the British Royal Air Force and United States Army Air Force planes on widely spread-out targets, including Dresden.

Jan, always in too much of a hurry, was kicked by the grey in the soft part of his leg. Fortunately the injury was not serious, but was, as would be expected, quite painful. Jan was unhappy! To top it all off, my little horse Anmuth got loose overnight. We found her the next morning with a fist-sized wound on her hindquarter. She had been kicked by one of the horses, which had been shod with caulks (for extra grip on the ice). From my travelling apothecary, I applied Rivanol, cod liver oil and Morphanil Prontalbin powder on the wound. Eventually the wound healed, but for the time being we could only be thankful that she was still able to hobble along behind us. The big, red, flesh wound in her black fur looked terrible!

We carried on in this sad and sorry state, stopping on the 17th of February in Mückeberg to grease our wagons once again. Until this time, we had had luck with the evenness of the countryside, for none of our wagons was equipped with brakes. Now, however, the land became rolling and hilly, and the horses had to stop to rest half way up a steep hill. Jan laid a stake, clumsily between the spokes of his heavily loaded wagon, and bang, one spoke was broken! My father was worried, for we owned no proper tools to make roadside repairs. With much trouble, the wheel was temporarily fixed, and after a good hour's delay, we continued onward. After this, we took a great deal more care with our braking methods!

A mass camping place for refugees, prepared by the German army, was located in Bad Liebenswerda. It was a grisly looking spot, but here again we were lucky for my mother and Gerhard found some kind people who took us into their own house. To a large degree, the horses did not fare so well. The countryside was poor, and there was not even straw. We, however, had coffee served with both our evening and morning meals. How wonderful that tasted! What a tremendous luxury coffee was!

Early on the 18th of February, we broke camp and headed for Torgau. We met a different troop of pitiful-looking figures on the road. They were English prisoners-of-war, who dragged themselves along, carrying their few possessions in little boxes, suitcases, and sacks. They were a grey-green column of helpless sufferers, with, at best, a few footsore guards. As their prisoner-of-war camp had been evacuated, they found themselves neither with means of transport, nor with any destination. One had the impression that not one of them knew where they were going. "Away from the Bolshi," seemed to be the one driving force for us all.

The guards suffered as much as the prisoners from lack of sleep and nourishment. Bad Liebenswerda would somehow have to feed twenty-nine thousand people, but where, without any preparation, could they find so much food? The head of the welfare department, to whom we also applied, was desperate. Finally, the prisoners-of-war were allotted a big deserted hay shed, where they spent the night. On their departure, they were each given one piece of sausage and a piece of bread. These were their provisions, but no one knew for how long this small amount had to last.

Our teams soon overtook this long, grey procession. We noticed a small horse-drawn cart carrying the sick, straggling at the rear. It seemed to take us an endless time to leave them behind. Upon fear of grave punishment, we were not allowed to talk to these pale, lost-looking men. I longed to chat a little with them to inquire into their fate. As our trek continued, we came across a place where a similar group of prisoners had stopped and discarded the things that had grown too heavy for them. Jan and some village boys, who had also discovered this treasure-trove, excitedly searched through the abandoned effects. I saw one happy boy with a newly acquired accordion. I was presented with one of the items from Jan's harvest – a boot brush with "Gift from the Red Cross" inscribed on it.

Having reached Lönewitz, we tried in vain to find a place to warm ourselves as well as our food, although we did not want to spend the night. After long discussions at several places, we were allowed to cook our potatoes at an inn. In addition we received coffee and a bit of meat, so that, quite strenghtened, we continued to Neiden, where certificates for accommodation were issued. We had the good luck of finding space to stay the night with a confirmed bachelor who lived quite alone. It was evident that he ran his household with perfection, as everything was clean and tidy. He gave us fresh fruit, drank home-brewed cider with my father, and was uncommonly gentle and attentive. Certainly we had to sleep in cold and close quarters, but his treatment was really heartwarming. After a long time of travelling and meeting all kinds of humanity, here was a sensitive person who sympathized with us, showing us that he understood our position, a fate that could easily become his own.

Generally speaking, during this period of time, the people we met made few mentions of flight. The further west we went, the better was the care given to refugees. Here, one was not merely issued room coupons but also food coupons. The homeless did not have to rely for the daily necessities of life, solely on luck or charity or on the noonday soup of the National Safety Service. As we immediately took advantage of these latest coupons, we were able to enjoy a memorable meal of breaded veal cutlets at an inn called *Zu Pretsch an der Elbe*.

Since Torgau, we had been on the left bank of the Elbe River. Who would have thought, how difficult it would be to get back again to the other bank? Fritzi, my brother's wife, was on the right (east) side of the Elbe River – that was our goal. I had to go to her, for only there could I hope to receive news of my husband. In the letter I was able to send him from Lissa, I had told him that Leitzkau was my planned destination. There, I hoped, to find some news.

We arrived in Dorna that evening. We had telephoned ahead from Neiden for reserved rooms. It was a strange feeling to be able to telephone again, if only over a short distance. When we arrived in Dorna, however, no one seemed to know anything about us. The innkeeper mentioned, in a huff, that he already had a hundred Black Sea Germans under his roof.[7] However, the Bürgermeister was kinder. He found us shelter at a little place owned by an especially helpful woman called Frau Gammel, who, in reality, had no room for us as she had already taken in so many others. Still, she invited us in, with great generosity, and gave us a huge evening meal consisting of bread and sausage, along with potatoes and quark. The following morning, she supplied us with coffee and fresh eggs. This sheltered feeling, of course, was restful and recouperative, but still, during the night, we could hear the rumbling of heavy planes, the growling of bombs, as well as the sound of far-away shooting. Again, we were spared.

I found out that it was possible to send telegrams from Dorna, and we immediately dispatched one to Fritzi in Hohenlochau, as well as another to my sister Nita in Munich. As we discovered later, however, this latter message never reached her. Strengthened within and without, we quickly covered the fifteen kilometres to Wittenberg, arriving early on the 20th of February. It was a picturesque old town situated on the Elbe. In spite of the damage caused by the war, the very air breathed history. The cathedral was untouched, seeming to look down gloriously and majestically on the small pathetic victims of war who hurried through the town. We felt distressingly homeless and displaced as we drove down the streets in the midst of the endless streams of other refugees. We went straight through, for it was not

---

7 Black Sea Germans were descendants of Germans from Schwaben [Swabia] who, under a decree by Catherine the Great, were settled in the area of the Black Sea. These people were among the other refugees of German descent from the Eastern Front who were fleeing from the Bolsheviks.

advisable to stop in bigger towns. My father was also impatient to get to his last destination, Leitzkau.[8]

We had crossed the Elbe. Did we know how difficult, if not impossible, it would be to come back to the west side? The landscape was especially beautiful in the brilliant sunshine. The winding Elbe River flowed quite near the road, and then out of sight again. We ate our lunch at an inn located in Cosswig, and then continued through the woods, where army engineers were practising dynamiting. In the *Stumpfen Eck* restaurant we found two rooms, but the nearness of the big towns of Dessau, Magdeburg, Wittenberg, Halle, and Leipzig filled the night with the howling of air-raid sirens. We did not go into an air-raid shelter but lived in a new world of horror, both real and imagined.

Wednesday, the 21st of February was the last day of our trek. While we drove through Zerbst, I remembered little Allo, my brother's child, who had died in the hospital here a few months ago. What a sweet child he had been.

I still had no news of Else.

---

8 Leitzkau was the final destination, as Martha von Rosen's sister-in-law, Fritzi von Kügelgen, lived there on the estate of Hohenlochau. As other family members knew of this address, Martha von Rosen hoped for news of her husband there. As they then envisioned this as the final goal, the travellers were naturally anxious to reach it.

✸ 3 ✸

AN END TO FLIGHT

How strange it seems now, but I did not look forward at all to our arrival at the estate of Hohenlochau. I simply wanted to find letters from Jörn, but sadly there were none. Hohenlochau was a very attractively laid out property. On one side of the estate buildings were the dark woods, while the green fields came right up on the other. Yet the main house seemed unfriendly, for it stood right among the workmen's quarters, which somehow seemed to make our homelessness even more apparent.

Fritzi was living in the foreman's house, where she had one room to herself, besides two rooms upstairs for the children and Ulla, the nanny. It was difficult for her not to live in her own house, and she felt most uncomfortable. My parents had a room in the manager's house. Unfortunately, he and his wife were not very pleasant people. I slept in the same building as Fritzi. First I was in the living-room with Gerhard. I did not have much with me, but the little I did have, I did not know where to place. Then Ulla had the generous idea of giving up her room upstairs, and we were allowed to move in there. What a relief that was!

Fritzi was a good friend of the Baroness Münchhausen, whom I also knew from the old days in the Baltic. She lived with her husband in the century-old castle Leitzkau. Baron Münchhausen took my horses over for his farm work for it was now spring and every extra horse was useful. He left me one for personal use and said that he would always have another, if there was a crisis.

After having had to sit still for so long, Gerhard was very happy. He found a charming playmate in his cousin Sandy. Ulla even gave him his very own toys, selected from among her children's less popular ones. We were endlessly grateful for having arrived, but I felt uncomfortable in the strange unfriendliness of the whole place. I did not want to go on travelling at this time, my main thought still being to continue the search for my daughter Else. Just how I was going to go about it was still a complete puzzle. The addresses I had been given by the officer in Schatzdorf were all lost, except for the one in my pocket which was in Wanzleben near Magdeburg. I decided to drive there with my team and Baron Münchhausen kindly lent me his little shooting trap for the journey.

First of all, however, we were invited to Baron Münchhausen's for Sunday lunch, where such luxuries as whipped cream in coffee were reminders of another world! I met Herr von Harpe from the estate of Engdes in Estonia, with his daughter-in-law. He was worried by the constant air-raid alarms, and since he could not stay there with his eighteen horses, he had decided to look up some friends further north and find better accommodations.

Everyone told of their various experiences of the past months. I talked of my missing Else, only nine years old, who had fled with the von Rosenstiels. On the following day, the von Harpes drove on to Stendal and I carried on with my travel to Wanzleben. I went through Magdeburg, where one could still drive undisturbed over the bridge, but on the roads people were constantly endangered by the strafing of the planes. Sometimes we were warned to stop immediately and to look for the nearest cover. The first time I did not understand this. The sirens howled penetratingly and my carriage rattled noisily on the pavement of Ottersleben. I should have crept away somewhere, but my primitive thought was to get away as quickly as possible. Luckily I was set straight by some passers-by and ended up pressed against a house wall, trembling all over. There I remained until it grew quiet again.

Despite the number of refugees living there already, I found a friendly welcome in the over-filled castle of Wanzleben. The hosts were kind, but there was no hint of the whereabouts of Else. That night we experienced two more air-raid alarms. I quickly put something on and stumbled tiredly with the others into the over-full cellar. As soon as the "all clear" sounded, we climbed back into bed, more sleepy and tired than before. I was there for only that one night, but how wearying it must have been for all those others, week after week! For years, people living there had been in terror of these nightly raids on the big towns. We were luckier on the right bank of the Elbe. The danger of bombing there was not quite so great, nor was it so overcrowded.

So I drove back to Hohenlochau again. Another alarm sounded as I passed near an army station. I would gladly have left the road and taken shelter in the trees, but deep ditches on each side made turning off impossible. This time I heard them announce low-flying strafer planes. I stood still, helpless, and could already hear the sound of the swooping aircraft coming nearer. Suddenly a thick impenetrable fog developed. I did not know it then, but the German army covered valuable stock areas with synthetic fog! This district happened to be an especially tempting target because of all the large warehouses. After dipping down and rising again a few more times, the pilots gave up, and I drove on to Hohenlochau.

On my return, I wrote letters to all the addresses, newly acquired at Wanzleben, asking about Else. Whether those letters ever arrived I have no way of knowing, for too many connections were already broken. English and American troops pushed nearer from the west, but no one knew exactly where they were. The Russians came from the east, and all were dropping bombs on Germany, which was squashed between the two fronts.[1] It was very clear to me that we could not stay here much longer, but I thought only of Else.

One evening when I had been back a mere two days from my latest search, I received a telephone call from Lotte Baroness Münchhausen's sister, Christa von Lilienfeld – no more than three kilometres away: "Please come and get Else."

There are no words to describe the emotions that I felt at that moment. In an instant I became a little miserable heap of humanity. My knees became jelly-like, my voice no longer sounded – only the tears ran over my face. One cannot grasp anything, except that the greatest of God's miracles has happened!

"My Else, my Else, my child, Else…" I could only sob over and over as I threw myself into my parents' arms.

Jan hitched up quickly and my willing horses made good time, but my heart flew ahead, as if on wings. How is she? How would I find my beloved child? Well and healthy? I was not kept in suspense long, before I held my happily sobbing child in my arms. The terrible need, which she had locked

---

1 Military history records that on 10 April 1945 the U.S. Ninth Army took Hanover and on the following day reached the Elbe south of Magdeburg. On 16 April 1945, a tremendous bombardment took place along the Oder and Neisse Rivers. Zhukov and Konev were breaking out of their bridgeheads and were driving northwest for Berlin, hoping to reach it before the Allies. Zhukov reached Berlin first on 21 April, so Koniev drove westwards and reached the Elbe at Torgau on 25th of the month.

up in her frantic little soul, could finally come pouring out unhindered. When people dare to tell me there are no miracles, I do not have to answer, for I know that I was allowed to experience at least this one!

The von Harpes, our old friends from Estonia, had driven 111 kilometres north from the Baron Münchhausens' to Nahrstädt (near Stendal), to visit Frau von Cramm. I had not listened carefully when they had told me where they were planning to go. Frau von Cramm was the sister of my dear friend, Frau Gutti von Rosenstiel. In Nahrstädt, the von Harpes were introduced to the old lady, Frau von Rosenstiel, and they asked her if she, by any chance, knew a lady by the same name, who had brought a little girl called Baroness von Rosen with her.

"That is I, and the little von Rosen child is in the next room," was the immediate reply.

As the von Harpes were returning in their coach the following day, they decided to take Else back with them to Leitzkau. The drive had been full of exciting experiences, as a foal had been born en route. There had been an air-raid alarm in Burg near the airfield, they had watched an air battle over their heads and had seen the German aircraft give chase, eventually shooting down the enemy planes.

My little child had lived through hard weeks, for even at a mere nine years of age she was old enough to understand the desperate seriousness of her situation. On Friday, the 19th of January, she had been brought from Lipie to the Hohensalza train station. There were five children, the nanny Kohli, and the grandmother in the party. The train was overflowing. Else constantly kept her little suitcase clutched tightly in her clamped hand. She had her total possessions in there. There were not many of them, but among them was her only book of *Grimms' Fairy Tales*. Kohli tried more than once to take it out of her hand to put it with the other luggage, but Else would not let go. She was eventually proven to have done the right thing, as part of the luggage did get lost on the way. After many changes, they reached the estate of Gorgast, their property on the Eastern Railway Line.

There, they waited for the parents von Rosenstiel, who planned to follow them on Saturday with horses and wagons. They waited, and waited, but no one came – only the word that the Russians were coming ever closer. When the city of Landsberg had been taken, the grandmother at last decided to give in to the constant urging of the army contingent stationed there. They were brought to Berlin in an overloaded army automobile and then they drove through the badly damaged streets by streetcar. The metropolis looked frightful from the constant bombing. How they actually reached Stendal, I do not know.

Nevertheless Else was very unhappy. Kohli constantly made it obvious that she was not a member of the family, seemingly begrudging her every bit of food. During all this time the old lady had stayed away from the nurse and the children. Her concern over her son and daughter-in-law, who she now believed could surely not have escaped in time, was simply too much for this old person. No one ever heard of her son again. After five nightmarish years of Polish imprisonment, her daughter-in-law returned to her children, who were by then scattered to different homes.

Our little daughter wept alone over her terrible troubles. She cried into her pillow so that no one would know how desperate she was to have lost her '*Mutti*,' for she found Kohli hard, sarcastic, and quite devoid of understanding. She wanted to leave the others, being confident that alone she would find me. And now God, in His wonderful way, had solved her dilemma.

Now that we were all together again, we could have trekked on, but the air-raids had increased. The low-flying planes were known to follow single vehicles found on the roads to strafe them. Added to this were my worries about the failing brakes. I was, quite honestly, too scared to go on, so I hesitated, thereby missing the chance when it would still have been possible.

My big, strong, grey mare gave birth to twins, but both were dead. My horses, stabled with the oxen, were fed by the stable boy. As I judged him to be no animal lover, I often sneaked into the stable in the late evenings, finding them thirsty, hungry, or with mouldy feed in their mangers. The next shock came in the form of Anmuth's illness. She developed badly swollen glands. I nursed her myself, and with daily special care I managed to keep her alive. She infected the other horses, however, which caused an indignant hue-and-cry from the Baron Münchhausens who had counted on having healthy horses that could be put to work.

Along with all these troubles came the catastrophe of the closed bridges. Due to the threat of troops advancing from all sides, the shattered towns and the fleeing people, the habitable area west of the Elbe River was getting tinier every day. As there were war manoeuvres on every side, in the air, as well as on land, the SS had closed the bridges, so that only under certain conditions was it possible for eastern refugees to come west. The Russians seemed, momentarily, to have been held up, after their first rapid advances. We heard, however, that the English and Americans were steadily advancing in our direction, so we decided that the best thing to do would be to wait for the Allies right where we were.[2]

It was already the end of March. My father diligently built brakes for the work wagon. It was rumoured that all who did not, or could not trek any further would lose their horses and wagons. Since our horses were again fit for work, we wanted to be prepared. During this time, I received the first mail from my husband, in reply to my letter sent from Lissa. I had written to him constantly, telling him of every plan and move we made, but I had not known whether anything had ever reached him. Now that we were in contact again, he knew that we had gotten out safely. At the same time, I got a card from Kottbus, from a certain Dr. X, with the following message:

> "The Hospital of Jarotschin passed through Kottbus and had to leave part of their belongings here. Dr. Tucholsky wrote me to tell me to pick out certain things of his and in doing so, I came upon your name and address on a trunk full of valuables. When could you possibly come and pick them up?"

The message was dated the 26th, March 1945.

I fought a hard, if short, battle with myself. Kottbus was almost two hundred and twenty kilometres to the East, and the Bolsheviks were known to be a mere thirty kilometres from there![3] I had already sacrificed most all the family treasures that remained in Geppertsfeld. In the haste of the last-minute departure, I had left behind countless valuables, in addition to irreplaceable mementos. Should I also be the one who would now cause the family silver to be lost? All the beautiful von Rosen silver, as well as the silver my parents had given me for our wedding? When my father-in-law had to leave Riga in 1919, he had managed to save some of it. My husband treasured it. I resolved that this family treasure should not be lost because of my fears! Against better judgement and common sense, I planned to travel back into the environs of the active front, to retrieve these heirlooms.

I asked Baron Münchhausen, who was in the yard, to allow me to take my fastest horses, and borrow the shooting trap again. He acquiesced unwillingly. An hour later Jan and I were, once again, driving towards the east.

---

2   The Soviet military, however, cleared both German strongholds – the Küstrin on 12 March and the Glogau on 30 March - and thereafter had the Oder-Neisse line under control.

3   The Soviets were holding the Oder-Neisse configuration at this point. The town of Kottbus, about 25 kilometres west of the Neisse River, constituted a strategically important place, lying close to the Breslau-Berlin autobahn. It was a dangerous location for any refugee.

My father was also very much against the whole idea, but my ever-understanding mother gave me her quiet blessing, and we drove away in the firm conviction that I was doing the right thing.

On the first day we drove as far as Rosslau. It was late, but the route was familiar, as was the stable where we had stayed five weeks before. We put up the horses, whereupon Jan and I slept on the straw in the passage. At the last minute my mother had given me our fur sleigh-rug, which I used to cover myself; however, of all horrors, Borowiak had used it on the trek, and it was full of lice! I realized where the trouble lay far too late for action, for at first I had blamed it on the straw. The whole next day was misery, therefore, for I was unable, while driving, to wage war on a hungry pack of mites. I had no choice, but to throw the whole thing out, as there was nothing else I could do with it!

We went a long way that day, for the horses had only a light wagon to pull. How still the land was – how peaceful. We saw no tanks, no soldiers. They were probably all concentrated closer to the real zone of fighting. It was springtime. We saw curlews and larks. In the evening, we turned off onto the property of some unusually charming and gentle people, the von Marées. They were landowners who wished to remain on their own property regardless of what happened. Here you did not rub shoulders constantly with your neighbours as they generally lived a distance away. Furthermore, they felt that the chances of fleeing were almost impossible. I was deeply ashamed to come into such a welcoming and clean house bringing my lice! I could only hope that this hungry infestation would remain with me when I left, saving me the embarrassment of being a louse carrier. After supper, I was led to a room, highlighted by a snow-white, freshly made bed. When at last I was alone, I put a sheet on the floor, and standing on it, took off my clothing, piece by piece, examining each item singly. The victorious result was that I spent a naked and peaceful night.

The next day we drove to Uckro, a railway station from where I hoped to reach Kottbus. I would need much luck. I would have to change trains. It was late in the evening when I found a place to leave Jan with the horses. I queued up in front of the ticket counter.

"What do you want in Kottbus? Only those living there can buy tickets!"

Not knowing what to do next, I turned away, when suddenly a man beckoned to me, offering to purchase a ticket for me in his name. The ticket got me only as far as Kirchhain, where I had to change trains in any case. Once there, however, I had no more trouble, finally actually sitting in the train headed for Kottbus.

It was six o'clock in the morning when I arrived. I hurried straight to the place from which Dr. Tucholsky's message had designated. What a dismal picture of a town Kottbus made! Only here and there, a house had been left standing among endless reaches of ruins. I did not have far to go, and the household seemed quite prepared for early visitors. At eight o'clock that same morning, another train would be going back west. If I could not catch that one, I would have to wait until the afternoon. So I had to hurry.

The woman at the address given to me was in a dangerous situation. Her husband was in the SS and she herself was a leader of the *National Sozialistische Volkswohlfahrt* and was known to have affiliations to the party. She was an obvious target for the advancing Bolsheviks, and local Bolshevik sympathisers would be expected to point her out.

She offered me an aromatic cup of refreshing coffee and I again recognized the special luxury. Then we immediately hurried to the open coal cellar, where I found my trunk. I hastily tied it up with string, and then asked if there was any possible way to transport it to the station, for it was, after all, a steamer trunk and more like a little chest than a suitcase. There were neither horses nor cars available. In fact, I doubt that there was a single vehicle left in the whole town. After much trouble, the obliging woman succeeded in mobilizing a fourteen-year-old boy with a hand cart, and together we pushed it to the station. It was now nine o'clock and I was certain that the train must have left. Yet, suddenly an attendant beckoned me: "Right here over the tracks, but quickly…." Led by him, we hurried, over a network of rails, directly to my train, reaching it just as it was gearing into motion. Fortunately for me, it had been unaccountably delayed!

Also I found unexpected help changing trains in Kirchhain. I had in exactly twenty-four hours of unspeakably good fortune accomplished my mission. When I arrived, I simply threw my treasured trunk out of the train, for, as it was pitch dark, I was certain that no one would steal it in the short time that it would take me to go to fetch Jan and the team.

Jan and I started our journey home that same evening. It was Thursday in Easter week. I hoped to be back with my family by Sunday. With our well-rested horses, we made good progress, but as always, I kept them constantly at a walk to save their strength for an unexpected emergency. We did make it back in time to celebrate Easter with my loved ones, but we all agreed that it had been the very last possible moment to drive back toward the East.

I was barely back when the German army called my horses up for inspection. They took three of my best draught horses away from me. I fought hard for my little Anmuth, for she was, after all, a mere 1.35 metres high, and therefore under the required height. "But she is the most perfectly proportioned animal here," said the SS Chief.

I realized this, of course, and the tears rolled down my cheeks for I would never have such a horse again. She had a large proportion of Arab blood in her, like so many of the horses from the Warthegau. To ride her gave one a sensation akin to flying! In addition to being a first-class puller, she was a lively, temperamental saddle horse. Quite recently, she had impishly run away with me during a ride through the woods, when she was surprised by a wild sow with her young. For quite a distance, we had raced next to the sow and her litter until they crossed the path and disappeared into the thicket.

Of all those whose horses were requisitioned, I think I was the only person who was recompensed. I received 3,500 marks, but to do so I had to persistently follow closely behind these men, not relenting, until I received the cheque in my stubbornly outstretched hand. I also cashed it on the very same day, which, as I later heard, was the last opportunity to do so.

Now the idea of continuing became even more remote, as the whole situation was becoming more critical for us all. Military men were quartered in the courtyard, making our position an obvious target for the approaching Allied troops, who had pushed as far as the Elbe and were shooting at the castle of Leitzkau, right over our heads. While they were damaging it, they also severely bombed the whole surrounding neighbourhood. The mistaken Allies imagined that there were news stations and observation posts in the castle towers. Daily the heavy bomber-planes passed over us on their way to attack Berlin, flying over Hanover and Braunschweig. Magdeburg and Dessau were also subjected to heavy attacks. Like that night near Dresden, we were on the outside, as we watched those awe-inspiring 'Christmas trees,' thrown like a horrible blanket over Dessau. It was like a vivid nightmare, the spectacle of those flying Porters of Death with their weapons of murder, and yet it was hypnotically impressive, almost to the point of beauty.

The increasingly frequent gunfire, soon made us extremely irritable and nervous. Immediately outside the high, grey, clapboard fence, surrounding the estate buildings, my father dug a pit, deep enough to stand in, covering it first with planks, and then topping it with straw. This became our home. He planned to put earth on top of this later. There was already a so-called air-raid shelter in the house, but that was no more than a re-christened vegetable cellar, always overflowing with panicky people at the least sign of danger.

I did not want to risk going anywhere with the few horses the military had allowed me to keep. Fortunately, however, I had acquired a bicycle left by a German soldier, who had wished to swim across the Elbe. With this I went to Leitzkau to buy bread. The bakeries were still open, in spite of the daily bombardments. I had just reached the town when I heard the sound of the ubiquitous dive-bombers. I quickly turned back. They had been known to hunt down even a single person on the city streets, as well as on the open roads. I pedalled as hard as I could. I was only half way home, however, when I heard the unmistakable sound of the 'diving of the *Jabo*.'[4] In panic, I leaped off my bicycle and rolled into the ditch. Directly above me, the shooting began with a permeating "prr ... prr...." I stumbled along a few steps further in the ditch, first into the little brook, and then under a stone bridge. There I felt a bit more protected, for the wet grey stones were sizeable and heavy. Two or three times more I heard the sound of diving and shooting, probably at my bicycle. I crouched in the cold water of early spring, waiting. Only when everything was quiet, did I dare to come out. My knees were shaking and I was trembling all over from fear and cold.

When I reached the farmyard, I found that I was not the sole creature who had been through an unpleasant experience. There had been an attack on the whole neighbourhood, and on yet another road, the *Jabo* had hunted down and senselessly shot at many harmless pedestrians. The yard and the buildings were riddled and whipped with bullets. Our top-storey apartment was also stuck full of them, and in the bathroom alone, Gerhard collected eight bullets. The only living things visible in the yard during the attack, two big Alsatian dogs, remained chained-up and unharmed. Many cattle and horses were killed in the fields.

My mother, with the children, had hurried to the pit, from which they waved white pieces of cloth. The pit, which served as our subterranean living quarters, being located outside of the barnyard, lay, as we hoped, outside the destructive path of the strafers. The straw on our pit roof, was not yet covered with earth, and as the strafing flyers had included incendiary tracer bullets with their ammunition, we had reason for concern.

---

4 *Jabos* (or [hunter] bombers, i.e., low-flying fighter planes) carried air to surface weapons for ground attacks.

In the middle of the yard, horse-drawn wagons loaded with ammunition were camouflaged with straw. Fortunately only one straw-heap had caught fire. During one of the brief pauses, while the airplanes were circling for another strafing run, one of the soldiers came out of hiding and calmly doused the burning straw that covered the munitions' supplies with buckets of water. There had been no serious accidents, and only our Buda was irreparably shot up. How faithfully it had served us over those many kilometres!

I experienced still another air-raid in Leitzkau. Once, when I had bicycled there to get provisions, I had discovered a completely abandoned state-owned provisions camp and was told that anyone could go there to fetch whatever they wanted. I was amazed by what I found. How many millions of refugees had neither knife nor fork, yet here, going to waste, was everything that a household might need! Now that there was extreme danger in moving about, everything was available – what a shame.

I put together a rucksack of all the most urgently needed articles but I had barely gone twenty steps when an air-raid began. Even on this diminutive, narrow street I was directly shot at! I left my bicycle and rucksack lying there, burst into a nearby store and down into its air-raid shelter. There I found other horrified souls who had been even quicker than I. In the dark and narrow room, we cowered, waiting – endlessly. I finally dared to go home under the cover of dusk. An aluminium spoon, a big meat cleaver, and many memories came with me from that trip, brought eventually even as far as our new home in Canada.

The tiny area of unconquered Germany became steadily smaller. We could not understand, however, why the Allies did not approach faster. One heard the droning of guns in the East, from the big battles of Treuenbrietzen, and the continued bombardment of Leitzkau. The latest edifice, that had been ruined, was the beautiful old church tower. One had to clamber over heaps of ruins and crumbling rubble to get from one house to the next. As a precaution Lotte Baroness Münchhausen's grandmother, old Frau von Grünewald, was moved into a workman's house in a quieter district of Hohenlochau. We all felt like cornered animals.

At last Fritzi, my sister-in-law, and Baroness Münchhausen entered the British camp at night. The two women talked openly to the Allies, Fritzi herself being American. They asked if they could find living quarters with them and the Allies agreed, but told them that they should come without any luggage and without the children's nurse. This Fritzi did not want to do, as she had two little boys and was carrying an unborn baby.

It was by now clear to all of us that we could expect not the British, but the Russians here. How could we have known that the Elbe River had been the prearranged boundary line for the advancing troops?

My Buda was virtually in pieces. The German soldiers had confiscated the wagon, along with my father's beautiful new brakes. The sole remuneration I had received for all this was enough horse-hair from their horses' tails to make a floor broom, artistically constructed by Jan. We still had four horses and one wagon, however. We loaded whatever we could, including remaining horsefeed. On the back, we tied a basket with our five newly acquired hens. We tied a young sheep to trot along behind. The general mood was scary. Bolshevik-oriented individuals appeared from nowhere. The wagon was heavily loaded with the trunks we had sent with Fritzi when she left *Warthegau* in August of 1944. As well as this, there were all the things that my mother had sent on ahead with Fritzi in August 1944. The wagon was simply overflowing. Sadly, we decided to leave five cases of books behind, along with Frau von Stritzky's big trunk, which I left in the responsible care of old Frau von Grünewald. I overhauled my own luggage, and gave Borowiak, who had decided to remain behind, a few of my husband's clothes and some money.

Heavily laden, we ultimately drove off on the 20th of April. My father, both children, Jan, and I walked, while my mother sat amid all the luggage. As Leitzkau was still being bombed by the Allies, we skirted it on small country roads, coming out toward the North, where we found the hard-surfaced road which led through Gommern. Here we saw where the Nazis had hanged a twenty-one-year-old boy because he had dared to say that there was no longer any hope of a German victory. As a gruesome warning example to other Germans, they had left his body dangling for all to see.

We aimed for the Elbe River. Somewhere, we thought, one must be able to cross it. Fritzi had two heavy draught horses from the Baron Münchhausens', and a flat wagon, which was much more practical for loading than the wagons we had. A young friend of Fritzi's from the Rhine River, Herr Kames, was the driver. We reached the river, but no arts of persuasion helped. We were not permitted to cross a single bridge. Without warning, the Allies had left their position on our side of the river and had withdrawn to the left bank.[5]

---

5 The Elbe River had become the boundary between the Allied Forces - Russians on the east side, British and Americans on the west side. The Russians occupied the east even though the Americans had previously crossed over to that side.

I was very glad to be out of Hohenlochau, for it had not been an agreeable time for us. Towards the end, the foreman had been an especially unpleasant neighbour, as he had only been interested in making up to his future masters, continually making us feel unwanted.

No one wanted to stay behind with the Russians, and thousands of people crowded together on the banks of the Elbe. I remember that there were many Dutch people also, for one of them helped me out of a very difficult situation. The road leading to the Elbe crossing went slightly downhill, before reaching a small village by the river. Else sat on Delight, who was hitched up with Udine, as the first two horses of my four-in-hand. The rear pair could not hold the heavy rolling wagon back, and the swing bar hit Udine in the heels. She became frightened, jumped, and shied. Delight conscientiously followed suit. I was fully occupied with the rear team and could not go to Else's aid. Then quickly a considerate Dutchman jumped in and saved the little girl from the by now quite wild horses. I drew the wagon to the side of the road, and together we brought it to a standstill.

This village contained a really strange mixture of people. Friends of the Bolsheviks appeared like fleas out of every crevice, and even though we too had lost everything, we were still the hated *burshui* (elite, bourgeois) to them. Many of them had spent time in concentration camps and prisons. Some were simple working people who had been forcibly taken from their various homes. As no one had any more use for them, they were unwatched and unguarded.

En route, we saw strange figures half-hidden in heaps of straw or in unused barns. The village was overfull, but we succeeded in finding room in a stable. Our method was to simply lay down on the straw covering the warm manure in a horse stall. Yes, the most important consideration, still, was warmth. The horses were stabled in another, if excessively narrow, stall.

We continued to look for a crossing place, but the whole area had been sealed off tightly. At last, we heard that there was still a possible gap at Pretzien. There were supposed to be moored barges, which could transport both wagons and horses. So there was renewed hope, but when I went into the stable the next morning, I found that one of Baron Münchhausen's big horses had kicked Delight in the shoulder, making her so crippled that she could not move. Initially, I hoped that she would be able to hobble along behind us, but she just stood sadly and watched us go. I took down half a sack of oats, on which my mother was sitting, and gave it to our host, the Bürgermeister, begging him earnestly to save this valuable animal.

We started off with our three horses. My parents sat in the wagon with Gerhard. Mother put down her hand and felt the seat, because it had suddenly become so slippery and strange. In pulling out the oat sack, I had tipped the syrup container, and my poor mother, in her beautiful seal fur, was sitting in a sticky, sweet mess! A little springtime stream of water ran next to the road. We stopped and I washed frantically, but the melted sugar stuck hopelessly to the fur. Due to our two stops, we quite lost sight of Fritzi and we did not get as far as Pretzien that night, stopping in an army camp instead. A friendly nurse helped as much as she could and found us a little water to wash out the miserable syrup, which by that time had soaked right through to my poor mother's skin!

The next morning we continued to Pretzien, a little industrial town on the banks of the Elbe. We drove our big covered wagon into the yard, in front of the locomotive repair shop, where the little country train, used in the lime quarries, had once been serviced. Fritzi had arrived the day before, and had made herself at home in the locomotive shed. From there, she had tried to locate the barges, now our last chance of reaching the other side.

I ran alone through the village, and from there to the river. The barges could be seen strewn along the banks. Thousands of people waited under the open sky for departure time. None of them had a plan. Everything seemed vague and frustratingly unpredictable. The only certain thing was that everyone wanted to leave the minute the Russians occupied Pretzien. It was said, however, that the Allies were definitely opposed to the idea of having all the refugees from the East with them!

Fritzi had her wagon standing directly in front of the train shed. We put ours in front of the warehouse. Jan slept on the wagon because we had to be very careful of thieves. We settled down on the straw-strewn floor in the tiny mechanic's office – five of us. There was just enough room for us to lie next to each other.

Wild gossip travelled ahead of the Russians. Some people asserted that they had already seen Russian tanks in the town itself, but one could not believe everything one heard. The railway yard lay on a side road that meandered through a little wood and onto meadows and fields, eventually leading to another village. As it was not a major road, we missed all the main traffic. We were soon to find, however, that the dreaded enemy feared for so long, had, as fate would have it, overtaken us.

I will never forget that night. We lay quite still on our beds of straw. With the coming of darkness, ghostly figures started to move about. We heard the sound of feet running to and fro, rattling noises, shouts, and eerie calls. I drew Else and Gerhard hard against my side, and asked God that if we had to die, at least let us die together. Despite all the confusion, I could distinctly make out the sound of unrestrained robbing and looting. Then the door was fiercely forced open and an icy white floodlight shone on our 'sleeping' faces. The single word, *spjat* (asleep), was uttered before the door closed, leaving us on our own to listen in the darkness to the greedy steps running up and down the stairs repeatedly before receding.

Slowly it grew still and we could breathe again, but none of us dared speak. Like trapped mice we lay, not daring to go out until daylight came. However, we could not get out, as the door had been barred from the outside. Labouriously I crawled through the narrow window and found that luckily the key had been left in the lock. I freed the others, and we took stock of the situation that had befallen us during the night. My father's coat had gone from the front of the door, and they had stolen the sack containing all our footwear from the wagon. From then on my heavy ski boots were all that I had for footwear! Poor Jan, who had been threatened loudly, was frightened and very agitated.

The night visitors had taken every stitch of clothing they could lay their hands on, along with any other object that had appealed to them, whether belonging to local people or refugees. Later we heard that they had been a group of prisoners-of-war (presumably Russian) from the nearby (German) concentration camps, accompanied by a few Russian soldiers.

Fritzi's wagon had been placed so far back in the yard that it had not been noticed, and she herself was unharmed. She now decided to leave immediately. Having already been to the Allies, and being certain of a friendly welcome, we encouraged her in her plans. In retrospect, I now realize, inasmuch as the Allies did not bother at all about individual refugees, we could all have joined her on the barges and landed safely on the other side. As it was, we remained behind, thereby sealing our fate.

Fritzi left with her team, along with two of my horses, in case we should cross the Elbe by walking across the bridge sometime later. Herr Kames helped with the loading. So did Jan, but later he was so frightened by the sight of approaching Russian tanks that he crossed over to the other side as well. We never saw him again. Herr Kames left with my horses, ultimately safely reaching his home in the Rhineland.[6]

---

6 Apparently Martha von Rosen, hoping eventually to cross the Elbe to the west, thought it wise to have two horses at her disposal on that side of the river. Kames agreed to take over and leave them with a farmer. Probably thinking that he would be unable to locate such a farmer, and knowing them to be valuable horses, he decided instead to take them home to the Rhineland. Martha eventually made a special trip to receive compensation for them.

We tried to arrange the situation as comfortably for ourselves as we could. First of all, we decided to move into the big locomotive shed, a move which the pompous young superintendent, Herr Elsner, generously permitted. There had been a dining room for hired hands located behind the big repair shop, and we used this for our bedroom, lying on straw, of course. In the front we set up tables. The big hall became our dining room and hallway.

We were told that we should never keep any valuables on our persons, as the Russians took everything. So I gave my father my wedding ring. He placed it in his vest pocket, because he was confident that no Russian would ever bother him. To this point, however, we had heard nothing but conflicting rumours, and apart from that one wild, night visit, we had seen nothing. The unreliable radio service was still reporting German victories and organized retreats, inasmuch as it was reporting anything at all.

My father decided to go into the village to reconnoitre. As we begged him not to take anything valuable with him, he hung his vest in the back room, over a chair, and walked away. He was stopped by no one, nor was he searched, although he came across many Russians in the streets.

Then they began passing by our yard. We were not near enough to the highway to see their tanks, but they drove by us in their little horse carts in an endless stream. Else and I busily buried a box-like trunk of wheat and bacon in the slag heap between the rails, while the little jewellery box was placed in a crack in a board in the yard. I put my bicycle in the furthest and darkest corner of our huge hallway. We put the carpet and the three big cabin trunks into a locked grain bin. The innocent hens ran around happily outside. Moritz, our last lonely horse, having somehow hurt his leg in all the excitement, stood sadly holding out his swollen limb for us to see. All reminders of the past trek were gone, and that was as it should be, because we had heard that the Russians showed no sympathy for those who had fled from them.

We had hardly finished our feverish activities, when a column of small wagons stopped in front of our gate. Soon the yard filled with dirty dishevelled fellows, who had obviously found our little road an easy one to travel. We addressed a soldier and his captain, and they were overjoyed to hear that we spoke Russian. Our first meeting thus turned out quite differently from what we had fearfully imagined. For the moment, the Russians were tired of fighting and plundering. They had reached a physical and mental climax. The Elbe region, appearing to be the current border, provided a place where they could settle down for a while and rest on their laurels.

We thought that we had stored our trunks safely in the locked shed, but before we realized it, the Russians had broken in and forced open the trunks with their bayonets, rushing off with sacks full of our goods. My father, who was interpreting for an officer at the time, saw it all happening and protested indignantly. The officer gave an order to have the thieves caught, but nothing came of it. It was like a second-rate movie, with much yelling, shouting, and futile rushing about, but there was evidently no real intention of catching the culprits! We sadly gathered our remaining possessions, consoling ourselves that the ignorant robbers had carelessly thrown away the heavy silver platters. Because these were dirty, they were not at all attractive to these unschooled people. My husband's clothes, as well as those of my father, were gone. Only a single shoe remained! We quickly packed the left-overs and took them into our back room. A soldier helped me to carry the trunk in, and another hurried helpfully beside us.

I was told to go outside, where another translator was needed. My parents were occupied elsewhere in a similar manner. When I returned, I understood. The whole thing had been a carefully planned trick. While we were in the back room, one of my helping 'friends' had opened the little window from the inside and had then detained me at the door, while the other had crept in unnoticed! With a sure hand, he had stolen my father's gold watch, along with my rings from the vest pocket. He also found my mother's watch and mine, and took my father's little suitcase with all his medical implements and toilet articles. Our old coach clock remained, nothing else. Later in the garden, in front of the window, we found a little *Tujas* (a box of birch-bark, made in Siberia) – full of cuff links and buttons. That was all. Our buried jewellery was the only remaining cache that they had not discovered!

We had hardly recovered from our sudden loss, when a soldier called me, telling me I was to come and act as a translator. I was ordered into a truck, where I sat in front together with three men, while another sat behind us. We headed for Gommern, the little town through which we had trekked only a few days before. I was abruptly told to find beds for them. I said that I could translate for them, but not assist them, as I was as much a stranger there as they were.

First we drove to the prison. Every one of its former inmates had been set free, and now the only remaining prisoners were the former wardens. The moment we stopped, the soldiers jumped down and left me sitting alone. A few went looking for more watches to steal. I caught sight of a beautiful collection, which one of them was admiring lovingly in his little sack. The others were probably on a different kind of a hunt! I felt helpless and very unsure of myself. I remained in the truck simply because it seemed to represent the best chance for me to get away again.

After an extremely long delay, the organizer of this expedition, came back with a local man, and my help as interpreter was finally required. He said that there were no beds here, but was clever enough to describe a place where we had a good chance to find some. There was, he said, a big discarded warehouse, which had belonged to the *National Sozialistische Volkswohlfahrt*. Luckily this contained not simply beds, but many good ones, and the warehouse custodian was sensible enough to co-operate. As a result, everything went smoothly, and soon we were back in the truck.

The soldiers behaved perfectly with me. On the way back, one of them asked me if I was afraid. "Afraid?" I answered, "Of what? You aren't going to do anything to me, and surely would protect me if it became necessary!" It was not until later that I realized how the Lord had held His protective Hand over me at that moment, and how much cause we all did have for real fear.

When we arrived back in Pretzien, I found that my chickens were gone. That made me uncontrollably furious! Had I not helped the Russians? They could at least watch over my things while I was gone! In my righteous anger, I held back no words, and we were soon all hunting together to find the chickens. In the end, they were not stolen at all, but sat quietly hidden in the overhanging branches of the tree next to our wagon! Although it was already dark, we managed to catch them all and carried them into the big workhouse. I led Moritz and the little sheep, who were already the greatest of friends, into a shed.

At last, we laid ourselves down on the straw, tired and weary after that first wild day of Russian domination. It was merely one day of a full year that still lay ahead of us....

✷ 4 ✷

LIFE UNDER SOVIET OCCUPATION

In May 1945, a foreign wave of humanity, termed the Russian occupation, poured over the land. Certainly one spoke of the "Russians," but this word described only one portion of this strange mass of peoples. In addition to all the different races that made up European Russia, there were also the countless tribes of the huge area that was Siberia inhabited by the Kirgisers, Tungusers, Kalmuckers, Tartars, and Mongols. I do not know them all. Many spoke only very broken Russian. On the whole, only their uniforms remained the same. These were made of a good khaki material, and consisted of a loose shirt, knee britches, and high boots. They were an amazingly undemanding people. I have seen soldiers simply lying on boards in an open shed, sleeping with nothing but their coats to cover them from the night cold.

Our family, residing in the train yard, was soon well known and respected. My parents, were especially popular and were often called on to translate conversations, which usually ended in the much greater responsibility of having to settle disputes and of setting various matters right.

The roomy engine hall, with the centrally placed, enormous, elongated table, now became a principal meeting place. Germans as well as Russians came to us. We were busy from morning till evening, constantly dealing with matters at hand, whether large or small. There were many amongst the Russians, who, probably being fathers of families themselves, found great joy in my children. I never allowed them out of my sight, however. On the second day after arriving, one of the soldiers had invited them to accompany him on a boat ride on an arm of the Elbe River, directly behind the house. The boat was no more than a little flat river raft. There was no rudder, but they zigzagged back and forth. The children, of course, were absolutely thrilled. I was elated and understandably comforted, when I had them safely back again.

My father was constantly employed mediating and interpreting between the disagreeable, self-important, young superintendent of the locomotives, Herr Elsner, and the Russians. The question of guns arose, "Did he possess any other weapons?" Herr Elsner stubbornly denied owning anything, without paying any heed to my father's wise advice and constant warnings to never hide anything nor to lie. Naturally, the Russians found the hidden guns without any difficulty, consequently placing father, as an intermediary, in a very dangerous position. At first, the Russians wanted to lock up both men! There were some very tense moments before they could be dissuaded. It was only thanks to my father's wonderful way with people, that the whole affair did not end in tragedy.

They also found Herr Elsner's radio hidden in the garden. All radios were supposed to have been promptly turned in. I watched tensely as the Russians systematically searched everywhere. With long, pointed iron prods they poked around in the garden. Loose earth, immediately suspect, came promptly under further investigation. I, however, was very proud when they did not find our bacon, hidden in the ashes and slag of the locomotive tracks. How often a soldier stood leaning against the post under which we had buried our jewellery!

A very agreeable person called Frau Dümelin had asked for and received shelter in the Elsners' house. Formerly from Magdeburg, she and her two little children actually had a room in Gommern but unfortunately happened to be in Pretzien when the Russians arrived. Her daughter was seven, while the son was but a few months old. Frau Dümelin begged us to hide her husband's military medals, as she feared being found with anything that would reveal his position as a high-ranking German officer. This pitiable, brave woman had to travel constantly between Pretzien and Gommern, to get groceries and supplies. At first, she went by bicycle and later by foot – nine kilometres each way. After the bicycle had been nearly torn from her, she begged me to take it for safe-keeping.

Still another woman, living on her own, Ingrid Baroness Wrangel (von Brevern, by birth), came to us for protection. She was a former friend of the Baron Münchhausens. She had been stranded in Schloss Leitzkau, where she had worked as a secretary until the tower in which she lived was so badly bombarded that everyone had to pack up and flee. She arrived with a little wagon, pulled by two Warthegau horses just as the bridges across the Elbe were dynamited. Now she marked time, as did we, on the east bank. She had found herself not far from Pretzien with her team of horses, two children, and an Estonian maid, when the Russians came. As there was a little horse-drawn caravan located in the woods for the forestry men to live in, she moved into this, thus at least having a roof over her head. The Estonian maid was, unknowingly, a source of protection for she soon had her 'own' Russian soldier, who jealously chased away all others. This, however, did not last long as she soon returned to Estonia, leaving Baroness Wrangel alone.

Once again, her situation was now really critical, but again luck saved her. A high-ranking Tartar officer laid a telephone under her caravan, with the instruction that, without his permission, no one was allowed near it. The Tartar himself, however, often came to play with her children. He seemed to like nothing better than to be able to get away from the other soldiers and join the warm, friendly little family group in the wagon. This saved Ingrid from the otherwise inevitable attacks from the mob of unbridled primitive *soldateska*, which roamed around the countryside. The greatest danger for her occurred when she had to go away from the wagon to find food. Once she came to us, shaking in fright, for a rider had chased her mercilessly on horseback. My father accompanied her back, for she simply did not dare to go the three kilometres alone. After that, my father often went there and brought her the extra food we occasionally had left over.

Baroness Wrangel asked two young men, who swam across the Elbe, to tell her father in Zörbig, five kilometres away, of her plight. Until now, he had known nothing of her whereabouts. One of the boys reached Herr von Brevern (her father), who then, together with his son, travelled, first by wagon and then on foot, to try to rescue her. Obtaining a boat and hiding it in thick reeds, they arranged a daring plan. Ingrid got the news by *Wasserrufpost* (river mail). This ingenious method of communication was devised by the women on the opposite side of the Elbe. They spoke in a low voice, yet very distinctly, with their mouths quite close to the surface of the water, and the waves carried the words across to the listener's ears.

Thus, on the appointed day, Baroness Wrangel stood on the bank with her two children, pretending to be cutting grass, so that her presence should not appear prearranged. However, nothing happened. No one came for her. It was after a few days when she heard that the boat, found by someone else, had been stolen from its hiding place. Shortly after this, the Russians themselves crossed the river. Changing her plans, Baroness Wrangel went alone to her former home in Berlin. She left her children temporarily with newly made local friends, until she could look after them again.

However, to return to our unfolding story. The Russians set up a bakery in our yard, where one could find occasional work loading or unloading the bread. For this, the worker was paid by the loaf – oh, what riches! There were also other tasks one could undertake. The Russians loved to eat wild sorrel, a plant, with a pleasantly sour taste, that grew along the roadside. It had to be picked by the sackful and was paid for with bread. Not being able to perform all this work without help, I hired big, strong, refugee children (refugees could be found everywhere), who earned bread for themselves. I received some bread for being the mediator. The same held true for the laundry. The Russians brought me their dirty things, and an older refugee woman was glad to wash them in return for a share of the bread.

As the Russians, at this time, still had plenty, they were very generous with gifts of all kinds. Big German warehouses had fallen into their hands. They revelled in rice, almonds, raisins, honey, and similar things, and they gave us some too. I had a special friend in the warehouse. He bore 'tender' feelings for me, although always from a great distance and with even greater tact. He was called Salnikoff. He spoiled the children dreadfully! He gave me one of the most valuable commodities of the time – dried yeast. This made it possible for me to bake bread for my mother, who could not tolerate either the soldiers' or the bakery bread. Frau Elsner, in her kindness, baked it for me in her oven. As I knew how to stretch the yeast with potatoes, this small package lasted a long time.

One soon learned that all previously held ideals and morals had completely changed. There was only one 'law' – take and possess. Our beautiful carpet vanished right after we moved into the locomotive shed. We found pieces of it much later, on the walls of a dug-out which the soldiers had excavated in a knoll, into which they carried everything they fancied like packrats. My wagon was also simply pulled away, though, thank goodness, neither my saddle nor any of the other tack were taken. I had laid these under the straw on which we slept. One of us always remained at home, for we had learned from our repeated losses.

I was always surprised at the frequent contradictions. One day, the soldiers plundered the cellar of the Elsners' house, which was stuffed full of things belonging to different refugees. They came out with a beautiful fur coat. "You can have that," said a soldier to me. Being too stunned, however, to think clearly, I instinctively refused. How stupid I was, for I should have taken it to be able to return it to its rightful owner. Nevertheless, I learned quickly how to cope in these times.

One day, with much yelling and cracking of whips, a great herd of plundered horses was driven past our yard at a gallop. Two of them split away from the main herd and came, unnoticed, into our yard. As there were no soldiers to be seen at that moment, I quickly opened a door leading to the coal shed so that the frightened animals ran inside. I immediately locked it behind them, and the whole short incident went unchallenged. We had to shovel away much coal to make room for them, but we did it gladly, as we were now again supplied with horses should the opportunity arise for us to drive on. The horses had been stolen from abandoned estates. For a short time, I kept the animals, ultimately lending them to a farmer. Horses were, of course, rare and greatly valued, and these were exceptionally strong and heavy.

There was still a war going on, however. The battles, fought near Magdeburg, were the last desperate, defensive, efforts by the German troops, and on the 7th of May, the "Terror without End" turned into the "Terrible End." There would be no more shooting, for this was unconditional surrender![1]

The joy of the Russians was primitively loud and generously wetted with alcohol. In need of something, I went to the big warehouse, where I discovered a heap of soggy Russians sitting and drinking to victory. A Finn, an officer with cold, blue eyes, roughly invited me to sit down to drink with them, which I promptly refused to do. Whereupon Salnikoff, raising his glass, said: "How can you expect Maria to drink to our victory? We should all be grateful that the war is over, and this she will realize and agree with." I was amazed at the fine sensitivity and tact of this otherwise simple man.

With the Finn, however, our different opinions did not end here. "Do you believe in God?" He attacked me. "Naturally, I believe. Why shouldn't I?" "You call yourself an educated person, and yet you believe in God?"

When I looked down at myself, I was surprised to still be called an educated person! My, once elegant, wool suit had sacrificed its beauty more than once, as in the dirty stream during the air-raid, and my work trousers were obviously tired of work! For footwear I had the choice between my

---

[1] The first armistice was signed on the Lüneburg heath on 4 May, 1945. The unconditional surrender was signed by Generals Jodl and Eisenhower at Rheims on 6 May. A surrender was also signed by General Keitel and Marshal Zhukov in Berlin on 8 May, 1945.

old ski boots or my old slippers, the ones Salnikoff had found for me. My hair badly needed a hairdresser, and the tortoiseshell comb, which I used to keep it in place, was broken. I did not miss my coat any longer, as it was now turning into a warm summer. At that moment, I did not find myself very amusing to look at.

Moreover, Else's little dress was torn and getting too small for her. I gathered small pieces of material, which the Russians had left lying about. I found a torn blue and white tablecloth, which an energetic refugee woman gladly sewed into a sweet little skirt with suspenders and a little white blouse. Later on, when they temporarily opened the school again, Else had something pretty and clean to wear. Small blue trousers were easily and quickly made for Gerhard, who was quite content with the carefree gypsy existence.

It was not at all fun to try to stay clean all the time! Living next to heaps and heaps of coal was a great comfort on the one hand, but the coal produced layers of dust and ashes that filled the shed and everything we touched.

Not long after the big victory day, the yard suddenly filled with cattle. These poor animals, mostly beautiful cows from valuable herds, bellowed restlessly as they had not been milked for a long time. Many of their udders were already hopelessly swollen and painfully inflamed. A big, blond officer said that whoever wanted to, could milk them, so I lined up with the others. Some of the milk cows still had their stall chains around their necks. I took advantage of this and kept the chains to help me catch others. As I was busily milking, the same lieutenant came and told me to take twelve of the cows and drive them into a small pasture. There they were to remain under my control to be used to supply the Russian troops stationed here. The choice of the cows was left to me. We knew of well-fenced and excellently kept pastures behind the little wood. One of these was designated for our herd. It lay about one-and-a-half kilometres away from the locomotive yard.

Immediately, with the help of the children and using my newly acquired chains, I began catching cows. My experience at Geppertsfeld stood me in good stead, as did a great deal of luck, I am sure, for I ended up with a really excellent herd of cattle. Now came the next order. I should not milk them myself, but had to find people that would do so: "You have shown that you don't mind working, and know how to milk, now this Baroness can do it," he said, and pointed to Frau Elsner. This poor soul did not know one end of the cow from the other!

I took Herr Krause as my helper. He was one of the quarry workers whose life had become very difficult now that all work had come to a standstill. He proved to be a first-class choice. He quickly found women who gladly took over the milking, for which they received milk and bread in return. The Russians obtained milk cans, and the milk was brought to my so-called 'cellar.' This was the hole in the smithy where normally the mechanics stood to service the locomotive from underneath. Most of my time was spent in catching the cows. I did this together with Herr Krause. The poor cows, quite bewildered, behaved like completely wild animals. We were kept at a constant trot, running back and forth between house and pastures.

I had strict orders from the Russians not to give milk to anyone other than the milkers. The soldiers could come and fetch it any time they wanted to, but they made little use of it. This was so typical of them – generous and wasteful, on the one hand, and then miserly and full of revenge against the *Njemtsy* (the Germans), on the other.

Soon, I had more milk than I knew what to do with. At night, a few silent figures, who found their way to us, would receive some secretly. Among those was Frau Dümelin, who's little baby was already quite blue and bloated from lack of proper food. I made butter with one of the big butter churns the Russians had seized from the Nazis, but this I made for us.

The whole business lasted about two strenuous weeks. Then suddenly we got orders that the cows were all to be driven away. I could choose two animals as payment for my work. With little hesitation, I just grabbed the first two at hand because the Russians were already there with long whips, on foot and on horseback! Without Herr Krause's help, I could not have succeeded in separating those cows in time. One of them had just given birth to a calf. I gladly accepted this extra bonus!

They also took the cows from the neighbouring fields. One had just calved there also, and the soldiers had to leave her behind, shouting to me that I could have her also. In this manner, I now had three and gave the last one to Herr Krause, who apart from his milk ration, had received neither thanks nor payment for his work. I bedded down my latest acquisitions in the coal shed. This was located in the middle of the yard. Now, I was the proud owner of two cows, three horses, five hens and one little sheep, yet all without one square foot of land!

The soldiers were not yet finished driving off the cows. They took them, whether the animals wanted to or not, over a narrow railway bridge that led over an arm of the Elbe. There was much shouting and pushing, and the poor beaten beasts responded to each wave that drove them on from behind. One of the cows ended up with her stall chain caught behind a loose board in the middle of the bridge. She could go neither forwards nor backwards, and stood helplessly in the middle of the span. Eventually, in her frenzy, she tore up the board, and fell through the decking, hind legs first. There she hung, for many frightful minutes by her front legs, kicking with her hind legs, all the while attempting to regain a foothold. Ultimately, her strength gave out, and with a huge splash, she fell into the water, far below. We all looked down breathlessly. The Russians, on the other hand, were quite undisturbed. The water, fortunately, was deep enough that the cow, unhurt, came up and swam to the near bank. Apparently unharmed, but somewhat shaken, she continued with the others.

Another one had probably suffered a similar fate somewhere else, for later, we found her lying, dejected and miserable, in our yard. This one too was 'given' to me. I gave this cow, as well as my calf, to the mayor for his people, asking for, in addition to a piece of the meat, a piece of a field for my animals, in return. Meanwhile, Herr Krause searched around for a small wagon for me, as my big one had been taken by the Russians. We needed a cart to carry all the grass that we had to mow daily to feed our cows. The arrangement was that, as Herr Krause helped me with the cutting, besides all the other work, we would drop a portion of the grass when we passed his place on the way home.

My cows proved to have been well chosen, and gave plenty of milk. We had no further orders to desist from giving any away. I already made butter, as well as something akin to condensed milk, from the surplus. A few men came again to work in the yard, and we shared with all who came, without asking any remuneration. This happy time did not last long, however, as even though I tried to distribute milk to everyone, someone must have felt left out, for there were many communistic reactions among the people even then. The result was that I received a letter from the chief Bürgermeister of Gommern, accusing me of possessing stolen cattle and ordering me to come to defend myself.

I did not wish to travel to Gommern, as it was nine kilometres through woods, within which soldiers were always wandering. I felt half safe in our yard in Pretzien. Here I was at least under the protection of my parents, but outside I would be at the mercy of the roughest soldiers of all. We had all heard of the many experiences of the women, and had no one to thank but God that so far we had been spared a similarly unhappy fate. Nevertheless, I now had to venture out of this protected area.

During this scary walk to Gommern, I saw far ahead, on a long, straight stretch in the woods, a soldier sitting on his haunches just alongside the road. I went on, bravely, without looking at him. The moment that I was abreast of him, however, he jumped up, grabbing me by both wrists, saying: "*Frau, komm!*" ("Woman, come!"). Right away I retorted in Russian: "*Ostaw menya w pokoi.*" ("Leave me alone.")

Surprised at being shouted at in Russian, he let me go, just as quickly. I took full advantage of this short moment and ran as fast as I could. I had my light slippers on, and he, his heavy boots. In spite of all his swearing and panting, he could not catch up to me. I could sense him, slowly lagging behind, and then, at last, a turn in the path hid my last exhausted efforts from his eyes. I ran on, but with only half the speed.

In Gommern, I found myself facing the Bürgermeister, an extremely unpleasant man. He was half-Jewish, and therefore had suffered grossly in concentration camps. "Where did you get these cows?" the Bürgermeister started. "As payment for my work for the Russians." "Then you are a recipient of stolen goods." "But I worked for them honestly." "People who never owned cattle before don't need them now." "That does not apply to me then, for I left a whole herd behind." "It would make things quite different had you taken them with you."

Carrying on in this fashion, I finally managed to keep at least the horses and the sheep. I had come to Pretzien with three horses, and no one here knew that the ones I now had were not the same ones. The cows were handed over to the mayor of Pretzien and ended up at a farm, where the farmer offered to sell us a litre of milk daily.

I had to run through the woods again to get home. First, I went to Frau Dümelin's while I gathered courage. My fear was simply too great for me to continue. My loving and thoughtful father must have had a premonition of my fears, for just as I started out, he came to meet me. Slowly we walked home, where we arrived safely.

We had no more fresh milk, but also much less work to do. Without having to bother with feeding, finding grass and all that milking, I almost felt as if I were on a holiday.

Then I had another stroke of good luck. The soldiers, having plundered a large herd of pigs, had slaughtered them one morning quite near our house. They made a fire, using straw, in which they laid the carcasses, burning off the bristles. Then the heads and feet were cut off, the animals' entrails taken out, and only the carcasses taken away. All else was left lying on the ground. Gathering the heads, the feet, and everything that was of possible use, I carried these to my 'cellar.' From this windfall, I was again able to feed many hungry friends. There was an engine driver whom I was especially glad to help, as he was always cheerful and helpful. He, with his wife and fifteen-year-old son, belonged to that group with whom I was willing to share, even to the last. Naturally, this applied also to Frau Dümelin, this dear, brave person who continued to come to Pretzien, at first because of the milk, but later for other things that she obtained from other people willing to help her. Whenever it was possible, one of my parents accompanied her to Gommern.

Once, while they were walking through the woods, a troop of soldiers suddenly stopped her and my mother. One of them laughingly drew a wheelbarrow up in front of them and jokingly said: "Come Babushka, get in and I will push you!" "Very well, but my friend must come with me, for I will not go without her," my mother answered.

Over wooded paths, up and down, over bumpy roots they went – my mother took it all in the best of humour. Frau Dümelin held tightly onto the sides of the wheelbarrow, and they arrived in Gommern unharmed.

Not only on the wooded paths did this woman show her unusual courage, from time to time she even found ways and means to get to Magdeburg, where her husband lived in their home. This was always a dangerous undertaking, for she ran the risk of being taken by either the Russian or the English guards. She would go to the Elbe secretly, hiding in the reeds until it grew dark. There she would remain unseen, hardly daring to breathe as the river guards passed by close enough to touch her.

When it turned dark, she would wade into the water. If a guard noticed her and started shouting, she would splash about in the deep water, crying for help as if she were drowning. Otherwise, there was a prearranged signal and immediately a boat would come from the other side to pick her up! One time she took letters from us, for we hoped that they could thus be relayed to Fritzi, who was in the English Zone and could forward them to Nita.[2] Frau Dümelin brought back a letter from Fritzi, dated the 16th of June. She wrote that Kames, the helper whom she had left on the ferry, had

---

2 These letters were addressed to Martha von Rosen's sister, Nita Lindenberg, in Munich, Bavaria, located in the American Zone.

gone on to the Rhineland taking my horses, and that she was working as a translator for the commandant in Ottersleben. She did not manage to realize her goal of reaching Munich until towards the end of June. She did this by truck. Travelling was only possible with a permit, but naturally people often went without one.

My parents tried to help wherever they could. The mayor of Pretzien, Herr Schulz, had been jailed by Hitler for being a Social Democrat. He also managed to get into trouble with the new rulers, the Russians. He had taken over a warehouse of household goods, which had been in the care of his associates, and shared out the contents very fairly among the needy. This displeased the Russian commandant, and Herr Schulz was summoned and sentenced to be locked up. My mother was asked to go as interpreter.

The commandant accused the mayor of stealing Russian goods. The old man was quite bewildered, for what he had distributed had belonged to the village. My mother attempted to make this humane and unselfish act clear to the Russian official. Slowly he grasped the situation and retracted the accusation. Herr Schulz, deeply grateful, frequently took occasion to show it later on. He was a good and righteous man who had undergone many hardships in his life. The commandant was thankful as well, for he now realized that my parents acted without fear or selfishness. He often called on them to act as judges and mediators, and always as interpreters.

The first commandant was soon replaced by another. The new one had gone to literacy school only in his adult years. He was nonetheless an actor and theatre director by profession. He wrote very questionable, long-winded poems to his various lady loves, which my father had to translate! An amusing figure, small and graceful, very temperamental, he was always very much an actor. He was very gracious towards me and never overbearing, which I can honestly say held true for all soldiers I was in contact with in our yard. Whenever one of them dared to get fresh or cheeky, he was immediately put down by the others. "Leave Maria alone," or "With our Maria one doesn't talk like that." Why they insisted on calling me 'Maria' I have no idea, as 'Marfa' ('th' in English translates to 'f' in Russian) is also a Russian name, and would have been the proper translation of 'Martha.'

Frequently I had to cook for them, as they often came to have tea with us. When they wanted to drink vodka, we sternly pushed them outside. They were like big children, and on the whole not at all difficult to handle. Whenever I cooked for them, they usually gave Gerhard and Else bits of their food, even though the two children never asked for anything.

Only once did I meet a soldier with a distinctly unfriendly attitude. Late one evening, some officers came, bringing all the required ingredients and made me bake endless amounts of pancakes. It was already dark, and I baked the pancakes in the 'dining' room of the big locomotive hall. The children stood, watching silently. One of the officers stood nearby, following our every move. Not even a single crumb should come to us. This was unusual. One noticed clearly that the soldiers were now being checked much more strictly – the first weeks of crazy luxury had come to an end. The strings of the feed sacks were being drawn tighter, even for them!

Amongst our many acquaintances was a German engineer, with his wife, who had also arrived as refugees. He, crafty and cunning, had juggled with adversities even in Hitler's time. It was amusing to talk to such a man, displaying his special kind of intelligence and ability for self-preservation. That he had lost none of his guile was demonstrated one hot and sultry day at the end of May, when we got the order that all men between sixteen and sixty should report to the commandant's office to be registered. After former experiences of this kind in the Baltic, we knew enough to be wary and distrustful. One had to be very careful of the Russians in such situations! We warned everyone we saw, but they did not believe us. Herr Krause went in his wooden clogs and shirt-sleeves. He went as so many others did, queuing up in front of the commandant's door. It took a while for them to wonder why no one ever came out again.

The sad answer to the riddle was that this door opened into a room to register in, while in front of a second room stood a guard with a fixed bayonet. It was into this room that everyone had to file eventually. All our new acquaintances strayed into this trap. Not one of them had listened to us, or even thought to prepare themselves for a 'journey.'

Desperate women arrived in the evening, searching for their men, but they were roughly driven away. Later, this pitiful band of men was herded out like cattle, heavily guarded, shouted at, and pushed about. In spite of all the deterrents, some women attempted to give them some bread and, here and there, a jacket.

Mercilessly the guards drove these blameless, helpless people at a trot in the direction of the east. Included were old men, as well as children. Some of them were war amputees, a number of them were already sick. The shock that this senseless act of brutality left in the village, I will never forget. Why? Why? What was the reason? What had they done? We never found answers to any of these questions, other than that eight other villages and towns suffered a similar fate during that same period.

As so often happens at this time of the year, the weather suddenly changed. From the glowing hot day, it turned into a cold, rainy night. Our men lay under the open sky, their teeth chattering with the cold. To have a minimum of shelter and warmth, they laid themselves back to back. To quench their thirst, as they had been forced to walk for three days without food or water, they used tin cans to catch raindrops.

They were driven to the town of Treuenbrietzen to join a huge camp for civilian prisoners and prisoners-of-war. This was the place where those who wanted to go east of their own free will were released. The main interest of the guards was to keep the count of their prisoners steady. If one of these succeeded in escaping, or if one of them died – as did a badly wounded soldier from Pretzien – they would pick up a harmless peasant working in his field the following day! The count had to remain constant.

This brings me back to the clever German engineer. He was successful in feigning illness, consequently landing in the hospital of Treuenbrietzen. He impressively impersonated a man with serious tuberculosis, faking high temperatures each morning by surreptitiously rubbing the thermometer. Then he would hold his breath to build up his phlegm and would cough prodigiously and noisily when the medical examination took place. How he managed to do it I do not know, but after a few weeks he was the first one back in Pretzien. He stood before us and told us of his experiences during the evacuation.

He did not stay long, however, for he soon disappeared across the ever more closely guarded Elbe. People were constantly managing to cross over in boats, but these were mainly younger, single people, not a group such as we were, with my mother of seventy, my father of seventy-four, Gerhard six, and Else nine years old.

It was evident that the taking of the men had not ended, for now the Russians were also collecting the women, forty years and younger, who were capable of working. This almost included me, for I was forty-one that June. Now our escape plans became more urgent.

One clever workman had not given himself up with the other men, saying that he did not live in Pretzien. Actually, his home was a river raft on the Elbe River just outside the town. He also owned a boat. He knew the same policeman who had earlier brought me news about my cows and the

Bürgermeister. This policeman had formerly been in a concentration camp under Hitler's regime. He coveted my little sheep.

At this time, mid-June, we noticed a great deal of shifting and reappointing of the Russian personnel. Many of the occupation troops were called back, including Salnikoff, who told me that they would be returning the next week to take more equipment further east. The yard was emptier, and we felt less closely observed. The policeman and the boatman were both willing to help us, so my mother and I secretly decided on a plan of escape.

On a prearranged afternoon, we would go on a walk, as if strolling to a picnic. My parents would care for the children, while the policeman and I would take the little wagon, scythe and fork, to show that our intention was to cut grass. There would already be some grass on the wagon, which we hoped would go unnoticed. We would have to leave several belongings behind, but other items would be hidden under the grass. At a secluded spot on the Elbe, about three kilometres away to the southeast, the boat would wait for us. Since I did not want to be stranded when we reached the other side, I decided to take along a horse, the big, strong, chestnut mare, which I demanded back from the farmer who had her on loan. The hens were put into a sack. We did not tell my father until everything was ready, because we wanted to spare him as much excitement as possible.

Everything went like clockwork. Our vehicle looked absolutely innocuous. We met at the edge of a thickly wooded, dark, damp bank of the Elbe, and went up the river to a deep side-arm where the boat was hidden. A second, older man was already in the boat, to help row against the current. We had to crawl up a little hill, under branches and over roots, to reach the edge of the river. Our hearts were beating almost audibly. We were frightened and exhausted, but at last it seemed as if the other side was almost within reach. We crept, whispered, and silently carried our things down to the boat. The horse stood hidden in the dark shadows of the trees.

On the other side of the river's arm stood a little house, which we could see quite clearly. "What is that house?" "A watchman lives there." "But he can see everything we're doing!"

Just as we finished our feverish efforts and as we were ready to push off from the shore, a man emerged from the woods on a bicycle. He wanted to join us, but we had to refuse, as the boat was already too full, considering the strong current. I held my horse on a long lunge-line made of laundry twine, and we pushed off.... At that moment a Russian soldier appeared from behind a boulder on the opposite bank of the small arm of the river!

Stunned, turned to stone, we stared at him. He stood on the edge of the bank and motioned to us that we should take the bicycle rider with us. Then we had to cross, not the Elbe, but the side-arm of the river, whether we wanted to or not.[3] With a great burst of energy, the horse reached the other side ahead of us, where it was immediately caught by yet another soldier. Slowly the bank drew nearer, and with it, our fate. As a snake stares at its victim, so this merciless figure stared silently at us, as if at a welcome prize. As the first one to land, the bicycle rider was taken roughly away. I gathered all my persuasive talents. I begged and pleaded but to no avail. My father had warned us repeatedly of the hazards, and now I was terrified that he might have a heart attack from the excitement! Dejectedly we stepped out of our barge, a group of unhappy and desperate people.

We had to go through a systematic and thorough inquiry in the guard house. As the bicycle rider proved to be an SS man, they suspected that we all belonged together. He was rather awfully treated, before being taken away. The same fate befell our two distressed boatmen.

They could not really have been so stupid, those helpers of ours! We did not know the countryside, as we had never lived here before, but these people came from Pretzien! Any other place than the one they had chosen would have been a safer spot to attempt the crossing! Why had they chosen to embark right under the very eyes of the river patrol? Could it be that the policeman in Pretzien actually informed the Russians of our plans, possibly to not only rise in their estimation, but in addition to acquire the belongings that we left behind?

We were thoroughly questioned and did not try to hide anything. For a while they put us in a room that we were forbidden to leave. The soldier who had caught my horse was in the farmyard. Later, I went to him asking to have my mare back, claiming that I had gotten so terribly attached to it. It seemed to work, as he disappeared right away and came back after about an hour, riding the mare and wearing a proud and happy face. As far as the Russians were concerned, I could take the mare with me, but not so with the local Germans. The mayor of the village said the horse was in his village

---

3 At this point the von Rosens were on the east (Russian) side of the Elbe River, at the confluence of a tributary. Both shores of this side-arm were controlled by the Russians. The west shore of the Elbe River represented the safety of the Allies. The Russians, evidently having been alerted to the clandestine crossing, had lain in wait to catch them in the act of fleeing.

and he would not let me have her back. I simply could not prevail against the German communists.[4]

Crushed and disappointed, after we had believed ourselves to be almost safe, we spent the night in the appointed room, alone with our thoughts. Behind a barred window, in the cellar of the same house, we saw our three unhappy companions sitting together and managed to whisper a few words to them. We were treated a little better than they were for our door was not locked. Our things were in a shed on the other side of the yard. Our chickens walked about freely. I crept, like a thief, to our baggage, for we wanted to have at least something to eat. My saddle had disappeared! The same friendly soldier showed me a looted saddle in the barn, advising me to take it instead, which I immediately did!

As soon as we were allowed to return to Pretzien, we were told to appear before the commandant. After a short family consultation, my mother went alone. The commandant began by saying that they had planned to send us further east that evening, but as Hitler and Stalin had made an agreement in 1939 that all the people of German extraction from the Baltic countries, were to be exchanged for the Russians who were in German-occupied Polish areas, he had changed his mind.[5] These Baltic countries had been occupied by the Russians that same year, so it had been decided that the Russians no longer had authority over the German Baltic people, and we could therefore remain here! This was the first inkling we had of what had transpired behind the scenes, when all the Baltic Germans had been resettled.

I had no energy left to take up a fight for our survival. The policeman did have exclusive knowledge of our plan to escape, and now we all realized that he had certainly double-crossed us! He had acquired the sheep as a payment from me, but he must have helped himself to many of the belongings we had to leave behind as well. He avoided us from then on, for he had surely never expected to see us in Pretzien again. The poor boatman had also been betrayed by him. He and his companion sat in prison for a whole week and were very badly treated. He also lost his boat!

---

4 There were obviously Germans who supported Nazism and others who leaned to Communism. Some of the latter were possibly card-carrying Communists, while others probably simply disliked the bourgeoisie and hoped for a better life under the Bolsheviks, once they defeated the Nazis. In the hope of gaining support from the ruling forces, these supporters often acted harshly against property-holding Germans, as well as against refugees.

5 Reference here is to the Molotov-von Ribbentrop Non-Aggression Pact of 1939.

✻ 5 ✻

MARKING TIME

If we could but have seen into the future! Merely a few days after our 'picnic' on the shore of the Elbe River, we noticed new activity among the Russian troops. It was a reversal of what had happened at the beginning of May. The present situation was the same as at the time of their arrival, except that now they went in the opposite direction. They drove in an endless column of little wagons towards the East. Could it be true that they were leaving? Why? No one was driving them away. They spoke unkindly of the English and the Americans and were very annoyed that we had tried to flee to them, but this was no reason for them to leave.

Soon the answer became clear. The Russians were going across the Elbe. It was an agreement that they had made with the Allies. The Americans and the English withdrew to the demarcation line laid down in the Yalta Agreement and left the overseeing of this area to the Russians. Further east up the Elbe, there was a pontoon bridge across the river. Other troops crossed over the provisional bridge near Magdeburg. What a stupid and even clumsy moment for us to have chosen to flee!

The area was suddenly so empty of soldiers that I found the courage to try to drive to Hohenlochau. When we had left Hohenlochau in April, we had driven in large circles, for days, and now we were living, here in Pretzien, no more than nine kilometres away from Hohenlochau, the estate from which we started. I borrowed a bicycle and pedalled off through damp fields and wooded paths full of wet and heavy leaves. The countryside was fantastically lovely.

Nothing more than a heap of paper lay where our five book cases had stood in Hohenlochau. The Russians had broken them open, thrown the contents on the floor, trampled on them, and torn pages out of the books. Only a few volumes could still be called books. I was especially happy to see the *Bogislaus Rosen*, a book about a famous ancestor. As only forty-two copies had ever been printed, obviously the book had special value as a family treasure.

Then I looked up Frau von Grünewald. There the looters had robbed nothing except the von Stritzkys' trunk. The almost illiterate manager of the Münchhausen estate had greedily collected a large library for himself, among which I saw many of our books! I was disgusted by this audacity, but could do nothing about his impudence.

Frau von Grünewald told me that the Baron Münchhausens had been arrested and imprisoned. This courageous eighty-year-old lady had driven the ten kilometres to Burg in a small country vehicle on uneven roads to persuade the authorities, in her quiet and determined way and in perfect Russian, to set her granddaughter and her husband free. Before the Elbe River was closed, Baron Münchhausen had contrived to send a good load of valuables to friends in the British Zone. Otherwise, he would have lost everything.

I returned safely with my treasures with a new outlook and full of new courage and ambition. The Elbe was no longer a barrier, so we could make a new attempt at trekking further. Munich, that distant goal, hovered before my eyes again. In Munich I could wait for my husband.

So again we had to prepare a team and wagon. I had complained bitterly to our Russians about their having taken my wagon, with the result that they had promised to leave me a little rubber-tired one. The mayor had also cast covetous eyes on it, and he won, as he was hard competition. Since, however, he did want to help us, he allowed me to have an abandoned caravan, in which the Russian soldiers had lived. My father, always a keen and helpful companion, went with me into the forest to see what the mayor had given us. To ensure against draught and instability, the Russians had buried the caravan up to the floor in sand. My father began to dig it out then and there, while I ran back to the village to rent a team, so that I could drive this new treasure into our yard that very night. There were just too many competitors for us to take chances.

It turned out to be a real little house, about eight metres long and two-and-a-half metres wide, with iron-rimmed wheels. Although rather worn, everything was still very functional. We were very excited and found a worker from the smithy, who gladly agreed to repair it. Windows and doors were missing, but the worst drawbacks were the broken brakes. For some technical reason, these had been mounted behind, and were operated simply by pressure on the drive shaft. We discovered much later that they were quite inadequate even when repaired. At this stage we were exceptionally thrilled with our latest acquisition. I still had my ugly Moritz and the second of the looted horses was beautifully suited to him in size.

We planned to drive with them towards the Harz Mountains, there to find a mouse hole in the border, allowing travel further south. In our covered van, we would be quite self-reliant, and would not need to worry about finding places to stay. We installed a small stove, on top of which we put our cheap cooking apparatus, or 'kitchenette.' The mayor made out a licence to prove that the little van now legally belonged to us.

When not working feverishly on the wagon, we took little walks with the children in the surrounding countryside. We especially liked a certain area in the stone quarry. It was so beautiful, and at the same time so interesting, to climb around on those lovely sunny afternoons. A few terrified refugees, who disappeared as soon as anyone came near, lived in a narrow corner of the quarry. One really no longer knew who to fear.

On the path lay a little button, which my mother picked up with the half-superstitious but sincere wish: "Werner, my Werner...." Here in Pretzien we could not hope for news of my brother, who had been last reported in Berlin. No one knew his whereabouts. We lived as if on an isolated planet.[1]

We wandered back, slowly, picking some seeds from an especially beautiful hedge. Just where they would ultimately be planted mattered little. It was already late when we arrived home. My father met us, his face alight with emotion. Behind him, like an apparition, was a tall figure – my brother Werner! It was unbelievable! What an overwhelming experience and what joy to be able to see him again!

My brother had been sent on a special army mission in April, but on his return had become separated from his unit. He found himself near the property of his good friend Baron Engelbrechten and had gone there. This friend was also a soldier fighting on the front. His wife was there alone and helpless. She had been overjoyed to see Werner. There was no fighting front there – merely lost soldiers.

---

[1] The last time Martha von Rosen had seen her brother, Werner von Kügelgen, was in 1944 in Geppertsfeld, on the occasion of the christening of his three sons.

Werner had waited a few days in the safety of her house. When the Russians came, he had burned his uniform, transforming himself into a civilian, courtesy of the clothing of his absent host. Through his clever way of handling people, he had managed to prevent disagreeable things from happening in the house. He had posed as a doctor, which was true enough. He naturally did not stress that he was a doctor of political science! For the Russians a 'doctor' was always a doctor of medicine. As a 'doctor,' he had even often been called to look at various patients. With his unusual compassion and good common sense, as well as the medical knowledge he had picked up during the one-and-a-half years he had lain badly wounded in a hospital in Eusskirchen, he had proved himself a successful healer! That there was a doctor who had not been drafted into the army did not seem to be unusual to the Russians.

Three months of play-acting had been enough for him, however, and he had decided to look for his family. He had started out with a bicycle, but this had finally become less of a help than a hindrance, so he continued on foot. In Hohenlochau he heard about our whereabouts. Here he now stood before us, alive and well, owning nothing more than the clothes he wore.

Immediately we planned to include him in our trip. He took the little wagon and Moritz and drove to see the manager of Hohenlochau, where he hoped to get our books back from the new 'library' of this despicable fellow. Werner showed him where his great grandfather, Gerhard von Kügelgen, and his English grandfather, Trewheeler, had written their names in the books. The man still had the cheek to insist that they all belonged to him! Werner managed to save several of these books eventually, however, and amongst these were a few volumes that I had personally bound for my parents. Werner also visited the grave of his child, Allo, who is buried in Leitzkau.

Every moment that passed in the Russian Zone was a great danger to Werner, but our preparations and the caravan were not quite ready. He decided, therefore, to visit Baroness Wrangel. This attempted visit, however, almost had him hung. A Russian guard arrested him, and it was only with a great deal of difficulty that the baroness rescued him. After this narrow escape, my brother departed alone without even telling us the reason for this sudden decision. He wanted to spare our parents extra anguish. He was able to cross the Russian border unseen, but at the British-American border he walked straight into prison. After three days, he managed to gain his release, continuing on to Munich by train, arriving there not long before his daughter Andrea was born in September.

Our preparations were nearly finished. We did not bother to ask the mayor to change our travel permit on which Werner was also named. We carefully arranged all our things so that they could serve as seats, a table, and the like.

We said our good-byes, and I went to hitch up the horses. The looted horse could only barely be pulled out of the stable. He dragged his feet and stood with hanging head before the wagon. We gathered around him, quite bewildered. What had happened? Realizing that we certainly could not go like that, we had to unpack again.

After managing to get the animal back into the stable, I called the veterinarian. The horse had contacted equine typhoid, an illness as dangerous as it was rare. The veterinarian seemed to have no knowledge as to the duration, nor the final outcome of the disease. My parents occupied the smithy again. I stayed in the wagon with Gerhard and Else. I nursed the valuable workhorse day and night for about a week, wrapping his legs with wet cloths. He got no better, but he continued to eat. One day as I crouched next to him with my head pressed against his body, busy tying the cloths, I suddenly noticed him wavering. I jumped back into the concrete well ring, which acted as a hay rack. A minute later and I would have been crushed under the heavy body! He fell, never to get up again.

What a labour of Hercules it was to drag the heavy body out of the stall. Fortunately for me, the villagers took over the job. Now I was left with a covered van, and only one horse, that would have been better called Harlequin than Moritz, for he was a clumsy-looking animal. Any hopes of continuing were gone again! Regardless of our present immobility, I wanted to find out at least which would be the best route to take – the one through Magdeburg, – or the one over the pontoon bridge at Aken? Again I travelled on a bicycle, which a friendly woman had lent me. My path took me over beautiful meadows skirting the river. Much of my trip was lonely and only once did I hide when a Russian vehicle, which I recognized as such by the loud voices, rushed past me. Thankfully, I escaped detection. The pontoon bridge was wobbly and had a steep step, so it would be no good for our covered van. I pedalled over it, and onward into the little town of Aken. No guard or any other obstacle stood in my way. What a strange feeling to be on the other side of the Elbe! I almost feared that my emotions would be too obvious, but I returned quite unnoticed. The Russians were, after all, the rulers on both sides.

I discussed the situation at length with my parents and decided to look at the bridge of Magdeburg before we made any definite plan. I got onto the borrowed bicycle again, starting off early in the morning. These trips alone were not enjoyable. I always hated them. On and near the bridge there were soldiers, a few pedestrians, and otherwise no movement at all. No one looked at me. I went through the hopelessly deserted streets of a once beautiful city – everything was dead, everything empty. All there was to be seen anywhere, were the many Russians in uniform. A town of ruins. How the people must have suffered – first in the air-raids and afterwards in those final battles that had taken place here. So many had given up their lives, like our friend Graf Stollberg, whose horses had meant so much to me.

The way via Magdeburg was our only real choice, but we still lacked a horse. I decided not to return right away, but to stay on the Magdeburg-Altkönigsborn road, planning to swing north from there to see what had happened to my wounded Trakehner mare, last seen in April.

For a time I travelled unhindered, but then I came out onto a long bridge that crossed a brook and a stretch of swamp land. Here the crafty Russians had placed guards and blocked the way. I hesitated. They had posted themselves at the other end of the bridge. I got off and thought it over because I had noticed a little path leading into the woods just ahead of the bridge, but already a Bolshevik guard was coming commandingly and quickly towards me. He called to me when he was still far away. I waited for him, still undecided about what to do. He, however, took all the decisions into his own hands, grabbed the bicycle and ordered me to follow him, not over the bridge to the guard-house, but down the path into the woods. Was his commander there?

I held onto the bicycle hard by the saddle seat. He shouted at me to let go. I had decided that this was the one thing I was not going to do. "What do you want? Where are you taking me?" He was angered most of all by the fact that I wouldn't let go of the bicycle.

I knew that I was in a serious predicament, especially as there was not a soul to be seen anywhere. We continued in this manner, walking quickly further into the woods, with me constantly fighting for the bicycle and demanding to know where we were going. The path was narrow and the trees got ever denser. Then suddenly the fellow threw away the bicycle, grabbed me by the arm and said the dreaded words: "Woman come!" One never knows where the right answer comes from in these moments, "I am ill, be careful!" "What do you mean, ill?" "Just that. You know, sick!" "That has to be reported immediately. You have to go to the hospital!" "Yes, but not like that – just sick!"

The man became distinctly uneasy. Wordlessly he picked up the bicycle, retracing our steps quickly to the bridge, which we crossed over. I stayed behind him holding onto the seat, quite determined not to give up the bike. Once in the guard-house, he disappeared with the bicycle, while I was taken over to an officer, who asked for my destination and where I had come from. Then I was ordered into the house and told to wait. Why, exactly? I told the officer that I wanted my bicycle back, but nothing happened. After a while I was told that I could go, but I refused to leave without my bicycle! Another hour passed. I sat alone, thinking. Next, I was told the bicycle could no longer be found. I said that I had seen with my own eyes how a soldier had carried it into the house, so they told me to look for myself, which I did. I found it, along with many others in a little back room. In the end, when they saw that I was really quite determined not to go without it, they let me have it, but only after a nerve-racking two-and-a-half hours!

That was the last time I dared to borrow the bicycle. I was terrified. I simply did not want to go exploring alone ever again! The Russian hunters of women, as well as of bicycles, were apparently becoming a menace in the countryside.

There was still another policeman in the village, a quiet, old man who had previously helped us in small matters. I now turned to him to accompany me to the village where Delight was. He came very gladly. We hitched up Moritz and drove off in the little carriage through the beautiful summer countryside and were bothered by no one. How different the place looked. How empty! In April so many people had thronged along the banks of the Elbe. The mayor, no longer in his official capacity was, however, still living in his house and still had my horse Delight.

Two days after we had left her there, he had decided to have her put down. Then the Russians came, and no one had taken the time to bother with the horse. After the first of the victors' wagons had gone by, he was astounded to see that her strong, youthful nature had won out and that she had decided to live after all. She had spent the whole summer out in a farmer's field, and, after allowing her three months to recover, her new owner had decided that it was time to hitch her to a plough. As soon as the going got too hard, she had refused to pull and all his thoughtless, cruel beating proved useless. By now, he was overly eager to be rid of an animal that was without value to him. I paid him 800 marks for my horse, who was, however, quite different from my former Delight. Her only value now was as a beautiful-looking and very well-bred, brood mare. An incurably stubborn horse paired with the ungainly Moritz were not what I had imagined as draft horses for the journey.

After a few try-outs in the yard, I realized that we would need a much stronger team for heavy going along the rough country roads. We would have to rent horses to take us as far as Magdeburg. It was August and harvest time. All the horses were in constant use. In our yard, the Russians put up three thrashing machines that worked day and night. The commandant organized and supervised the work himself, being impatient that the harvest was not going quickly enough. It rained a lot and the grain was wet, but there was simply nothing anyone could do about it. The big machines were constantly plugged up with wet grain. The harvest wagons stood heaped and ready, and valuable time was lost. At night, lamps illuminated this busy, yet badly organized, scene. Only our chickens profited. Gluckschen, a hen who had turned into a real family pet, had nine little chicks, and this happy group virtually swam in grain, ignoring all our extra gifts of food.

My horses were now also sleeping on straw and not waste paper as before. A paper factory had hoped to save its store of paper by packing it in our complex, and now all kinds of stationery was available, ranging from costly note paper to rolls of unprinted newspaper. Paper was normally very hard to come by. We supplied ourselves plentifully with stationery before the Russians commandeered the rest. The newsprint, in place of bedding, had been a miserable substitute for the animals, but better than nothing at all.

Day after day, we watched the thrashing, lived through the terrible noise and dust, and waited. We also saw the return of two of the arrested men who had been taken away. First came Herr Krause. I looked him up immediately, but the unlucky man was so completely disturbed that he refused to answer any questions, and we never found out what had happened to him during those three disastrous months. The next one to return was the engineer who worked with the quarry engines. He was quite depressed and shattered, but spoke openly of what had transpired.

His fate touched me deeply. During his absence, some Russian soldiers had ordered his son, together with his friends, to go fishing with them. Fishing with the Russian soldiers meant that they threw dynamite into the water, and then gathered up the dead fish that came to the surface. This time, they chose one of the deep water holes which had been created during the quarry work. The soldiers placed a big box full of dynamite on the bank and threw a large charge into the water below. The detonation caused the whole contents of the box to explode. One soldier and one boy were thrown backwards by the air pressure. Our friend's son and one of the soldiers disappeared into the big hole. Its banks proceeded to cave in. No trace of the bodies was ever found. After hearing of this additional shock, the unfortunate man had hardly even a painful smile left. All the light-heartedness was gone from his formerly cheerful mien.

Tensely we listened to the descriptions of his horrible experiences. In Treuenbrietzen, the collection camp where they had been taken, one hundred thousand men lay in the open fields, carefully guarded – civilians, as well as prisoners-of war, young as well as old, all waiting for their fate. They believed that they would eventually be sent to work somewhere. There had been so much destroyed in the war – bridges, streets, and everywhere there was rubble to clear away. They were almost happy when they heard that they were to collect their things and prepare to move on.

They marched in the direction of Frankfurt on the Oder. Surely it was to be one of the big Oder bridges that they would have to repair. But no, from Frankfurt they went to Posen, during which time they suffered much hardship, sickness, hunger, and lack of care and attention. In Posen, they were pushed into another huge camp. By this time, the engineer had lost contact with the other men from his village. Many died, others were marched further on. In Posen, they sat in the glowing hot summer sun, in a camp surrounded by barbed wire and guards. Stomach disorders weakened and wore down the strength and spirit of these destitute, unhappy men.

Then one day, they were, once again, ordered to get ready. By now, they actually had nothing left to prepare. They were driven out into the dusty road, in their dirty rags, a mixture of wavering, filthy, suffering figures. Now it surely would be Siberia, where they would have to do the work that was constantly spoken about. As the grey group of men moved out of Posen, they did not go towards the East but towards the Northwest.

The heat was solid and searing. Everyone was yearning for water. No one was allowed to carry water with them nor to stop at the lakes and streams they passed. They halted only at dirty ponds and ditches. The younger ones, some still merely boys, could not stand the thirst and repeatedly tried to run to nearby streams, though they knew that the guards would shoot immediately. They had seen this happen already to many of their comrades, but the thirst was simply unbearable. Other prisoners were ordered to bury the corpses and then rejoin the ranks further on. They did not dig deeply, for there was neither the time nor the strength. Apart from these occasions, no one was allowed to leave the ranks. The last ones waded knee deep in the filth and dirt, and stomach illnesses raged wildly among them all.

When they were finally allowed to stop to drink from some dirty pond, the parched men threw themselves down sucking at the filthy slime like cattle, for they had really become little more than a mass of suffering beasts by this time! Those who were sick and unable to go on were treated as if they were already dead. As this was their doom, the prisoners supported each other as long as possible. Our friend had a wound in his hand, and the infection took the form of a red line up his whole arm. His glands were swollen and very painful. He felt feverish. He tied up his arm with his suspenders. His companions begged him to bear up. They dragged, pulled, and supported him.

"Just don't give up. We're going in the direction of home...."

After an endless march under heavy guard, they arrived in Stettin. Here, instead of coming to a prison or camp, they were told to go wherever they wanted! Sick, penniless, every stitch of his clothing dirty, he found a sympathetic person who bought him a ticket to Berlin. Once there, he searched the streets for a doctor as he feared losing his arm. He never found one, but discovered a trained nurse sitting on the sidewalk. She took him home and nursed him, and as soon as he was capable of travelling again, this charitable soul found him the means to go home. After many other unexpected events by rail and on foot, he finally reached home. We never found out what Herr Krause had experienced. From all those who had been driven away from our village, only one other came back while we were there.

Many of the men in this part of the country were greatly influenced by communism. They had expected their 'Red Paradise' to turn out quite differently!

The hectic harvest in Pretzien was nearing its end, and at last, the grain was thrashed. I was given the name of a farmer on the other side of the village, who owned a strong pair of horses. I went there and a very kind refugee woman, who was looking after the house, advised me to come again the next day as the owner was away. The following day, I met a woman there, who pointed to a tiny house a little distance away.

"A friend of mine lives there. She lays cards. I think her advice will be helpful to you." Right away I made an appointment to see her the next day. Else came with me.

It was very interesting and, in short, she stated the following:

"Through every difficult experience runs the red thread of good fortune. Everything will turn out for the best. An older, married couple stands behind you with all their love and affection. You are filled with concern for your husband, but he lives and you will soon find him, but you must first shed tears of joy. A woman friend will prove to be your saving angel, as will also another friend, who is a man. There is a house waiting for you, which will be your next home. You have made many attempts to leave this place. Now is the right time and you will succeed...."

To my question about what I owed her, she replied:

"From you I can take nothing. It was my pleasure to do something for you. You will soon leave Pretzien, but remember that even if there are difficulties that thread of luck is on your side...."

I thanked her warmly, asking her to tell me something of her own life. The great courage of this woman impressed me, for her husband belonged to the SS and had been captured by the Russians. She had no children, knew nothing of the fate of any of her relatives, and had no one to whom she could go. As she owned nothing any more, she could well have asked me for money, but her only desire had been to help me. Often since then has she been on my mind, for it all happened as she foretold, with the exception that there were many more than just two helping angels! I have often wondered which ones she had meant. The woman angel was surely Lee Sherman, who appears often in my story and is still my dearest friend.

The farmer agreed to let me have the horses, in about a week, as soon as he was finished with his harvest. Delight stood, well-fed, in her stall, so we decided to ride her. She went well under saddle, with merely a slight limp in her left foreleg to remind me of her bad accident. Else was overjoyed, sitting excellently in the saddle by herself. She only rode behind the house, where the best trails were. However, one day Delight came galloping back with an empty saddle – what a fright! Else had not ridden for so long and was out of practice, thus the mare had thrown her. She bravely mounted again, continuing to enjoy her little outings. Even this joy ended one day, when, without warning, she was pursued by a mounted soldier. As the front gate had been closed, she had to ride all the way around the complex to get in by the smithy. A frightened girl flew into my arms. After a similarly bad scare occurred to me, we decided to give up this entertainment.

✴ 6 ✴

NEW SURPRISES

September came with its clear air, heralding to the birds the time to head south. The farmer harnessed his two strong, well-fed horses to the caravan, to which I thought we would also hitch my light ones so that the heavier ones would pull as the leaders. When I approached the front of the wagon with my team, however, the farmer contemptuously waved them away. As his horses did not need any help, mine could follow at the rear!

Our little caravan wagon was very neatly and comfortably arranged. In the rear section, which was separated from the front by a thin wall, lay our sleeping bags and blankets filled with dried clover. The clover, besides serving as bedding to sleep on, also provided excellently nutritious horse feed. There I slept with my two children. In the front section were two small cupboards, as well as the camp beds for my parents. During the day, these became our sofas. Our few pots and pans were stacked tidily in the open cupboards. It all looked very neat as long as the caravan was standing, but travelling on the village streets was like being on a stormy sea! The wheels rattled, things flew about, the house wobbled and swayed dreadfully, and the noise was deafening. My mother, as the sole passenger of the moving caravan, sat in the centre of this instant chaos. As she could not possibly have walked the twenty kilometres to Magdeburg, she just had to manage as best she could fending off the pots and pans! Fortunately, only the road through Pretzien was especially bad, so that everything that was going to fall did so in those initial kilometres!

Our friendly farmer brought us safely across the provisional bridge which crossed the Elbe. No one so much as looked at us along the way. The man with his team of horses kindly drove our caravan through the town, onto the wide solidly surfaced highway. After thanking him for his help and paying him for his services, we bade farewell, and we were left to our own devices.

It was afternoon, our own horses were fresh and the road was excellent. It graded slightly downhill, and, with the slightest nudge of the horses into their harnesses, we began moving. We felt entirely carefree, and mightily pleased with ourselves. However, this soon came to an abrupt end when the horses were asked to really lean into their collars, which they needed to do to pull us up the next incline. Delight greeted this new development with an annoyed shaking of her head. She made a little jump, and then stood still. That was the end. After an advance of a mere kilometre, we now had to search for a different means of locomotion! Moritz, choosing to pull only when his partner did, loyally and gallantly copied all the bad manners Delight had learned during her sojourn on the farm.

We were in a truly ridiculous position. There was nothing to be seen, far and wide, to give us some sort of push, pull, or other impelling force. After one long hour, during which we had repeatedly attempted to set the caravan in motion again, a farmer with his team came driving by, pulling an empty wagon. We used a chain that we carried to hitch his wagon in front of ours, whereupon Delight immediately followed his team quite willingly, now that there was no pressure on her harness. This pleasure lasted only until the farmer had to turn off this main road. Once again we found ourselves on a small incline, having managed to continue for merely a short distance. As it was already nearing evening, I chose, at the next protesting equine head shake, to quickly turn the caravan onto the roadside. We had no choice but to spend the night here.

The horses, soon unhitched, grazed in front of the caravan. The chickens, swiftly let out of their cages, contentedly replenished their needed pebbles and grass. Once our stove was lit with the wood and coal we had brought along, we settled down to enjoy our little house. This was so much better than having to beg for shelter, or needing to rely on other people's questionable charity. If our animals had pulled, this whole trip could actually have been enjoyable!

We spent a peaceful night with not a soul on the road. We could have been the last people on earth. We did not hurry the next morning, as we had only to be ready in case someone appeared who could provide us with the indispensable jump-start. Again, we realized how fortunate we were, because a team of oxen came by, plodding along on their way to their daily ploughing. After they helped us into motion, the horses hardly felt the weight of the caravan as it rolled on the smooth road that branched off to Ottersleben – that was where Jan, our Estonian farmhand might be. With almost a bad conscience, I drove past, heading south towards Bernburg, the town that was so closely tied to the history of my family, since the von Kügelgens had resided there.[1] Proud of our brakes, we still felt that we could conquer the Harz Mountains, making grandiose plans as to exactly where we would slip across the border.

On the second day, with a little help, we found ourselves at a farm. Here, we noticed to our great consternation that a rim of one of our wheels was loose. The friendly foreman allowed us, with the help of his mule, to drive into the middle of the yard, where he left us parked next to the dung heap. Once we were stationed in that position, we had no way to move away!

A few days before our arrival, all the property owners here had lost their land titles and deeds.

We encountered a number of communist 'representatives' and 'overseers' with labelled armbands, swarming around the yard. The real owner had received a bad concussion after falling from his horse. Since he had been unconscious for three days, he knew nothing of what was transpiring on his usually well cared for and perfectly run operation. His wife was a prisoner in her own house. She could neither go near the garden nor the farmyard. The manager was basically decent, but had to conform to the communists' wishes, as he was constantly being watched.

Our horses had a grand time in the stable, which they shared with the owner's saddle horses, as well as his daughter's two lovely carriage ponies and two goats, which pulled a little rubber-tired cart. Like her mother, the little girl was not allowed to show herself outside the house, but in the dark of evening we saw her climb over the fence to steal walnuts out of her own back garden.

The village blacksmith was supposed to fix our wheel for us, but said that he neither cared to, nor had time to do it. When, at last, he did get

---

1 Bernburg was first under Allied and later under Russian occupation. The final division of Germany into zones of East and West, through an accord between the Allies, differed from the initial layouts of the occupation. The Potsdam conference of 1945, for example, shifted 69,866 square miles of Poland to Russia, giving Poland 38,986 square miles of land east of the Oder-Neisse that had previously been controlled by Germany. The joint Allied-Russian control over Germany fell apart when Russia withdrew from the governing council.

around to taking off the wheel, he noticed that other things were also wrong. The caravan, having originally belonged to a group of circus players, had been built only strong enough to stand up to the rigours of traversing the short distances between the railways and the performance areas. The first several kilometres of country roads, during which it had carried our home with all our belongings, however, had undoubtedly been too much for it!

While the smith tried to repair our caravan, we watched the German communists, with their armbands, disrupting the well-run operations of the farm in every possible way. All their attempts at organization were made in an ignorant, pompous manner and failed accordingly.

'Regulations' did not allow one to stay longer than three days in any one place and every location was overfilled with refugees. No one welcomed newcomers. For ten whole days, we were forced to be unwilling witnesses to the agrarian reform of the Eastern Zone. We were given ration cards while we stayed there.

Our caravan was ready to roll again and a good mule, shaming my stubborn horses, pulled us onto the road until we reached a favourable decline. This time the hill was quite steep. My father wanted to manage the brakes, while I was to control the team. I would rather have had it the other way round, but the fresh and rested horses made my father uneasy. I believed that I had them well under control, but to my bewilderment they accelerated, commencing a gallop, until, finally, I lost control. The caravan, swaying dangerously from side to side, rolled onto the heels of the horses, causing them to grow even more frightened. Did the brakes not work? "Stop! Stop! Stop quickly!" I heard my mother's anxious voice, but I was helpless as we raced on.

A glance behind me showed that my father must have fallen, as he was lying far behind us on the road. I pressed the reins of the racing horses into Else's hands, and rushing to the back of the caravan, turned the brake handle as hard as I could. Finally, we fought the horses to a standstill. Then I tore back to my father, who was slowly getting up. Through the exertion of walking behind and watching the brakes, he had become overtired, resulting in a small heart attack, and he had fallen down unconscious.

My mother and I helped him to his feet. We all slowly walked back to the caravan. Else successfully held the team during this time and continued to handle them to the bottom of the long grade, with me working the brakes. It was very difficult as the drive shaft was now bent and badly wedged. From then on, we were very careful, even applying the brakes whenever we were at a standstill. Even so, the caravan still moved freely enough downhill. Of course, going uphill we, as usual, had to wait for assistance. We really had not expected to have such a trip! This stopping was punishment and terribly humiliating!

As we stood by the side of the road, waiting for help, my mother read from the rescued copy of the famous book, *Reminiscences of his Youth by an Old Man* by Wilhelm von Kügelgen, especially those sections concerning Bernburg. At least in our imagination, we could reach our next destination, but it was simply fantasy, for the road was lonely and still, and all our patient waiting was for naught.

At last, my mother decided to go for help to a nearby army encampment, just visible from the road. A Russian soldier with his two horses quickly brought us, with much joking and laughter, the short distance to the outskirts of Bernburg. It was already evening, and we could see the lights of the town winking below us. After all our bad experiences, we decided to wait until morning, before trying the descent. We had our own little house and went to bed, glad at least to have reached the town of our forefathers. Quite an achievement to have come thirty kilometres in three weeks!

The next morning was the 19th of September. I took both horses, without the caravan, and went to look for a stable. It was exceptionally fortunate that we had not attempted, the night before, to drive them down the mountain, for the grade was very steep and long. Half way down lay a farm which had not yet fallen under the new occupation laws. The manager, Herr Spreter, saw Delight, with her beautiful conformation and Trakehner brand, and wanted to buy her.

"No, I would rather buy another horse myself, but I do not want to sell either one of mine," I answered.

So he found lodgings for us and kindly hitched up his heavy plough horses, pulling our caravan to another nearby farmyard that belonged to the same owner. It was a generously laid-out estate, with a stable lying near the other sheds. Our little covered caravan was dwarfed by these new surroundings.

Meanwhile, my parents had gone straight into Bernburg to visit the original von Kügelgen house. The memorial plaque of Wilhelm von Kügelgen and his beloved father-in-law, Pastor Krummacher was welded to the front door. They found the current clergyman, Pastor Schröter, to be a cultivated and kindly man, who expressed great sympathy and understanding for our present situation. He invited my parents to return and enjoy a cup of coffee with him that very afternoon. They sat in the living room, where our forefather had lived a hundred years before. A friend of Pastor Schröter, who worked as a translator for the Russians, was also invited. Herr Frauenstein, as he was called, was very impressed on hearing how many languages both my parents spoke. They, in turn, were happy to now be with educated people, in a cultured atmosphere.

Originally, it was planned that I would go with my parents to visit my ancestors' house. But knowing that we were not allowed to stay in any one place longer than three days, I had to act quickly. In Bitterfeld, some 50 kilometres away, was Dr. Herman Kienast, whom I had known quite well in Estonia. He had two horses, which he did not need any more, as he was working in the hospital. I arrived there by train, taking Else with me. Herman Kienast's wife was hopelessly distraught by their flight with all its terrible experiences. Her fifteen-year-old son cared lovingly for his little two-year-old sister, doing everything that one would naturally expect of a wife and mother. Herman's team was now stationed at a nearby farm. After he had heard of our unwilling horses, he gladly offered to sell me his two.

Coming to an immediate agreement with him, we set off for the farm with him. Here agrarian reform was raging at its wildest. Two things worked wonders for us. The first was that Herman was a doctor, so the authorities knew that he really had nothing to do with agriculture, and the second was my travel pass from the mayor of Pretzien. Printed on it were the weighty words: "Help and protection is to be given...."

The two unexciting, plain-looking horses really offered no advantage to the land- and booty-hungry new rulers. I acquired them easily and hitched them immediately to a little farm wagon. We climbed in and drove away that evening.

It was quiet and cool when we started back to Bernburg. The big road was still empty. My obedient little brown horses advanced step by step. What a difference from mine! Now, again, we had horses that went willingly. It had been a stroke of pure fortune! Where else could I have found even half a horse? We arrived at a farmyard late that night. The house stood unattractively next to the road, and the farm buildings separated us from any view of nature. The night watchman advised me to stay outside of the courtyard, as the Russians were constantly going in and coming out of that house. I therefore made a soft and sheltered nest of straw in the wagon, putting the horses in the narrow stall. During the night, drunken soldiers came past, disappearing into the house. Else and I lay as still as mice. The moon stood big and bright in the sky. In the very early morning, the night watchman gave me my two good horses again, and we started off for Bernburg. There I found myself in a new dilemma.

A Russian officer had come in my absence, taking my mother to work in the soda factory of Solveigh to help as an interpreter. Herr Frauenstein, having spoken of his talented new acquaintances, alerted the Russians to our language qualifications. They quickly took advantage of this valuable information. They also wanted my father to translate English and German into Russian, and to type out his translations right away on a Russian typewriter. My mother was to translate French into Russian, for as the factory belonged to a Belgian firm, the books, magazines, and instructions were often written in French. My mother wrote by hand, on many pages of duplicating paper, and had to translate all the technical terms with only the help of a small Larousse dictionary. They worked for ten hours a day. They were treated very well, and the improved food rations were certainly a boost to their health. They were also allowed to eat their meals in the officers' restaurant, where the food was excellent and plentiful.

At first, I refused to believe that my dream of going on had again come to an end. With my four, albeit, mismatched horses, I had already believed myself half way to Munich! We afterwards heard that the Russians did not prevent people from going towards the border, but then would grab them at the crossing point only to take absolutely everything away from them at the very end.

Complaining, but quietly to myself, I finally gave in to the hard facts. The farmer took over my horses gladly, in return for a daily kettle-full of workman's soup, a twice-weekly litre of skim milk, and occasional supplies of dried peas, groats, flour, and the like. Our main preoccupation was getting our daily bread. Through the work of my parents, we got permission to stay where we were and had a regular supply of food coupons. These were divided into different categories. The lowest category was for non-workers, such as housewives and old people. These were also called 'Graveyard cards': "Not enough to live on, only enough to die by." The next group were the children's coupons, which were also practically starvation coupons, – there were no milk products at all. Then followed the different grades of workers' coupons. The heavy manual labourers, for example, were issued Coupon #1. My parents soon received double the amount of the best coupons, as well as other free meals. This was thanks to the kindness of the Russian professor, who was positioned at the head of the department where they worked.

I was also thankful for our carefully buried bacon from the summer before, which was nourishing, even if a little rancid! Our chickens also occasionally laid an egg. I still had chicken feed in the form of the oats, originally intended for the horses, and the wheat in which the bacon had lain. All but one of Gluckschen's chicks turned out to be cockerels. Since I still had left-over clover, I made a sad and misguided effort to trade them for some rabbits. I was badly taken in, acquiring a band of sickly little beasts, which promptly died!

The weather became increasingly autumnal. We had been in Bernburg nearly fourteen days. The cool days of October were drawing near. On the 5th of October, Else had her tenth birthday. With the remaining dried yeast, the little white flour, and the one egg, I secretly made a *Butterkringel*, our traditional birthday cake, though naturally without a speck of butter or fat. A friendly baker offered to bake it for me. He gave it a beautiful icing all his own, which made the otherwise tasteless, uninteresting cake seem quite wonderful! As a surprise for all of us, we also had guests. The pastor's wife came, bringing a down pillow for Else, who kept this gift for the rest of her life, especially treasuring it. I can still see this beloved woman clearly before me, standing in our narrow little camping caravan, in her big, black decorative hat, from under whose brim her intelligent brown eyes looked out at us with so much sympathy and understanding. She was also a Baltic person, born a von Harten, from Ösel (Saaremaa) in Estonia.

She brought still other visitors with her: a very musical, well-educated woman called Fräulein von Oppeln, who gave Else a necklace of very beautiful stones, and Frau Krause, who lived in the pastor's house. My mother had hand painted a deck of *Schwarzer Peter* cards, copying the figures from one of our few books, *Hänschen im Blaubeerwald* (Jack in the Blueberry Forest). We served coffee, not made from beans, but from barley and dried roasted buttercup roots (our own harvest), with skim milk and sugar. And best of all, the *Butterkringel*! It really turned out to be a very festive birthday party. At the end we all played *Schwarzer Peter*.

Soon after this, I visited the pastor and his wife. Both of them understood our situation well – the crowded life in the confines of the little caravan which had been bearable as long as we had been travelling, but was simply too small a dwelling place for five. They had a room, which they could empty, and they wanted to take my parents in. It was not large, but quite sufficient for two old, undemanding people. There were two beds, chairs, a small table, and a stove that easily warmed the room. It really was high time that they had their own corner under a real roof, where they could be properly cared for once more.

As the pastor and his family did not want to leave me on my own with the children in the lonely, far-away farm yard, they suggested that I move, like a snail with my house, into their yard. It was a wonderful idea, but the yard was very small, and I felt bad about taking up all the space with my monster. But they were quite ready to do it. It was, however, fortunate that we thought of first measuring the width of the gate, which, as it turned out, was much too small, and furthermore, the mobile home much too high. As one could neither make the century-old gateway higher, nor my caravan any lower, and moreover the lane leading to the entrance was too narrow to turn around in. We simply had to abandon this plan.

The pastor's yard, surrounded by a high wall, included a garden. This divided the yard and contained a garden house. With its high windows and doors, it had evidently not been built for habitation. Yet, for no visible reason, it had a chimney. Our new friends immediately thought of a new plan. The two children and I should move into the garden house. They soon found three beds. Our little iron heater, in addition to the cooker, was, for the time being, to be our stove, as well the source of heat. We had our sacks of hay and plenty of blankets. It was roomy with very high ceilings, and as yet not too cold. It was like the most beautiful fairy-tale palace for us! It was a personal, private home, including even our own kitchen. I simply had to run across the yard, up a flight of stairs, and there were my parents, whose little household I could now manage.

We were mid-way through our moving activities when the pastor's children surprised us with a wonderful concert of: "Now praise we all our God," played on the cello, flute, and violin! One could not have wished for anything more beautiful to make us feel really welcome.

For my children, this meant the beginning of a real childhood life again. Pastor Schröter had four children, aged from ten to seventeen. The youngest girl, Renate, was the same age as Else.

Even our chickens were well taken care of. They joined those of the pastor, and both our families took care of them. Our crafty little Gluckschen, our pet chicken, however, soon found out where we were located, and flew daily onto the sill of the window facing the yard. The garden gate was opened, but she was not the least bit interested in the tempting looking garden, but instead proceeded to go straight into our house, where she received an extra ration of wheat or corn. On days when she laid an egg, she was determined and incapable of distraction. She would first slip under a chair, snuggle into a cardboard box to deposit an egg there, before returning to the crowd of other, less tame hens.

Gerhard was seven years old in March, so he too would have to go to school. Else, having previously had plenty of experience with several different schools, was mature and sensible in this respect. I had really wished for a different first school experience for my son, however.

He would have to attend a public school in this place with teachers, who were not only complete strangers, but also chose to punish children with beatings. Gerhard, however, took it all with the joy and equanimity with which a child greets something new. Only when it came to his vaccinations did his self-confidence leave him, and he lamented miserably, despite my presence in the same room. I did manage to be with him, despite the rules. His school equipment was very poor. He did not have anything even resembling a school knapsack, and had to make do with a cardboard book-cover in which to carry his copy-book and pencil. His pencil fell out frequently, even though he clamped the book-cover tightly under his little arm.

There were many cold and wet days. One day, we had snow. I waited patiently with lunch, but my little scholar did not appear. Eventually, I went looking for him. He had discovered a mound of earth covered with a bit of dirty new snow, and he blissfully slithered down the slope, enjoying the two-metre-long ride on the back of the school coat given to him by some kindly person. The book-cover lay on one side, open and discarded in the dirt and snow, but at least nothing had happened to him. We lived in unsafe times and such a delay could have had so many other much more disagreeable causes. It was a happy, though very dirty child whom I took home!

My main daily chore was to keep my family healthy and warm. We had brought a few coal briquettes with us in the caravan, but they were soon gone. It was imperative when coal was on one's ration card to act immediately, as the supply was always short. When successful, I laboured home uphill with a joyful heart, dragging my black treasure. People stood in long rows, each with a sack, and if they were fortunate, also with a little cart. Besides this source, I walked daily on the banks of the Saale River, where the big trees mercifully lost a branch or two. I saved even those sticks with dimensions no thicker than fingers. I felt fortunate if my shopping bag was half filled after many hours of searching. There were so many people on the move, all intently looking for every twig they might find to kindle the wet coal.

The soup had to be fetched from a far-away location, and I had to do this alone. The rectory was established on a little hill above the river, while the farmyard lay on the other bank on the edge of the town. It was a long but beautiful walk, over the old stone bridge, up hill and down. Twice a week, I was fully occupied this way. As well as the soup, there was also the skim milk. This was rationed out by the spoonful into our coffee cups. At first, we found the soup quite marvelous, but since there were only two different varieties, we could soon bear neither the taste nor the smell of it! Perhaps we were no longer hungry enough. At the pastor's house, however, it was still a very popular dish, so Bernhard, the fifteen-year-old second son, took over the job of fetching it by bicycle.

One could buy beetroots and carrots by the sackful. I made a hole in the garden, burying some to keep them fresh. Together with the rancid bacon, they remained the mainstay of our diet. The yeast flakes were unrationed, making a wonderful addition to our meals. I also learned how to make a paste-like spread out of pressed yeast, as this was now also available. We became owners of some sugar, thanks to a very fortunate incident at the farm. A big trailer truck, having been unable to brake successfully on the long hill by the farmyard, had overturned with its valuable load. The burst sacks lay all over the road. Everyone had raced there with bowls, buckets, and cloths to harvest the treasure. We had done likewise and now had a good supply.

Soon after our arrival in Bernburg, we received our registration papers. They used English forms for us, as Bernburg had first been under Western occupation. By the end of October, we were asked to register again, as Russian papers were already in use. Another obligation for everyone was the compulsory vaccination against typhoid fever. My father wrote out a statement for me, saying that I had already had typhoid. I had a close call with it in 1919. He used his official medical stamp, which fortunately he still carried with him. It worked, and I was spared. We also managed to arrange for Gerhard to obtain his inoculation at home. Given Gerhard's delicate health and hypersensitivity, my father was afraid of an unexpected or bad reaction when the inoculations were done. He made sure, however, that he really pricked the little fellow the three required times so that the child had the lasting impression that he had been inoculated, should anyone ever ask him.

✵ 7 ✵

RECONNAISSANCE

As there was still no mail to the other side, I was constantly ill at ease, waiting for the moment that would bring news from my husband. I now wanted to find a way to go to Munich, alone, as it was obviously impossible for us to travel any further together. Pastor Schröter's wife, understanding fully, generously insisted (rather than merely offering to take care of my children, as I had hoped) on having them both come and live with her. She would make a bed for Gerhard in the bath tub, while she would have Else sleep in a hammock above Renate's bed. It is hard to describe how deeply touched I was by this kindness, at a time when so few hearts and doors were opened to strangers any more.

It was the end of October. With a beating heart I sat in the train going through Güsten, Sangerhausen, Nordhausen, always towards the West. There were murmurs about secret crossings in the Harz Mountains, but where were they? How would I be able to find them? The train was full of restrained people who distrusted each other, sitting in silence. What were they planning to do? Where were they going? Above all, I had to know where to change trains, for only the little side-tracks led to the secret crossing places. So far, my only help was an old atlas, *Deutsche Heimat*, but this showed neither the present borders nor the Russian guard stations. The countryside was completely foreign to me. I attempted to listen to the whispered conversations of the other passengers, but the place names that I managed to overhear could not be located anywhere on the map.

A man, with a closed, secretive face, caught my eye. He sat as silently as I did, with a deliberately expressionless face. He surely had the same aim in mind that I did – to cross 'black,' or in other words, clandestinely, over the border. I had no luggage with me, merely an empty rucksack with a little food in it. I sat on the edge of my seat, ready to jump at any moment. We passed a small station and my new guide, for I had decided to make him such, leaped off the train. "May I go with you?" The question and his answer were unnecessary for he long ago seemed to realize what I wanted.

Having passed a few more stations, while riding on a tiny country train, we disembarked at a place that was little more than a stopping post. We hurried down into a damp meadow transected by a deep ditch. The man was curt, but not unfriendly. A few other men also attached themselves to us, unasked. Obviously, all had the same idea. The ditch offered us some slight protection and cover. Soon after passing through a few bushes, we clambered onto a slightly higher area, covered with trees. We were motioned to stay hidden, while our guide scouted ahead. The watch tower could be seen quite far away. It was already late afternoon. Would there be patrols? The watch towers were not near enough to each other to close off the border by themselves. We spoke only in whispers, lying, as if glued to the damp ground.

There was the crossing to freedom! There was the British Zone, but what obstacles and what surprises still stood in our way? We lay breathlessly until our guide came back, telling us to crawl after him. I sometimes wonder why he came back for us at all. He could so easily have continued on alone, for he had not asked us to come with him, and we were certainly no less than a source of danger and inconvenience to him.

Now we went in another direction – more to the north. The protective shrubs came to an end, so we continued in a shallow ditch. We hardly noticed the dampness of autumn. I cannot recall how long it all lasted, but to me it seemed an eternity. Then we found ourselves out on a hard-surfaced road. What road? Was it still under the Russians? Or – one hardly dared think of the fantastic alternative – was it already under the British? Yes, we had managed after all! Just exactly when we had crossed the border was, however, unclear.

All our inner tensions, doubts, and repressions were suddenly loosened. Now we could talk openly. I found that I had picked my leader well. He was an army major who had dared to come back, in disguise, into the Russian Zone, to find a higher-ranking friend whom he even now hoped to bring out eventually.

Not far from where we had come out onto the road, we found the registration station of Bremke. From there we were driven in a truck to Friedland, where we found everything wonderfully organized for the endless streams of refugees who managed to cross the border daily. This was a daily occurrence, despite all the preventive measures taken by the Russians. More stamps were put on our registration cards. After I had spent an almost sleepless night in a huge tent camp, a train took me to Göttingen. There I visited some acquaintances, Herr and Frau Adelheim, who were very happy to hear of the well-being of my parents and told me of other friends of whom they had news. The next day, I took a train to Kassel, the border station between the British and the American Zones.

At this time, the British were really very decent, allowing refugees in from the Eastern Zone with no difficulty at all. But the Americans were quite the opposite. I had already been warned about them: "They shoot and send you back to the Russians."

I, personally, had really expected no trouble in passing from the British into the American Zone, hence one can imagine my surprise when I was roughly ordered off the train, to be inspected on the platform outside. Whoever could not prove their identity was immediately arrested, and those who carried Russian identification papers were sent back to the Russians.

My first Russian identification card, the one which had been filled out on an English form, had the big stamp of Bernburg on it, but as the geographical knowledge of the American comptrollers was not great, I was permitted to pass on.[1] Trembling inwardly, but managing to stay quite calm on the outside, I continued, eventually boarding the train again, on my way towards Munich. There were endless changes, hold-ups, and stops, for many bridges had been blown up, but I did not care, for at last I was moving and going somewhere!

It took three long days, but then came the big moment: I stood on the train platform of Munich. What a shattering impression the state of the city made! There were ruins on top of ruins. One could not recognize anything. There were still occasional taxis to be found, and I took one to Laim, where my sister lived on the Vohburger Strasse. Crying tears of pure joy and relief, my sister Nita and I threw ourselves into each other's arms. My

---

1 This sector of Germany, first occupied by the British, was later to become part of the Russian Zone. Thus, there was a carry-over of British official documents into the Russian regime.

first question was almost fearfully asked: "Do you know anything about Jörn?" But no, she knew nothing.

How much there was to tell, how much to talk about. The poor thing had experienced many terrible moments during the constant air attacks. She lived quite near the Laim train station, the surrounding area of which had been laid flat by the ceaseless bombing. During these attacks, she would sit in the dark, narrow air-raid shelter, singing hymns with her six children. This was the best way to keep their minds occupied, as they were all very musical. When a bomb fell in the proximity, hitting a neighbour's house, for example, they would all fall on their knees, reciting the Lord's Prayer together.

The wonderful days we were able to spend together passed by much too quickly. I took the day train from Laim into Munich, as there were no street cars running in the bombed streets, and walked to Tengstrasse to see Werner and Fritzi. Here again there was an overwhelmingly joyous reunion. One of the biggest surprises was that Thechen, our beloved governess from childhood, with her daughter, Ilse, was also there. The hours flew by. Every three days, I had to go to the supply station to report to the authorities, for one could now no longer stay anywhere without a permit. I managed to extend my stay to twenty days, but they were so short. My main purpose was still to hear from Jörn, or better still to see him in person.

During this time, Hillo von Rosen, my sister-in-law, and her mother, arrived from Göfis, a little town on the border between Switzerland and Germany. This place had the advantage of still belonging to Austria. They felt that from that spot it would still be possible to flee, yes, flee, for no one really believed in any form of peace any more. Their final destination was to be Sweden, where Hillo's sister lived.

Baroness Daisy X, another close friend from Estonia, also living in Göfis, knew nothing of her husband's whereabouts. He had remained in Estonia to fight against the Bolsheviks. I greeted every scrap of news with the feeling that each located friend had been resurrected from the Beyond. Then the time came to say good-bye. I was at Werner's for the last time, when by chance, Ursula, his children's nurse, dropped in. A soldier had left her a piece of paper for me last September, and that piece of paper was somewhere.... Here ... she found it. My hand shook with joy and excitement. It was in my husband's handwriting! The note consisted of only a few lines legibly written on the dark grey cardboard, dated the 2nd of September 1945.

I read the following with anticipation:

"Frau Martha von Rosen, at:
Lindenberg, Vohburger Strasse 9, München
(Borstei) or Ried near Dietramszell near Holzkirchen
from: Obergefreiter. Jürgen von Rosen"

Then there was a different handwriting:

"Denkstrasse 27 (Werner lived in Tengstrasse!) Kügelchen"

Then again, in Jörn's writing:

"My dearest love, I am well and hope that you are all well too. A week ago we returned from Italy to be discharged, but now we are going on after all; where to, none of us knows. On the side of our car is written: 'Champagne, France....' I still hope to spend Christmas with you and the children. A thousand good wishes and kisses for the children.
          Love from your Jörn."[2]

How was it possible? How could they have kept this jewel, this *everything* away from me for all this time? Still, the answer to this question was not important. My whole trip to Munich, which I had undertaken exclusively for him, was crowned and made completely worthwhile by this little message!

A soldier had found this piece of paper near the railway tracks at the main train station, tied onto a small, dry biscuit (the round type with the central hole), along with the following instructions: "I beg the finder of this letter to take it to the above address. As thanks, I can only offer this biscuit...."

As there was no tram running, the obliging man had walked with it the seven kilometres to Laim. There he had been sent to the wrong address by an unthinking housekeeper – to Denkstrasse instead of Tengstrasse. This stranger having walked there also, delivered his precious gift without having received one word of thanks. If the immeasurable gratitude still in my heart could ever reach him, he would be well rewarded today for all his selflessness and trouble!

Now that I had the greatest gem and riches in my hand, I went flying home, only making a short detour by way of Stuttgart to see Nita's son, Christoph, who was going to school there, and lived with dear old friends of my father. This town also was unrecognizable. Every-

---

[2] See p. 200 of Jürgen von Rosen's diary in which he describes throwing the note out of the train window.

thing was in ruins and looked so strange, so uninhabited. Stuttgart lay in a topographic depression, reminiscent of a bowl with the bottom blown out of it!

I did not have any difficulty returning to the Eastern Zone. The Russians gladly took in everyone who wanted to come.

A young Swiss friend of Nita's had brought back wonderful things from a visit to his native land, as a result I had been given chocolate, cocoa, dried yeast cakes, dried milk, and even Christmas candles! I had also brought along a collection of children's books from Bengt, Jörn's brother, and his wife Tatjana, which would really make our Christmas a festive occasion. My suitcase was now so full, that it was much too heavy for me to carry the two or three kilometres of 'neutral zone' where no trains operated!

It was a dark November evening as I got off the train and started dragging my suitcase rather helplessly behind me. If only I had a little cart, or something! Then I stumbled over that 'something' in the dark. I could only feel its outlines to find out what it was, for it was much too black a night to see. Truly, it was a wonderful little wagon! It must have been abandoned by its owner, who had not been allowed to take it on the British train. My suitcase now lay on a narrow board, on four tiny wheels and there was even still room left for the bundle of another woman who was also having difficulty. She helped me pull our load across the bumpy, uneven country road. I used my lovely British pass and crossed the border without being stopped. Again they did not realize that Bernburg was in the Russian Zone, except that at this time they stamped it with the words: "Taking up final residence in the Russian Zone."[3]

How wonderful it felt to be back with my children and my parents again, for every separation was almost like a physical strain on my heart. But I had brought back what we had all hoped for – I brought news!

The children and I moved back into the garden house. We covered the walls, the big glass doors, and the windows with blankets, rags, and pieces of carpet. My small heater did its best, but could not cope with the winter cold, a situation we endured until our dear pastor organized a wonderful

---

3 Martha von Rosen's passport, of British vintage, showed that she came from Bernburg, an area first occupied by the British. The Russian officials, however, did not realize that this city now lay in the Russian Zone, and that Martha was actually returning to the Russian Zone. Her passport did not show legal exits to the West from the British Zone, however, and this could have raised awkward questions about her travel in the easterly direction across the border.

iron stove. Then we were warm. At the same time, I had the good fortune to have found a source of brown coal, needing special permission, which we obtained as a result of the work of my parents for the Russians. The manager of the farm was willing to fetch the coal – he was smart enough to get a wagon with a trailer – the wagon for us, the trailer for himself. He went twice, and the second load we gave to our dear hosts.

The brown coal gave little heat, and as it was very wet it took much coaxing to start burning, but, once we had glowing coal in the fire box, it all worked very well. From the farm I managed to get a load of corncobs as my fire starters. I was even able to pick off quite a few kernels that had been missed – these were wonderful both for us, and the chickens!

Christmas drew near. I had hidden what I had brought with me, and this became the basis of our celebration. Christmas service was held in the magnificent old church. We all went there in the greyness of the late afternoon. (We were warmed to know that here, over a hundred years ago, our ancestors had also come to worship the Christ child.) From the church tower the trumpeters blew: "From the heavens high, I come to Thee." Out in the darkening night, it was cold, but, inside the church, it was warm, thanks to our gift of coal. Pastor Schröter spoke to us seriously and yet with hope. He was the mainstay and shining example to so many people during these difficult times.

Our room, the garden house, was altogether Christmas-like. It had a small fir tree with Swiss candles, a tray with good things to eat, and a table with gifts. We sat down to our Christmas dinner. Paula von Rosen, a cousin who lived in Bernburg, and Fräulein von Oppeln were our guests. We sat on our beds, two chairs, and a few boxes, arranged around a small improvised table. The weight of what stood on the table did not strain it very much, but we were proud that everyone had something to drink from, and that there were enough plates, even though they were only enamelled ones!

The traditional *rassolie* (a potato salad with beets) had been prepared. Beyond all these blessings was, however, the greatest one: the great gift of all of us being together. The children's father was not with us as he had hoped to be, but we had him nevertheless constantly with us in our thoughts and hearts.

Dr. Schauer, the esteemed old dentist sent with his maid some sugar and an attractive bowl filled with marmalade, while we were all sitting there together. What a kind and thoughtful Christmas gift! I will never forget it, nor the sender, who looked after all our teeth during this time, becoming a special friend as well. That marmalade bowl still has a special place in my house today.

After supper, we continued our celebrations by the Christmas tree. We lit the diminutive candles, sang our favourite old carols (which no flight or war could take from us), and shared our humble gifts. The picture book and coloured pencils were for my son, who showed his disappointment in spite of all his efforts to hide it. A knapsack had been his big wish, but where could I have found such a prize? Then suddenly, the door opened, and the tall, second son of Pastor Schröter, Bernhard, came in, carrying on his back a school knapsack, very obviously too small for his towering figure. Gerhard welcomed the fifteen-year-old boy as the veritable Santa Claus! So we celebrated together one of the most significant and joyful Christmases I have ever known.

A cold January followed. Six days a week my courageous parents went to their work, holding onto each other. In the evenings, I cooked potatoes in their skins, and fried the bacon left from our cache in Hohenlochau. It had not held up too well in the now mouldy wheat, and I had to serve it with plentiful portions of onions to hide the rancid taste. Our room was warm, thanks to the coal and the stove. My father usually brought home some useful household items carrying them generally in his coat pocket. For example, he brought detergent from the soda factory, which became such a great help for the laundry.

There were also books to be had. They lay in big heaps in the cellar of the factory, left behind by the scientists who had either been captured by the Russians or had fled to the West. Most of the books had been taken away or destroyed by the soldiers. Although my father never managed to find a complete set, he did locate two volumes from a very beautiful series by the famous German author, Stifter.

When the Russian professor who headed the department wanted something for himself, he always asked my father to smuggle it past the watchman for him. Once he wanted a certain cardboard filing cabinet. As my father carried it by, he was asked: "*Djadushka*,[4] what have you got in there?" "That I can't possibly tell you," said my father with a sly look. "Oh, please, let me see...." "That is impossible, because I have got something in there that's called ...," and then in a whisper, "My intellect!" Then very excitedly and seemingly very cautiously, he opened the cabinet and it was empty! All laughed at the joke and no one realized that it was the cabinet itself that had been taken past them!

---

4 *Djadushka* = grandfather.

It was always so very important to know how to behave towards the Russians. A poor German worker having found a pair of rubber coveralls in the air-raid shelter, rather than reporting them, had instead hidden them in a box, hoping to smuggle them out of the factory after work. The Russian guard caught him and locked him up in the very same air-raid shelter for the whole night. The following morning he was dragged before the head scientist. As he could speak no Russian, my mother was called to translate. Shaken and stammering, the man spoke foolishly and clumsily, for he well realized that he could be locked up without a moment's hesitation. He was the father of a large family that badly needed his small earnings. My mother, realizing this, translated his words generously, and to his advantage. The Russian scientist noticed what was happening, and said accusingly: "Anna Petrovna, you are not translating literally and word for word!" "No, but much more efficiently and better," my mother answered without fear, and the scientist, who was basically a decent person, understood and gave the command to let the man go.

The condition of my mother's overworked hand worried me. She could only use it with the greatest will power, and yet was still expected to write from eight o'clock in the morning until six in the evening.

Our days ran together uneventfully with the daily routine. The highlights in our lives always came in the form of letters. We were now able to get letters from the Western Zone. Regular reports came from Werner and Nita, but the letters always took from two to three weeks to reach us.

We also heard from Dr. Fritz Kienast[5] (brother of Herman) and his wife, Cora. He was stranded in Schwerin, and it was delightful to have located yet another old friend. He asked for my father's help, for he was critically ill, and no one had been able to diagnose his sickness. He begged my father to write to him, telling him what was wrong, and suggested many possibilities, among which was undulant fever. There was a period when the questions and answers went back and forth, during which time Fritz was taken to the hospital in Schwerin. Although both he and my father were medical doctors, each of them being well-known diagnosticians, they could not find the cause of the illness. We suggested that Fritz and Cora should come to Bernburg, where we had a better chance to nurse him back to health.

---

5 Dr. Kienast, a radiologist, was Martha's friend from Estonia. They were confirmed together in the Lutheran Church.

The former pastor's widow had an unoccupied room that she would gladly give up for a while. It was sunny and the entrance gave directly onto the lovely old parsonage garden. How happy I was at the thought of having my best and oldest friend with us, as we had remained very close to each other since the time of our youth. I eagerly looked forward to his arrival, but the good Lord willed it otherwise, for, in the middle of January, Fritz died from a tumour on the brain. What a loss to all of us, for he was an especially fine and talented person, and very dear to us all.

In the end Cora came. This had been Fritz's last wish. As her relatives had all remained in Estonia, she had nowhere else to go. My parents found her a job in the soda factory, for without work one received no food coupons. She fitted in well, and was fluent in Russian as well as in German. After about a year, she married a fellow-worker from the factory.

✻ 8 ✻

REUNION

The small piece of paper dropped from the train window in Munich, remained, until January, the only sign of life we had from my husband. Finally, in about January 1946, we received a letter from Jörn by way of Nita's address in Munich. The return address was that of a German, who also worked in the coal mine but was not a prisoner of war. Prisoners of war were completely shut off from the outside world. Jörn had cunningly overcome that problem with this letter. He wrote about himself as if writing about another person to let us know that he was working in a coal mine with little food, while going through hard times. Then he referred directly to himself with news of little importance.

Our joy at hearing from him was indescribable. We now knew where he was and that he was still alive! I wrote an answer to the given address, giving his prisoner's number, but it came back unclaimed, as I had feared it would. Prisoners of war were supposed to write on specially prepared letter paper containing pages on which the receiver was supposed to answer. This was totally in theory, however, for in practice they never got any letter paper at all! I could visualize his desperation and worry at not hearing anything from his family! All of us, having tried to be brave, would need to continue to be stalwart – that was the solution of paramount importance.

On the 2nd of March, we received a package of medicines for my mother from Nita. As usually happened, when my parents came back, exhausted from work, I had a warm room and something to eat waiting for them. Today we had not received any of those letters that were always greeted so eagerly, but at least there was a small parcel. My mother opened it and discovered that there was a short letter enclosed, which simply read:

> "Yes, here he is in front of me – quite unchanged and well! How superbly Jörn has managed it all!"

My mother started, looked again – none of us could understand. What did she mean? The name 'Jörn' stood clearly there! What had he done that was so wonderful? How could he possibly, in an instant, appear in front of Nita? Could we indeed dare to believe it? Was it really he? We were not kept wondering very long, for an 'express boy' brought the following card the same evening:

> "Rulli, Rulli, (that was my nickname) Jörn is here! Jörn – he is sitting next to me! He is well. He looks healthy. He is so dear to me – I nearly smothered him to death with my kisses. I cry and laugh and run about and don't know what to do in my joy. I'm half crazy with happiness, and should write you more important things than just how I feel. Jörn is here and we are doing everything – everything to make a new life possible for all of you! Have patience! I am telegraphing right away to Graf Keyserling, that he should find a place for you as quickly as possible. We'll try everything at this end. He is free! How wonderful! Just received Mutti's letter of the death of Fritz. It seems that there can be no happiness without pain ... Rulli, bless you ... I share your joy. Oh, Rulli!
>
> Your happy Nita.
> 5 March 1946."

So he had escaped! My husband! How brave, how clever! He was healthy, safe, and now no longer lost to us. We started to make plans immediately. It was the 18th of March. Jörn could not, under any circumstances, risk entering the Eastern Zone, regardless of how great his yearnings were to be here with us. We had to do everything to get to him. Above all else we needed permits and papers. Since he had escaped, Jörn possessed no documents at all, except a card to prove that he was a member of the Red Cross. Nita ran from one authority to another, while her husband, Dr. Horst Lindenberg;, and Fritzi stood as guarantors for Jörn.

Fritzi's statement was especially important as she was an American. She wrote:

> "I have often stayed with my family, in the house of J.v.R., whom I have known personally ever since he moved away from the Baltic, in 1939. He had to live under difficult conditions, for he was not given his own piece of land like the other new settlers, but he was always willing to help in every way. He knew that I (Fritzi) was married to a German, but had kept my U.S.

Citizenship for my children and myself, but he never feared the consequences that this might have caused him with the authorities. I know that J.v.R. did not carry out any of the policies which the Nazi Party or any of its branches suggested to him. By his whole manner it was obvious that he found everything to do with the Nazis or the military despicable. He loved the peaceful work on the farm of Geppertsfeld near Jarotschin. He was bitterly unhappy when he had to become a soldier. I bear witness to the fact that J.v.R. has a great feeling of responsibility and an attitude towards his fellow-man which an American would call completely and fully democratic."

My husband received an identification card as well as a residence permit for Ried, my sister's refuge in the country. It was still impossible to stay any longer than three days in one place, without such a permit. One also could not get anything to eat; there was simply nothing to spare! One had no right to exist. Frequently homecoming soldiers without the required paperwork (being the *Zuzugsgenehmigung* or residency permit) could not even join their wives and children, although the latter already had coupons.

My main problem was to find a way across the border that would allow us all to slip through more or less officially. My first impulse was to travel to my husband immediately and alone, as I did not see any way I could manage it with the children. Else was, fortunately, very much against this plan, and after a while, I capitulated. I went to the local refugee agency and wrote to our cousin Eva von Rosen, who was stranded with her children not far from the border at Kölleda. I put out tentative feelers in every possible direction.

On the 18th of March, we got the news. I planned to be ready to leave on the 2nd of April, and we actually managed to stick to this deadline. I constantly packed, sending only small parcels (*Pfundpäckchen*, or pound parcels), for one was not allowed to mail anything heavier than a pound. This was a terrific and tedious task, but to carry everything would have been impossible, and I knew that one could not take over more than one could personally carry across the one-kilometre-wide neutral zone. Eva wrote, informing us that an extra train of refugees was supposed to leave Kölleda at the beginning of April. It was felt that enough people were expected there by then to make a whole trainload full.

I showed the refugee agency a letter from Jörn in which he said that he had a residence permit for Ried, and on the strength of this they gave me a travel permit. What I did not tell them was that the residence permit was for him alone! The main thing was that I got permission to go, and my omission could be pardoned under the circumstances.

Now that I realized that our future travels would not be by horse and wagons, I sold all four horses to the manager of the estate. In this manner, I suddenly had the money necessary for the expenses.

However, my joy was lessened by the knowledge that I would have to leave my parents behind. They could not come with us for many reasons. First of all, they had no residence permits for Munich. Furthermore, they could not simply leave their work with the Russians, for, without an official leave-of-absence, one could not get a travel permit. Moreover, where to go? Nita's country house was tiny; besides, who knew whether we would ever get there? It was a comfort to know that Cora would, like a real guardian angel, look after my dearest parents. She had her room close by and was able to cook, bake, and tend to them when they came home exhausted from their strenuous work. No loving daughter could have done better. So one sunny day, on the 2nd of April, the three of us left Bernburg.

The farewells stuck in my throat. How would we find each other again? We had very few belongings, but even these ended up being too heavy to carry. I simply was not capable of handling the rucksack, suitcase, and bundle all alone. Else's small suitcase, with the woven pattern, was small but not light. Gerhard had a small, yet weighty, iron toy winch – his most precious possession, which a child at Pretzien had given to him.

At the beginning of our journey, while on board the train, we thought exclusively of our destination. Our final goal was clear, but the route and manner to reach it were represented only by a dimly exposed image, and only the Lord knew whither our travels would take us. Luckily, we could not possibly foresee all that was to transpire.

First we had to change trains at Güsten. It was almost too easy, for the next train was stationed so near. On the stretch to Sangerhausen the train started to fill with people and their luggage, along with wild rumours. Kölleda was reported to be a huge camp, a camp whose reputation aroused horror and fear. There were about six thousand people hoping to find a solution to their difficulties, trying to achieve a release from this omnipresent turmoil, a deliverance which they hardly believed possible any more.

Still, we changed course, heading towards Nordhausen. Again we swapped trains, not so easily now, for the closer we came to the border the fuller the train became. Nevertheless, after much pushing, shoving, and crowding, we were standing, at last, squashed together in the train. Another transfer faced us at Leinefelde. While standing on the platform, however, I was faced with the throngs of people waiting there, and became oppressed with the certainty that we could not possibly all fit into the next train! People with even more luggage had been waiting for a week, or more, under the open skies, with no one to care for them – all of them homeless, frantic, and without solution.

We went right up to the edge of the platform. Perhaps if the train was a long one, we would have a chance here. There – it came puffing along! People hung-on like grapes on the outside steps, and even crouched, in the hundreds, on the carriage roofs. Those who wanted to get out of the already over-crowded compartments could only do so through the windows. A crying, yelling, fearsome horde of helpless, frightened humanity greeted our eyes.

I held the children close to me, terrified of losing them in the turmoil. "Here, Else … Gerhard, quickly…."

To reach the other side of the long train, we scampered across the railway tracks, around the front of the locomotive, where, as a total surprise, helping hands reached down to us from the top of the coal tender. Hurry! One child, another child, rucksack, sleeping things, suitcase, Else's little case, and then the precious toy winch, and lastly I quickly got on. The miracle had happened! We were all sitting on top of the coal tender, perched on top of the pile of coals, immediately behind the steaming locomotive, spewing continuous showers of sooty sparks mixed in with the clouds of steam! Precariously perched, attempting to gain footholds in the crumbly coal, I made certain of the safety of my loved ones. Soon we left the wailing, complaining, and desperate cries of those who remained behind, and with trembling, yet thankful hearts, we continued our odyssey.

The spring landscape flew past us. How well I knew this part of the country! There was the Schloss Bischofstein, where Werner had been in boarding school! I had never seen it from so high up. We did not have much time to look around, however, for we were kept busy trying to keep our balance just to stay on board. I had to hold onto the children, as well as to look out for burn marks resulting from the flying sparks, which rained on us with every puff of the engine. I spread an old military blanket of Werner's over us like a tent, but then the blanket started to ignite. Still, that was better than our hair! Our coats also had large holes burned in them. All this time, it was impossible for us to move, for we sat on a closely piled mountain of coal with nothing to hold onto. Yet that was so much better than having to hang, with only one foot on the steps, or trying to perch directly on top of the slippery roof covering one of the passenger cars!

However, like all the others, this trip too, came to an end. In Heiligenstadt, we found out that, as there was no further train service up to the border, one had to take up one's bundle and walk there. At Arenshausen, a small border crossing, we had to show our papers. No one could tell us beforehand how the border crossing would be arranged, for the procedure apparently changed daily. Inasmuch as the endless stream of people moved slowly forward ahead of us, we could only hope that today the border was not closed.

Big posters of Stalin and Lenin looked down like symbolic and merciless giants on this pitiful herd of little people who could be destroyed by one stroke of a pen. The tension was terrible! Moreover, our physical strength had been overtaxed from the ordeal of carrying our luggage so far. Who would stop us? The Russians, the Germans, or the British? There were many stories about the actions of all three, but we did not hear anything negative about the British. Would this be a closed crossing place, or was it the hoped-for gap in the border? As fate would have it, it turned out to be the one we had prayed for. We had withstood all the required tests — all our documents were accepted and stamped, and we stood shaking on free soil. We were on the "other side," in a free country — at least at that moment we believed that we were.

My father had made out an affidavit that stated that we were "germ-free and clear of all infectious diseases," for, without this precious piece of paper, we could not even have bought our train tickets. As this, however, seemed to carry little importance in the British Zone, we underwent immediate and thorough delousing.

I do not think that the lice would have been very impressed, had we really managed to collect any en route, for the whole procedure seemed amazingly ineffective. We were sent up a pathway, where we had to open up our clothing. To the right and left stood people with large spray cans of powder: 'Poofing' this, they covered us with clouds of the white dust. It was certainly much more unhealthy for us to inhale than the non-existent lice! I would have enjoyed a hot bath ever so much more!

We were then told to wait in the camp town of Friedland for transportation that would take us further. Here and there were huge tents, or lean-to-like structures containing scaffolding arrangements for sleeping. I never would have believed that one could sleep on such an apparatus, but we were all so tired that we could have slept almost anywhere. The care that we got was wonderful and everything was beautifully organized. We listened intently as monstrous loudspeakers broadcast exact instructions about how we were to proceed. After we had listed ourselves among those waiting for transportation to Bavaria, we had been told nothing further than to go and wait. Well-trained in such matters, we waited. On the second day, we were told to get into a train. Even though we could not find out its exact destination, we were still glad to be heading anywhere that appeared to be in the right general direction. First we passed Göttingen and then continued along the Leine River. We enjoyed the scenery, even though I noticed that we were going in a northerly, instead of southerly direction, for I felt that in Hanover we could surely get a connection bringing us south again. By the time we reached Nordheim, however, I had become perplexed, as we had now started heading west (perhaps to the American Zone?), but supposedly not by way of Kassel, my destination. The train took all kinds of detours, passed all stations without stopping until it ultimately reached Paderborn. It was not until then that we were told that the train's destination was the Rhineland!

As I really did not want to go there, I made a quick decision, grabbed our belongings, and we soon found ourselves, standing albeit somewhat helplessly, on the platform. Gerhard and I had been coughing since leaving Bernburg, and recently Else had started too. It was chilly, there was no train, and we were having to wait again. A very kind woman, employed by the railway, came to our help, and took us inside. It was already late in the afternoon when, at long last, a small train came by. We took a fond farewell from our latest helper, who had even found us something to eat and was now busily stuffing the remaining bread into the children's pockets as they climbed into the narrow compartment.

We puffed slowly back again in an easterly direction through Altenbeken. Here the rails came to an abrupt end. We had to continue on foot to reach the next connecting train, a distance of two kilometres away. Everyone had to cross over a long, narrow dam, because a bridge had been demolished. It seemed an endless distance.

As I found it impossible to carry our luggage all at once, I had to do it in stages. First Else stayed behind and guarded the bundle, while Gerhard and I walked a short distance with the other bundle, rucksack, and suitcase. Empty-handed, I then returned to Else, while Gerhard waited ahead. This went on and on, over and over again. All the other passengers were able to carry their own suitcases, so I was left far behind, terrified that we would miss the train. This method of running back and forth worked very well for us while we were walking on the raised roadway. However, when we reached the crevasse, where the bridge had fallen away, we had to cross on a dangerously steep and narrow embankment. Shaking from sheer exhaustion, we really were the last ones to reach the train. Nevertheless, we made it in time and undauntedly continued our progress to the Warburg station on the British-American border.

We had to change trains eleven times during the five days en route, but we were always drawing nearer. Only the American border remained to be crossed, and then, soon, we would be with my husband. We entered Warburg. "Everyone out of the train. Produce all documents!"

Since the previous week, it had no longer been possible to go freely from the British to the American Zone. It had now become necessary to have a special entry permit! This I did not have. We were told to go to an old convent in the encampment, a mere ten minutes away. We walked and walked, and walked some more, but saw no trace of a convent. Eventually, not able to carry my things any longer, I leaned all the luggage up against the wall of a house, sat the children on top of the heap and went on alone. What a relief, when I found the convent – an hour's walk away!

It was now night and very dark. I was worried about having left the children so long, but, instead of finding them crying and upset upon my return, I encountered two quite happy little people waiting for me. They were eating chocolates, which a passing British soldier had given them. They immediately stuffed some of these delicious morsels, which they had thoughtfully saved for me, into my mouth. Then we got up and dragged our things to the convent, only to fall, worn out and weary, onto the scattered straw.

I inspected our surroundings more closely the following morning. There were over thirty people in the *Oberschule* (high school), as this camp was called. The real convent turned out to be in another wing of the building. The whole complex, constructed in the sixteenth century, lay high above the picturesque little town. The massive, thick walls were steep. On these, we hung out our blankets, letting the accumulated clouds of dust blow away in the clean spring wind. I inquired everywhere, but no one seemed to know what was planned for us. The *Amis* did not let anyone in without this latest visa, and I could not find out how to get one. We heard that they were waiting until there were enough people to make up a trainload – the old story. What did they mean by 'enough'?

Our coughs got worse and now my ears started hurting. It was too cold outside, while inside the air was thick and unbearable. My concerned Else sensibly forced me to frequently go out into the fresh spring air. We could not stray too far from the camp, for the orders to move might be given momentarily. In their desperation, people started foretelling the future from cards, whether they knew how to read them or not. All kinds of oracles appeared and were asked for, but it did not help the waiting.

Full of envy, we once watched a private car arrive and drive off with a married couple from the camp. Relatives of theirs who owned a car had come to take them into the '*Ami Zone.*' It seemed that they were not so strict in their control when it concerned traffic on the paved roads, yet it would be impossible for us to try this on foot!

There was only one room to wash in, for use by both men and women. The cutlery, pots and pans, laundry, diapers, and everything else were also washed in this room. The food, not bad, was almost sufficient, besides which I still had some rolled oats for the children, and we ate them raw like cake.

Gerhard found this life simply wonderful. He played with the other children, and showed off his precious winch. No one pestered him with such procedures as washing, getting up on time and other annoying routines. He lived a free and carefree life. I read to the children. They had coloured pencils for drawing. We wrote letters to their father, as well as to Bernburg. The friendly atmosphere in our communal living room was exceptional. There were about thirty-six of us inhabiting the one room. A small partition ran down the centre, but the men and women mixed, as families always lay together. Slowly the building filled. Finally, more than five hundred people were staying there, awaiting an unknown future with all that it might bring. Then the rumour started that the Russian border had been closed again, and that the *Amis* were letting refugees in exclusively for trade and for barter.

Day after day, we waited fearfully. We had arrived on the 6th of April, and, at last, on the 15th we heard that we should get ready to leave – and now of course it was 'immediately,' and in the greatest hurry. Oh how gladly we hurried! Everyone ran hither and thither, asking, shouting, and looking for things, as well as one another. There were cars ready and waiting for the luggage, so we took the hour-long walk to the station, unencumbered. Once we arrived there, the pace was naturally not nearly as rushed as we had been told it would be. We stood around for many hours, waiting, but eventually we ended up sitting in a small train. Departure – arrival – it came too soon, for it was no more than twelve kilometres before we reached the vital U.S. border-crossing, which already had caused so many people an exceptional measure of unhappiness and misunderstanding.

Here we were in for a new surprise. We had to pay for our tickets! I fortunately carried money with me. I also had hung a bag with money and various addresses around the neck of each child, for children could so easily get lost in the crush. Many of the refugees had not a penny, and once again were, hopelessly and frantically, stuck. Then it was over, and we changed trains for the thirteenth time. What a feeling! No more borders to keep us from Jörn!

The train pulled into the station at Kassel. It was very late. The big hall was overfilled with American soldiers – black as well as white. A furious black soldier swore at me, for apparently I had opened an forbidden door. I looked desperately for a place to spend the night. To whom could one turn? Our next train left early the following morning at four o'clock.

An approachable conductor who ultimately saw our plight, invited us into an empty freight car, where we laid our blankets on the floor. I held a child tightly on each side of me, and this helped to keep us a little bit warmer.

At two o'clock the next morning, there was a sudden loud banging on the sliding doors, which we had closed so that no one could get in. "Get off, the freight train is pulling out right away!"

We stumbled out over the dark rails and platforms looking for our train. Perhaps one could already get on board?

Suddenly I heard Gerhard's wail of misery – his winch, the precious treasure, was still in the freight car! I raced back and fortunately was able to find it. He held it tightly from then on. We located our train after worried searching, and to my surprise it was already open, yet still quite empty. We sat down comfortably and in leisure. It was three o'clock in the morning. Suddenly there was a jerk and it began to move! How were we to know that this was the night when the general time change occurred? Yes, in the spring, "spring ahead one hour." In the fall, "fall back one hour." The departure of the train, therefore occurred earlier by one hour. Had our sleeping quarters not been shunted around, waking us at this early hour, this could have surprised us also. As the many others who had also wanted to take this train obviously had not been warned, they did not even realize that they were being left behind! We had no one to thank, other than our friendly freight conductor, and our good fortune. How much unhappiness we must have left behind us, as we sat in the almost empty compartment, tensely awaiting the future.

It was already Wednesday of Easter week. I had our travel permit, which made it fairly probable that we would be reasonably well taken care of at the different stations. How many more times would we have to change trains? No one seemed to know anything, and no one gave me any definite answers. All the direct connections from Kassel to Munich had been broken. It was amazing that there was any traffic at all, as there was so much that had been damaged! The trains travelled at a nerve-shatteringly slow pace, and all the itineraries were completely unreliable. In any event, we reached Frankfurt that same day, without having to change trains.

How heavily that town, too, had suffered from all the strafing! Every waiting room was filled with throngs of people. I knew that we had to wait for our train until the next day. We eventually crept into one of the crowded, stinking, waiting rooms. People lay on the floor everywhere. We zig-zagged around tired bodies trying to find an empty corner and, exhausted, lowered ourselves amongst the others on the dirty stone slabs. We could be thankful that we were able to be under a roof at all, not having to stand outside throughout the whole night.

We crawled out again the next day. The sun was shining. I went to look for food. Else and Gerhard sat on our belongings beside the big entrance. They leaned against the sun-warmed wall and slept, forgetting their hunger and weariness. Our train arrived. Was this to be the last stage of our journey?

We travelled through the night, arriving in Munich at an uncivilized hour the next morning, the 18th of April. We knew that my husband was in Ried, but we decided to go first to Nita.

Her house was full of wayward, homeless children whom she had generously sheltered. As we should have arrived long ago, I had to tell her everything in detail. They had been expecting us daily. We were worn out, but she strengthened us with a good breakfast. Now all that remained was the last, short distance, the forty kilometres to Ried.

On this sector of our odyssey, we travelled by bus, sitting in the last vehicle of our long journey towards our final goal. We enjoyed looking out at the beautiful Bavarian countryside. How peaceful! Here there was no sign of war anywhere.

It was late that afternoon when, thank goodness, we turned up in the unscathed, tranquil, little village. What a contrast with poor destroyed Munich. Leaving our luggage at the village store, we walked towards the setting sun. The suspense in our hearts was unbearable. One-and-a half kilometres. Then a small path across rolling meadows. There it was – the little cottage my sister had built as an escape for the eventuality that bombs would fly at Munich, causing them to lose their home. It was called *Der Kirschgarten,* the cherry garden, for its one cherry tree amid well-tended pastures. Suddenly, my Jörn, light-footed with joy and happiness, appeared. His great, strong arms opened wide and enfolded the three of us. All sorrows, all anxieties, had been overcome. At last we were together again.

✸ 9 ✸

THE LAST RETURN

We were together. We felt so hopeful. In spite of the hardships that still faced us, we were ready to contemplate making a fresh start.

After Nita had helped Jörn obtain an identity card and a residence permit, the next step was that of obtaining ration cards. Again, my sister came to our help, and we soon had our own supply of these vital coupons. The local farmers had enough food for themselves but were outnumbered by a growing body of refugees. Furthermore, they were unwilling to share unless you worked for them. You had to be very lucky indeed to find a job.

But fortune continued to smile on us. After a few weeks of intensive searching, Jörn found work as a hand on a farm run by a woman. The owner was absent as he had been arrested as a Nazi supporter. (Two years later he was declared innocent and released.)

We were squeezed into two tiny rooms. Even so, we would have been the happiest people in the world, had not the knowledge of my parents being cut off in the Russian Zone gnawed at me relentlessly. Yet, how could I leave my two children unattended, while I went back to retrieve my parents?

As it happened, my own dear governess, Baroness Thea Stromberg, was now in Munich, staying with her daughter. Her husband, Dr. Schröder, had died. She had managed by a miracle to escape the bombing of Dresden, having jumped on a freight train, which left the fatal train station only minutes before death engulfed the thousands of refugees awaiting transportation.

Thea was overjoyed at the thought of coming to the farm to care for the children. I now set out to retrace my footsteps, with the intention of bringing back my parents. Even though I had every confidence in Thea's kindness and ability, I was leaving with a heavy heart indeed. The feelings of that occasion when I took farewell of my husband and children remain to this day as a painful memory for me.

First, however, I sought to settle the matter of my horses, which I had earlier entrusted to Herr Kames, when he had fled across the Elbe. He was now living in the Ruhr area, where he had managed to re-establish a semblance of domestic normality, including a beautiful flower and vegetable garden, which in itself was a remarkable oddity, considering the heavy bombing of the industrial heartland. Not only had he already sold one horse, but he presented me the other, a formerly beautiful brood mare, in poor condition. All her papers had been lost. Herr Kames agreed to pay me for both animals, but a miserly, small price. The 'HORSE' chapter of my life – always capitalized in my mind – was concluded for the time being. At least I had some money to carry on.

I took the train eastwards, getting off at a small village in the Harz Mountains next to the Russian Zone. What to do next? I was searching for a cue. As everyone with seemingly secret tasks was reluctant to speak, I could not very well make inquiries. All I was able to do was to listen carefully for whatever hint came my way. Then, knowing in which direction the Russian border lay, I decided to investigate on foot. All I had with me, apart from the clothes I stood in, was a little knapsack with a tiny piece of bread and, good for bartering, a small package of tobacco. My sole outfit was a light cotton dress and some extremely ill-fitting shoes.

It was so peaceful, so quiet, nothing moved. My route took me through some meadows, intersected by alders and birches, which were rather more bushy than full-grown. Where my path would lead to, I had no idea. It was all very uncanny, but I was spurred on by the thought of my stranded parents. Suddenly, out of nowhere, shooting began everywhere around me. Startled, I hurled myself to the ground and lay motionless. Sometimes the firing was close by, then further away, but it did not stop. I could neither discern its source nor its intended target. I do not recall how long I remained there, hardly daring to breathe and unable to escape from the stinging nettles that were tormenting my legs. Then, as suddenly as it had begun, the shooting stopped. The ensuing silence was unbearably eerie. No longer sensing any movement near me, I ventured to get up on my stiff, badly stung legs, and made my way back to a sort of inn. There I put up for the night in the hall.

I was informed of the British military manoeuvre, that very afternoon, into the middle of which I had strayed. Inwardly shuddering, I reflected on the perils into which my ignorance had led me. Listening to the people around me, however, I soon understood that they had the same aims as I did.

Moreover, now it was time to make new plans. The general advice, from those who shared my objectives, was that one should not try to hide, as the Russians would find you anyway and dire consequences would ensue. Thus, on yet another warm day in May, I again walked eastwards along a wide paved road and I was soon joined by two young men. Obviously, we had the same goal. After a few kilometres, a roadblock of huge trees indicated: "This far, but no further." Undaunted, we marched on, climbing without hesitation over the obstacle.

Then, some distance ahead, I spied the peak of a Russian military cap, along with the outline of a pair of binoculars, gleaming in a ditch alongside the road. My two companions proceeded unruffled, possessed, I think, of an almost fatalistic yearning to find freedom. I told them to offer cigarettes to the guards, and that I would repay them from my tobacco supply later. As a child, I had played "cops and robbers"; now it was "robbers and wanderers." But this time the game was a little too realistic. Nevertheless, I managed to remain calm.

As soon as we were abreast of him, the guard got up and started interrogating the boys. He was joined shortly by another soldier who had been hiding. The questioning was brief, and, as one of the militiamen understood their German explanations, the two boys were soon released. Then it was my turn. I feigned ignorance of the Russian language, but understood all too well what they were saying about me – they could make use of women in many ways. I told them the truth: "I want to rejoin my parents, who are old and still working in a factory office for the Russian authorities."

One of the soldiers wanted to release me, while the other had plans to set me to work. At last and thank goodness, the kinder of the two prevailed, advising me to skirt the village that lay ahead to avoid being seen by the local commander. He also told me to obtain a good supply of cherries from the people who were picking them. When I hesitated, he said: "I will watch you to make sure that you get some."

Eager to follow orders and do as I was bid, I made a wide arc around the village, hastening along to the next hamlet. This was closer to the railway. Fortunately, the pain in my blistered legs was bearable, as long as I was walking. After several hours on the road, I reached the station, only to find that there was no train until the next day. For a small cost, I was offered an attic room, but sleep was out of the question as my legs still stung viciously.

The journey by train to Bernburg to return to my parents was soon accomplished. They had been awaiting news from me, yet had not expected me to arrive in person. Our reunion was overwhelmingly emotional and we hugged each other joyfully. "We must begin to plan. Without delay!"

When I had left with the children for the Western Zone, my parents had been refused permission to accompany us due to their indispensable work for the Russians at the factory. Even though most of the assigned interpretations had now been completed, and although the Russian officer in charge was a gentleman and understood my parents' predicament, it was still astonishing that he had actually given them written permission to leave.

The greatest obstacle had been overcome, yet we still faced the problem of recrossing the border. Every one of my spare forms had been used up, and were all decorated with a departure stamp from the Russian Zone.

Wishing not to waste time, we promptly packed and left. We still had to choose which possessions to pack, including our valuable family books (inscribed by my great-grandfather), which my brother had earlier rescued from the 'library' of the impudent farm inspector. Sadly, I could only bring a few of the books, because of weight constraints.

The train quickly reached the boundary: "*Aussteigen! Inspektion! Papiere nachprüfen lassen!*"[1]

Everyone had to alight, with all their bundles and baggage, to have their travelling papers validated. As we stood waiting for further instructions, my father, growing bored, wandered off into the local village. My mother, guarded the baggage, while I attempted to find out what was happening.

There was a long low fence separating us from the train. It was guarded by a patrolling soldier. At the exit, gate the militia were checking the documents as the people sluiced through to the waiting trains. Those with the necessary permits were allowed to pass through; the others had to surrender their documents and to report to the police. I knew how hazardous that was and recognized our possible fate. Do anything, I urged myself, but do not get caught in that trap. Deciding to approach the police myself with my precious, albeit inadequate, document, I went to the guard, as he was

---

1 I.e., "Get out! Inspection! Show your papers!"

pacing up and down, patrolling the fence line, and asked: "Where is the police post, please?" He showed me the way: "Go through this gate (the one he was guarding), and turn left in the tunnel." I thanked him and proceeded on into the tunnel. After making sure that no one was watching me, instead of turning left, I bore right. I realized that I would thereby come out where I wanted to be, that is, where the trains were boarded.

I hastened back to the entrance, to where I knew that the dangerous checkpoint was located, except now, of course, I was on the proper side of the fence. My mother, at first aghast to see me there, soon grasped the situation. Loudly, yet casually, I called to her: "Give me some of the luggage. It will be quicker if I take it to the train right away." Zealously I darted back and forth with the baggage. My father soon returned and we all carefully assumed innocent faces lest we betrayed our deception in passing through that fateful gate.

But the Russians were very thorough. After a short time of travelling, we again had to climb out with all our luggage, and were shepherded into a large building. Yet another checkpoint!

Resorting again to my strategy of going on ahead to reconnoiter, I pushed my way through the milling throng. On the far side was a high counter, like a loft, on which sat a row of officials checking through the documents of the endless queues of people standing before them. As I started back to my parents, I caught the sound of an unhappy, lost child wailing for its mother. I stopped to console this bewildered, fearful creature, who had been shoved back and forth in this forest of muddled humanity, and picked her up. I walked alongside the counter scrutinizing the tense, efficient, and impersonal faces of the inspecting officials until I reached a woman who somehow seemed friendlier, kinder, and more approachable. As I lifted my little charge up for her to see, I implored her to announce its whereabouts over the loudspeaker. This was done, and in no time the child was back in the arms of its distraught mother.

However, this did not solve my problem. I found a corner for my parents to sit and pondered our plight. Then I went back to this kind official, telling her how hard it was for old people to stand around in lengthy lines. Could she not attend to them first? Without demur, she agreed. After she had assisted my mother and father, I edged closer to her and whispered: "Please, help us." With a fleeting glance at me, she ornamented my invalid document with the valuable stamp. There can be no doubt that I owed my good fortune to the little child, who had made the first contact. These are our invisible, yet visible guardian angels!

The next train ride was equally short. Once again we had to clamber out with all our baggage. Even when one possesses so little, there is still too much to carry. A three kilometre-wide strip of no-man's land lay ahead, with a single sentry standing guard on the imaginary boundary line. To our delight, a horse and cart appeared, as if from heaven, and relieved us of our luggage and anxieties.

I now renewed my acquaintance with the British refugee camp on the other side. How much it had changed in the short time since the children and I had stopped there. Everything was better organized, including the delousing with DDT and the accommodation.

The rail services to Munich similarly showed better organization, and with little delay, my little family was fully reunited. Even though all of us were squeezed into two tiny bedrooms on the farm, we were content. At least, and at last, we had all survived the ordeal and were free.

Before long, however, we moved on again. Over the next little while, through the work that Jörn and I were able to obtain, we had just enough to keep the family going. He was a poorly paid worker on a cow farm, and I was an energetic, but honest searcher for food supplies. Eventually, we managed to acquire a small flock of sheep, which were an invaluable source of milk and wool. Poor we may have been, but we seldom went hungry, even though there was hunger all around us. The children resumed their schooling, and before long Else was attending the high school at Wasserburg, on the River Inn, some fifteen kilometres away.

At last, after all the hardships, uncertainties and deprivations of the past few traumatic years, a measured rhythm was returning to our lives. Sadly, my father did not survive long to enjoy it. His old heart, already troublesome during our extended flight, had been grievously overtaxed. The attacks grew more frequent, the pain more intense, and there were no remedies available to make life more bearable. Then one day, while I was away visiting Else, who had been hospitalized with appendicitis, he closed his eyes for the last time. It was a terrible blow, for we all had benefited by his presence, his advice, and his wisdom.

Now Mother had to carry on alone, but she found great solace in the icons she painted. Individuals and public institutions gladly bought them. As a treasured memento of this period, I still have a series of postcard reproductions of those of her works which the famous old Bavarian monastery of Ettal had purchased.

THE DIARY
OF JÜRGEN VON ROSEN

INTRODUCTION

by Elvi Whittaker

In the waning months of the war, while Martha von Rosen was struggling to keep her small bedraggled band of fugitives together, and trying to escape the imminent Russian advance and the fate of being cut off from the Western world forever, her husband had his own hardships. Jürgen von Rosen and his family had for some years now been powerless pawns in German military policy. First they had been forcibly dispossessed and "repatriated," not to fatherland Germany as they had expected, but instead to a neglected farm in Poland. In 1942, this powerlessness was further exacerbated by his being conscripted, against all of his strong philosophical convictions, into the German armed forces. He was now to fight in a war in which he had no political commitment. To do so he was given the rank of *Obergefreiter*[1] in a heavy anti-aircraft unit of the Luftwaffe in Italy. This was

---

1 *"Obergefreiter"* corresponds to the rank of corporal in the British system, or to private first class in the American ranks, and has been also translated as "leading airman." Von Rosen's wartime correspondence with his wife has been lost; thus, accounts of his life in the Luftwaffe are not available. His rank is taken from his Iron Cross citation, dated 13 March 1945 and signed by "General der Flieger u. Kommandierender General der dtsch. Lw. in Italien," which gave his affiliation as "dem Obergefreiten l./schw. Flakabt. 311 (v)" (see p. 134). By his wife's account, his unit was attached to the Afrika Korps, but the expected actual transfer to North Africa did not occur. It appears, from later accounts of the war in Italy, that the Italian partisans played a significant part in deterring this move during the African campaign.

IM NAMEN DES FÜHRERS
VERLEIHE ICH
DEM

Obergefreiten
Jürgen von Rosen
1./schw.Flakabt.311(v)

DAS
EISERNE KREUZ
2. KLASSE

Gefechtsstand, 13. März 1945

(DIENSTSIEGEL)

General der Flieger
u.Kommandierender General
der dtsch. Lw. in Italien

(DIENSTGRAD UND DIENSTSTELLUNG)

Certificate to accompany the Iron Cross awarded to Jürgen von Rosen on 13 March 1945 for his courage in single-handedly defending an embattled military train by firing at the strafing jabos with his army rifle.

not the final blow, however. He lost control over his own destiny completely when he became a prisoner of the Allies when the Germans surrendered in May 1945.

In April 1945, German resistance in Italy was beginning to collapse as many Italian cities (Mantua, Parma, Verona, Genoa, Venice) were "liberated" by the corps of the American Fifth Army, Eighth Army, together with air support, in their spring offensive. On April 29, 1945, the surrender of German forces in Italy was signed at Caserta in the south. It was on May 2 that the surrender was actually ratified at the front, and at noon on that day, the surrender became effective. Six days later, at 11:01 at night, all operations ceased in the European land war and the Allies claimed victory.

However, as von Rosen's writings show, the conditions of war remained. The captured German forces had now to contend not only with their captors, but also with the unpredictable actions of the Italian partisans. These partisans were the guerrilla fighters who had vigorously opposed the Axis forces and now continued to act on their own in situations which, as von Rosen's diary shows, seemed often to be outside the formal end of hostilities.

The diary begins with the German surrender. It is a rare document in that it is a testimonial to one man's experience of military imprisonment. Even more pointedly, it chronicles an experience quite foreign to our conventional knowledge of the fate of those we considered the enemy in the immediate post-war years. Moreover, it reveals expected perspectives on the conduct of the Allied forces towards these captives. The histories constructed and institutionalized by the Allies, like all accounts, are, after all, politically constructed, and have been widely disseminated as the official and true accounts. Von Rosen's contribution, therefore, is that he reveals in painstaking detail the experience of a German soldier at the mercy of his American, British, and French captors. His writings depict a man diligently working off his one hundred days of forced labour, which he believed would earn him the promised repatriation. Instead, he is continually disappointed in this expectation, finally losing hope, and becoming one of the nameless thousands who inhabited prisoner-of-war camps in Italy, Germany, and France. The usual acknowledgments of humanity one would have expected from their captors, or the Allies as we know them, seemed to be absent. The diary shows that the ordinary privileges permitted prisoners by the Geneva Convention, such as having shelter, receiving and sending mail, possessing writing materials, and having food supplies of acceptable quantity and standards,

*Baron Jürgen von Rosen, 1942,
in one of the few photographs taken of him.*

were missing.[2] Added to these deprivations, von Rosen and his fellow prisoners are forced into long marches to places unknown, to be followed by further marches, and yet another uprooting for yet another march somewhere else.

---

2 The qualities of justice, humanity, and charity conventionally attributed without question to the Americans have been seriously challenged in James Bacque's *Other Losses* (1989a). See also Bacque (1989b), Fraser (1989), and Gault (1989). These works made an impact in publicizing what some have come to call Eisenhower's "death camps." It should be noted, however, that at the time of publication of this book, historians are undecided about the status of the claims made in these writings. It is clear from von Rosen's diary, however, that while he seemed to escape the most horrible of the experiences supposedly meted out by the Americans, he did have to endure the absence of the most basic of human comforts, such as shelter and food. According to Bacque, these conditions were reserved for Disarmed Enemy Forces (DEF), a special status created by General Eisenhower in March 1945 for those who surrendered at the end of the war. The reminiscences of Helmut Horner (1991), also a German prisoner of war, supply the details of a parallel experience.

Introduction

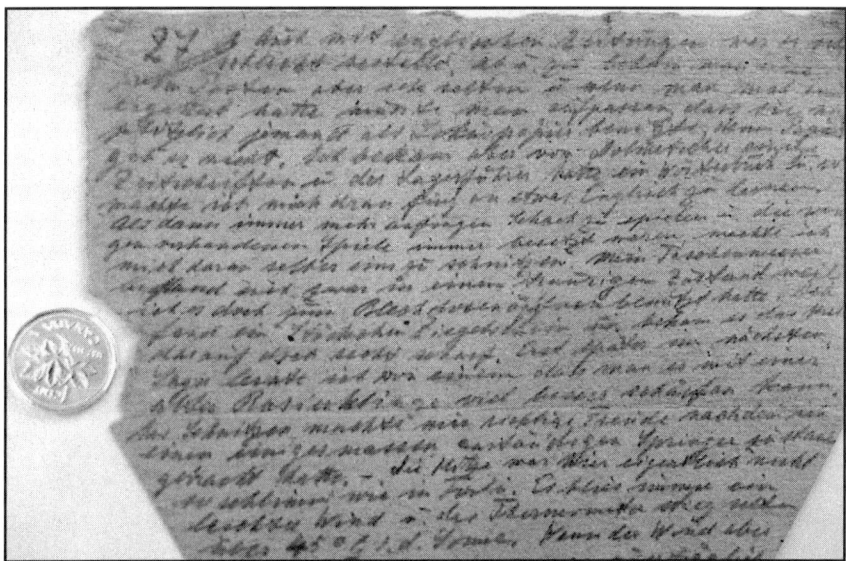

Fragment of Jürgen von Rosen's diary.

His writing was done furtively, during whatever private time he was able to garner. Lacking paper, he salvaged any paper products he could – pieces of cardboard, discarded bureaucratic forms - all of which he then divided into as many sheets as the poor quality of the material would allow. To these precious sheets he then applied his one pathetic pencil. This was a treasured stub which he sharpened regularly to permit the finest of scripts, one of the many methods by which he managed to conserve writing space. The writing, too small to be easily legible, ran in smooth lines across the dull, rough surfaces and badly glued seams. Parts of the diary are written on greyish, abrasive toilet paper, others on parts of packing material. In the last months of his imprisonment, the prisoners were finally permitted paper, and even some lined white paper, though the latter was of inferior quality. This too is to be found among the fifty oddly shaped pieces that make up the original diary.

Quite surprisingly, the diary survived detection during repeated searches of its owner. It accompanied its creator on long imposed marches, on the unpredictable relocation from one camp to another, and on his final escape. How and where he was able to hide this bulky collection defies the imagination.

It is obvious that the compulsion to produce this record, and to protect and preserve it, was all-important. He wrote a few parts of it as a letter to his family, addressing them as "you," but, perhaps most importantly, he wrote it to occupy his mind during long periods without diversion or congenial company. The commitment to this enterprise is also evident in the large amounts of time he devoted later, in the relative comfort of his early years in Canada, to transcribing the original diary, in a legible hand, into school exercise booklets. It is these inscribed records that Martha von Rosen later translated into English to be ultimately reproduced in this volume.

The diary is uncut, in order to be true to the nature of the original experience and its immediacy, but also to allow the character of the writer to emerge with as much fidelity as possible. Clearly Jürgen von Rosen made himself into an impartial observer. With an objectivity that any scientist would recognize, he records not just the dramatic events of his imprisonment but, even more importantly, the wearisome round of daily life. The occasional slow pace of the diary reveals, more pointedly than anything else, the meaninglessness and loneliness of a prisoner's existence. Despite the inevitable separation from the world as he knew it, and the dehumanization engendered by the experience, von Rosen's diary is a testimony to human resourcefulness. Although his trials and disappointments were harsh, he was able to give the reader a strong, and unexpected, sense of inner peace.

✳ 1 ✳

BELLARIA, CAMP 14

August 3, 1945

When I look back now, after three months of imprisonment, I realize that some of the events are about to escape my memory – events which at the time of their occurrence, I believed could never be forgotten. Now I feel sorry that I did not start writing the diary right away. However I will try to recollect the events following the general breakdown, and will relate them briefly.

That a general collapse of the Southern Front was expected, was quite apparent to me and most of my comrades, after we heard the news that Kesselring had been recalled.[1] His successor, Vietinghoff, would hardly be able to hold the front. We were happy when one day, about the middle of April, an unexpected order was peremptorily given for the FMG (anti-aircraft radar tracking system) to be readied for removal to another location.[2] That the move would be northwards was self-evident, especially after

---

[1] April 1945, Kesselring was the *Generalfeldmarschall* (field marshal) of the Axis Southwest Army Group. After being injured in an accident, he became Commander-in-Chief, West, in March 1945, replacing Field Marshal Gerd von Rundstedt. He proved unable to stop the Anglo-American drive into Germany, however, and surrendered the southern half of the German forces on 7 May, 1945. Kesselring was replaced by Vietinghoff, as field marshal of the Axis Southwest Army Group.

[2] FMG (*Funk Mess Gerät*) refers to a radar aircraft tracking device, stationed near the anti-aircraft cannons (five in number, named *A, B, C, D, E*, i.e. "Bertha," and "Dora," etc.). The firing aim of each anti-aircraft battery, consisting of several cannons, were dependent on the one FMG.

we had heard that the FMG's with the other batteries of our detachment had been given the same order.

This very special and precious apparatus was to be removed to safety. The only question was whether we, the attendants, would accompany it, or stay to help man the cannons in the final ground battle. Meanwhile, we started with great gusto to shovel the entrance to the FMG free, and fetched the two trailers that were stationed in a farmer's shed, located about 300 metres away. Two days later, however, the trailers had to be returned to the barn, and generally it looked as if the whole withdrawal would have to be abandoned, as there were no heavy tracked vehicles available to pull the trailers (carrying the FMG). So we went on living out of half-packed rucksacks, except now we were very badly protected against shrapnel because the entrances to our shelter were exposed. However, as we experienced very few attacks, we concluded that something was happening at the front. We always noticed when the *jabos* (the airplanes which normally strafed our positions practically each day) sometimes did not appear, and those turned out to be the times when something special was happening at the Southern Front.[3] Thus the *jabos* were probably busy there.

Because the freshly dug soil made our position conspicuous, we had to haul branches from some distance away to hide our equipment. Young alders and aspen trees were placed against the FMG, but had to be removed at every alarm to enable us to turn the tracking device.

So we had to wait in vain until some vehicle arrived to move us. The news from the other fronts got worse every day and letters from home became very scarce. Nevertheless, I felt happy to realize that *meine Lieben*[4] were in safety. I was hoping so intensively from day to day to receive the news that you had reached Nita. This last reassurance was, however, not mine to receive, I have, nevertheless, lived in the secure belief that you are in Ried.[5]

---

[3] The battles at the southern front flared up on April 2, 1945 when the Allies pushed northward, generally holding the orientation of the east-west "Ghengis Khan Line," and breaching the strongly prepared Axis positions just south of Bologna. They had almost encircled this city by April 20th.

[4] "*Meine Lieben*" = "my loved ones."

[5] This part of the diary, like some of the other parts, shows that von Rosen was writing it as a letter to his wife. Nita Lindenberg, Martha von Rosen's sister, owned a country home near the village of Ried, Bavaria. Her city address was in Munich, Bavaria.

One day, a rumour arrived that the British were just south of Verona. We laughed this off at first, when, however, two days later the army news reports from the front stated that the enemy had built a bridgehead across the River Po, having widened it the next day; this made it scary indeed and our thoughts were directed towards the earliest retreat possible.[6] The so-desired vehicles did not arrive, however.

The partisans had become very active, not only in the mountains but also down on the flats. However, we were assured that our retreat highway remained open. Which route that was, was not disclosed to us. The AE1,[7] which had first been formed to guard us when we had landed at Comacchio Lake, was reassembled in Arkade. About sixteen to twenty persons, some German and some Italian, joined it from our battery. Before that, about April 20th, an armed truck from our unit had driven some thirty kilometres past Belluno into the mountains, a route often attacked by bandits[8] However, it returned the same day without spotting any. About April 24th, our interpreter, Sergeant Major Scholefield, and an Italian dressed themselves as civilians and started out into the mountains on bicycles to investigate the strength and mood of the partisans. After several days – we thought they would never return – they brought news that the mountains north of us were full of bandits, estimated to number more than 30,000. Six thousand were expected to occupy Conegliano the following day. The bandits had asked the two men to stay with them, but they both declined and were released unharmed. Meanwhile, the AE1 fought several engagements against the partisans. Castelfranco was cleansed of bandits and about thirty German soldiers and women communications messengers were liberated. Conegliano was recaptured, some bandits were hanged, and Germans were freed. What was clear, however, was that there had not been 6,000 partisans in the town.

---

6 The British had managed to cross the Po River, against the defence of the Axis forces, and in this case established and widened the ground held on the opposite side.

7 AE1 (*Alarmeinheit* 1, or alarm unit 1) was an emergency response team created by borrowing personnel selected from batteries, *Operation Todt* (OT), and elsewhere to be used for quick deployment to points needing defensive action. The battery consisted of a single FMG, acting as the radio detecting and ranging device used to target approaching aircraft several kilometres away. It was connected by cables to several anti-aircraft cannons (8.0 cm). Four or five such batteries would be coordinated from a central command post as, for example, at Arkade.

8 "Bandits" is used interchangeably with "partisans." The original diary uses the words "*Banditen*" and "*Partisanen.*"

We have not been able to hear the *Wehrmachtbericht* since about the 26th. The last we heard were the speeches of the *Gauleiter* and *Bürgermeister* of Munich after the *Putschversuch*.[9] At first, we did not take this seriously, but after the same speeches were repeated all day, we realized that the situation was rather serious. That was the last we heard from Germany because the Italians cut off our electricity soon afterwards; in any case, we lived in the dark and without news. Our only information now was what the Italians told us. They mentioned that Mussolini had declared that, when Berlin was seized, Italy would no longer be bound by the alliance with Germany. This was discussed feverishly by our Italian soldiers and we were not at all sure how they would behave towards us if the situation deteriorated.

The Italians from the AE1 were the first ones to disappear. Some of them were impudent enough to go straight to the commander, declaring that they were quitting. He was sensible enough to let them go unimpeded. On the 26th or 27th of April, we got the message that the Sergeant-Major (*Spiess*) of the 3rd battery had made *avanti*[10] during the night, taking the whole crew, including the cash from the till. We were especially shocked as the 3rd was our sister battery, with which we had, all this time, cooperated as a *Grosse Batterie*.[11] We had been together all along, relying on each other, and the 3rd had only recently been moved to Spresiano.

The activity of the partisans increased steadily despite the efforts of the AE1. As a rule all of AE1's attempts proved ineffective. The partisan situation was elastic like rubber. AE1 was able to capture a settlement, but as soon as it left, the partisans were back again. From Treviso came the message that our 4th battery, which was positioned there, was surrounded by partisans. They had planned to move but had no trucks, so, to come to their aid, five people from AE1 were sent with the heavy traction engine from headquarters. En route, they were naturally attacked by partisans, one man was wounded and the rest were taken prisoner. Just as the partisans were about to leave with their captives, an SS Panzer came by and three of the prisoners took the opportunity to disappear into the ditch. The partisans ran off and the

---

9 *Wehrmachtbericht* is the official armed forces newscast. *Gauleiter* means "leader of the district," in this case, probably Munich and its surrounding districts. The *Putschversuch* was a failed attempt at uprising against the regime, carried out in Munich.

10 "*Avanti*," is an Italian word used sarcastically by the Germans, meaning "desertion."

11 Literally "large battery," that is, several batteries working in unison.

two other prisoners (the driver of the heavy engine and one of our own men, originally from Köln followed them. The three others were unable to operate the tracked vehicle, especially as one of them was badly wounded. So the Panzer retrieved them (albeit very reluctantly for lack of time). A trained driver and an assistant were sent out to get the heavy-duty haul machine, but, as could be expected, the partisans had taken it in the meantime. By this foolish action we had lost the only heavy-duty haul machine.

One evening in Arkade, there was a loud noise and a huge blaze of fire from where the division command was stationed, about two kilometres away. At first, secrecy prevailed, but after a while the news trickled through – the partisans had detonated the division's gasoline stock. Our chances of getting away were thus worsening.

On Thursday, the 26th of April 1945, the Italians received news that Mussolini had been taken prisoner and that night about half of our Italian gang had disappeared.[12] Now, because the gun crews were inadequate, new members were recruited, only Germans, by taking the whole baggage crew, along with all the FMG attendants, and stationing them with the cannons. At night the sentries were doubled as we counted on partisan attacks. The Italians were no longer deployed as guards, and again, during that night, several of them deserted. (At the other battery the Italians had already made *avanti* much earlier.)

On Thursday the site construction crew from Nervesa hurriedly made *avanti*. A detail from our battery went there with two horse-drawn vehicles to inherit some of the remaining supplies. They returned with two barrels of dynamite, some cigarettes, and other trivialities. They told us that the section leader of the site construction detail in Nervesa, a party head[13] who always zipped around in a car and got drunk in our canteen nearly every night, was totally beside himself and could not take off fast enough. The OT people from site construction detail were ordered to the *Volkssturm*.[14]

---

12 During the whole period of the war, Italian partisans had acted as guides and helpers to the Allies, and on 28 April a group of them captured Mussolini and his staff, including his mistress Clara Petacci. The next day, they shot all of them. Mussolini had been captured before but escaped, resuming his activities with new vigour. This was the second capture.

13 I.e., Nazi party.

14 *Operation Todt* (OT) was named for Dr. Todt, a civil engineer, who was the Reich Minister of Armaments and Munitions from 1940 to 1942. He supervised the work of the OT which was responsible for providing the labour for building the West Wall. *Volkssturm* literally means

(The fat party activist, despite his overdone haste, did not manage to escape after all, for we met him later in the lime plant.[15])

On Friday, April 27th, Sergeant Major Scholefield went, together with a few of our men, to Nervesa to deliver the mayor an ultimatum, telling him that if the partisans harmed any of our people, Nervesa would be flattened by our cannons. Most of our people thought that this unwise move would provoke the bandits, but maybe it had a positive effect as the partisans never did appear.

Another commando was dispatched to Nervesa where a train with rifles had arrived. (Where this train had suddenly come from is difficult to imagine, as the movement of trains has long been dead.) However, everything useful had already been taken by the partisans and our men only got a box with a brand new 2-cm cannon. On their return trip they had an encounter with two armed partisans who, when challenged, did not stop, and were shot, but otherwise they got back without mishap.

A number of trucks, carrying ammunition, eventually arrived on Friday morning – ammunition that they had retrieved in time from the batteries on the River Po. That gave us, nevertheless, more courage. Now at least we had enough ammunition. Before this we had to economize and were mostly not allowed to shoot at all when the *jabos* attacked the bridge.

On Saturday we learned that Spresiano itself – the village en route from Treviso to Conegliano, about five kilometres from our position – was occupied by partisans. With that, our main line of retreat was blocked. We heard some shooting, but not much. We were given orders to move the FMG to our central command in Arkade. Rather senseless orders, we thought, but at least we did not have to worry about demolishing the equipment. As there was no way of pulling the FMG away, neither with a tractor nor by any other means, we decided to take our two strong battery oxen.

I went to the gun-carriage storage area, which was also the location of our mess kitchen, about 500 metres distant in a farmer's yard, to fetch the battery's draught oxen. Just when I reached the yard, I heard a pistol shot and had a weird premonition, which soon proved to be correct. The cook, having shot one of our oxen with his pistol, was readying himself to slaugh-

---

"peoples' storm." Towards the end of the war, when manpower suitable for combat became scarcer, Hitler ordered that people from all forms of pursuit should join the *Volkssturm*. This was a civil army, consisting of males and females, many of very young age. They were sent to the war, often close to the front, or even at the front itself. The women were usually employed in telecommunications, in messenger services, in nursing and the like.

15   As a POW.

ter it. I asked him whether he was crazy, as right now we badly needed these animals. He very calmly replied: "Better we eat him now, instead of the *Tommy* later on."[16]

Now we had only a little horse and a donkey in the barn, and they were far too feeble to pull this heavy equipment. One strong draught horse, which we still possessed, had been taken away on some other errand. Sadly I went back to our position and, after some discussion among us, the *Unteroffizier*[17] went with another man to get oxen from the next available farmer.

We were still busy rolling up cable and packing the ancillary equipment when a farmer coming by, stated that the war was over. Yes, yes, for sure, he had just heard it over the radio, and the peace bells were ringing also. And truly, we suddenly could hear the church bells ringing in Spresiano, Arkade joined in, then Nervesa, and finally the air was filled with the ringing of bells. Yet, suddenly the bells were drowned out by the crackling of shots. Also audible were 2-cm machine-guns and, from time to time, single rifle shots. The firing was quite close to Arkade, and came from the side towards Spresiano. Closer and closer it came until it was apparently between us and Arkade. We asked the farmer if that sounded like peace, and he hurried away. Arkade's bells also stopped ringing, as if from fright. We were immediately placed on alert and manned our peripheral defences, which commanded all approaches. Rumour had it that the headquarters were surrounded by partisans and that the telecommunication lines had been severed. We had been ordered to fire the mortars, at a high angle, in the direction of the HQ, a 2-kilometre distance, whenever the commander there signalled with a red flare. The telephone operator finally got through to HQ via a different line and we were told that negotiations were in progress.

Meanwhile our *Unteroffizier* had returned, but without any oxen. They had gone towards Arkade and just when they were about to bring the animals out of the barn the shooting started quite nearby. They retreated rapidly and we decided to leave the FMG right where it was, as it was late and getting dark. In Arkade we heard a few more shots, and then there was quiet. Later we found out that the shooting had started during an attack in which only fifteen partisans encircled the HQ, demanding all weapons. The demands,

---

16 *Tommy* was the commonly used nickname for the British.
17 A non-commissioned officer.

of course, were refused, and the whole thing ended with the capture of the partisans, whereby two or three who continued the offence, were shot.

The anticipated attack on our battery did not occur that night either. While I was standing guard, I considered how simple it would be to overrun the whole battery. It was rather dark and I had no contact with the neighbouring guard positions. It would have been easy for the partisans to approach along the ditches and mulberry hedges and without detection get right into the centre of the battery.

Trucks were moving past all night on the highway near Spresiano. It was most unlikely that the partisans were driving in such numbers, so it could only be German troops and I could not understand the situation, as Spresiano was supposedly held by partisans. It was likely, however, that they felt too weak, and just allowed our columns to drive through.

While I was standing there on guard, I thought, "There they go with their heavy trucks, and the last chance to take our cannons! If we want to get out of here alive, we should be leaving with them." Instead our battery slept unconcerned and awaited orders which never came, because the responsible officers had left long ago. (To be sure, the columns did not get much further, for later in the POW camp I slept alongside a few of those who had passed us during that night. They informed me that many of them had been from a pioneer unit, as well as a marine trucking company. Both had plenty of fuel and ample loading space, and would have been happy to haul all our ammunition in addition to our six cannons. They also said that they would have been happy to have this heavy ordnance with them, as they would have had a better chance to fight through the partisan resistance. They all got stuck in the mountains, and were taken prisoner by the partisans who later delivered them to the British.)

It was Sunday morning when the order came to prepare for the move. Our rucksacks, of course, had been readied long ago, and repacked repeatedly to meet the different requirements of driving or walking. Because no one could, as usual, provide any certainty on this matter at this time, I had placed the necessities into the rucksack, as well as packing a day bag, just in case I could drive. The FMG was finally to be removed in the morning. We had several battle station alarms, and once the *jabos* came straight at our battery, but without offensive action. However, in Arkade they shot with onboard guns at the transports exactly as the FMG arrived. Our cannon fired once, at close range, and that was the first and only time that I have stood next to a cannon in action.

It was announced that our regimental commander was at section headquarters. The *jabos* had destroyed his car, nevertheless, he and his adjutant were left unscathed. He mentioned that the army had continued to withdraw the troops across the River Po, with very few casualties and that the retreat was carried out according to plan, etc., etc. We were supposed to move into a prepared position in the lower Alps, but as there were an insufficient number of vehicles, we were to carry out our retreat by being transported in a staged manner, alternately with 5th battery. The latter was located in Treviso. This 5th battery was meant to be moved to its new site this Sunday, and we were hoping to follow under cover of darkness. We were certainly comforted in the knowledge that a higher-ranking officer was finally with us, as we were now sure everything would be properly organized. The 4th battery, still captives of the partisans in Treviso, were to be left behind, as was the 3rd battery in Spresiano, since they had already decamped. We thought it very fortunate to be located so close to the command post, as this would enhance our chance of being taken along.

Until this point we had been inhibited about firing at the *jabos*. Now, by contrast, we had orders to shoot as much as possible, first of all to get rid of the ammunition, as we had no means of transporting it, and secondly to intimidate the surrounding partisans. However, we never got another chance to fire. The *jabos* circled incessantly near Conegliano, apparently the site of quite a bit of activity, but they never flew within range.[18] The bridge was of no interest to them anymore.

Our Italians had disappeared by now, and the only two faithful individuals who were still with us were officially sent away.

At noon on Sunday, April 29th, we were given the order to get each of the cannons ready for the move. *Dora* was to be readied for immediate demolition, but *Bertha* was to be pulled out first, while the rest of them still remained in readiness in case of an attack. So we all started digging, opening up both approach ramps – a torturous task, as the cannons were well backfilled with dirt. As soon as we were ready, we were told that as *Bertha*'s barrel was not the best, she should be destroyed as well. However, the other

---

18 Conegliano was a centre of activity as the retreating Axis forces defended their positions at the rear against the advancing Allied forces. As the Axis forces were heading north into the mountains, they were being attacked in the rear guard. Conegliano was one of the last of such skirmishes before surrender.

four were going to be transported. So we went to the next cannon and started shovelling, all over again.

A very foolish and conceited *Unteroffizier* already started to get the blast charge ready for the two cannons, as well as for the piles of ammunition. And in his overambitious manner allowed a heap of ammunition to explode right in the middle of our battery. We all had to take cover and sit waiting for the detonation. We waited and waited, but nothing whatsoever happened. Obviously he had not ignited the end of the fuse properly. Finally he dared to go back again, and lit the fuse properly. This produced a deafening concussion, yet not by any means were all the grenades destroyed, it continued to burn and smolder, and every couple of minutes a hand grenade would explode. This was very unsettling as they happened right inside our battery; it was a miracle that no one was hurt in all the hustle and bustle.

The stock from the canteen was distributed in the meantime – everything that the mess stock handler had been sitting on until now. I had asked for a vermouth on Saturday night, but the canteen master served only sour red wine. I told him, "Beware, tomorrow you will be glad to give the vermouth away for nothing." Not only did he give it away, he simply poured it out! Everybody was given one bottle of cognac and one bottle of liqueur, and in addition, a few hundred cigarettes. We did not know where to put the stuff. To fetch our supplies from the canteen we left our digging position one at a time. And most of the soldiers started drinking right away, and either never returned, or if they did, were drunk and did not do anything.

All along we heard a deep rumble sounding from the north of us behind the hills. First we thought it was the enemy's tanks trying to cut us off. Apparently it was only *jabos* chasing the last of our fleeing vehicles.

Right after lunch some farmers had been corralled along with twelve weak draught cows and they were soon busy trying to pull the gun carriages from their hiding places, to move them over to the cannon positions. It actually took all afternoon as the farmers – probably on purpose – acted very stupidly. Furthermore, they also had to take a long roundabout approach as a result of the burning ammunitions heap. It was not until late in the evening that we were finished with the digging and mounting the cannons. It just had to be that the twelve cows were hitched to the most inconveniently located cannon and, naturally, were not able to get it loose. Enough people were finally called together and after much pulling, yanking, and yelling, we could get the cannon to break free. And, carried by momentum, the cows raced pulling the cannon across the small meadow. Beyond this, however, lay a narrow bridge over an irrigation ditch, on the far side of which the road turned left. The cows at the front were thus unable to pull anymore and so the cannon got stuck. Now the cows were hitched to the rear and pulled the cannon back off the bridge – and then again at the front. This went on and on. Hitch one way and then back, with great zest forward, only to get stuck again at exactly the same point. Again people were called in to help – but in vain. Finally it grew dark and we had gotten nowhere. The cows lowed hungrily, and were useless for pulling.

In the meantime, a commando, who had been sent to find draught oxen after we had given up hope of finding suitable vehicles, returned. The oxen for the task had been commandeered several days earlier; however, the farmer had removed them immediately, and now maintained that the partisans had taken them. (By the way, our second massive battery oxen was stolen by one of our own Italians during the mix-up of Sunday.) After the commando unit had returned empty-handed, everyone dropped their hands dejectedly. Even if we got the cannon to the hard-surfaced road, it would be for naught as we had no draught animals and no vehicles to pull it with any further. The twelve cows, having worked all afternoon, would not in any case have pulled the cannon any farther.

Now, at last, our two officers appeared, after being invisible all along. One of them had only recently been assigned to us and appeared to be a big "zero." The other one, Lieutenant Schock, actually the mess-officer, was commanding our battery because our first lieutenant had gone as replacement commander to the 5th battery in Treviso. By now he probably was already far away and we were all rather annoyed with him. He had left us, his original battery, helpless, and had not sent back the vehicles to fetch us as earlier agreed.

Our little Lieutenant Schock was not liked by the crew because of his exaggerated, militaristic manner. He was 150 per cent Nazi and lectured every Sunday about contemporary political concerns. This he did up to the very end. We finally thought every Sunday morning: "My God, what matters of positive value could he relate to us anymore?" Still, he was an eloquent speaker and possessed unshaken faith. However, this was the first Sunday that he did remain silent, showing total dejection. He did, however, give us a speech stating that he had received orders from the section commander to retreat across the Piave River with four cannons, in order to establish an anti-tank defence position there. He asked us to do our utmost to get at least this one cannon out. How else could he face his commander if he had not fulfilled the orders? How he intended to move the cannons without the wherewithal to do so, he did not divulge, nor how he imagined that a tank barrier could be formed with only one piece of artillery. Generally speaking, there was much ill feeling all round as our heavy guns were not equipped with anti-tank armour, while the other batteries, which had left earlier, had been thus equipped so that they could fight the ground battle. Nevertheless his speech moved us enough to start again with renewed gusto. In any case we all had only the one thought in mind: "If we are at least gone from here, then things will work out further on." Even the last work-shirkers were rounded up, the cows were totally unhitched, and with a 'heave-ho' things got moving, and with the same momentum using the unified marching step the artillery piece was pulled out and onto the hard-surface road. Everyone heaved a sigh of relief and hurried back into their abodes to fetch the rucksacks. Meanwhile it grew pitch dark. I hurriedly removed all inessentials like a second set of underwear, and the like, from my rucksack, which I now foresaw I would have to carry myself. With a heavy heart I left my fine writing paper, all the blankets, my tropical shorts, and many more things, and still the bag was noticeably heavy. We left a terrible mess at our encampment. On the table stood a big bowl of sugar. They had suddenly dispensed it out at lunch, even though in the recent past they had always denied having sugar supplies.

By the time that I got back to the cannon it was festooned with dangling rucksacks. I found a spot for mine to dangle but had to run back in the pitch darkness to fetch my steel helmet, which I had forgotten. My gas mask, I deliberately left. When I returned we were told that the cannon would be demolished right where it was, as there were no oxen to pull it. Well, that was what I had said in the first place, and we could have spared ourselves this torture. So I shouldered my rucksack and was soon made to realize how heavy it felt. One Italian rifle with 120 rounds of ammunition, two hand-grenades, and the steel helmet. At least I had abandoned the gas mask. Meanwhile the wagons from the artillery transport storage place[19] arrived: a pair-driven cart, pulled by our own unmatched pair of horses, was loaded with provisions and had a field-mess hitched on behind; our little donkey pulled our office paraphernalia; a farmer with two oxen pulled a four-wheel wagon loaded with two 2-cm artillery pieces; and then there was still another farmer with a two-wheel cart, pulled by a little donkey.

---

19 In the farmer's shed.

Everything was already loaded to the hilt and the rucksacks were packed everywhere and dangling all over. Nevertheless, I succeeded in dangling my heavy rucksack from the field-mess.

Then we were classified. The interpreter, Sergeant Major Scholefield, was to lead and precede us with our vanguard. Then, to follow, was a second security section, and the vehicles of the baggage train brought up the rear. As not enough people volunteered to join the vanguard, the younger ones were appointed and every one over 35 was relegated to the baggage train.[20] We walked about one kilometre and then waited for the demolition detail. We waited endlessly as the stupid *Unteroffizier* demonstrated his lack of skill. As he had all afternoon to prepare and attach the charges, all he had to do now was to ignite the fuse. Yet, apparently he set off each explosion singly, taking shelter before each blast. Probably he had occurrences when the fuse did not continue burning after ignition, and so on. Hence the delay seemed endless. We sat there in the roadside ditch, waiting impatiently for two or three hours. The command at HQ in Arkade had already finished the demolitions in the afternoon and everything was now totally quiet from that direction. No sound was to be heard from the other batteries either, as they had probably retreated beyond many hills by now.[21]

While we were sitting and waiting, I came to the conclusion that being in the vanguard should actually be the best choice. If there were an attack by the partisans, they certainly would initially concentrate on the wagons, and the leading troops would have the best chance of advancement. Therefore I moved right up to the front. My calculation soon proved to be the correct one, for the sergeant told us that he would march ahead and parlay with the partisans whenever we encountered a blockade. If the partisans opened fire, we should return fire and by all means attempt to battle our way through. The baggage train would be left to its own devices.

Finally, at long last, we started out, walking in attack form, single file at five pace intervals along the road side, whenever possible in the shade of the trees, because we now had bright moonlight. From behind us we heard the creaking of the wagon wheels. Every now and then, came the subdued call, "Slow down, slow down."

---

20 Jürgen von Rosen turned 38 in 1945.

21 *Über alle Berge* (literally, "over every mountain") is an expression meaning: "They left a long time ago."

And thus, despite our impatience, we moved like snails through ill-famed Nervesa and onto the *Ponte Priula* across the River Piave.[22] It was quite an elevating feeling to be finally on the move and I told myself, "With every step I am coming closer to *meine Lieben.*"

Feeling rather adventurous by this time, we were disappointed not to come across a single partisan. Before reaching the bridge we came upon the main highway. It lay there totally devoid of traffic. It was deathly quiet. "Certainly we must be the last ones, and only the *Tommy* is behind us."[23] In the middle of the cross-roads, in front of the bridge, lay a bag of sugar. I pulled it aside, filled my cap, and nibbled as I carried on. Undisturbed, we crossed over the unscathed auxiliary bridge which lay alongside the damaged main bridge. A car was abandoned half-ways in the ditch. We pulled it out and vainly tried to start it. We totally immobilised it with the help of a hand-grenade. A little further on, lying next to a bomb crater, was a motorcycle with perfect tires. I wanted to pick it up, but decided against it. No doubt, it will not run anyway.

Now we were on the wide asphalt road, marching pretty heedlessly in the bright moonlight. Only when a *pipo*[24] flew over, did we momentarily seek cover under the trees. But even that was most likely superfluous, as the normally terrifying *pipo* was not doing anything this night. Evidently he was afraid of hitting the partisans instead of us. Someone behind us apparently had picked up the motorcycle and came running with it. Every now and then it made the sound, "puff, puff, puff," and then it stopped. Subsequently the rider gave up. However then the *Fähnrig*[25] took on the challenge, using undefatigable stamina, with very little result.

About four kilometres past the bridge near the outskirts of Susegana, the lieutenant came forward and instructed us to look out for the commander.[26] I thought to myself silently, "My God, are you really so naive as to believe that the commander would sit here waiting for us! They are, without a doubt, beyond all the hills." If he had in fact moved only this far, it would

---

22 Nervesa was ill-famed in the eyes of the Germans, possibly because of the incessant encounters with the partisans at that place.

23 The *Tommies*, at this point, were probably through the Adige Line, heading past Padua towards Treviso.

24 *Pipo* = night strafing plane.

25 *Fähnrig* = ensign.

26 From Arkade.

have been easy enough for him to dispatch the motor vehicles back to fetch us. Of course, nobody from our command was found in the village. The place was dead still with not a soul to be seen.

We halted at the far end of the village. An empty house was forced open and we moved in. We were all deeply distressed by this decision as we had hoped to make quite a bit of progress under cover of night. The fact was that the *jabos* were masters of the road by day. Had we not merely covered about ten kilometres. The lieutenant was set on searching for the commander the next morning. However, as we found out later in the POW camp, having decamped already in the afternoon, they had followed a route on the opposite side of the Piave River leading to Montebellino,[27] and had not taken the Susegana road at all.

The regimental commanding officer, on whose ability to organize we had banked so heavily, had in reality only caused the opposite. He had ordered the unloading from half-loaded trucks of equipment that he regarded as unnecessary. He thought other things to be more important, hence those had to be loaded instead. After he had thoroughly confused our section commander, he sat himself along with his officers in our department's personnel carrier and took off. He, most likely, did not get very far before driving into the hands of the partisans, and the same probably happened to our divisional command staff.

It must have been around 0500 hrs when we halted at Susegana, after making only about ten kilometres in three hours. What a pitiful start! The horses were unhitched, guards were posted, and we segregated ourselves into the various rooms and lying on the floor, slept wonderfully.

I felt as though I had slept a long time – in reality it was still early in the morning – when a horde of soldiers making a lot of noise and with cheerful salutations came storming in. It turned out to be the 4th battery, which had been surrounded by partisans in Treviso. After lengthy negotiations, they had decided to surrender the cannons to the partisans. (The *Verschlüsse* had been buried earlier.) Then they were allowed to leave with their light armour.[28] They had been awarded a special piece of paper, the possession of which apparently would cause all the partisans they were to meet to allow them through. A partisan escort

---

27 Now called "Montebelluna."
28 A *Verschluss* is that portion of the cannon that is closed after the shell is inserted in the breach.

had always taken them from one partisan post to the next and they had only been on their own since the bridge.

Now our lieutenant appeared outside, telling us to prepare to leave immediately, as the lieutenant from the 4th battery had advised him that the enemy had passed Treviso already. Tonight would be too late. As we began to leave, we all heard the shout of, "Partisans, partisans!" I looked out the window and saw a bespectacled civilian, apparently the spokesman, accompanied by an unkempt fellow brandishing a white piece of cloth in the one hand and a hand-grenade in the other, half-afraid and half-swaggering, rush into the yard. The lieutenant from the 4th battery stuck his document in front of his nose, but it appeared to not make much of an impression. In any case, an endless negotiation ensued. The partisans demanded that we surrender all weapons, after which we could proceed unscathed and all other partisans would let us through as well. We refused because, unarmed, we would be plundered right to the skin by the next partisans we met. The oxen driver also entered the discussion, asking to be released, and his request was granted. The man with the donkey had been discharged earlier, immediately upon our arrival. After lengthy discussions an agreement was somehow reached. The two 2-cm artillery pieces were to be abandoned – we had no means of moving them anyway. The 4th battery's document was signed again by the partisan chief and we got ready to move. The *Verschlüsse* were removed from the guns, and the carts were repacked. The field mess cart had to be left behind as well, and only the two two-wheeled carts remained, each pulled by a single horse.

It must have been 0800 hrs when we were finally ready. The 4th battery was in the lead, and we, the followers, were to profit from the *bumage*[29] by declaring that we were all from the same battery. From now on the lieutenant of the 4th battery (who spoke some Italian), so to say, took charge. As it seemed unnecessary to our interpreter Sergeant Major to remain, he took off on his own. It was with heavy heart that I saw him leave as I held appreciably greater trust in him.

I now shouldered my rucksack after long deliberations regarding how I could lighten the load. A good tarpaulin was all I felt I could spare and even then the weight remained unchanged. We now proceeded to walk in the ditches making columns on both sides of the road stretched out for a long

---

29 *Bumage* = document [in Russian].

distance. The two wagons were to precede us to be between us and the 4th battery. We were headed towards Conegliano. Two armoured troop carriers came from behind speeding by, filled to the brim with mostly officers. When we saw them approaching, we had the satisfying feeling: "So we are still not the last ones." However after that changed as they had passed. Filled with envy we saw them leave, thinking: "Now we are definitely the last ones."

Soon we left the highway, continuing to the left along a small side road. After only about one kilometre I already overtook one of our wagons. The poor little horse was drenched and breathless. No wonder, for the load on the cart was great, and on top of it still lay the slaughtered ox. As there was nothing that I could do to help, I went past this and on my way, certain that as soon as we got into the mountains the little horse would be too weak to pull even an empty cart.

I hurried on as the 4th battery, with which I did not want to lose contact, was far ahead. But before long, I heard the command from behind, "Get provisions for four days ahead."

So I returned to the wagon, took four packets of biscuits and one can of meat, placing these in my rucksack. I discarded my little sewing box, although it weighed virtually nothing, and pressed on again.

A few kilometres further on, I caught up with the other wagon. As the road was rather steep here, even the big horse could pull no more. I could see how the tins of meat were being thrown to the women surrounding the wagon. I would have liked another can myself, but I was already sweating enough, and refrained. Besides, I wanted to make haste, as the 4th battery had disappeared. The road, getting progressively steeper, also became very narrow, with thick hedges on both sides. In the middle of this sunken road was a huge army truck, blocking the way completely. I reasoned that the partisans might have placed it there, and noticed some suspicious figures loitering behind the hedges.

Squeezing myself past the vehicle, I hurried on. "I hope the others are sensible enough to leave the wagons behind," I thought to myself, "as they can never get past this obstacle."

The road now went slightly downhill, and with some relief I made out the rearguard of the 4th battery in the distance. I tried as hard as I could to gain on them, but, apparently in a great hurry, they disappeared behind the next bend in the road. Behind me there was not a sign of our battery. Soon the road became steeper again, winding uphill. On the crest was an old fortress from the top of which the Italian flag flopped in the wind. "That looks to me like partisans, again," I thought as, sweating profusely, I dragged myself uphill. The road now widened slightly between two rows of houses, and I was finally able to reach the 4th battery as they rested in the shade of the houses. I immediately followed suit.

The negotiations with the partisans were apparently over and we were waiting only for our battery to catch up. It did not come. Seemingly it had been held up by the truck. The lieutenant was about to cycle back to help them with his precious document, when an Italian rushed onto the scene and said that a partisan general had called by telephone with instructions for him not to let us go, but to keep us waiting. Again there was endless discussion. We cast off still more superfluous articles. Most of us still had many of these and they were given to the women. Some men even gave away their pots and coats. After some deliberation, I too parted with my coat.

While the lieutenant was still bargaining, our stragglers arrived amidst a great commotion, without weapons, and escorted by automatic pistol-carrying partisans who were being led by a youth, actually theatrically waving a huge green, white, and red flag. There was much applause and the women, who a minute earlier had been begging from us, clapped their hands in approval. The conferring continued, the partisans wanted to let the disarmed men go but wished to detain us. But then the lieutenant became more energetic and we simply left. Nobody made a move to stop us. As, again we went downhill, we felt more rested and encouraged. *Jabos* flew above us, and when they approached too close, we sheltered in the ditch. In front of us, beyond the mountains to the right, we heard protracted shooting, continuing for some time. This must have come approximately from Conegliano, which meant that the enemy had advanced that far already. Their tanks must have gotten past there shortly after we left the highway. There was no time to be lost, if we were not to be cut off. The enemy would not stay in Conegliano for long and now everything depended on whether he chose to go towards Udine, or into the mountains towards Vittorio Veneto. Meanwhile the partisans sent messengers ahead of us to announce us to the next position. A padre on a bicycle and a harmless-looking limping civilian passed us. We met both of them at the next partisan post about six or seven kilometres further on. From afar we could see the flag fluttering in the wind, but this time it was on a church steeple. The road led straight on towards it. We were ordered from afar to stop. The lieutenant advanced on his own to negotiate, and again there was endless waiting. Meanwhile we noticed that a machine-gun was placed and barricaded in the area in front of the church.

Finally, we were allowed to go on. The chief, a tall thin Italian officer, waved to us jubilantly and shouted that the British were in Conegliano. It had certainly now become very quiet in that direction.

At long last we proceeded down the steep mountain side along the serpentine road into the valley, where we met with a highway. I had a premonition that at any moment enemy tanks would arrive from Conegliano to our right, and thought to myself, maybe if it is only a weak spearhead we could seize the captured vehicles to drive onwards. Then we could speed by all the partisan posts and would soon reach the Alps.

But when we arrived at this road crossing we saw a large throng of people in the distance, gathered on the main road much farther on and to the right. The lieutenant instructed us to wait while we found out what was happening, especially because the last of our men were still far behind and furthermore unarmed. So we waited again, even though we wanted so badly to move on. As this crowd approached, we recognized German uniforms.

They waved a white flag, and thus were apparently harmless. Nevertheless the lieutenant waited for them to approach more closely, and then talked with them endlessly. It seemed to be a variegated bunch, tossed together from anywhere. Many were already in civil garb. They had already turned in their weapons to the partisans in Conegliano. As we stood there, a three-wheeled motorcycle, carrying two Tito partisans, approached from the direction of Belluno.[30] With long hair and red neckerchiefs, they hesitated and made a move to turn around when they saw our group. However, when one of the crowd waved his white kerchief, they were emboldened to speed past us in the direction of Conegliano.

"Well congratulations," I thought, "if the *Tommy* is not coming here on his own, *they* are going to fetch him now!"

Finally we trudged onward again. We followed excruciatingly slowly behind a soldier waving a white handkerchief. Still, every now and then a call came from behind, "Slow down, slow down."

I thought it was rather selfish to slow everyone down because of those few. If they had brought too much to carry, all they had to do was discard

---

30 Tito partisans were probably partisans of Yugoslavian origin, taking their name from Marshal Tito (Josip Broz), the head of state at that time.

the excess, or sit down and wait for the *Tommy*, instead of delaying us all. It was evident that we would not get very far at this snail's pace.

The same three-wheeled motorcycle returned from behind, only this time the riders were bolder. They stopped us and told us that their checkpoint was not far ahead, but that there were no partisans further on in the mountains. They wanted to take our lieutenant along, so that he could complete the formalities there. However, when the lieutenant refused, they demanded the automatic pistols that he and some others were carrying. They did not get those either, but left with two Italian rifles, which they had taken from two of our men who had been foolish enough to surrender them. They also offered to give a ride to some footsore people. However, nobody accepted, and they drove on to take their messages to the outpost. Incidentally, this time there were four partisans, two of whom had bicycles strapped onto the back of the motorcycle. These they unloaded and rode back towards Conegliano (obviously to inform the British).

We now passed through a bigger village without challenge, but two kilometres further on, there was a tank barricade consisting of large boulders, evidently built by the partisans. It was so arranged that horse buggies as well as motorcycles had to squeeze by. After we had passed this barricade, I remarked to myself, "Now I feel much better, because if the tanks approach from behind they may be delayed long enough until we have turned off this highway." (Our intention was to turn off to the right and, using small trails between Vittorio Veneto and Belluno, to get over the mountains.)

We had advanced no farther than 100 metres – the last ones had probably just reached the tank barrier – when around a bend in the road, we were taken by surprise due to the poor visibility and we were faced with another partisan checkpoint.

The lieutenant, once again, advanced to negotiate. This seemed to be going more quickly than before. Just when we were relieved and under the impression that we were allowed to proceed, we heard a deep rumbling sound issuing from behind. Because of the bend in the road our view into the distance was obstructed, and I listened to the uncanny sound with foreboding. The rumbling sound was approaching steadily, when the partisans shouted out, "*Inglesi, Inglesi!*" Sure enough an armoured reconnaissance vehicle appeared from behind the barricade. We could not see how many more vehicles were following it, but I felt that we could overpower it. After all, we still had several anti-tank bazookas besides one machine-gun. However, the officers shouted, "*Nicht schiessen, nicht schiessen!*" (No shooting, no shooting).

So we simply resigned ourselves to our fate. A very suspicious-looking Englishman came forward, inviting our lieutenant to go and speak to his commandant. Our lieutenant ordered us to put our weapons down and went to the rear to negotiate. Two more Englishmen, with red butcher's faces, now appeared. They forced their way among us, removing wristwatches wherever they could find them. I marvelled at their routine – with one grip they got the watch, and it simply disappeared into their pockets. The partisans approached from the other direction, wanting to seize the weapons, but the British chased them away. This time the bargaining took no time at all. We had to pick up the weapons, keep them in our hands, and retrace our steps along the same road into British captivity.

The lieutenant assured us that it was a great honour to be taken POW with our weapons in our hands. The simple fact of the matter was that the English were not equipped to transport them and did not want them to fall into the hands of the partisans.

The partisans were now called on to remove the tank barricade. That was done in the twinkle of an eye. A single patrol car went on along the route that we had been taking, while the rest turned around and followed in their wake.

Those with sore feet were given a lift on the tank. Initially they took us only to the crossroads, where we had met the highway. There we rested in a meadow lying between the road and a little stream. We were told that trucks would come to rescue those with sore feet. One patrol car parked on the highway alongside our meadow, and the others drove into side roads bringing new prisoners from virtually every direction. Soldiers, a troop of railway workers, OT – every type imaginable. All the while groups of partisans kept arriving and delivered a few prisoners. It was now 1600 hrs, we had left at 0800 hrs. We now enjoyed our involuntary rest and ate our food without haste. Then our master sergeant gave us our last pay. Each of us got 300 lire. (Incidentally, the two partisans on the motorcycle who had left on their bicycles were on the tank when they caught up with us. They had informed the British while the others detained us, preventing us from proceeding.)

Finally a truck arrived, the supposedly footsore people squeezed in, notably young ones, and drove off in the direction of Conegliano, which apparently was our destination. We formed a long train of about 400 to 500 men, and followed the scout car, from which dangled more 'footsore' people (mainly officers and sergeants, including our so-important *Unteroffizier*, who hung on like burdock). To our dismay, when we reached the crossroads, the scout car turned onto the serpentine trail which we had only

160 A Baltic Odyssey: War and Survival

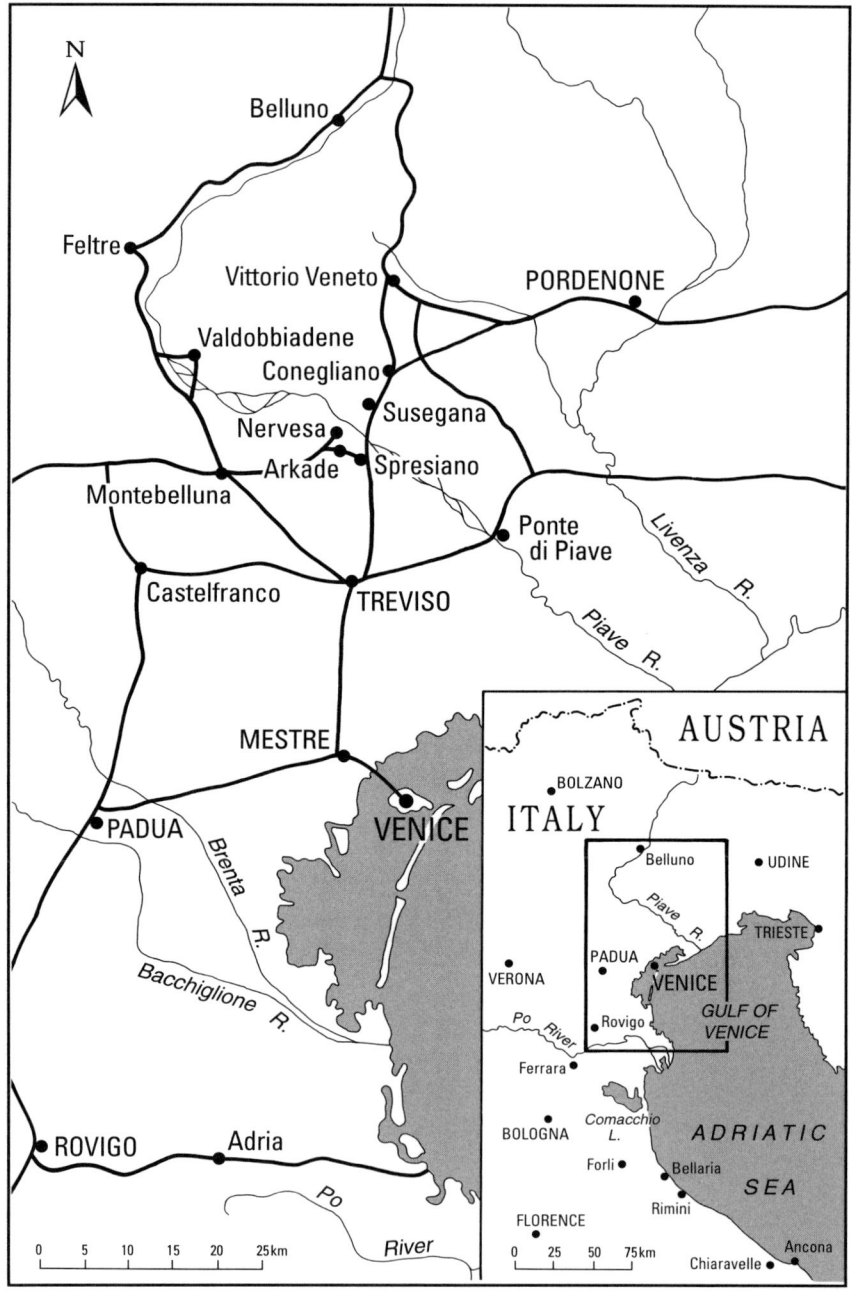

Map 3. The capture of Jürgen von Rosen (Piave River Valley, Italy).

recently descended. So the climb started over again. As we walked, we plucked our cartridges to pieces and threw them away. We had already thrown a portion of them into the creek while waiting in the meadow; however, the children ran into the water and gathered them up. The reduced weight relieved us noticeably. I had earlier allowed my helmet to roll down a hill while we were descending the curved road. Finally I figured that it was useless to carry the rifle, and I put it on the scout car. Now all I had was my rucksack, a manageable weight. The commander of the scout car, a young and very congenial-looking lieutenant, got off the truck and walked alongside the vehicle. No guards were posted at the end of the convoy. It really did not seem too difficult to sidle off into the bushes, an opportunity that some tried to take. These included our master sergeant, who already had civilian clothes in his rucksack, and our little lieutenant, who had been completely crushed and silent since the other lieutenant from the 4th battery had taken command. He and some of the others lingered further and further behind, and finally disappeared. I doubt that they made it to Germany, as the locals were too hostile, every civilian was a partisan, and the country provided no cover as the hills here at the base of the mountains are covered with meadows or vineyards. The forests start much higher up the mountains. One of the escapees was delivered to our camp as early as the next day, and had been completely stripped by the partisans. They had taken off all his clothes and then given him a ragged civilian suit. The master sergeant and one other man were also returned in the next little while, but immediately escaped again the next day.

I too toyed with the idea of escape a hundred, no a thousand times, anything to join *meine Lieben*. But now it was the love of family that restrained me from attempting something so utterly unsafe. The chances of success were practically zero. Besides, we figured that the end of the war was imminent and we counted on only a short imprisonment. This little detour was the safest, we reasoned.

We marched uphill and downhill. In the beginning the road was familiar. Then we left it and marched on and on. We passed out of the hills and dropped down into the open country of the Piave valley. The scenery was not at all familiar to us and it must have been quite a distance upriver, near Feltre, that we finally reached the valley. Meanwhile we had stopped off at a well for ten or fifteen minutes, but the Englishman urged us on as we had to reach our goal before dark. However, he did not reveal the whereabouts of this goal. We passed through many villages where impassive Italians stood in front of their houses. Further down the valley, however, they became aggressive. After we had passed one village, somebody in the rear shouted, "Hold it, hold it!" The procession stopped and our leader strode back energetically with his revolver in his hand and dispersed some Italians who had thrown rocks at those of our men who were bringing up the rear. A little later this conduct was repeated, and the English officer hit a knife-wielding onlooker with an upper-cut that sent him staggering backwards.

Suddenly, some well-armed partisans, feeling very important, appeared to escort us to the next and larger village (Valdobbiadene, I think). The Englishman allowed them this privilege, but when we reached the market place, we met up with a machine-gun emplacement. The scout car halted and stayed put until the whole procession had passed, and remained stationed at our rear. Now we were safe from attack from behind. The lieutenant marched alone in front. As it had already started to get dark, we hoped that this village would be our goal. Instead we marched on out of the settlement and further down the Piave River. It grew darker and we were at the end of our strength. My legs simply would not carry the weight any more, and the rucksack pressed me down like lead. Without the rucksack I could have walked endlessly. Every time that we stopped for even a moment, I immediately sat down on the bank of the ditch. The lieutenant, who had originally led us and who had been marching in front with the British officer, told us not to be dismayed. The Englishman had shown him our goal on the map and it could not be more than two or three kilometres away. Yet we marched four and five and six kilometres and still there was no goal in sight. Again he said there could not be more than two kilometres. After we had covered another ten kilometres, and it was pitch dark, we simply sat down in the dew-moist grass and refused to go any farther. The British officer must send the scout car ahead to fetch some trucks. After some discussion, he agreed. The scout car left and the officer remained alone with us. I stretched out on the grass and fell asleep, but was soon awakened again by the sound of cajolery. Our lieutenant was trying to persuade us to walk on slowly. The vehicles would soon arrive and we would fall sick from sweating and lying in the grass. Finally, everyone actually got up and the procession moved on. Quite soon afterwards, we made out some lights ahead of us. Our scout car was returning with a large tank and a truck. Everybody immediately stormed them. I managed to squeeze myself into the truck, which was extremely tightly packed. Manoeuvering endlessly back and forth, the truck made a U-turn on the narrow road and we finally moved off. We all hoped that this ride would not last long, since this part of our journey felt worse than anything that had gone before. Half-sitting, half-standing, half-hanging, I was hemmed in and could not move. I became nauseous and was afraid that I would throw up. Moaning, swearing, and whimpering could be heard. We stopped twice, everyone rejoicing and wanting to climb out, but the driver had simply missed the turn off. With a great deal of back and forth, he struggled to turn around. Finally we arrived, and practically gushed out. What a relief! At first we were completely disoriented in the dark. Cars and tanks stood around, and we were directed into the beams of a car's headlights where we were cursorily searched. That did not take long. They were mainly interested in the money in our wallets. I had only the 300 lire just received. They did not remain with me any longer. A soldier searched my rucksack, but when I told him that it contained only provisions, he was satisfied and I returned into the darkness. Soon I discovered a water wagon and filled my field bottle. Then I waited for my comrades from the FMG, who also had to be searched, after which all of us went to find a place to sleep. Eventually our eyes became accustomed to the darkness between the car beams and we could make out densely packed human shapes rolled up in blankets, lying between some bushes in a depression to the right of the road. There was no room left, so we continued along the road. To the left were dilapidated houses and everywhere, between the rubble and bricks, people were huddled together. In a relatively undamaged room, officers[31] were sitting around a candle. Another 500 metres further on we reached the end of the allotted territory, marked by a tank whose light beam constituted the otherwise unmarked boundary. To the left of the road, on a knoll of rubble, there was still space left between some bramble bushes. As we had neither blankets nor coats, I rolled up in my tarpaulin and we lay down close to each other and fell asleep instantly, despite the uneven rocky ground. However, when we awoke early in the morning, we were shivering from cold and started running around. It was like a beehive, as most of those lucky enough to be with blankets, were just as cold, and thus had to move about to keep warm. I tried to establish where we were but everything was unfamiliar. There was a dam and, very likely, a river behind the row of houses. Then the light suddenly dawned; we were near Susegana, quite close to our Piave bridge. That

---

31 German POWs.

meant that we were back where we had started our long journey! *Tommy* had brought us back, by a hugely circuitous route, so that meant we had covered about 100 kilometres in twenty-four hours. The 4th battery from Treviso had actually covered 115 kilometres, although in more than twenty-four hours and without the two hours of sleep that we had enjoyed in Susegana.

I had expected to be absolutely lame in the morning but my legs were only slightly stiff. Otherwise nothing was wrong and I had no sores on my feet. I was about the only one who had no blisters and most people had severe footsores.

We had to sit and wait for developments to unfold. As it grew warmer, I lay down to snooze. Around midday we were told that fifty men should line up to collect provisions. We joined the others and were moved to the opposite side of the dam. There we were searched again. The rucksack was only superficially checked. Even so, my good nail clippers were removed. Full of sadness, I watched them disappear into the pocket of a British soldier. He weighed my rusty knife for a moment in his hand and then returned it. It was not worth taking. Now we lined up again and marched across the bridge. We had to wait on the other side as one troop after the other followed, always fifty men. It soon became evident that all this was not for food. The camp was simply being dissolved, and we were being formed into a long column in sections of fifty men. As we stood and waited, we marvelled at the speed with which the damage, inflicted on the bridge by *jabos*, had been repaired. There was much traffic across this bridge, always in the same direction. Traffic taking the opposite direction used the German provisional bridge. After everyone had lined up, we started out along the highway towards Spresiano for a few kilometres. We halted at a lime plant. Again we were searched, this time we had to empty our rucksacks, but the British soldier was very kind. He wanted to confiscate my penknife, but I told him I needed it for eating, so he returned it to me.

Whoever was ready was led to the yard, the *Unteroffizieren* to one side and the common soldiers to the other. (Later on, everything got mixed up again.) We sat down and started to eat, for we had carried enough provisions with us. When it started to cloud over, we took refuge in the hall, where four big lime kilns stood in a row. Other people erected tents outside. Then the downpour really began and we soon discovered that the rain leaked in everywhere. Fortunately I had a spot where I could squat without getting completely drenched. At night the rain stopped.

Having been told to collect food, we duly lined up outside, forming a long column. It took hours, yet we finally got there. Each group of ten was provided with a pot of jam and some biscuits, which then had to be distributed among the individual members. Everyone got two biscuits and a large blotch of marmalade.

Newcomers arrived continually, mostly in trucks. We were about the only ones who had had to march the distance. The British encircled our camp with a white ribbon and the place grew very crowded as more and more moved in.

Because rain still threatened, we suspended our tarpaulin slantwise from the wall of the hall and lay down under it to sleep. It was so crowded that you could neither stretch your legs, nor could you easily roll over, but at least it was warm. Soon it started raining again, continuing all night. All the newcomers were drenched, and clustered in the hall. By morning they stood shoulder to shoulder, cursing their comrades who had managed to lie on the floor.

Two cakes and a blotch of marmalade were again distributed in the morning. The white ribbon was extended as the space was now impossibly crowded. Two water tankers fetched water incessantly, and each time they arrived, you imperilled your life when you got near them. Although we always watched our rucksacks, my canteen was stolen this morning.

After the white ribbon had been shifted again, we left the hall, and erected a tent in the farthest corner of the yard. We were now in a vineyard, lying on one of the intervening strips of rye grass. We had six tarpaulins to provide shelter for the seven of us. It was very congested, but nevertheless we could all stretch out, arranged like herrings in a box. The two of us lying on the outside had coats to cover us, but those in the centre had nothing and were extremely cold at night. The next day I managed to obtain some straw from a neighbouring farmer, so that at least it was warm from underneath.

The guard would permit the prisoners to go under the white ribbon at one spot to get straw from a farmer. When the first one returned, the next one was allowed to go. It grew to be such a throng that we had to wait for hours. Once the designated straw pile was exhausted, you had to guard your own straw supply against theft.

Now divided into *Hundertschaften*,[32] we were led by an officer to receive our provisions. These groups were further subdivided into groups of ten. By now more provisions had been brought in, which was fortunate as our own were finished. Everyone was given one package of "*keks*"[33] (twelve pieces)

---

32 *Hundertschaften* = groups of one hundred.
33 *Keks* = crackers.

and one tin of canned vegetables, which included some meat. Water was a constant problem, as the two water wagons could not cope with demand. Across the road was a well with a winch, where endless rows of soldiers gathered. Two guards were positioned nearby and only two men at a time were allowed to cross over. Bringing the water up with the winch was a tedious task, as the well was very deep. We lined up alternately, filling our canteens and mess pots, as we had no larger containers. We drank most of the water and hardly anything was left for washing. Matters improved slightly after we obtained a cracker container. The crackers were packed in big twenty-five litre tin containers which were perfect for fetching water. Thereafter we always had a good supply.

Meanwhile the ribbon had been moved a few more times, and each time the masses swarmed into the new territory, devastating everything like grasshoppers. People who had no tents broke off twigs from the mulberry trees and built shelters. Others, who had obtained shovels from somewhere, dug holes for warmth. In no time the whole vineyard was devastated. Finding tent poles was extremely difficult.

We had the most favourable impression of the British. The guards were kind, immaculately clean, and well shaved. The officers were initially identifiable by their walking sticks. Towards the Italians they displayed great reserve.

We tried to obtain news from the guards about the situation in Germany, but they did not seem to know very much. As most of the information was contradictory, we were left groping in the dark. A guard gave me an English newspaper, which reported the capitulation of the Southern Front. I concluded that the Southern Front no longer existed, and that everybody was imprisoned. I regretted not having attempted to make my escape, but the accounts of the others convinced me that it was impossible to elude the partisans. Contrary to what we had been told, the Tito outpost, where the British caught up with us, was not the last one.[34] No, the further one went into the mountains, the greater was the number of partisans, all of them equipped with every kind of weapon and always in radio contact with the British.

Where more powerful German units and columns tried to force their way through, they were destroyed in no time by the British *jabos*, within fifteen minutes, as they had been called in over the radio by the partisans.

---

34   Probably one of the outposts manned by Yugoslavian partisans.

The demobilization of this provisional camp started on the 4th and 5th of May. Those from our unit, who were still in the hall, were the first to be moved to Conegliano. We were happy to see them go and wanted no further contact with them. Our *Unteroffizier* was a most uncongenial and unlikeable cheat. He had behaved so foolishly during the demolition and after he was captured he promoted himself to the higher rank of Sergeant Major. As for the rest of them, we did not much care for them either.

Now we had our own little group of seven, only one of whom did not fit in too well. A real sneak, he fell ill and was taken to the military hospital, so we were rid of him as well. Now we had more room in our tent. Fortunately he had had no tarpaulin and our tent remained intact.

I inherited a large paper bag from one of those who had left (he had used it at night as a foot muff); now at least my lower parts were no longer so cold.

We were the last to be moved. It was the 6th of May. We had to clean up before leaving. All the tins were thrown into holes, and the ground was levelled. The farmer would not have much fun ploughing later.

We were counted as we were marching through the gate. Then, much to our satisfaction, we started out in a northerly direction. Again we crossed the Ponte Priula and proceeded to a silk factory in Susegana. The partisan chief, whom we had encountered earlier during the bargaining session, was at the gate. Evidently he was either the director or the owner of the factory. The first arrivals had already reserved the spinning halls and were about to settle between the spinning wheels. Silkworm cocoons were used for mattresses, and curtains for blankets.

We moved to a lovely meadow behind the factory and erected our tent. Along the meadow was a wide ditch with fairly clean water. Now at last we could wash and even take a bath. It was high time that we washed our clothes as well.

We were provided with sufficient food and I felt we had cause to be grateful. Only our officers disturbed our peace with their German Military Regulations, dividing us into companies, according to rank, such as Master Sergeant, Sergeant Major, etc., and holding roll call. The latter was apparently ordered by the British, as we had to be counted daily. In addition, the latest news was read to us – not much news, but at least some. The one good item was that the Italians had asked that German prisoners be supplied for work on reconstruction projects, but the British had declined. Our hopes were raised that we would soon be able to write letters. In any case the next camp would be a main camp, where we would certainly have the opportunity to write.

We were not able to enjoy our lovely meadow and the abundant water for longer than two days. We departed on the 8th of May, but this time heading southwards. We were told that our destination was beyond the Po, and that the room and board would be better, as the supply depots were closer there, and because the multitude of destroyed bridges had made it difficult to ship a sufficient quantity of supplies.

This time we were loaded onto trucks before being driven to Mestre. Here, for the first time, we were surrounded by barbed wire, in a rectangular area approximately 100 metres wide and long. We were released into this area. Initially we were few, but during the day more and more men arrived until we felt like penned-in sheep.

Now we were real prisoners. The field was trampled, rock hard, and it was evident that many had been here before us. It was only a transit camp and we thought it futile to erect a tent because we would not stay for long. Besides, we had no tent poles, and we simply lay down on the hard ground. Of course all kinds of rumours went around.

Many maintained that we were assembled here to be loaded onto ships bound for Africa. Others thought our destination would be Forli. Two British soldiers constantly walked through our crowd proffering "lice powder," a reddish powder which they distributed with a spoon from tins.

I was surprised to see how many people accepted. Until now I had believed that lice were only abundant in the East.

The next morning, we were ordered to gather, in a very humane manner. An Englishman walked through the camp calling, "Get up, get up!", and gently pulled those who were fast asleep by the legs. A German would certainly have run through the camp with a whistle.

We were loaded into an endless row of trucks, driven by dark-skinned men. The leader of the column was an imposing figure with a fat belly, a big black beard, and a white turban. Right away, we nicknamed him "Maharajah." Until now the British had performed everything in a very quiet manner, without any shouting. Now, by contrast, there was a noisy commotion before we started out.

Unfortunately the trucks were covered so that I could not see much during the drive. There was only a small opening at the front and at the back. We crossed the Po near Ferrara and proceeded further south until we reached Forli in the afternoon. This was a much larger camp, with a maze of barbed wire. Immediately after entering a small fenced-in square, we had to line up. Once the space was packed, we were led farther back along the barbed wire fence into a slightly bigger yard. We passed many similar yards, some totally filled, others fairly empty, along the way. We glimpsed a few members of our original unit, who yelled to us that they had been here for two days, and that Austrians and Sudeten Germans would be separated from the others.

At the time we numbered about 1,000 men, and all of us stayed in this fenced-off area of not quite one hectare. Two rows of grape trellises extended through the compounds, affording at least some shade. However, as all these locations had all been taken, we simply settled in the centre. We thought back longingly to our green meadow in Susegana.

We had imagined a main camp to be totally different. Very soon we learned that, as this too was only a transit camp, we would be transported still farther south to the real main camp. Rumour had it that this would be at Ancona. Now the calamity with the water recurred along with the crowding when the water wagon arrived, as it did about three times daily. We were able to save some washing water in advance, after we had organized another biscuit container. The food was no better than at the previous camps, possibly worse. Yet we could live off it. We even had sugar and real tea, which we were left to our own devices to make. The advantage of this was that paper, as well as anything else combustible, was collected and used for cooking, thus leaving the camp cleaner and more orderly.

It grew frightfully hot during the day. The temperature in the sun registered at 55°C, as measured on the thermometer I had taken from the silk factory. We lacked tent poles to erect a shelter for shade. A few of the guards found some peas on the other side, and pulled out the supporting stakes, which they threw over to us. Now we were able to erect the tent for protection against the sun. As we counted on being moved again soon, we did not put up a real tent. We each intended to take one pea-stake with us on the next move.

There was a lively trade in cigarettes with the guards. Although they asked exorbitant prices (1,000 lire for 40 cigarettes), there were always buyers, and I was astonished at how much money some of them still had in their possession. Some of the guards attempted to pry more money out by saying, "If you go to Africa, you won't need lire." This, of course, set wild rumours going.

Two days after our arrival, the call came that Germans originating in Poland, were ordered to report. They were assembled in another yard where they, evidently, had better care and different food, along with ready-made tea and coffee. One heard only Polish spoken in that compound and we understood that the men had enlisted in the Polish army.

The day thereafter the Austrians, Sudeten Germans, and Baltic Germans were summoned up to report. At first I hesitated to move. Nevertheless, I decided to go in the hope of meeting someone, perchance from home. There were two of us from our group, the other one from Sudetenland. We were taken into a large, crammed corral. There were many railway workers, as well as all kinds of foreigners who spoke many different languages. That night we were asked if we wanted a blanket, but the interpreter said that those who had been issued with blankets the previous night were scratching badly. Consequently I declined the offer. We lay down near two Germans from Sudetenland and tried to keep a distance of 50 centimetres from our neighbours, who looked very unkempt. We were shocked to see the company we now had. There was no sign of the Baltic Germans. I tied my rucksack, my shoes, and my pot into a bundle, keeping it under my head – a very sensible precaution, since many were missing their belongings the next morning. One man even lost his shoes from his feet before he could react. The authorities searched the camp, finding the shoes but not the other items. We watched, in disgust, how people near us started to catch lice. One man sat there for hours over his dirty shirt, crushing them one after the other. That is why we were glad to line up for another move. We had to march a long way to the railway station – a pile of ruins. The train was already waiting there with, fortunately, open-roofed cars. We were told that we would go to Ancona to an international camp, which was near the sea and had two-man tents. Our morale rose at the prospect of being close to the sea. High-spirited, we drove south, savouring the beautiful Adriatic landscape. This part of Italy was familiar, as two-and-a-half years ago I came here from Foggia.

Our disappointment was naturally keen when we turned right, eight kilometres short of Ancona and drove another ten kilometres inland. It was pitch dark when we arrived in Chiasavalle.[35] We were unloaded and walked the short distance to our new camp, which, also, was divided into many small sections, but this time they were a bit larger. We were allocated a

---

35 Or "Chiaravalle."

newly demarcated section, comprising half an alfalfa field and part of a field covered in wheat stubble.

Next morning we had to line up segregated according to nationality. As there was nobody from the Baltics, I stayed with my comrade from Sudetenland. Then a German, in British uniform, arrived and declared that there were no longer *Sudeten-* and *Volksdeutsche*, only Czechs and German nationals.[36] Furthermore, the latter should join the other Germans "on the double." Thereafter the people in the crowd announced that they were Czech, and I escaped to a small group of people who, like me, did not know where they belonged. They were Germans from Rumania, but denied being Rumanian when asked. Consequently they were sent to join the Germans from Germany, the German nationals. I was sent along with them. These Germans were quite a stately crowd, partly "blue" railway workers, the other half mostly members of the multitude whose arrival here was inexplicable.[37] We settled with the navy. Now we were divided into blocks of 100 men, each under the authority of a Sergeant Major. The only officer, who had accompanied us from Forli, was now removed, presumably to an officers' camp. Then a long list of illicit items was enumerated, which would have to be surrendered, after which a march would follow. The pile of surrendered goods, quite impressive, consisted mainly of penknives and pliers. I had been unjustly relieved of my nail scissors, since they were permitted. The same rules applied to watches. I broke the big blade off my penknife, and was thus allowed to keep it. Next we had to spread out all our belongings, but only spot checks were made.

We were now informed that German nationals would be removed to another section, so we just stayed and waited. However, as nothing had happened by afternoon, we erected our sunshade once more, using the available metal tent poles.

Nothing further transpired about letter writing, because this was only a transit camp, and again the rumour arose that we would soon be moved to a

---

36 Hitler chose to make distinctions to recognize ethnic and national differences in the German armed forces. He thus separated *Volksdeutsche*, German-speaking peoples living in countries other than Germany proper, and *Sudetendeutsche*, those German-speaking people living in the Sudetenland, the region of Bohemia near Czechoslovakia. The separation in the POW camp was made by sorting out the Czechs proper from the German-speaking people.

37 The "blue railway workers" were probably railway construction and repair crews akin to, or affiliated with, the OT people. The term "blue" originates from the colour of their uniform.

main camp. However, nothing happened for quite a while. First of all the French, Spanish, and Croatians were taken out, and replaced by Czechs. Our number therefore remained at about 1,000 men. Our enclosure covered a three-hectare triangle, so that there was sufficient space to move about.

Eventually we were allocated tents, and soon felt quite comfortable. The water supply was good, and deliveries were well organized, with the water being distributed to blocks and groups. Among the water drivers was a small, very efficient Negro boy who drove back and forth more often than the British. On the days when he drove we always had plenty of water. However, it was another story with provisions, as these were much worse than before. In the beginning, they still distributed crackers so it was not too bad, but later on we were given white bread of the same weight, and we all felt terribly hungry. At lunch six men were given one loaf of white bread (one pound) plus one tin of corned beef, while at night four men received the same amount. In addition to this there were two or three figs or some raisins, and half a teaspoon of marmalade. On some days lunch consisted of warm soup, brought in big pails. Sadly, this was worse, as one-half of my mess bowl was filled with liquid swill, which replaced the bread and corned beef, and I was even hungrier.

Sometimes there was very strong tea with a tinge of milk, a great treat. Anyway we could exist on this ration as we had no exercise. Most of the day we passed lying down, and I slept more than I thought possible. One had to be very careful indeed when getting up, and hold onto something. For example, I felt very giddy and everything spun around when I arose. In the mornings and evenings we had to line up to be counted by a magnificent-looking sergeant. That was quickly over and took no longer than a quarter of an hour. This sergeant was universally popular. He looked like a lord and I was quite impressed by his appearance.

He was very obliging and all the British here were very kind. But actually he was a cheater. There were complaints about the provisions and one day he arrived with a list of our rations. He remarked that there must have been a mistake as even their own soldiers did not receive such generous rations. There was just not enough to go around and they could not distribute more than was available. Yet in the evening he took one box of corned beef to the "staff tent," where the camp leader and the interpreter (both Austrians) stayed. The provisions were sold at 300 lire per tin of corned beef. Eventually it grew to be a real trading post, where one could purchase provisions, and there were still a surprising number of capitalists who possessed the wherewithal to acquire extra things for themselves. Popular anger was aimed at the camp leader, but the main culprit was the sergeant, who pilfered the provisions from the supplies and embezzled the money. Under these circumstances it was no wonder that our food supply was inadequate.

After we had been there for quite a while, the sergeant instituted boxing matches. Many participated because the winner was awarded one loaf of bread and a tin of corned beef, and the loser half of each. During the event the sergeant distributed more prizes in the form of one thousand lire notes. This gesture was greatly applauded. I thought to myself, "First he skins you, and then you cheer him. The money came from your own pockets to pay for goods he has stolen from you in the first place. On top of it, he gets his money back in a few days." (In other camps, the commerce in provisions was even worse. We heard later that some German camp commanders were shot because they had sold provisions to the Italians.)

We had further experience here of the German officers trying to make our lives unbearable. Our German camp commander issued the order one day that no one could lie down in the morning between 0900 hrs and 1100 hrs. Blankets had to be folded, and our belongings had to be stacked in a prescribed manner in front of each tent. At 1100 hrs we were allowed to put everything back. An *Unteroffizier* was appointed to stand guard at the entrance, and to whistle as soon as an officer entered the camp, so that everybody could spring to their feet. The German commander maintained that this order originated with the British authorities, but no one believed him. Our section leader was sensible enough not to take any notice of the order. (Perhaps he was scared of our rage; the people were furious enough already about the sale of rations, and rumours circulated that the camp commander was secretly a Gestapo.)

A genuine company Sergeant Major was the leader in the neighbouring section. Here, everything was performed by the letter. The whistling never stopped and each morning the poor inmates had to stand for two hours in the glaring sun beside their belongings, until the final whistle sounded, and they were allowed to put their effects back. Some people speculated that this order originated with the camp physician, because of the supposed benefits, which were airing your belongings regularly, having something to do, moving around, and improving your digestion. More and more prisoners were suffering from constipation.

However, I think it was not so much the lack of activity but starvation that caused poor bowel movements, and the body's digestive organs felt

Chess figures carved by Jürgen von Rosen in prisoner-of-war camps in Italy, 1945.

Pieces carved by Jürgen von Rosen out of boxwood and used in German games such as "Dame" and "Mühle," while he was a prisoner in Italy, 1945.

that they were superfluous. It would have been more advantageous if the doctor had recommended figs to counter constipation. I soaked three figs every night in water and ate them first thing each morning. As a result of this I was just about the only person who had something for breakfast and no calamities with my bowels. I still had a few cigarettes which I sometimes bartered for extra figs from habitual smokers.

From time to time we were led to bathe in a little stream flowing about half a kilometre distant. It was not too enjoyable as the bottom of the brook was muddy, and those people downstream had only churned-up mire to wash in. But I was always glad to go as I got some exercise and could wash my clothes. I could also bring home some reeds, which I dried and used for bedding.

In general there was a great lack of reading matter. Nevertheless, we were always reassured that there would be a library when we reached the main camp. Later on we were told that this camp would become the main camp and then we could enjoy all the proper facilities. Still, nothing improved, not even English newspapers were available. From time to time a guard would give you one, but this did not happen often. If you did get one, you had to watch that no one snatched it for use as toilet paper, which was a rarity. On one occasion the interpreter gave me some magazines and the camp leader lent me a dictionary, that was when I started learning English.

People began playing chess, moreover, because an ever-increasing number started to participate in and even enjoy the game, chess sets were always in demand. I began to carve my own, using my little knife, which was in a very poor condition as I had always used it to open tins. Nevertheless, after an exhaustive search, I was happy to find a tiny piece of brick, which I used to hone it. (Only later, in the next camp, did I learn how to sharpen the knife with an old razor blade.) I enjoyed the carving, especially after my success in fashioning a respectable-looking knight.

The heat at this place was not as bad as at Forli. There was a constant breeze and the thermometer seldom rose above 45°C in the sun. On the other hand, the dust was unbearable when the wind blew. It penetrated everything and there was no escape. It took no time for eyes and ears to be filled with dust, as were the blanket and rucksack – everything was permeated by it. My eyes burned like fire when I arose the next morning. Fortunately the wind usually abated at night, but it would return day after day for long periods of time.

A camp with better facilities, including kitchens and showers, was constructed not far from our place. Polish people were installed there. They had to line up repeatedly to sing and have religious services. After a few days they were taken away to Mailand, where they were supplied with clothes and given training.

Right beside us was a Russian camp where a red flag was displayed on a pole. Before long the Russians were also removed, apparently to Tarent, where they were met by Russian ships which bore them away. The guards accompanying them told us that the Russian prisoners had to be forced onto the ships by the Russian soldiers, who shoved them with their rifle butts.

The Austrians were removed from our camp, whither I do not know. They were happy to go and were convinced of their early release. Disappointment probably awaited them. – Now the camp was quite empty for a while and we had room to move, but not for long. Sudeten Germans, actually most of them were Czechs, were moved in. They certainly were dirty and louse-ridden, but fortunately they were in the other section and the assembly square lay between us. The success of awarding many prizes to boxers resulted in the staging of other tournaments. Prize *skat*,[38] prize chess, prize carving, and so on. I wanted to enter the chess and carving competitions, but was thwarted. One morning when we were lined up, the surprise order was issued that we were to pack right away. This time we headed North and there were rumours about Trieste.

I nearly forgot to mention something else. The long anticipated registration had occurred about a week earlier. This allegedly heralded the first step in the progression from transit camp to main camp. Everybody had to fill out a questionnaire, which contained three sections, and our hopes and resolve were fortified. This was surely a step closer to release. Moreover, it was said that the home address provided would be used to notify relatives, and we had great hopes that families would be informed of our whereabouts.

Then one day a mass of newcomers was brought into the neighbouring camp – unkempt German soldiers and Italians in uniforms and civilian clothes, more like rags. Rumour had it that they were partisans and they certainly looked the part. The soldiers who had banded with the partisans in the belief that they would receive better treatment, were to discover the opposite. We had earlier had one of these types in our camp. First he boasted

---

38 *Skat* is a card game.

about his heroic deeds (killing imprisoned officers, etc.), then, when he received no positive response from us (he was nearly beaten), he grew uncomfortable and made plans to flee. The English somehow discovered what was happening and our sergeant removed him.

One night, five men from our area made an attempt to flee. There was much shooting and they were all caught. The result was that the barbed wire fence was reinforced.

A large labour detachment that was recruited from our neighbouring enclosure worked daily to construct new compounds. Corrugated iron barracks were erected and every building was encircled by an impenetrable fence.

We decided that the British would not go to so much trouble if they intended to release us. However, the rumour then circulated that it was built to house the SS. That was some consolation to the doubters among us.

Well, on the 6th of June we were abruptly moved. Walking the short distance to the railway station, we were loaded into box cars that, unfortunately, were covered. The doors were locked from the outside and now we felt truly imprisoned. In one corner stood a big slop pail, in the other two were boxes of supplies, along with two canisters of water, all indicating a lengthy journey ahead of us.

First there was a prolonged discussion about how long we would have to make our provisions last, and finally, after more debate, we unanimously decided to distribute everything right away. As there were fifty men in the wagon, there was only a very small amount for each of us and most of us ate it immediately.

It was stiflingly hot and airless. We were sorely pressed for room. Even so, although happy, we were soon to be disappointed when the "long journey" promptly came to an end at Rimini. We had all hoped in our hearts that even if our destination was not Germany, it would still be closer, being farther North.

After we were unloaded, we marched through a city of ruins. First we thought that we would be engaged in cleaning up. However, we passed right through the city, out beyond its limits, and on an endless asphalt road into the dusk. First we cheerfully carried our belongings. I had brought quite a lot of stuff along. Besides my rucksack, I had an empty corned beef box and some little boards for use as carving material, and a carton – we had all counted on marching only a short distance. Except for the first march, we had always been transported by some means or other in the past. This time we were wrong because we went on and on. At times I thought of discarding the box, but then mused, "I have taken it this far, it can't be too much further."

It grew dark and night fell; we asked one of the guards how far we still had to march and he replied about two hours. If I had believed him, I would have thrown away the carton as well as the box, but we all thought that he was fooling us. On the distant horizon there was a searchlight and I was sure we did not have to walk as far as that. It was pitch dark. We could hear refreshing, gurgling springs, but as soon as we attempted to go and drink, the guard intervened furiously and hurried us along.

From time to time someone collapsed. First the guards tried to egg the victim on, but when they had no success, he would be picked up at the rear and loaded on a truck. The heel of my left boot started to loosen. The leather was so dry that the nails no longer had any grip. Eventually they pierced my heel. On top of that, I had taken my shoes off while we were in the train, and we were unloaded so unexpectedly and hastily that I had no time to put rags properly on my foot, before donning my shoes. Now my toes were painful.

The searchlight drew closer and closer, then we were abreast of it, and then even more searchlights came into view. Still we marched on and on. Then to our left we saw a barbed wire fence and the indistinct outline of tents. Oh well, we thought, what a relief! Yet, no, the barbed wire ended, and we had to keep on marching. We had several short breaks, no longer than five minutes, and then on and on. Again there was a wire fence, but we walked past it.

Finally, we saw those ahead of us turning to the left. We entered a fenced enclosure, just beyond the gate to which was a ditch streaming with water. Everybody rushed forward to have a long-awaited drink. After quenching our thirst everyone sank down, refusing to stir. A German officer came to lead us on, but he was met with scorn. Patiently he persuaded us to get up and we proceeded for nearly a kilometre, before he allotted us a strip of field between two ditches, and we were all able to settle down.

Next morning we discovered that we were in a huge camp about a kilometre square in size. There was lots of space in which to roam and one hardly felt as if one was in a camp. The frail fences, quite unlike those in Ancona, surprised us.

Nothing was provided and we had to accommodate ourselves. Only the camp administration and the nursing units were supplied with tents. Most of our men were shocked, but I was quite happy since I figured we were not going to stay here too long.

This camp contained mostly SS men and those from the police force, all of whom were soon going to be transported to the South. Apparently this move was in exchange for us and they were going to the better fenced permanent camps.

We started to work right away. Following the example of the earlier inmates, we made dug-out hovels, or created adobe walls over which we could hang tarpaulins. Some built walls of clay and old tin cans.

I rejoined the marine drivers with whom I had been in our last camp. I had the tarpaulin and they had a sheet, both of which sheltered us from the sun. It was evident that this was only a transit camp and we would not stay here for long.

The provisions were far better than in Ancona. Initially we were shocked to be given everything uncooked – raw vegetables, raw meat. Up till now we were used to eating from tins. However, we soon learned to find the means to prepare our meals. We were provided with diesel oil, and we managed by combining it with pieces of cardboard and boxes. The ten of us used a biscuit canister as a pot. Other blocks possessed field kitchens, but those served by them did not fare too well.

The process of dividing the provisions caused frequent quarrels and disputes. First, provisions were distributed to the blocks (1,000 men), then to a division of 100 within each block, and then to groups of ten, and finally to the individual man (if cooking was not done by the group). Some supplies never reached us, largely because of our block provision distributor. He had erected a small tent in a far corner, surrounded by barbed wire. The provisions were delivered there, and while he was making his distributions, nobody was allowed to approach. The provisions were brought in by German trucks from a stock under German control.

On the highway there was heavy traffic, consisting of all kinds of German vehicles, trucks, cars, motorcycles, and horse-drawn vehicles, none of them closely guarded. We soon realized that we were in the midst of a huge number of camps. We were in Camp 11 and the many encampments we had passed at night were all grouped together.

The so-called German HQ Bellaria administered all of this and was headed by a tank general. The British guards here were rather reserved and unfriendly, quite unlike Ancona. Apparently the prohibition on fraternizing with prisoners was more rigorously enforced.

The morning and evening head count, of course, took much longer than in the previous camp. British officers, accompanied by two soldiers with their machine-guns at the ready, ran from one block to the other with unbelieveable speed. Our block commander, a first lieutenant, commanded, "Attention!", and reported to the British lieutenant, who then chased along the front and counted the rows of ten. After he had passed, everybody had to sit down and wait until a general signal was given for them to return to their places. The whole procedure lasted about one hour.

The SS and the police force had generally surrendered in group formation, and the SS staff from this formation constituted the camp management, while the police took over the policing of the camp and wore white armbands bearing the inscription 'MP', military police.

They patrolled within the camps and were posted at places like our provisional camp, which was located in a shelled-out farmhouse right in the centre of our camp. They also had to guard the detention cells. These were wire cages about 2 by 2 metres, surrounded by a 3-metre-high wire mesh fence. A few of these cages were almost always occupied at this particular time by an *Unteroffizier*, who had promoted himself while he had appropriated all kinds of medals and decorations not belonging to him. He was, moreover, demoted to the lowest rank. Such punishments were executed by the German camp commander. After this event all self-promoters were ordered to submit to registration by a certain date and were guaranteed immunity from punishment. Certainly a few came forward, but definitely not everybody. For instance I later met our demolition expert who still wore the insignia of his self-promotion.

The partisan from Ancona was suddenly detected in our block. He must have been imprisoned there all by himself, but somehow had managed to get into our transport. He habitually stayed by himself and was very quiet. The block commander reported his case to the camp authorities, and he was placed in a cage. He managed to escape at night, but was recaptured by the British the following day. Where he finally ended up I do not know.

Another partisan was detected by some soldiers in the neighbouring camp. They had watched him shoot several German officers when they were being taken prisoner by the partisans. He was badly beaten and I could hear him shrieking like a little child. Then he was taken to the commander and guarded by the SS. His fate was not known to us, but the SS were most assuredly not kind to him.

The following happened the day before we arrived at this camp: a man from the SS, a Frenchman, approached the British authorities with a long list of SS members in his unit, whom he accused of some infamous deed. He hoped thereby to gain favour with the British, but instead they returned him to his camp where a sergeant ordered him to prepare for a march. His rucksack was filled with rocks and he had then to march. When he fell he was beaten until he got up and resumed marching. After this cruel exercise he was taken to hospital where, according to our information, he died a few days later.

Another person was beaten to death in our neighbouring camp because he stole some crackers. This did not, however, deter people from thievery. Most culprits were those who, having exchanged their biscuits for cigarettes, then stole crackers from their neighbours when they felt the pangs of hunger.

The water supply was excellent. On one side of the camp stood a huge water main with two taps at every 100 metres. We could wash and splash to our hearts' content. Rows of latrines were positioned on the opposite side of the camp. As our block was next to the water taps, we had a long way to go to the latrines, about 1,000 metres. There were quite a few stinkers who were too lazy to go to the latrines at night, and instead used the ditches which criss-crossed our area.

I had a real aversion to these disgustingly dirty people. The worst part was that you had to lie next to them with their lice and other vermin, which survived despite the lavish dusting with powder. A motor sprayer drove through the camp dusting all blankets and clothing with a white powder – but they could do nothing with these unkempt people. I was surprised that I still had no lice. However, I had contrived to lie next to a very clean comrade, a very open and neat labourer, and Social Democrat, from Mannheim. Generally speaking he had very sensible political ideas and could lecture for hours. Only when he started to talk party politics did he become narrow-minded and sullen, and as pugnacious and quarrelsome as a rooster.

German HQ Bellaria started to publish a camp newspaper which was read to us daily at roll call. Now we could at least learn something about world events, even if the news was rather sparse and contradictory.

Eventually we began to be sorted out. SS, police, and parachutists were taken from our block and sent South, where they were reunited with those who had moved earlier. Not everybody co-operated, however. Some mingled amongst us in the hope of escaping detection.

It was quite possible to go unnoticed because those who had been captured by the partisans no longer had their soldiers' paybooks. These men were given interim identification papers by the camp authorities, and many of those wanting to remain anonymous simply destroyed their salary books and were granted temporary papers.

Next to be removed were the OT people, and finally the older men over forty-five years, as well as the young men under twenty.

Then the plan was devised to sort the people by alphabet. These camps still contained mainly military units and it was hoped by this stratagem to tear them apart, thereby promoting demilitarization. However, this last idea was dropped and the next plan was to sort people by alphabet. This became an endless undertaking.

Meanwhile, the last of the SS people were taken away, and a new camp command and police force were established. In addition, a football field was laid out. There were always enough volunteers for such jobs, since extra rations were granted to those who volunteered for any job lasting more than four hours.

To our great surprise, we were told that we would be going to the Adriatic for a swim. I had no idea that the sea was so close, only about one-and-a-half kilometres. We had merely to cross the highway and the destroyed railway tracks to see the water. Of course endless roll calls preceded our departure.

Fifty men out of every hundred men were selected to go. However, not that many chose to do so. We marched to the gate where more endless waiting followed. Finally we exited and the combined column marched to the beach. There must have been several thousand people simultaneously rushing into the sea. Despite that, it was gorgeous. Unfortunately this pleasure did not recur very often. At the time that our block was selected for the next beach outing, the British authorities were annoyed about something or other, and after waiting at the gate for one hour, we were refused the pleasure of proceeding further.

One night we had a thunderstorm, accompanied by a downpour. Those without tarpaulins got soaking wet. I packed all my belongings in one pile and sat on top of it, pulling my tent cloth over my head, thus staying reasonably dry. Far worse was the dust storm which struck a few days later. Instantly, the camp looked devastated. Tents sailed away and the air was so filled with sand and dust that you could not see your own hand in front of you. Once again I packed my stuff in a pile, and covered myself with the cloth. From this experience I gleaned some notion of how terrible a desert sand storm must be.

Rumours had always circulated that farmers would be the first to be released. Until now no trades people, including farmers, had been registered, and there was no interest shown in the rumour. Health personnel had been moved to a different camp. The same happened to reporters. Railway employees had already been registered and counted several times over. It was only the farmers in whom nobody appeared interested.

One day we were moved again without any prior notice. The young and the old were to take our compound over. We left on the 20th of June, leaving only the young and the old behind. We thought that they would be released soon. As we were marching North once again, we derived some satisfaction that we were at least heading homewards. For about seven or eight kilometres on our march we passed many camps, set back from the road. We crossed the railway, which there was no apparent intention of restoring, since asphalt had simply been poured over the rails. Among the sand dunes between the highway and the sea there was a *jabo* airport crowded with planes. The air was filled with them and their noise. The landing strips consisted of rolls of wire covering the sand, a simple and effective technique.

We stopped at Camp 17 on virgin soil, being as we were the first inmates. The camp administration and police, having arrived earlier, were there to receive us. In layout, this camp was the same as the last one; about one square kilometre in area with taps on one side and latrines on the other. The grass was still green and untrampled. For the most part it was knee-high swamp grass, and there could be no doubt that this was a swamp. We were taken to the far end, where there were no reeds, only rock-hard dry mud, cracked into pieces.

At first we stood dumbfounded in this rocky yard, but we soon started to build walls, the soil underneath was softer but dry. The mud slabs were white and about 20 to 30 centimetres thick, very similar to the limestone slabs at home, and were ideal for building walls. It took no time to build a big square, and erect our sun protection over it. Soon we had a genuine room to ourselves, exceptionally cozy and private. I shared the room with the former group of three marine drivers. We were on a vast plain, devoid of bushes and trees. To one side was another camp, and adjacent to that an additional one, which was still unoccupied. On the other side was a transit camp. This vast plain was one huge swamp, but I deduced from several plants that this had once been farmland. One could see sugar beets, beans, pumpkins, and the like that lay scattered in the various cracks between the mud slabs. The field was also traversed by ditches. It resembled a tract of land that had been ruined by flood, very possibly caused by the warfare that had raged in the past and had resulted in the demolition of a dam or a sluice.

The place was perfect, as long as it did not rain, and we did not doubt that we would be released before the onset of the rainy season. We realized that a single rain storm would be catastrophic for us as the walls of our 'adobe' shelters would just melt away.

The catering seemed to be even better than in Camp 11. Noodles and rolled oats were provided and we were able to make a lovely thick soup for lunch. To top it all off, there was a professional chef in our group, who expended much love and attention on the preparation of the food. Unfortunately there were no more good coffee beans, only German tea. In addition, we laboriously harvested sugar beet leaves to extract some sugar. I also took the young sugar beets and cooked them with their leaves, thus producing a wonderful vegetable that was not, however, appreciated by the others. As a result of this extra nourishment, I was able to save my crackers, and to stash away a carton of fifty, either against a "black day" or possibly to take home as a surprise for my children.

We had a young, vain, and self-important first lieutenant as our block commander. I could not dispel the suspicion that he had promoted himself to this rank. He did not look as though he had been at the front, and he certainly was never available when he was wanted. He had no uniform but wore an elegant garment, similar to a blazer, that he had obtained for his escape and which was now ornamented with epaulets. He did have a commanding air, and fortunately he only appeared at roll call.

Counting here was done differently. Every leader of a division of a hundred men had to report to the British, and somehow the system did not work as well as in Camp 11, since quite often the procedure had to be repeated because the total did not tally. (The counter made a note of the numbers of people in his one hundred group, and then all the counters retired to the administration area where endless tallying began. The whole procedure recommenced when the expected total was not reached.)

For roll call we had to be fully dressed, an order ostensibly issued by the British. But I think it was more likely that the German love of orders was the real culprit. I believed that if the British authorities truly wanted this they would have given the command themselves. Consequently, I always attended barefoot and shirtless, without comment from the British.

One day a second lieutenant was appointed to our group of one hundred. A tall spectacled man from Saxony, he made an empty speech to us in which he suggested that he was willing to be helpful. Apparently his great way to help was by holding many roll calls, during which he repeated to us what the other lieutenant had already told us in the morning.

We were taken for swims more often. However, this stopped when two parachutists attempted to escape, only to be immediately recaptured.

To our delight, we were entertained by a musical band from the camp. In addition, talks were started. An African explorer provided us with a very interesting series of lectures, which were given over three evenings. This did not lead to further activity because the camp was broken up. After five days (25 June) we marched back along the same road, past Camp 11 to Camp 14, a few kilometres further South.

This camp was constructed for continuous use, with hard, trampled soil, but in between were very small sections of green corn which had been more or less saved, a fact that I greatly marvelled at.

Here we were torn apart alphabetically, and the *R*'s were taken to the farthest corner of the camp, which, I noticed with satisfaction, was the best corner. We arrived at a badly trampled alfalfa field, next to which was a turnip field, as well as tomatoes and beans. Interspersed were rows of tiny fruit trees and grapes. All these should have been left alone, but everything edible had been torn off too early to be of any use.

The *R*'s arrived at a corral where a complete command structure had existed from the beginning, with the officer and company leader acting as block commanders. Immediately after their capture, all these men were brought here and had remained ever since, while we had been chased from one camp to the next. This indicated that the other alternative did exist as well! However, after a few days this company too was torn apart and divided alphabetically.

During those first days, I explored our green corner, finding peppermint, clover, and the pointed-leaf plantain, which I dried, having enjoyed delicious plantain teas in earlier times. These tasted so much better than the German tea in Camp 17.

I also cooked my lunch myself and collected greenery as fillers – sour grass and nettles, which yielded an ingenious soup. After the new alphabetical order had been effected, a field kitchen, which I utilized, was installed. The cooking was by mass production, without personal care or touch. Obtaining fuel was a chore. The crude oil ration for each person was insufficient to cook the hard peas that were apportioned almost daily. If one was unlucky, one obtained water rather than soup. Consequently I went to collect my slop at the very end, in order to get to the thicker sediment at the bottom. The coffee was a sad excuse, a great pity as it was actually brewed from beans.

The sorting by profession continued. SS and parachutists were still being asked to register, and railway employees were required to register incessantly. Then they looked for truck drivers with a view to forming a drivers' company. Other trades like locksmiths, masons, and carpenters were sought for possible work in the camps. Only the farmers went unregistered, but we were consoled by the thought that we were together with the blue railway gang. They surely, would be the first to be released, and as long as they were among us we certainly had not reached a dead end.

At this point I stayed alone under my triangular tarpaulin, which protected me from the southern sun.

I sat in its shade and carved. My comrades admired my perseverance and suggested that they did not have the necessary patience to do likewise. My ready comeback was that, to my mind, it took a great deal more patience just to stand around.

One fellow from my area really irritated me, for he stood about all day in front of his tent, with his hands in his pockets, moaning that he wanted at least one chance to be on the outside of the barbed wire enclosure. Yet whenever the call to go swimming in the ocean was made – an opportunity for him to leave the camp – he never seized the chance. Ocean bathing was somehow unpopular. Initially, each group of 100 men was ordered to provide ten people for the swimming detail, but as only a few volunteered, a daily squabble about who was to be designated ensued because the men simply refused to participate. Incidentally, I soon stopped volunteering, as it always entailed the odious process of roll call. The whole procedure not only necessitated waiting for the selection of ten men from our group of 100, but also waiting in line until a total of 100 had been chosen from the other groups. Then we marched to the entrance gate where we had to wait yet another hour to be counted again. All the while we recognized that the whole outing might be aborted at the last moment. To circumvent this whole performance, I would often venture off on my own, showing up at the gate at 1000 hrs, when I would tag onto the end of the line. In this way I was always able to join the excursion. More and more people began to do likewise, so that this method became standard. Soon the insistence on a specified number of participants was abandoned. Thus it often happened that only a small group would go out, except on Sundays, when there were usually more candidates than were allowed.

The suspension of the quota may have been related to the drowning of five men from Camp 11 one stormy day. Ten others were rescued only just in time by some able swimmers. Initially I could not understand how this could have happened until I too experienced the strong pull of the surf.

Our bathing area was at the mouth of the Rubicon River which was practically dry during these summer months. But on one occasion, following a heavy downpour during the night, the river became a powerful torrent, and the sea turned chocolate brown for quite a distance along the coastline. It was so dirty that some men decided against entering the water. The current surged along the coast past our bathing area with tremendous power. At some point it turned out to the sea, and here a weak swimmer could easily fall prey to the elements.

One day, when I was totally engrossed in my carving, a voice in Rhineland dialect asked if the space next to me was free and if the owner of the voice could lie down. I answered without glancing up, "Yes, but where do you come from? There has not been a new intake." He replied, "From the detention cell." I must have looked at him rather doubtfully, as he went on to add with some embarrassment, "On account of a dispute with one of these dammed people."

That was reassuring, for he was an honourable man, and not one of the biscuit thieves. He had been in Camp 17, living adjacent to the tent of the block leader. There he and his comrades had noticed how the block leader always put aside some of the provisions in his own tent. After observing this repeatedly, he demanded an explanation from the culprit and quite a hefty dispute must have ensued. The upshot was that the quartermaster sergeant laid a complaint with the camp commandant. When the comrades were questioned, they suddenly denied seeing anything, and so he became the culprit and was placed under arrest for insulting a superior.

After Camp 17 was dissolved he came to Camp 14, and when he had completed his time in the cage he was sent to block *R*, for his name was Rosenstein.

This was the first really spacious camp, especially in our section, as there were relatively few people whose names began with the letter '*R*.' I certainly enjoyed the opportunity to lie all by myself. However, I could not very well refuse, especially as he had no tarpaulin of his own. So he now lay down next to me, in the sparse shadow of my triangular strip of tarpaulin.

The next morning he asked me to watch his belongings, as he intended to go to the employment agency in Rimini. One of the most prized work shifts was in the British supply camp. Only the day before he had been there and, by chance, a replacement was being sought for a man who had stopped working. So he registered immediately. Henceforth he would leave every morning, at 0630 hrs before roll call, and would return in the afternoon. He had to load provisions, was well fed, including extra camp rations, and could take home fruit and any slightly mouldy bread. Invariably he brought home box-boards or empty sacks, and nearly always something to eat.

I started to make a real tent from the sacks, fastening them, as well as the small pieces of board and the cardboard lids (these I had brought from Ancona), to my tarpaulin. Then we moved in together.

Moreover, British gas capes were issued to needy people and as we got one each, these served to shield our entrance. Now we had a protected home and awaited the rains to see if everything was truly rainproof.

We had no rain for many weeks, but shortly before we had completed our home there was a short but heavy shower. Both of us fled behind the sanitary tent. It was big and well-tethered, and because the rain was blown by strong winds from one direction only, we remained perfectly dry on the lee side. After the rain had stopped, we found disaster at our place. The storm had lifted one corner of my tent and everything was sodden. The rest of the night was wet and cold, and it was only during the following day that I was able to dry our belongings out in the sun.

A few weeks later our masterpiece was once again put to the acid test. One night a ferocious thunderstorm, with repeated lightning and gale-force winds, blanketed the camp. The clay turned to the consistency of gumbo almost instantly, and the tent pegs lost their grip. The storm pressed one corner of our tent downward, and we both squatted down grasping the fluttering corners in our hands. All around us we heard frenzied activity. People were bailing water and pounding posts. We stayed in our tent clenching the corners convulsively. The big challenge was who would stay dry during this furious night. The single dry place we could think of was the sanitary tent, which was the only closed, strong, and waterproof tent. When the storm had passed and we ventured to stick our noses out, there was absolutely nothing, the big tent had simply flown away. Now we realized how lucky we were. We certainly were a little wet, but our rucksacks were quite dry and, most importantly, our crackers were not spoiled.

Those who fared worst of all were those who had made the painful effort to dig holes. These were certainly great protection against the dust storms, but now the holes were filled with water, which the occupants had to bail out all night, and everything in their hovels was soaking wet.

From time to time Rosenstein was able to bring a newspaper or magazine from Rimini. I had plenty to read and my day was simply too short.

Every morning I went for a swim that took up half the day, including going and coming. We were now allowed to swim a whole hour. Initially it was only half an hour. In the afternoon I read, and in the evening we played chess. In this way the day passed in a flash and I forgot about being behind barbed wire. With all the additional food Rosenstein brought, there was enough to eat, and if only there had been news from my loved ones it would have been a lovely summer.

In any case there was far more freedom here than during all the previous years in the battery, where every step was dictated. I felt more like a prisoner there than here.

Rosenstein proved to be a very good comrade. He had been a tank driver and in the evening, at dusk, he would relate some very interesting stories, mostly about his war experiences. Six times his tank was shot to pieces, but he always managed to get out safely. On the sixth occasion, however, he suffered heavy burns. The first five tanks had been unable to destroy anything. His sixth tank was a Panzer, and with this he shot up twenty-six Sherman tanks before he was hit. He was in a defenceless situation because his own cannon's loading chamber had jammed. He thought there was no better tank than the Panzer.

His tank was shot up at the very front in France, and he was badly burned. Yet he crawled back to bring out his severely wounded commander – he had to drag him. The last of the retreating soldiers had seen his tank burn out and had reported the event to his unit. They were now convinced that he was dead and reported him as such to his home, where they held a memorial service and placed a cross with his name in the church.

He himself just made it to the ambulance as the doctor was about to move on. The doctor unpacked again and dressed the wounds. Meanwhile the British tanks approached and took them prisoner. The British lieutenant apparently did not want to be bothered with the injured. Whatever the reason, they were asked whether they would prefer to go to Germany or to prison camp. They decided Germany.

He loaded them onto his tank, and that night took them over to the Germans. (When the tank drove back some idiot shot at it.) In this way Rosenstein was taken to a military hospital in Germany without re-establishing contact with his unit, and when he was finally able to write home, they had, so to speak, already buried him.

The welfare division of the camp command was very active. They started a camp choir, and they practised diligently every afternoon. An ingenious stage was built, bricks for the purpose being carried from a dilapidated farmhouse inside our camp. The performance was not very good. The amateur performers did not really succeed and the various camp productions, including those that visited from neigbouring camps, were rather poor. I had enough after seeing the first performance. There was quite a crowd, which indicates that the show must have been worthwhile for some. I went to the weekly movies instead.

We had a film wagon which showed a film for four days at our camp, before moving on to neighbouring Camp 14a for another four days. They showed a different movie each time, fortunately all of them new to me. A good culture film was always shown at the beginning. Later on, on the orders of the British authorities, a newsreel was also shown. Once they showed a terror film depicting the happenings in the concentration camps – these were so exaggerated as to be unbelievable.

The general mood in the camp vacillated between high and low, depending on the prevailing rumour. One for instance was that the old and the young from Camp 11 had been sent home.

My former neighbour from the previous camp, who was now billeted close to the road, persisted with the story that he had seen these men driving by. (Later on we found out that they were prisoners who were joining a group in another camp.) Some maintained that they had been talking to people just under forty-five, who thought that they could slip in. The transport went to Augsburg, everybody was released, only those who were a bit younger were sent back and punished, with the result that they now had to wait until the very end. But after a few days we heard that all this was nonsense, just empty rumour. The younger men, as well as the older, were still in Camp 11.

One day, when everybody was talking about being released, the welfare division started lectures and graduate courses. In addition, I was told that the British authorities had informed those people, who had enrolled in the courses, to count on at least one quarter of a year before they would be freed. This was a blow to those hoping for an early release.

The participants in the graduate classes were taken to the lieutenant of Camp 5d. Our camp developed a kind of school, offering mainly commercial courses, but also classes in various trades, like masonry and carpentry. Additionally, there were a series of English language courses, which I joined initially. However, as all of them usually took place in the morning, I preferred my swim in the ocean, which I would otherwise have to give up. I attended only the agriculture lectures regularly. These were held twice a week in the afternoons and were rather interesting.

Although quite a few courses were offered, participation was comparatively poor. The pitiful multitude did not know how to make use of their time. They churned around after they had had enough of just lying or lingering about, and always lamented the presence of barbed wire wherever they turned. (I must say that I did not notice the fence any more.) Their favourite pastime was to collect cigarette stubs for barter, or to spread rumours.

Some went a bit crazy. At the other end of the camp there was a farmhand who stayed in an iron barrel for hours, never responding when spoken to. Then suddenly he would rush out and deliver confused addresses to the crowd, only to stop abruptly and crawl back into his barrel. (Apparently he had heard something about Diogenes.) Then again, he sat down and wrote endless long letters to the HQ in Bellaria, but the block commander did not forward these as they were too bizarre.

Eventually, a very welcome camp competition was started to beautify our "homes." Some had tidy and clean tents, with lovely front gardens, which they surrounded neatly with pebbles and planted whatever was available inside the camp – a tomato or a sunflower, whatever was not trampled.

At one time, it was rumoured that the Americans would take over the camp, however, it remained a rumour. What did change was that Italian guards now stood in pairs with the British. This trend continued until only the gate warden was British. The roll call was performed, as before, by British officers.

After Italy declared war on Japan, our Italians grew scared about being sent to the front, and some absconded. The result was that they were all dismissed as sentries and placed in a camp under guard. Consequently we were again guarded by British sentries, until they were replaced by Polish troops. We were shocked by this change and the initial days were rather disagreeable.

After roll call the first day, we had to parade again, and the whole counting procedure was performed repeatedly. No success was achieved and we had to stand and wait until late at night. The next thing was our swim hour, and again there were endless roll calls, not to mention restrictions, for we were not allowed to go further out than 100 metres. After a few days, however, everything calmed down and reverted to what it had been under the British.

Most of the Poles had served in the German army, and had become POWs during the war. A number of them had been captured together with us, and eight of them who were in our camp now reported.

In the evening after roll call, so-called "meetings of the mutual homeland" were arranged. It was a splendid idea because so many old friends and relatives were reunited. However, there were no other Baltic Germans. I went twice to the meeting for Germans from outside Germany, but these were mainly Germans from Poland and Sudetenland, as well as some resettlers from Rumania.

The different groups erected signs indicating the times and places of their meetings. Eventually there were numerous signboards, which became increasingly artistic. Some were real showpieces, displaying the characteristics of the relevant home city or landscape.

My shoes were my great worry. They were completely dried out and there was no grease. The heels were loose and the nails were ready to fall out. I went barefoot all the time, but I would need them if there was another move.

I had already taken them to our block in Camp 11. A shoemaker worked here; however, as he had no tools, the result was that after two weeks the boots were returned to me in the same poor condition. In this camp there was a big workshop tent, housing eight shoemakers, but these men were too few for 12,000 people, and they were drowned in a pile of shoes. Finally, just when I had nearly given up, the shoes were accepted, and after two weeks I got them back in reasonable repair. This was just as well because soon after we moved to Camp 17.

The Austrians were assembled in Camp 11a, which was intended to be a showpiece camp. They counted on being released soon. We counted on our release just as much as they did theirs, and conjectured that as soon as they had left it, we would have our turn.

My tent mate was in a quandary, as he did not know whether he should join the Austrians or not. His parents lived in the *Westerwald* in the Rhineland; however, during the war he had married an Austrian, and now he did not know which way to turn – to the Rhineland, or to Austria. He was told that if he chose Austria, he would have to stay there forever. So he decided to wait until he could return to his old home, whither he would bring his wife. Yet, after he was then posted to the labour battalion, he soon regretted his decision.

✳ 2 ✳

FROM BELLARIA TO ILE-DE-FRANCE

Sunday, August 12, 1945

The first Austrians from Camp 11a were taken away last Sunday. Truck after truck went by all morning, heading towards Rimini, where we figured the Austrians were boarding the railway. Many had little fluttering red-white-red flags. Hearsay had it that only those who originated in the American Zone were discharged and that they were destined for an American camp in Verona, but would be sent home from there very soon. The plan was for 3,000 men to leave Camp 11a daily.

It was on Wednesday that the first work battalion was taken from our camp. Where to, nobody knows, maybe to Germany. The British promised they would certainly not be going to the Russian Zone. Rosenstein was among them, and now I am alone in my tent, enjoying the space, although he was a very good comrade.

Assembled at much the same time, a second work battalion was taken away yesterday, Saturday. It was comprised of people from the seventeen- to twenty-five-year age group, although there may have been some over twenty-five as well. While the first ones were all from the Russian Zone, those in the second battalion were all from the Anglo-American Zones.

The wounded men finally got away on Friday. Very possibly they went straight home. We were all allowed to write a postcard, to be taken along by this group, to be mailed in Germany. I finally had a chance to write to *meine Lieben*. I dearly hope that this postcard arrives, so that she has at least some sign of life from me!

In any event things have started to roll.

This is very comforting. One day it will be our turn. Rumour has it that the camps here have to be disbanded by the end of the month, and that those who stay for the winter will be moved to the barracks in Rimini. This is reassuring because with the onset of the rainy season it is unbearable here. Of course most of us had hoped to be released before winter, and the thought of wintering in the barrack camps is no comfort at all.

Today we were counted according to the occupied zones in Germany, and those from the Russian Zone can apply for, and state, the addresses of relatives or acquaintances in the English or American Zones. It is stressed that nobody will be forced to go to the Russian Zone.

Wednesday, August 15, 1945

It is quite apparent that the discharges are beginning in earnest. On Monday it was rumoured that during the previous Saturday, an American commission had visited the camp, expressing its displeasure at the poor rations, the bad housing, and the dilatoriness of the discharges. They were also dissatisfied with the existence of work battalions, as we were designated internees and not POWs. (Most of the inmates of these camps had been taken prisoner only after the capitulation of the Southern Front, when there was no more fighting.) Whether those rumours had any substance I could not tell, but on Tuesday morning a good number of prisoners were unexpectedly called up to be transported – railway employees, miners, farmers, etc. And I was among them. We packed hurriedly. In the course of the morning we were told to be at the gate at 1345 hrs, and that we would be conveyed to Camp 17. That was our old swamp camp and we were rather doubtful about how it would look after the rain.

By 1400 hrs we stood at the camp gate, quite a sizeable group, comprising about one fifth of the camp.

We had been along this road before. It covered about eight kilometres and with our luggage it had been quite a strenuous march. My rucksack had definitely become heavier in the meantime, as I had been given two blankets and one gas cape. Besides these, I now had tent poles and a pile of little boards which I wanted to take along, as I felt certain that our stay there would be long, besides we would possibly have to cook for ourselves again. When a row of trucks arrived everybody heaved a sigh of relief, believing that at least their luggage would be transported. When the first people to be summoned were loaded along with their baggage, we were overjoyed.

We were loaded alphabetically and it was a long time before 'R' was called. We did not make the first convoy, and had to wait endlessly before the trucks returned from delivering the first batch. We nevertheless arrived at Camp 17 before dark.

We entered the camp from the back, past our old "mire castles." It was obvious that this camp had not been occupied since we had left. Our mud castles were somewhat dilapidated after the rain and looked rather romantic, like a landscape of antique ruins. As the far section of the camp was not in use, we were given the front area, which was to some extent drier.

A very sensible German major met us, informing us that this place had been converted into a discharge camp in great haste so that everything was inefficient. However, as we would soon be leaving, it would be wise just to accept the situation.

Relocation was planned to start on 17 August and it was envisaged that 15,000 men would be trucked daily to Verona, where they would be transferred to trains. An immediate start was made by filling in questionnaires. Finally we had positive and reliable news.

We were divided into groups of 100, and ordered to a particular spot. I joined an *Unteroffizier* whom I knew from other camps. We spread out our tent on a reasonably dry spot, and soon felt cozy. Intricate building operations were naturally not undertaken, as we hoped to be away within a few days.

That night we were issued with provisions, as the whole operation was apparently very well organized. Ordinarily we were not supplied with provisions before we left a camp and we got nothing in the next camp until food was distributed in the afternoon. If you had not wisely saved something beforehand, you simply went hungry.

What rascals there were among the German soldiers when supplies were distributed! Rations were given to every group of one hundred, and when the seventh such group approached to receive its rations, it was informed that these had already been distributed. Now all 100 people have to go hungry, and it is impossible to trace who had received their share. During the allocation it had started to get dark and, since we were all strangers to one another because of our being divided into groups, it was possible for a malefactor, or a group of them, to put the supplies aside. The same thing happened in the sector next to ours, only in lesser degree. Within each group of one hundred the provisions were divided into portions for ten people, and our group of ten did not get any dried milk, which we were told had been allocated to someone else already.

Here, by the way, we again encountered the civilians who were merged into Camp 11 a fortnight ago. We had watched them with envy when they left and I had given a Bavarian the address in Ried, and pleaded with him to write to my dear one. Obviously, they had gotten nowhere yet, and we may ultimately get home simultaneously.

Thursday, August 16, 1945

Today we were supposed to fill out the questionnaires but so far there is no sign of them. All that happened was that we had to confirm our relationship to the occupied zones. I doubt that the first departures will occur tomorrow.

Meanwhile we were told that we were to be transported by truck to Verona. The Americans will take over at that point and we will be conveyed by train to Munich. I cannot believe that we are really leaving soon! The joy and expectation are great, but the worry that has been lurking in my heart throughout has grown overpowering – what shall I discover and will I find *meine Lieben* again?!

Friday, August 17, 1945

Registration started today, beginning with those from blocks 1 and 2, going to the British Zone. They had to attend roll call with all their belongings and, following registration, were ordered to a specially designated area where they must await transport. Evidently this will only happen on Sunday. Positioned in the centre of the camp is a loudspeaker vehicle which transmits directives hourly.

More transports arrive daily from various other camps so that our camp has become very crowded and resembles an anthill. There are about 7,000 people here. As I am in block 2, I hope to get away early. Maybe they will select only those from throughout the camp who are going to the British Zone.

It is a pity that the swimming ended. All the time I was in Camp 14, I was able to enjoy a swim in the Adriatic. It was like a summer holiday, and I cannot understand why so few took advantage of it – only about one percent.

Sunday, August 19, 1945

Today was The Day that I went to register. The preliminary checks were fairly quick. After roll call first thing in the morning, it was our turn. Initially we were given five forms. One hundred clerks, who had to complete the forms in block letters, sat along four long rows of tables.

Then one filed through a corrugated iron barrack where an Englishman took four of the forms, after which there was a medical check-up, when one surrendered the fifth form. Thence with all one's belongings to the "louse chaser," where everything was showered with a white powder, and finally one was directed to new quarters. We are lying far too close together in these quarters, but hope that we will get away soon, maybe Wednesday or Thursday. The first 500 for the British Zone were supposed to leave last night, but nothing happened, and not this morning either. Rumour has it that the Brenner line had been blown up by the partisans.

At lunch time they finally left, 1,400 altogether. They will be loaded onto trains in Rimini, and will ride without break to the British Zone.; Hopefully everything will continue at this speed.

Wednesday, August 22, 1945

Today is the day that we will depart. I cannot believe that the day we have been anticipating for months has finally arrived. We sit on our packed rucksacks, waiting for the trucks that are supposed to take us to Rimini. It is 1230 hrs and at 1900 hrs the train is scheduled to leave. Which line, how far, and where to, is still written in the clouds, still we hope that the train will take us all the way to Munich.

The British have permitted everyone to take a certain number of clothes: two sets of underwear, etc. Any excess has to be left for the comrades who will stay, some of them for the winter. It is mainly tent material that is to be left behind. I had only what covered my body, so all I could leave was my piece of tent and my reading book, which had changed hands quite often.

Originally I wanted to exchange it for another book to read on the way, but those remaining have a greater need for books and we who are lucky enough to leave so soon can spare our copies.

All 1,400 of us were divided into sections of 200. The leader of our group is a fine major from the *Odenwald* – one of the few who really understands how to adjust to the changed circumstances, and how to adopt the right manner in dealing with the men. He takes care of everything and keeps order without fuss, and all the men listen to what he says.

People from the British, American, and French Zones are now registered alternately. Only those from the Russian Zone have not been registered yet. It has been repeatedly announced over the loudspeaker that they should not be afraid and that they will be released just as quickly. Nevertheless, yesterday they ordered the registration of some of the people from the Russian Zone, which indicates a measure of continuing uncertainty, and that these prisoners will stay awhile yet. Moreover, none of the arriving convoys were for the Russian Zone.

By the way, a novelty in this camp was the presence of a little boy of thirteen. As far as I know he was released with the first batch to the British Zone, along with his father. He came from Camp 11, and there was quite a bit of discussion about him, but I could not get his story quite straight. Evidently he came from Silesia all by himself to find his father. He was taken prisoner and delivered to Camp 11. His father was in fact discovered in a different camp and brought to Camp 11. The British gave them a two-man tent so that they could stay together by themselves. The two of them were exempted from roll call, the boy was allowed to roam freely, and even leave the camp. He was treated very kindly by the British and the guard at the gate gave him plenty of cigarettes for his father. It was a really beautiful family idyll.

Thursday, August 23, 1945

There was further great disappointment. Yesterday we left on time with 700 men at 2 p.m. It was a lovely drive, full of hope. We passed by the many camps and waved to the unlucky comrades who remained behind. At 3 p.m. we arrived at Rimini station, were unloaded, and the trucks returned to retrieve the other 700. Then we waited in front of the station for three long hours. Our train stood ready, the guards boarded, and enough provisions for several days were piled high on the platform.

Then suddenly the news broke: somewhere the railway had been disrupted (hearsay had it that the partisans had attacked it), and repairs would take thirty-six hours. When the truck convoys returned with the other 700 men, they had to turn around immediately to take these men back to camp.

After waiting awhile, the trucks returned and transported us to the camp as well. It was quite dark when we arrived, and we wandered back sadly to our familiar field. I found consolation in telling myself: "In this manner our sense of anticipation is drawn out, and who knows what awaits us in Germany? Now everybody places their hopes on tomorrow."

By the way, the Russians who up to now had been here in our camp, were carted away. They wore English uniforms and sang every day while exercising. Apparently they had not wanted to go back to Russia and had enlisted in the British army. However, they wore the Soviet star, and waved little red flags from the trucks.

Friday, August 24, 1945

It is difficult to appreciate how rushed everything has become. Yesterday at noon we received the sudden order: "In fifteen minutes everybody must be ready for loading."

And we had all made preparations for today, our rucksacks half-unpacked, and everyone clad in bathing trunks as we stood in line for our rations. In our haste it was difficult to decide where to put the blotch of marmalade, etc. The only solution was to swallow everything, get dressed, stuff our rucksacks, and head off to the gates.

After our dejected return from Rimini the previous night, one of our comrades had obtained a tent tarpaulin and the three of us had slept together under it. Now, as we were hastily leaving, one of the men who would remain behind, approached us asking for the tent. The "owner" promised to give it to him in return for his fetching our lunch from the field kitchen, since we would not have time to get it.

He gave him our three ration cards and field pots, and the man disappeared. I asked him if he knew the man and he replied: "No, I don't know even where he is billeted." The two of us remarked that the man would prefer three portions of soup and three filled pots to one tent tarpaulin. Then we teased him that he had taken the last movie too seriously. They had shown the movie *My Wife Theresa* in the camp only two days before. It was about a woman who was so kind-hearted that when asked by a poor stranger on a railway station for one mark, she gave him fifty, and requested him to get change for her. Shortly before the train left, he returned to give her the forty-nine marks change.

We were not concerned about the soup, but the field pots were another matter. However, sure enough, we experienced the same as Theresa. After we had given up hope of seeing him again, our man appeared, but without any soup. The first serving had already been distributed, and the second was not yet ready. So he got the tent tarpaulin and the ration cards, and we were greatly touched that decent people could still be found. He now informed us where he could be located. Later, after a vain hour-long wait at the gate for the trucks, we went back to this man, retrieved our ration cards, and by now the soup was ready.

We were able to enjoy a very leisurely meal before a huge column of trucks finally arrived and took all 1,400 men in one go. There was no waiting in Rimini this time. We were loaded onto a freight train, thirty-eight men to each wagon, and to our utter surprise the doors were left open. At 1930 hrs we left, filled with joyous anticipation. There was just enough room to half-stretch out at night and I slept well. This morning we passed Verona and now, in the evening, we are climbing towards the Brenner Pass. That means we will be in Munich tomorrow. I can hardly believe it! The train had provisions for four days, and they must be made to last until each of us has reached our destinations. On the way we saw German soldiers working on the line at several places. It seems that they were people from the Russian Zone. They called out to tell us that the Americans up here had long since released those from the Western Zones, the last a fortnight ago. What on earth had made the British wait so long?

Beyond Bozen we encountered the German population – many workers in the fields waved to us. We met many trains carrying returning Italians, most of whom were cheering and shouting noisily.

Saturday, August 25, 1945

Yesterday's jubilation was suddenly dampened. About fifteen kilometres from the Brenner Pass we were shunted to a side track, the locomotive disappeared, and we just stayed put all night, and all morning as well. Two other trains with German soldiers passed us. One was from Livorno and the other from Naples. We watched them with longing gazes. Allegedly the brakes of our train are inadequate for the descent down the Brenner Pass. We are told that another train is expected at 1700 hrs and that we will have to transfer to it. So we lay outside in the sun, admiring the mountains, which are really magnificent, and enjoying the pure forest air.

Yet somewhere deep inside us, a restlessness hinders our full enjoyment of the surrounding beauty. It is now 1400 hours, it has become too hot, and I have moved back into the rail-car.

The rumour spreads that in half an hour we will be moved to the Brenner, where we will possibly change trains.

Monday, August 27, 1945

Of course, everything took much longer and we sat, waiting all afternoon. Women from the Tyrol plied back and forth on bicycles bringing us fruit. It was only at night, after a wait of twenty-four hours, that we moved on slowly to the Brenner. There we had to get out, to wait for an Italian transport and then change trains. As our train lacked air brakes, it was not allowed to proceed further. So we sat in the midst of a dilapidated, totally devastated railway station.

Empty tins, all kinds of junk and dirt were everywhere, and the smell was horrible. At night it was cold so we made a fire – there was plenty of wood in the rubble. The Italian transport only arrived at 1500 hours. The transfer to that train was quick and continued without incident from the Italians. Then finally the train went on to Innsbruck where we stopped until 0600 hours, when our train was divided into three sections, as we had to take the precipitous route past Garmisch. The normal route to Rosenheim was obstructed by a destroyed bridge. Finally we rode into the beautiful morning through magnificent landscape. Now we understood why we could not have used the other train. The descent was uncannily steep, and our train was short and had two locomotives and good brakes.

The train was reassembled in Garmisch and, of course, there was more endless waiting. One Italian train after another rolled South, always amid loud shouts and noise, the wagons covered in chalk crosses. Here too the following transport from Rimini overtook us; it had left twenty-four hours after us. Once again it was late afternoon before we continued, but now we went quite a bit faster. People waved to us, everybody was dressed up for Sunday, and the landscape was so beautiful and peaceful.

Yes, it was Sunday and our first impression of Germany, the new Germany, was quite Sunday-like – there was nothing to remind you of the war. The train had to stop at several small stations and everywhere there were friends and relatives. While the train was passing through one station at a snail's pace, one man jumped out, kissed his wife who happened to be standing on the platform, jumped back in, and off went the train.

We were taken quite a bit more swiftly through Munich. The train halted briefly at Munich-Süd, and I contemplated whether I should simply get off. All the doors were open and the sentry did not care one bit what we did.

But then I reasoned that we would be released in a few days anyway, and we had been told time and time again that we could not obtain ration cards without the necessary discharge document.

We drove past Rosenheim to Aibling, which we reached at night. Again we spent the night in the open. There was space in the tent only for the sick and the old. At this time we are waiting to be screened and for whatever else is going to happen. First came the delousing, the same type of powder sprayer that we had met with in Camp 17 before our departure.

It is lunch time and our mood has deteriorated considerably. The release is much slower than we expected. First they sifted out the wounded, the sick, and those unable to work, and second they divided us into different trades: builders, drivers, etc. Then the great bulk of us were sent to a different section with small tents (made from buttoned-up tent-sheets) which were already overcrowded. We discovered that some of the men from Rimini, who had been discharged before us, were still here. And we had imagined them to be back home long ago. Now we sit and wait, and it looks as though some of those in the tents will be released today, and we can occupy the tents.

Naturally, all kinds of rumours circulate – for instance that work battalions are being assembled here too.

The sub-divisions here are very small and crowded, and the wire fence is so dense that you really feel imprisoned, especially after the freedom of Rimini.

Women and children are in the meadow outside the barbed wire – how they found out that their husbands were here is a mystery. They are not allowed to approach closer than 300 metres, and their calls are hard to understand. If, in their despair, they try to approach, the guards shoot all over the place and it is a wonder that no one is hit.

Now it is evening and we are still crowded like sheep in a pen. We are behind the latrine. It appears likely that we will have to spend the night here, as no one has left the camp yet.

The members of last "latrine parole" sound a bit more optimistic and say that registration will resume tomorrow. Numerous secretaries are ready and waiting, and the whole procedure in Camp 17, Rimini, is void – we start all over again here. People were once again sorted feverishly by occupied zone, with all the usual confusion, and releases to the British and French Zones will occur here as well. Anyway we all look forward to the next day with renewed hope.

During the afternoon some of the wives, displaying great determination and stamina, managed to reach the fence and throw small parcels across into the enclosure next to ours. This is less crowded, and its inmates are apparently Nazi party and the SS members. Possibly the intended work battalions will only comprise party members and the like.

The food is supposed to be worse here than at Rimini. However this morning we had a little piece of cheese, at lunch a really good potato soup (even if it was only a half-litre), and at night one two-pound loaf of bread for six people. However, it was really good rye bread. I ate it voraciously and it was far more satisfying than the air-filled corn stuff that we had in Rimini.

Tuesday, August 28, 1945

We certainly have moved from the frying pan into the fire here and I wished that those comrades in Italy who still enjoy the golden freedom to move, yet complain so much, would see what is happening here.

Here 5,400 of us were penned in an area about 100 by 100 metres, and those of us who were newcomers had, in truth, to spend the night on the narrow strip between the fence and the latrines. It was so congested that you could not even stretch out. Despite the stench and the constant clapping of the latrine lids, I slept well, thanks to the exertions of the journey. Deeply disgusted, we realized next morning that hordes of fat maggots with long, thin tails were crawling all over us. During the night they had deserted their breeding places in the cesspool in order to make cocoons in our garments.

Fortunately we were spared the ordeal of spending another night in this fashion. Allegedly this excessive accumulation of people over the last few days was caused by a change of secretaries.

Today processing has started again and there is more room. During the course of the morning we moved to the vacated tents and were at least rid of the stench and the maggots. It is still very congested as we are ten people to a tent, each of which is shaped like eight triangles.

If I had foreseen that developments would be so endless, I would have tried to mail a letter en route, either in Garmisch or somewhere else. Here we are hermetically isolated from the world. In addition, the most depressing fact is that no end is in sight.

Wednesday, August 29, 1945

This endless uncertainty is depressing and the perpetually circulating latrine paroles do not help to improve morale. We were so full of hope when we arrived here, and we counted on being released in one or two days. Now our disappointment is great because everything remains so unsettled and no release is in prospect. In any case only ten percent of those from our encampment who were screened yesterday were earmarked for release.

All the rest were sent back and confined to the enclosure next to us – the enclosure that we thought was reserved only for work battalion recruits. Once again the wildest rumours began to circulate. The classification of people seems to have happened entirely randomly. Only trivial questions were asked and no one seemed to bother about party membership.

Mostly sick and wounded people were screened today and very possibly they will be released. I was told that some of the injured people, who had left Rimini ten days before we had, are supposedly still here, with all the officers among them.

Nobody knows what happened to the postcards we were allowed to send along with the injured people. As there is still no mail service here, probably they ended up in a wastepaper basket.

Quite a few transports have arrived today, including one from Rimini. Now it is their turn to lie between the fence and the latrines amid the stench and worms, and we hope that we will be screened tomorrow to make more room. Apparently arrivals exceed releases, and everything is shrouded in secrecy. In the meadow behind our enclosure, new enclosures are continuously being fenced in, but even these cannot keep up with the inflow.

The complete isolation from the outer world is very depressing: no newspaper, no radio, only a loudspeaker playing the same records morning, noon, and evening. A voice, speaking between the songs on the public address system, informs us about which enclosure will receive food at what time. Food is cooked in huge battery kitchens and carried in large pails to the encampments. Cooking is done in three shifts and you are unlucky if you are allocated to the third delivery, because you only get your lunch at night.

Today I was one of the food haulers. The pails are very heavy and have to be carried quite a long way. You have to pass the hangars (the whole camp is on the airfield) which are occupied by the *Blitz Mädel*.[1] Apparently they are accommodated comfortably, sleeping in two-storey bunk beds. In any case, they do not need to fret about the rain, as we do in our primitive and crowded tents. We have, up to now, been very fortunate with the weather, with constant beaming sunshine and temperatures nearly as hot as in Rimini.

Thursday, August 30, 1945

Well, today we were finally screened and I, of course, was among the unlucky ones. Very few were selected for release, for it was mostly the blue railway people that were the fortunate ones.

There were five American officers questioning us about whether we had been in the party, the SS, or the SA, and then each of us passed along to be registered alphabetically. The few lucky ones were immediately directed into a different corner, where they received their papers. A fat man sent me to the black sheep. Now we are in Camp 13. In the morning, 2,000 were dispatched from this camp, nobody knows where to, nobody knows anything, and of course the weirdest rumours are going around about work battalions being sent to Frankfurt/Main or Belgium or God-knows-where. The mood has sunk to sub-zero, and everybody rails at the authorities in Rimini, who promising us our release, instead sent us into the deepest disappointment. If they had told us from the beginning that we would not be released, but must first go through labour camps, we would have been inwardly prepared.

---

1 *Blitz Mädel* = young women working in the communications corps.

Friday, August 31, 1945

We have more or less resigned ourselves to our fate and are now awaiting news about our future. Yesterday we obtained good rations, American cold rations, and that has helped to lift our spirits. Each of us also received six little tins of delicacies yesterday, and three today.

This morning at breakfast we felt as if it was Christmas. Everybody was busy unpacking all kinds of delights: candy, cocoa, cigarettes, crackers, and marmalade. Everything, of course, was in small amounts, but was neatly and invitingly packed. I would like so much to save some for the children, but I have no idea how long I will have to carry the things in my rucksack, which is already full.

Guarded optimism has again seized the latrine paroles. The 2,000 inmates who left yesterday only went to a new camp three kilometres away. That meant they had not yet been put to work. After assembling at the new camp they may even have been divided according to zone and released.

However, we have definitely been unlucky. The prisoners were freed continuously until just before we arrived, but we of course had to come upon this mysterious stoppage.

On the basis of much that we have heard on our way, I concluded that the general registration of civilians is currently in progress and that the release of the military will be delayed until the registration is completed. I keep hoping that the freeing of the military will resume by the 10th of September and that we will remain here until that date. Even so, I try not to get depressed, despite all the rumours.

There are now eight of us in each tent – not as crowded as in Camp 11. The members of our previous group have been reunited, except that two of our former number were suffering from some or other ailment and did not return from the medical check-up. Instead they went to join the group comprising dismissed people.

Saturday, September 1, 1945

Those who were registered after us had more luck than we did, as comparatively more of them were being released. Maybe the work battalions have their full complement now, and we just had the bad luck to be allocated to them.

Today we have sat since lunch with packed rucksacks, have been through the alphabetical roll call, and are waiting to leave. Whither? Nobody knows.

We had rain yesterday. The drizzle was light but our tent was reasonably rain proof, even cozy, and the weather was quite a relief after the excessive sunshine.

The provisions have improved – we are now given a double ration of bread and, in the morning, a milk soup.

Sunday, September 2, 1945

Well, we did not depart yesterday. Instead we returned to our tents at night and were awakened as early as 0500 hrs, were hastily served warm soup, and attended roll call in the previously finalized alphabetical order – but we were only loaded at lunch time. All of us remained hopeful that we would not be sent too far away, but on the outside of our train wagon is a note bearing today's date and the destination "Champagne/France." That killed the remainder of my hopes. It will be at least a quarter of a year before they release us from there – maybe before Christmas. There are quite a number among us who cannot believe the fact that they have brought us here from Italy, only to send us on to France, especially as we are farmers or belong to other specialized trades. In Munich I was able to leave two notes behind, both with the Munich and Ried addresses. One I pressed into the hands of a railway employee, and to the other I tied a biscuit before throwing it out the window in Pasing. Now I feel a bit lighter in my heart. Maybe one or the other of them will reach their destination, providing my love with confirmation that I am alive.

If I had any idea of what course things would take, I think I would have left the train after we had arrived in Munich, when hardly anyone guarded us. Now we are guarded so closely that it is useless to even try to escape. And besides, what could one do without papers? Sometime, somewhere, you have to report, and then you are sent once more to some place not of your own choosing.

Despite all that, I reproach myself that I did not leave the train in Munich. Quite possibly I passed close by *meinen Lieben*, and I cannot grasp why I did not try the utmost to reach them. Some inner voice kept me back. Maybe it was also the feeling that I could not leave my rucksack behind. It is disgusting how dependent one is on one's last earthly possessions. But my love's most recent letters and my carved chess figures are in there, and the biscuits which I saved for such a long time to take to the children.

Everywhere we pass, I can see many young people who have been released, and that fills me with a certain envy and I argue with fate. Why us – why should we have this misfortune?

The "consolation" parole has been told that every German has to work for three months, and that those released now will be recalled later to the work battalions. If that is true then, naturally, it is far better to complete my work obligation now, and should that take a quarter of a year, we will still be back with our loved ones by Christmas.

Tuesday, September 4, 1945

Yesterday we drove towards the Rhine River, stopping frequently along the way. The landscape was beautiful, with many laden orchards. People threw fruit into our wagons and there was much fighting and quarreling, for some filled their pockets while others got nothing. Time and again experience reveals that the German reputation for good comradeship is often far from true.

In the evening we crossed the Rhine at Kehl and suddenly there were no more waving onlookers. Kehl itself looked lifeless; probably only a portion of the evacuees has returned.

At night our doors are locked from the outside, but fortunately, during the day the door is open on one side.

Today we passed Nancy and Toul and soon we will have reached our goal. The American guards shoot incessantly at sparrows and crows, even house ducks, with their automatic pistols.

One hundred and forty men, from one of the earlier transports, escaped near Karlsruhe, and fourteen of them were shot. Possibly that is why the guards have been reinforced. In the centre and at both ends there are flat-decked cars with 2-cm cannons.

Seemingly the plan is that everybody must work for a quarter of a year.

We were told, by a woman at a railway station on the way, that, in her village, a man had returned after completing his work obligation, and that her husband, who had been released quite a while ago, had to go and replace him. We try to comfort ourselves with this fact, because if we were to be released now we would have to work in the spring, and that would be much worse.

✳ 3 ✳

FORCED LABOUR CAMPS IN FRANCE

Wednesday, September 5, 1945

The country is endlessly desolate, between Châlons-sur-Marne and Reims; huge ill-kept sandy fields interspersed with a few pine forests. All the big fields are separated by narrow strips, which you can still make out by the remaining weeds. Signs of some cultivation are visible on a few of the strips, but most of them were just wasteland. A handful of sad villages were all that was to be seen. In vain I looked for vineyards – I do not know where champagne comes from.

The soil improved past Reims, and the landscape was more beautiful; nevertheless, I could not discern any vineyards. There were deciduous forests on the hills, with interspersed luscious pastures and fields.

The villages looked far wealthier and the intervening estates bigger. Near Reims there are big prison camps and American warehouses where prisoners have to work. We were sure that we would be unloaded there, but after standing immobile for quite a while, the train went on again. On the way we saw many Germans working on the tracks, in a brick factory, as well as on farms. We all hoped in our hearts that we too could be allocated to the farms, as nearly all of us were farmers.

We finally arrived late at night, were unloaded, the pitch dark being lit up by a few searchlights (it was the tiny station of Vittichy). We were then marched uphill on a good asphalt road, leading out of a beautiful valley (or so it seemed from what we were able to see in the dark). To the left wooded hills, and to the right the valley with its meadows and bushes. After about an hour we arrived at a big camp, situated on a barren flat on the crest. There we were locked in an empty yard, and spent the night outside. It had been raining and the ground was muddy, but fortunately our yard was not too trampled, and sparse tufts of grass remained for us to lie on.

In the morning, to our great grief, we had to surrender all our blankets. Then we were dusted again with the louse powder, after which a search ensued. We felt as if we were back at the very beginning of our imprisonment, and this time the search exceeded all previous ones in thoroughness. Everything was shaken out, and even though I knew that I should retain nothing regarded as 'undesirable,' I, as a final precaution, hid my penknife with its broken blade, my Iron Cross, and my watch in my shoes. But I could not save everything and had to break off my fork from my lovely set, and give up my sewing and darning needles, which were regarded as terrible and dangerously sharp instruments. However, I was lucky in that the guard did not confiscate my store of biscuits. These I wanted so badly to keep for the children. Just that the rule here is that one hour after the meal is delivered everything must be consumed. So I decided to eat the biscuits myself. They say that if an American finds food while searching one's rucksack, he shortens the rations.

We are in a crazy camp. It is clean, I admit that, and very orderly, but everything is restricted, and every step is dictated. There are forty of us in low tent-like huts. Mesh wire covered with tarpaper is stretched over a simple scaffolding made of round stakes. Both ends are open, still it is dry inside and we lie on straw.

When it is not raining during the day we are forbidden from staying in this shelter. Moreover, we are not allowed to go barefoot or shirtless. Oh God! What wonderful freedom we had in Bellaria. We have to save water as it seems to be very scarce. There is only one small tap and most of the time it is shut off.

Why we have been brought here is a mystery, because apparently there is no work. Those who were here before us were just as idle as we were in Italy, and were simply waiting to be released. That seems to have been the case here from the very beginning. For instance, all the Austrians are still here, and we have again begun to hope that when the releases start we the farmers will be included. It will be worse if we have to wait here weeks or even months for some suitable work and then have to labour for three months, or half a year, so that we will have to spend Christmas behind barbed wire. But I don't want to abandon optimism, and have renewed my hopeful wait.

Thursday, September 6, 1945

This morning we were awakened at 0530 hrs, when it was still pitch dark. Watery tepid tea was distributed in the dark. Half an hour later, when the tea was cold, we received a small loaf of white bread for five men. And after consuming the bread, one herring was distributed to each of us. I do not know when I last ate herring; it was a real feast, only terribly salty and there was nothing to complement it. But the breakfast was so hearty it was a pity that we could not enjoy it all at once, like a real breakfast. Furthermore, it was hard to understand why it took place in the dark, since there was no work waiting for us.

At dawn the straw had to be piled up in the centre of our hut at one specified spot. Then the blankets had to be folded in a prescribed manner and the rucksacks lined up 20 cm from the wall. The end result was that everything looked neat and tidy, evidently clean. However, I dislike the fact that the blankets are all mixed up, and I have no chance of getting my own blanket back again.

At 0800 hrs you had to leave the hut and were not allowed to return before 1100 hrs. Outside the hut is an empty area where you can lie down, but because it was foggy and cool everybody ran around. Between 1100 and 1300 hours we were allowed to go back to our huts and were given one litre of very tasty noodle soup. The food is cooked inside our encampment in a capacious kitchen.

From 1300 to 1700 hours we have to leave the huts again and at 1700 hours there was some watery oatmeal soup, which we would have appreciated more in the morning, and the herring at night instead.

In the afternoon we were sorted again by zones, just as had happened so many times before. Our hopes of release rose. It was an administrative mistake for sure that got us here. The batch of prisoners that arrived immediately after us had not been unloaded in Attichy at all. Instead they had been provided with food and sent back, maybe only to another camp. This camp is assigned to the SS, so we expect to get away soon.

Friday, September 7, 1945

Last night we suddenly had to attend roll call with our luggage and were rearranged, again alphabetically, just like when we arrived. If they had not mixed us up when we came they could have avoided this extra trouble. It took them ages to straighten matters out and it was pitch dark before we were assigned to our new tents, which were in the same enclosure.

At lunch time today the sun finally came out and it has warmed up. At last we can see the local environs! Actually there is not much to see, we are on a plain and only to one side can we discern a wooded valley stretching away down the hill. The only other thing visible is the huge tented area, divided in sections. They say that 123,000 men have passed through here. At the moment a large part is empty. We heard that the rations had been very poor during the summer, the water supply in the hot summer was catastrophic. Most of our group now realize how good Rimini was.

Yesterday small "luxuries" were unexpectedly provided: two packets of tobacco, one cake of Palmolive soap, one razor blade, and one tube of toothpaste.

It is evening now. In the afternoon we became alarmed when we were given our small helping of evening soup at 1530 hours, and had to attend roll call with our luggage. We were taken to Camp 5, that is, the camp for the outgoing people. It is located alongside the one which we entered first. Then the same pattern ensued – no shelter. We were again sorted endlessly by alphabet whereafter we were left to our own fate.

I am afraid they will leave us here for the night, without shelter or blankets, as they took ours away on our arrival, and we had to leave behind those with which we were provided at Camp 14. Maybe that is a good sign, as those men who were released never had blankets, while those who went to labour camps were able to keep theirs. So there is hope and I do not mind being cold. Hearsay has it that 2,000 SS men have arrived today; maybe we will ride back in their train.

Saturday, September 8, 1945

The night was cold and moist, and was I happy to have kept my sacks. I crawled feet first into two of them, the third one I wrapped around my shoulders – a well-proven method – and the gas cape was around my body. Consequently I was able to get some sleep. By the morning the cold together with the moisture had penetrated everything, but this proved to be a good Kneipp cure.[1] The horrible cold I had caught at 0500 hrs on the first night, while I still had my blankets, disappeared just like that. Most of the others could not sleep at all and ran around all night. It was like an aroused bee swarm.

---

1 A hot and cold water compress named after the Reverend Sebastian Kneipp.

Two hundred men arrived during the night in Camp 5a, next to ours. They had been felling trees for three months. In the morning they were searched in the same way that we were searched before, only not by the American but by the German camp police, the latter confiscating far more than the Americans had taken from us – it was a real shame.

The sun came out during the morning and warmed us somewhat after the cold night, then we finally left at noon. We marched back down from the dreary plain into the beautiful wooded valley along the same picturesque road, and now we sit at the station at Attichy and wait.

To judge by the road signs, Attichy is about equidistant from Soissons and Compiègne.

It is 1700 hours and our train has just arrived. We all desperately hope that it will take us back to Germany. If not, there will be more terrible disappointment.

Sunday, September 9, 1945

Last night at 1830 hours, we left, and this time we are not guarded as heavily as on our way in. Moreover, the doors were not closed at night and this leads us to hope that we are going to Germany. But the guards are very unfriendly, much more so than those on our inward journey. Nobody is allowed to get off, not even to fetch water, and they shoot the moment you lean out. One person has already been wounded in the leg and will have to be taken to a field hospital, as the main artery has been hit.

We travelled back along the same route and passed Nancy at lunch time. Now, having covered a good distance, we have been standing for two hours. We are stationary at a siding at some small station, because the locomotive left us here. Just as was the case on our inward journey, we passed this section by night, making it difficult to establish if we were travelling homewards. This could be the route to Epinal, but that actually seems to be too far South. We hear the weirdest speculations as to our destination.

I still believe that we are heading towards Germany. Every rail car was given one lot of provisions, but we do not know how long they must last. On the way in we were given our rations each day, a simple matter to deal with. Possibly the rations must last for three days, but the amount of bread is especially small – three-fifths of a loaf for each person. I had two slices today and half the loaf is gone already – yet this is only the first day.

Monday, September 10, 1945

Last night we had a considerable shock when a locomotive came and was hitched onto the other end. Our trip took us back in the direction from which we had come. In Blainville we stopped awhile alongside a transport that had come directly from Aibling. They had arrived from Rimini on Monday, and were sent on to France on Thursday. They too were guarded heavily in the front and in the middle, and there was a platform-car at the rear carrying machine-guns, as well as two guards in every wagon.

In the dark it was hard to tell whether we were on the same track as before. Around 2200 hours we passed through Nancy and then came to a halt. When morning dawned, I noticed that we were apparently on former German territory, as we rode on the right track, whereas the French (in any event the railways) use the left side. That was quite comforting; we were not returning to Attichy. During the morning we stopped at a small station, St. Avold, thirty kilometres from Saarbrücken; here we were told to offload to be subsequently taken to a camp, twelve kilometres away. As we have been standing here for several hours already and the guard has given us permission to fetch water, we believe that we will travel onwards.

Well, they apparently did not want to accept us in St. Avold and now we are told that we will be taken to a French camp near Metz. The locomotive maneuvered back to the other end of the train, which faced towards Metz. Our morale sank to sub-zero. Where is our odyssey going to end? And why, with the lack of capacity on the transport routes, are they driving aimlessly through the whole world? The same applies to the many other convoys as well.

After travelling about an hour we stopped again. Again the locomotive was unhitched, a new one was hooked up to the other end, and we started out in the opposite direction. Well, it is not heading towards Metz, as we have turned off to the right, I guess towards Saarburg. Our hopes are rising. Maybe we are going to Strasbourg and across the Rhine!

Wednesday, September 12, 1945

Now a camp, a French camp, has swallowed us. We were unloaded in Saaralb on Monday night, and were marched through the little town to a camp barracks. For the first time since we were taken prisoner we spent the night in a room, and even without blankets it was fairly warm. As we were going to be searched by the French, I started to eat my hoard of biscuits with an aching heart, and feasted on the other good things.

Until now I had hoped to give the children a treat for Christmas, but we have been told that everything edible will be confiscated, so I consumed the lovely chocolate myself and decided not to save anything for the future. This decision was soon vindicated, because a morsel which I saved in my rucksack for breakfast was stolen by one of my comrades overnight. I came out quite unscathed from the search, but some people were really plundered – mainly food, tobacco, and cigarettes, as well as soap – all items which neither Americans nor British had shown any interest in during their checks. After the search, detailed screening and registration started again. I have not been in, as yet, and expect to be called sometime today. They are assembling work units here. The last transport went to Strasbourg, as far as we could make out, but with luck there may be a chance to get into the countryside.

My hope now is to obtain any sort work as soon as possible, so that I can quickly discharge my labour obligation.

Last night we had roll call again after a long interval. There was none in Aibling or in Attichy. Immediately after the roll call we had some exciting moments. All day there had been nothing to eat, as nobody had announced our coming and no one was ready to receive us. Although fires were forbidden, several men picked at the edge of the fence and found some dandelion leaves with which to make a green soup. The firewood was obtained by demolishing a shed, originally meant to hold provisions. Now there was the inevitable commotion, and the culprits were ordered to step forward, otherwise the whole camp would be punished. Nobody reported, of course. Some of those who had made the fires did come forward, but stated that they got the wood from somewhere else. Finally a deadline was set; the boards have to be returned by morning. This is hardly possible since most of them have been burned already.

I hear that some boards have been hidden for future use as firewood, and maybe these will reappear by tomorrow morning. Anyway, the German reputation for discipline and orderliness is questionable. Discipline only exists when somebody stands behind with a whip.

Thursday, September 13, 1945

Last night I was finally registered. Another form had to be filled out in the same way as before, with the same questions. I am now convinced that the discharge forms completed in Rimini, which lacked just our thumb prints, have landed in some wastepaper basket. After registration we were requested to surrender our money. I had nothing; they had confiscated my 300 lire when I was taken prisoner, without giving me a receipt, but I did not grieve over this small amount anyway. Some men had quite a few lire, and German marks as well, for which receipts were issued later in Rimini. The German marks were paid out when we left Camp 17, and a receipt was issued for the lire. Now all their fortunes have gone again, a fact that was recorded on their forms, but without receipts being given.

After the screening, we were allocated to a different group of one hundred in another building. That means that we have spent every night in different quarters, and tonight we are supposed to move again. However, nothing, as yet, seems to have happened. Last night was distinctly cold, since we lay on a concrete floor, and still had no blankets. My sacks are inadequate. When I place them underneath, it is cold from above, and when I use them as a cover, the cold comes from the concrete below. At least we have sunshine during the day and can store up some warmth.

I should wash my shirt and my underwear, but as I have no change of clothes, I would have to wait until they dry. Because we constantly expect to move, this is not possible.

The food here is very meagre. In the morning we are given a drinkable brew (somewhat better than the strange American coffee substitute that we had in Attichy), and at lunch and again at night, dishwater slop.

In addition, we receive a quarter loaf of doughy rye bread during the course of the day. No meat or fat is given; compared to this, even the soups in Attichy were an improvement.

They were looking for volunteers for the Foreign Legion today. Surprisingly, thirty-four applied, among them a family man with four children. The recruits have been promised leave for two weeks, and then have to report to Paris, where they will be given 9,000 francs, and will get their training in Marseilles. They have to enlist for five years and are thereafter French subjects.

Here (actually in Attichy) I met two men from Silesia, one a farmer, the other a farm labourer. They are not exactly "church lights," but they are clean, tidy, and decent. We will try to stay together. You are formed and moulded into a beast of the herd here, and I repeatedly ask myself why I, totally content to be a solitary person, have to be exposed to this herd life. Once again I feel like the fairytale character Zwerg Nase. I could flog myself for not jumping off the train in Munich. How could I pass by my love, and even do it twice in a row? Initially, when we came from Italy, we clung to the belief that we would be released in a few days, but I really cannot imagine what kept me back the second time, when we came from Aibling. Yet, the conventional wisdom (very possibly wrong) was that, as all personal details, including family addresses, were in their long questionnaires, they would know where to find us right away. It was also held that you could neither get a job nor ration cards without producing the necessary discharge documents.

In any case, I would at least know what had happened to my loved family and maybe I could have stayed with them a little while before reporting back again. The most they could do to me would be to send me back here, and I would have seen them. Maybe for some obscure reason it is better the way things have turned out; it is hard to keep your trust in God when you have experienced such bottomless disappointment, believing that you are so close to your goal of being reunited with your loved ones only to be thrown back into abysmal uncertainty.[2]

Friday, September 14, 1945

Yesterday some of those who had made the fires, were taken to the lock-up (for one to six days). A few of the boards were returned during the night and the whole affair has ended. Today one incorrigible inmate started another fire in a sheltered corner – he surely is inviting trouble.

Today we were paraded before a medical doctor, who selected the healthiest among us. I am in that group, but not my two room-mates from Silesia.

We are therefore torn apart from each other. I could have gotten around it quite easily, but I hope to get to work and away from here soon. We hear that everybody has to work 100 days and the quicker I start, the quicker it will all be over. In all probability we will be taken to a coal mine near Saarbrücken, very interesting, furthermore, I do not share the uncanny feeling of most of the others.

Although all the sick men and those unable to work for other reasons were weeded out in Aibling, some men are still being directed to Group 4 by the doctors, and they have a prospect of being released. For the time being they will remain here until enough people have accumulated to make up a transport, a possibly endless wait.

---

2 P.s. After I returned home, I understood that everything was God-sent, for at the time *meine Lieben* were still in Bernburg in the Russian Zone. There had been no message from them and nobody in Munich knew their whereabouts. Very possibly, I would have attempted to search for them and we would never have found each other in the chaos [Author's note].

There are still some Austrians among us here and they will be transferred to a different section.

Monday, September 17, 1945

I have a minuscule hope of getting out by Christmas. Some say that the 100-day period starts from the date of our arrival here, and that was 11 September. Others think they have heard that everybody has to serve 600 hours. Whatever the case, we could be eligible by the middle of December; yet, personally, I have a saddening feeling that January will be included. The plan is to take us first to a main camp in Metz, on Wednesday. Hopefully there will be a chance to write letters there. The Bavarian mail is working again.

Wednesday, September 19, 1945

Well, we are on our way again, and it seems unlikely that we are going by way of the main camp in Metz. Rather we shall go straight to the mine in "Klein Rosseln," on the border of Lothringen and the Saar district.

It is supposed to be only thirty kilometres from Saaralb, but we have been on the move since this morning and have made only a few kilometres so far. We have been standing at a small station en route to Metz, but we are not moving.

Last night we were divided into new companies, and those unfit for underground work were taken to another camp, and fit men were added to our group. These poor devils have been here for three weeks already, and are considerably weakened by the endless water slop that they have had for nourishment. The provisions in Saaralb have undoubtedly been the most miserable to date, and the soup consisted of clear warm water in which a few green spinach leaves were suspended. If you were in luck, you might come across a spoonful of potato peelings and a few noodles at the bottom. Hopefully the food will improve, otherwise not much work will be performed.

Those people unfit for underground work sadly stayed behind with their water swill, and I believe that we are the luckier ones.

The others may remain a bit longer with their slop, and then they may be sent to the main camp to be distributed to different work commandos. They will certainly be searched again and who knows when they will start to work?

Excepting the provisions, it has not been too bad in Saaralb, much better in any case than Attichy. We had more freedom and, apart from the nightly roll call, the French guards were unobtrusive. The days passed quickly, with standing in the food line-ups three times a day. Meanwhile I had time to darn my socks, and on Sunday I washed my shirt and underwear. There was nothing to read. Last night I exchanged two cigarettes for a book with a man from the neighbouring camp. I finished reading it on our railway trip, but at least I have something with which to barter. There are still quite a few people who have books, but these you can get only in exchange for another book.

Thursday, September 20, 1945

Well, late last night, in the dark, we arrived here in "Klein Rosseln," where we disembarked with much shouting from the French guards. We marched for about half an hour uphill, were met by a tinsel-glistening German company chief, and were led into a relatively decent barracks camp. The atmosphere is military, rather strange, since everything militaristic has been completely disallowed. In Aibling every ornament had to be taken off, while here the Sergeant Majors are full of glitter!

To our great delight, we were served coffee and everybody received a third of a loaf of bread. This morning the inevitable search was made, but not much was confiscated. There was nothing to take anymore! Still, this time they collected all our legal papers (the paybooks we had already turned over in Saaralb). It was here that they took my driver's licence away. I hope to get it back later.

There are several camps here. Ours has about 1,400 people and is called "Underworld," as everybody is working underground. Next to us is the "Rose garden," where the surface workers stay. The landscape is beautiful, with wooded hills all around, and you do not notice the coal pit. Some of the people in this camp have been here for three months already. It is rumoured that everybody has to work ninety shifts. The first men will have reached this goal on 10 October, and we are full of anticipation to see if they will get their release. A transport from Norway arrived just before us; clearly those of us from Italy are not the only unfortunate ones.

Apparently we are not provided with work clothing. In that case I will have to use my uniform. Until now I have tried to keep it reasonably clean, even if my shirt is falling to pieces.

Friday, September 21, 1945

Forty men, who were selected yesterday, left today to work underground. First they were checked over by the doctor, who rejected some of them. I have not been examined until now but I hope that my turn comes soon so that I can go underground, as it is likely that I will be released after ninety shifts. Besides, wintry weather is imminent, and there is more protection underground from the elements. In addition, the provisions are slightly better for underground workers. Beginning today, we receive 750 grams of bread, 50 grams of fat, warm soup once a day, and coffee twice a day. We get one litre of soup, but not many solids; at least the liquid is not as watery as in Saaralb. The others get 125 grams less bread and less fat.

Thirty-three men were taken today to build the barracks. We have to be content with our present accommodation in the so-called "dining room" until the barracks are finished. We lie on iron beds and have been promised straw bags. Unfortunately there are no blankets.

Those, who have not been appointed to any special job, are supposed to undertake general clean-up work. I reported to an earth-shovelling commando so that I would get used to shovelling again. I felt like a convalescent who, after a long sickness, tries to walk again. For nearly half a year I have done nothing physical, and my hands have to get used to holding a shovel. This short practice session is very useful; those who were underground today returned exhausted and with blistered hands. I am apprehensive of only two things, the dust and the low headroom underground. Some of the workings are only 60 cm high and I do not understand how one can work there. If you are lucky you can get into a higher working area, some of which are supposedly two metres high, and in these you would not even have to stoop.

I bartered a night shirt yesterday, in exchange for eight cigarettes. It will be good for my work, as the shirt from my uniform is disintegrating. Today I have started sewing work pants, which I am making from a sack.

Everyone was ordered today to the painter, who decorated our uniforms with a large "PG" on the back, and on the knees of the pants. I had hoped to be spared because the Americans put the "PW" only on the American garments that were given to the prisoners, but here they put it on German uniforms also.

The head of one of the young fellows was shaved yesterday – he was kicked and chased across the yard. He had stolen trousers from a comrade to sell them to a civilian in the mine. He will be taken away to serve in the search for underground mines. Hopefully his example will help to curb the stealing.

A person who had been recaptured after he had tried to escape was brought in during the evening roll call. First he had to stand barefoot in a big puddle in the centre of the yard so that he could be seen by everybody. Later his head was sheared and he was chased with a cane by the French. Quite possibly he too will have to go and search for mines. However, the new edict is that all escapees will be shot on sight – anyway that is what our German camp leader asserts.

Monday, September 24, 1945

Yesterday we were finally allocated. I am going to the night-shift in the Wendel shaft where I will work for the first time tonight. It is supposed to be the closest shaft, only twenty minutes walk away. The others are said to be quite a bit farther, up to forty-five minutes away.

We moved from the big hall yesterday and are now living with thirty-three others in a reasonably cozy room. I have my bed in a corner on the third level, have fabricated a shelf on the wall, and finally have my own nook. I do not need to live entirely out of my rucksack anymore. The bed is good, with springy wire netting, and I even have a straw bag, although unfortunately it contains no straw. There are no blankets. However, at the moment it is still feasible to do without. It will be different when the winter sets in. Hopefully we will be given a stove. The food is still inadequate as, in reality, we only live on bread. Today the soup was even more watery than in Saaralb; I found thirteen peas in one litre of clear water.

I have finished my sack pants and they definitely look good. I have been asked five times whether I am a professional tailor.

A stage was recently constructed. It was completed at the very last moment on Sunday, and was immediately initiated. It provides for a unique mixture of theatre and variety programs and these have turned out to be a real hit, much better than the silly variety programs in Rimini. Unfortunately it was too cold for me to sit outside without a coat.

Tuesday, September 25, 1945

Now I have experienced my first shift. It was very interesting and not as bad as I had anticipated. In the first place there was not as much dust as I thought there would be. But of course we did not do very much; it was enough of a test just to get used to the environment on the first day. It might be totally different when we are fully occupied.

The pit has not been in full use because it has been under water for a while, and they are only now starting to bring it back into production.

Well then, at 2100 hours we had to be ready. First came the roll call, then the French guards took over, and we marched in leisurely fashion down into the valley, using the same road that we had taken from the railway. Right behind the rails is the workshop, rather dilapidated and with the windows broken. The first act was to take a numbered tin disc from a big board in the entry room, where many chains dangled from the ceiling. Everything you want to leave behind you is hung on these chains, which are pulled up to the ceiling. This allows you to dry your work clothes overnight. Right beside it, is a shower with hot water, where you can wash after your shift. After having done this, you then pull down your clean clothes, change, and raise the dirty work clothes back up, where they remain until your next shift.

First I was undecided whether to go down just in my shirt or to keep my jacket. Some said it was cold, others mentioned that it was very warm. After debating this way and that, I decided to risk taking my jacket, and it was just as well, because conditions were very draughty.

Initially we had to wait a very long time; then we had roll call again in the corridor; then we passed through a gate and everybody was given a miner's lamp; thence to another gate where you left your tin I.D. tags and were given others in their place; and then along stairs and a passage to the hoist tower. Up to this point the guards accompanied us. Here we waited again before we entered the skip cage. This comprises three tiers of cages stacked on top of each other, each holding about twelve closely packed people. The ride down to 580 metres was very fast, and I knew from my experience of a visit to a potash mine that my eardrums would pop, so I had placed cotton in them.

At the bottom, we entered a vault measuring about five metres high. It was 2215 hours by this time. Again we waited before a civilian led us a little farther, to a machine room where we had a further wait. The civilian workers now arrived in dribs and drabs, until finally the shift boss arrived to issue the work orders.

By now it was 2300 hours. We walked along an endless passage, about three metres high. There was no masonry, but at three metre intervals there was an arch of strong *T*-rails behind which lagging posts were packed. Initially the walkway was dry, but then we came to a caved-in section where the *T*-rails were quite compressed. Half of the walkway had collapsed, and there was water and muck everywhere. Balancing on the ground rails, we managed to stay fairly dry, but it got worse as we proceeded further along. Altogether we walked about three-quarters of an hour before we reached a spot where a conveyor belt ran into a side gallery.

Here we turned and moved alongside the conveyor belt. Then we had to climb up a ladder, finally reaching the stratum where the coal seam was located. It was 2400 hours; two hours had passed already. Now our path angled quite steeply uphill. We had to crawl on all fours and it was very slippery. The whole area was supported by three rows of strong adjustable iron props (similar to huge jacks with cross-caps on top). The rows were about 1.2 metres apart, and each row was generally about one metre wide. To the left of the middle row was the chute, a metal conduit with a continuous chain located in the trough. At about one metre intervals along the chain there was an upright plate to rake the material along. The chain returns to the surface along a large pipe to the right, next to the chute. On the other side of the chute there is a pile of assorted broken rocks. Beyond the right hand row of props is the coal seam, measuring about 1.45 metres across.

We crawled along an endless uphill stretch, but not quite to the end. The whole length is supposed to be 280 metres. We were distributed at about two-metre intervals. Everyone had a big shovel shaped like a giant salad spoon. Then we sat down and waited for the conveyor belt to start moving. We waited until nearly 0100 hrs.

Meanwhile a civilian miner was busy working with a jackhammer, and it was fascinating to watch how the head bit in, as if through butter, and the coal fell apart. Then he shook the hammer back and forth gently, as if using an iron rod, and a big piece caved in. After the conveyor started, our shovelling was quite successful. Shovelling from a kneeling position was easier than anticipated, as we worked on an upward slant and the rock surface was smooth. Then you simply scooped the loose material, to your left, onto the slide; from there the rock glides onto the conveyor belt and falls into the wagons farther down. You have to watch out, when shovelling, that no big lumps are suddenly dislodged. My rock-blasting experience at 'Lepiko,' as we called our farm in Estonia, serves me well here, and if I am watchful I will notice the onset of crumbling. I was very careful in those places where the coal is about one metre from the support. With uncanny foresight, I stayed in the protection of the support. That proved to be a wise precaution. On one occasion a huge rock slab weighing several hundred pounds came crashing down right next to me. Of course that did not happen often. The civilian miner approached and, very impressed, reckoned that the slab could easily have crushed three people.

The rocks have to be thrown across the slide, a difficult task because it is very low and the opening is restricted by the compressed air pipe which runs above the slide. To top it all off, the rocks were as heavy as lead.

After two hours the conveyor belt stopped again and was idle for quite a while. Only at the very end did it start up again. At 0515 hours we finished and began to go back. All in all we had worked little more than two hours. Our return was slightly quicker than our entry. The shower was very congested, and once we were back in the camp we had coffee and lay down to sleep until 1430 hours.

Another person escaped, this time a worker from our cross-shift as it was returning from work. Now there will be more guards. Someone else was caught stealing bread. He was sheared and locked up. They should be punished more severely to put an end to the thieving.

Monday, October 1st, 1945

It is one week since I started underground, and up to now it has been very interesting. It is always midnight by the time we are allotted to, and arrive at, a workplace, and at 0500 hrs we start to get ready for our return; that means four to five hours of work. The civilians who work with us are mostly from Lorraine. They all speak German but chose to become French, and some of them are rather malicious. So far I have gotten on quite well with them.

I have been working together with another comrade at the same spot, a so-called "warp." An old, kind, and quiet civilian also works there. At this warp, which is in about the centre of the stratum, the coal is compressed and makes a bend downwards. As the chute cannot be bent, the rock above has to be removed to get a somewhat straighter line. The rock continues to splinter afterwards, resulting in more headroom so that I can stand upright at that spot. Working on the rock is not quite so dusty as with the coal and is more varied. Between times they blast and then work with the jackhammer, and the place has to be supported and reinforced with props. There is a helter-skelter of supports and posts and caps here, criss-crossed to suit the immediate need. Free passage is secured for the chute only.

At 0200 hrs there is a 20-minute break for our piece of bread, and our old co-worker always gives us a sandwich. On the whole, I do not think it is as exhausting as I had anticipated. Only the crouching in the coal seams is arduous. The most exhausting night for me was when I had to crawl down into the workplace and back out three times, simply to fetch some tools.

The coal layer in our eighth level is comparatively thick, about 1.45 metres. One can almost stand at the point where it has recently been removed. The rock under the coal is very slippery, and runs steeply upwards, so that you slide continually. In one stretch measuring 250 metres, the coal seam rises 80 metres. The pressure from above must be tremendous and the pieces of wood are quite flattened between the rock and the supports. Despite the iron props, the ceiling sags so much that you must crawl on all fours on the far side of the chute. When the latter is moved, the iron supports are hammered out and removed, while the wood, being left, is soon buried by the relentless pressure of the rock.

At some places the coal seems to be quite hard. This week they blasted several times at the entrance to the level. There was a weak and muffled detonation followed by a horrible choking stench. However, the draught is strong enough to dispel it quickly.

Then there is a kind of milling cutter or fraise which saws coal into layers. It is pulled up slowly on a rope and causes a fabulous racket and unbearable dust. It passes by our spot on the warp. Sometimes the sawed coal collapses by itself, making it difficult for us to get past; we have to crawl along the chute. Small people have an advantage underground and I have hit my head several times against the pieces of wood. I sewed a pad into my homemade cap today – I hope this will cushion the cracks to my head. In addition to my sack pants, I have now made a sack jacket to wear over my uniform. My pants have prompted a search for sacks, because everybody wants sack pants now. One of the men offered a half-loaf of bread for a sack, but that is real robbery.

The provisions are now considerably better. There was an inspection whose recommendations were that the soup had to be improved. It now contains noodles but no potatoes. We are supposed to get 100 grams of potatoes daily, but we do not get any. Nevertheless, we do get a half-loaf of bread (750 grams) daily, along with some fat and marmalade. Before this, there was either fat or marmalade, and the marmalade days were rather poor. On Sunday everybody was given a whole loaf of bread, and for once we were able to eat really satisfactorily. Reputedly the calories will be raised by about 1,000.

All kinds of rumours concerning our discharge have been in circulation over the last few days. As so often before, the cause is the sorting of people according to the zones in which they have their home addresses. Another rumour is that we will become civilians, to be obliged to work here for another three months. I do not believe anything that they say and still hope to be released after ninety days, during mid- or late-January. I have given up hope of being with *meiner Liebsten* at Christmas. If only it were possible to write.

Friday, October 5, 1945

Today is Else's birthday and I am totally with my little girl in all my thoughts. Four weeks ago I felt certain that I would celebrate this day with my family. Now I will not even celebrate Christmas with them. However, next year we will be together for sure. In a few days we will see if there is any truth in the ninety-day idea, because the initial arrivals will have accomplished their allotted tasks. There are many who doubt that a release will occur. We have a lot of new people, professional miners this time, who also believed that they would be discharged. When they arrived, they told us that they would be obliged to work here as civilians but nothing has happened – they are prisoners just like us. The rumour persists that they have come to replace those who have completed their time.

The food is not bad now, but very monotonous. In the morning and evening there is bread, and for lunch noodle soup. There are never any vegetables. We could have purchased some apples today, but we have not been given any money yet.

We are supposed to get ten francs per day, five francs to use in the camp and five francs to be kept until our release. Before now you could only get beer with the five francs camp money, but today, for the first time, there were apples (fifteen francs per kilogram). Hopefully there will be more fruit later, after we get our first pay. I do not care much for the beer.

Finally we have straw for our beds and we sleep like lords. Even without blankets it is warm enough. Those on the lower bunks do complain of cold though and would like a stove, but I hope it does not arrive too soon. I anticipate only smoke, fumes, and that we will suffocate in the upper bunks.

Monday, October 8, 1945

The second week has passed, and I think that the time has gone really quickly. After you have worked two shifts, it is already Wednesday, and then you start to look forward to the coming Sunday, when you can sleep blissfully for one night. Sleeping in the forenoon is unsatisfactory. In the morning between 0700 and 0730 hrs, we return from the mine, have coffee in the camp, and then wait for roll call. That is a nuisance as everybody naturally longs to lie down. This was allowed earlier. However, because some night-shift workers just stood around with their hands in their pockets watching roll call, the rule was changed and the French ordered everybody to attend. In the end it is always the thoughtlessness of some of the Germans that creates difficulties for the rest. The roll call lasts until about 0830 hrs. Our German camp leader protracts matters by wasting words on inessential issues. Then we can sleep until soup is served for the night shift at around 1500 hrs. The afternoon passes in a twinkling, without our being able to start anything worthwhile. At 1700 hrs there is roll call again, and between 1800 hrs and 1900 hrs the cold provisions are handed out. The rations have to be distributed to our rooms, and that is usually accompanied by quarreling. Then coffee is again served – accept, eat, and prepare to leave for work. At 0815 hrs the first night shift leaves for St. Charles. Luckily, we from the Wendel shaft have the shortest route and leave only at 2100 hrs.

Yesterday at roll call, the camp leader read a long address from the camp physician to the camp administration and the Red Cross. All the abuses and shortcomings were listed. Inadequate housing, poor barracks, no fuel (despite our being in the coal pits, the kitchen does not get enough coal for cooking, and no coal may be brought from the mine) no blankets, no overcoats, poor clothing, no change of underwear, poor footwear, no medication or bandages, poor provisions. According to the camp physician we get only 2,000 calories, while we should have 3,500. Whether this complaint was forwarded I don't know.

Maybe he read it to us to demonstrate his zeal and solicitude. I cannot help feeling that the German camp leaders are primarily eager to serve the mine bosses and the military forces. The good soup last week was served only because a commission had been expected. First a major came on Tuesday, and we had thick noodle soup. To our surprise it was still good on Wednesday and Thursday. But later we heard that a commission had been expected and that it only arrived on Friday – some civilians from Paris from the Ministry, along with some other dignitaries. So Friday saw an excellent soup, very thick. However, since Saturday we have been back to our slop – about ten peas, or beans, and some bran to make it look less watery.

Today there were even some bread crumbs floating about. When the mine management supplied more, in anticipation of the commission, our kitchen staff should have made an extra watery soup, to show how bad the conditions really are in this place.

I try the best I can to enjoy the "little amenities" of life. Foremost, the hot shower when you leave the mine. I pity those pigs who cannot even pull themselves together to take their dirty clothes off. Some merely extend their hands under the shower from afar, or, at most, strip only the upper parts of their bodies. And then they are surprised to find lice. It is horrible to see how many men are going to ruin. I don't think the Russians could be worse. Stealing too persists, despite all punishment.

I cannot stress enough how much I enjoy the beauty of our natural surroundings here. The camp is situated on a knoll, around which are hills covered with beech forests and only now are these starting to get their autumn colouring. All you see to the South is the towering chimney from the Wendel mine. Otherwise there is nothing to remind you of a coal district. The camp leads in terraces down the south slope and from here there is an unimpeded view into the valley, where the little town of Forbach makes a picturesque sight. (It reminds me of the other Forbach[3] and our friends von Cube, but I guess it is only the name, as that place had no beauty.)

This little town is about six kilometres away, and beyond it another wooded hill stretches towards the ruins of a castle. And beyond that is a higher, bare hill where the Saar boundary supposedly runs. I am immeasurably grateful to have this beautiful landscape. I can draw so much energy and confidence from it during this trying period, and I have the imperturbable belief that I will find *meine Lieben* again.

Along with all the other disagreeable facts we have had to contend with, there is the senseless gossip of my comrades. Either they were quarreling about provisions, or they were lamenting our hopeless situation. One hundred times a day they repeated what bad luck it was to be in French captivity, because the French had been the last ones to release their prisoners after the First World War - some had been repatriated only in 1923, – etc., etc. It is awful when people think that they must talk persistently and, lacking something to talk about, repeat themselves constantly.

Tuesday, October 9, 1945

Last night, to everyone's surprise, a truck arrived to deliver American provisions. These, subsidized consignments from the International Red Cross, were intended to build up the work force to help reconstruct France. These allocations will supposedly be made every day, mainly in the form of tins. By this

---

3 An estate in Warthegau.

morning we had already had a good creamy soup, and at lunch the soup was again good. If this keeps up at the same rate, we can be very happy indeed.

Today we were given a good, large piece of soap. Now everybody can keep clean, but I am afraid some rather prefer to remain dirty, and instead barter the soap for cigarettes. On our trip from Saaralb, it was pitiful to watch what a lively exchange of goods was conducted with the French guards. The French were eager to get soap and there were many idiots who exchanged the lovely Palmolive that we had just received from the Americans for a small piece of bread. Later, when they got dirty in the mine, they regretted this, and then they started to steal.

A little while ago all three of our mine commandos (Wendel, Kargan, and St. Charles) had to elect a confidential representative. He is supposed to be the link with the camp leader and the mine management. How the election was handled I do not know, as we had just returned from our night shift and had gone to bed. The early shift had gone to work so the election was left to the noon shift. I do not feel that I can confide in this representative. His first deed yesterday was to distribute some newly arrived coats, jackets, and pants. The best coats were immediately taken by the camp dignitaries, who already sit in the shelter. The camp police, who have everything in duplicate and possess fur coats and blankets, now show off in their new coats. The pitiful remnants were given to the representative to distribute. I was simply told: "Be happy, you already have a pullover," and I did not get anything. However, those who had earlier bartered away their underwear, were given clothes, which some men immediately exchanged for cigarettes and bread.

Yesterday, three people escaped. At night, one jumped onto a passing train on his way from work and was gone. For a person who has his own farm, his own work, and food, and need not report immediately to the authorities, this may be the best choice. However, this does not apply to me as I need release papers. I would have to report somewhere, then I would be returned to a camp like Aibling or whatever, and the whole odyssey would start all over again. I think it wiser to be patient and to endure the discomfort, because one day it must end. I am still hopeful about only ninety days of forced labour. And it is certainly possible to cope here at the moment. We have a good roof over our heads and do not need to struggle with tents and primitive huts in the cold of the winter, like in Attichy. Besides, if the food stays as it is at present, we can be content. I am certain that those of us who are in the mine are best off, with the exception of those working on farms. In other work commandos the provisions seem to be much worse. Some newcomers who have been working on a woodcutting detail are given only half a loaf of bread and a little watery soup, just as in Saaralb. At least we miners apparently have the best care, and the work is definitely bearable. In winter we even have a dry and warm workplace, and I would not like to change with those surface workers who are outside in the rain and cold, and lack proper clothing.

Wednesday, October 10, 1945

This week I am still working at the warp with the kind old man. As our workplace is exactly half way between the 560- and the 480-metre levels, we do not ride to the 560 level anymore, only to climb again. Instead we ride to the 480 level and crawl down-slope, and this is far more convenient. The 480-metre level is also much drier, warmer, and better to walk along. Down below at the 560 level, there is always an icy cold wind and you are frozen by the time that you arrive at your workplace. When you climb up again, you sweat. A warm draft blows at the 480 level, and I do not need to carry my uniform jacket with me anymore. If you are lucky, and the chain has been removed from the chute, you can just slide down there in a twinkling.

We were given new cardboard helmets, at the mine today. They are featherlight and should be good protection against head injury. (My padded cap had proved to be of good service as well.) Along with the helmets we were given English miner's lamps. These are attached like bicycle lights to the front of your helmet. The battery is worn at the back of your belt. You can dim the light or turn it off. They are lighter by far than the old ones, and much more convenient when walking or crawling, because both hands are free. The old ones were superior to work with as they could be stood- or hung-up, thereby lighting up the whole area. The new ones give off only one straight beam of light, like a bicycle headlight. Yet the old ones were heavy, four kilograms, and a bother to carry when crawling along. The real miners attached them to the front of their belts and they dangled between their legs, but I could not get used to this and carried mine in my hand.

Monday, October 15, 1945

Today the third week has passed, and twelve weeks remain for the completion of ninety shifts. Except now, I too, start to doubt these ninety shifts, as men who have reached that goal are still here, and nothing is heard about their release. Among the gossipers the rumour of the discharges has given way to a more exciting topic, discord between America and Russia. It is rumoured that the anticipated registration according to our military training and experience is connected with this. Thus, according to the civilians in the mine, the French newspapers talk openly of this imminent rupture. It may be that we can expect great turmoil, and the times seem to be working in favour of Russia, at least so it seems to us in the absence of unbiased news coverage.

It is interesting to notice the gradual change in opinion. At first everybody in English captivity in Italy praised the Americans. Supposedly everything would be better under them. Better provisions, earlier releases, etc., etc. After we came to the Americans in Aibling, full of expectation and hope, our disappointment was great – we had moved from the frying pan into the fire. Certainly, now that we are under the French, everybody agrees that our British captors were by far the best and fairest. Nevertheless there are quite a few who are convinced that the real saviours are the Russians – they expect their salvation from that quarter. There are allegedly several men from the Russian Zone and they reputedly maintain that the Russian troops behave very well. They display placards with the inscription, "Who has smashed Germany to pieces – we or the others?"

That, of course, impresses the average soldier. Only when these propagandists become too bold, by maintaining that Russia has already released most of her prisoners, do they meet with disbelief and ridicule.

Yesterday I slept through the entire Sunday and was interrupted only by the fetching of food and the roll call. I felt exhausted, possibly less from work than from a cold in my nose and throat, however, this was cured by sleep. Now I feel much better, I have washed my underwear and mended my work pants, the knees of which had become worn. Now Monday is over. No time is left for reading, even though the greater part of the day is not spent in productive work. Most of the day is passed away idling and on the walk to and from the mine, with all its attendant counting. The roll call in the camp takes longer each time because there is always someone missing. Sometimes, after a long search, they find him in the washroom or in one of the other rooms. Today the missing person could not be found and I presume he did actually escape.

There are a few lamenters who wail and complain all day. What we have to endure! What we have to go through! I can feel only sorrow for them and will not allow my life to be burdened by their persistent complaints. In general, life as a soldier was just as bad, and I try to focus on what has improved since then. What gets me down is being without news. Oh love, my love, when will we finally be able to communicate! When we at last have news of each other, everything will be bearable.

Monday, October 22, 1945

Last week we were each given two blankets, and they were actually new ones! Jackets and pants are also in prospect. Supposedly they are here already, but the paint, needed for the "PG" emblems, is lacking. We also have an oven, and apparently coal is being delivered. Now they produce heat senselessly and it is suffocatingly hot.

Because of the extra rations from the Red Cross, we enjoyed good food for a week. Initially these were supposed to last for three months, but the luxuries have ceased already. Instead, we are given vegetables and better soup. Unfortunately, the small soup serving we received in the morning has been discontinued. Last week one person in the sick bay died of diphtheria. Death is allegedly here in the camp. Will our relatives ever be told?

Letters are being forwarded now within the French Zone, but I have not a single address to which I can write. The only remaining hope is that deliveries will soon be made to the American Zone as well. How I wish to receive a Christmas letter from my love. I have long given up hope of being with my dear ones by then, but I count on being reunited with them by spring. The ninety-day rumour has been shown to be false. (There are many who have accumulated more than 100 days.) They will not keep us here forever.

Monday, October 29, 1945

Well five weeks have passed – thirty shifts. Time goes quickly. Supposedly the Austrians will be released, and this time the story seems to be true. That could mean that our own liberation is not too far off either. I count on about January or February. The Alsatians, followed by those from Lorraine, are returning home too, and there are even some transports from Russia. They were starved, and eighty men out of 1,500 died en route. The civilian miners, who are nearly all communist, have become rather demoralized and pensive.

Quite a few of the prisoners still attempt escape. The day before yesterday four, and yesterday two more. There is much talk about the practicality of escaping, but most agree that, without papers, you can neither stay in one place nor report anywhere. If part of Germany had remained unoccupied, most would certainly consider taking off. One escapee was brought back. He must have been short of wits, for after circling the camp three times during the night, he was recognized by a camp civilian in the morning, being seized forthwith. Most people lament the barbed wire, and the guards who always accompany us to work. I see neither of them, but I do suffer from the uncongeniality of my co-prisoners (the word "comrade" is not apt, when you consider all the quarrels, etc.).

Dirty, ragged, itchy and ulcerous – you cannot detect any German cleanliness. I guess it only exists when it is compulsory. I have come to the conclusion that one of the greatest evils is smoking. Many have given soap, underwear, and clothing in exchange for tobacco, and now run about in rags. In addition there is the garnering of cigarette butts. I thought only the most depraved beggars did that. The moment we get out of the pit and into the washroom hall, these people start to pick up scattered cigarette butts and, even worse, immediately place those that are still glimmering in their mouths – people without dignity and honour. Fortunately most of the men in our room are orderly and clean, although my bed neighbour smacks his lips so noisily that the sound penetrates to my very core. Often he saves a piece of bread, which he then devours with great smacking noises.

After some hesitation, I finally made an appointment with the dentist. One Italian filling has fallen out. Anyway, I have had some respite for half a year. We will see what the French dentist in Forbach accomplishes. It will be quite a while before I get my turn, and some men have already been waiting for four weeks.

There is much criticism of our German camp physician for discharging patients to the mine prematurely. Some were still half-sick and the French doctor in the camp had to send them back. He looks like a butcher, not a physician, but his task is not easy as there are many shirkers and malingerers. For example a man with a scratch on his hand made a red pencil streak on his arm to simulate blood poisoning.

Sunday, November 4, 1945

Today, Sunday, I had bad luck, for I had to work. Only four of us, selected from the whole camp, had to go. Sunday work has been generally discontinued. Another three men have been appointed from the two other shifts. The reason is that they have allocated too few people to the warp on the eighth level, and the men cannot keep pace with the steady progress being made. We have now encountered fifteen metres of pure rock, and the coal is at a uniformly greater depth. The rock is drilled and blasted, then the chunks have to be heaved across the chute, to be stacked on the other side. In general, I am quite happy with this job. There was one day when I had to erect a row of props, and that was much more exhausting. As these metal props weigh about a hundred-weight, there is too little strength in one's bones to handle them.

Thursday, the 1st of November, we had a day off. This did not work out too well for us from the eighth level, as our shifts had been changed, placing us now on early shift, so that we had to start early on Friday. The work is still the same. The midday shift is now the conveyor shift during which, to the accompaniment of much sweating and shouting, the men have to remove successive batches of coal. They come out black like negroes. The night shift readjusts the chute, while the morning shift takes out the props and resets them.

Generally speaking the conveyor shift requires the most men. Our detail consists at the moment of 150 men, which is about double the number on our previous night shift. This entails quite a few drawbacks. Endless delays in leaving, and great congestion in the washroom. You are lucky if you can emerge early, get properly washed, and can avoid rubbing against those men covered in coal dust.

But there is one advantage - you can sleep at night, even if you have to get up at 0400 hrs. Besides, the sleep is more satisfying than during the day time – you can never replace night slumber. A great source of distress at night is the overheated room. This foolish overheating is a real curse.

The weather is beautifully autumnal and still quite warm. The beech forests are starting to lose their gold, and it is hard to believe that they were still quite green when we arrived. Winter is approaching and this seems to have some bearing on the innumerable escapes by the prisoners. Probably they want to take advantage of the last of the good weather. Almost every day one or two people disappear from camp, or work, or while en route to work at night. The watch is getting more infuriated. Escapees' quarters are thoroughly searched, and all knives are confiscated. We have also been searched on our way to and from work. One escapee was wounded after being shot at, and four men were killed by hidden mines. It is too risky, and it is better to hold out a bit longer and keep your bones intact.

Sunday, November 11, 1945

Today we were supplied with form letters and can write to any of the zones. That kindles the hope in me that I will receive news from *meinen Lieben* in return. Only the Austrians and Saarlanders were not given forms, as they are going to be released next week for sure. They only have to wait for substitutes.

Escaping continues, despite the warnings of the camp leader. Today at roll call he gave a stirring speech based on his old slogan: "Endure, hold out, and keep your mouth shut."

He is absolutely right to remind us of the folly of risking being shot to death while attempting to escape, after having survived the war and ensuing upheavals. Yesterday another man was wounded while escaping. He died later. Three others were captured. Fewer people would attempt flight if the food had remained more nourishing. The soup is getting thinner every day. Instead of carrots, they use horrible water-turnips, and no flour or groats are added to give the food more body. I always try to save a piece of bread to crumble into the swill. You can manage on one half-loaf of bread. We don't starve, but we get inadequate food for our strenuous tasks.

The old civilian co-worker on our night shift did not stay with us, and we now have a false rotter at the warp. He was reputedly an overseer before the war, but because he had been a member of the Nazi Party he was not allowed to retain his rank. At work he is inconsistent, clumsy, and ignorant. I wonder how he ever became an overseer. Apparently all you need is a big, glib mouth. That, he certainly has, to ingratiate himself with his superiors, to tell tales behind his co-workers' backs, to discredit the Nazis when he was one himself, and now to be a great Frenchman. Watching him placing props at work makes me sick. He seldom gets the right measurements. When the prop is too long, he invariably cuts off too much. And when it is finally in place, he batters it just long enough to dislodge it. Then he positions it anyhow, hoping that nobody will touch it.

Since last week we have also had another disagreeable fellow at level eight. He has just become the overseer and was introduced by his predecessor. Possibly he will stay here. His nickname is "The Terror of the Prisoners" because of his sudden outbursts of swearing and shouting. Apparently he is somewhat crazy and our civilian co-workers do not take him seriously. Generally they are not too intelligent either. They know only their present skills, inherited down the generations – I think that with some common sense I could do much better.

Throughout, I was never given general guidance at our warp. Every shift worked on its own, and usually impractically. Neither of the overseers were able to follow a sensible line. At last a senior overseer arrived, raised hell, and imposed some order. As we progressed further and further with the "hanging wall," we blasted enormous quantities of rock, and did not know how to dispose of it. From below, we now concentrate on carefully peeling some of the waste rock from the "footwall," located underneath the fault zone, thus exposing the coal seam. An additional advantage is the closer location of the ore chute.

Monday 26 November 1945

Today it is my birthday. I know that my love is right here with me. My birthday wish is to get some news from my dear ones. Although I have the letters from them here with me, I will not take them out as I will be overcome by emotion. Those celebrating their birthdays here are allowed an extra scoop of soup. I have saved my helping of special carrot soup for tonight and will spare some bread for tomorrow. Instead of turnips, we now have carrots in the soup, which is sometimes quite thick. Today, for instance, it contained a little flour and Maggi.

Several truckloads of carrots arrived about three weeks ago, and were carelessly and foolishly dumped into big pits, where they were inadequately covered with wood shavings. Now of course they are rotting, steaming, and stinking, and have to be used at once. Even so, more than half have gone to waste.

Last Tuesday the Austrians got away for sure – the Saarlanders have to wait, but their turn should come soon. The rumours continue to circulate amongst the rest of us, one that is going around, for example, is that the SS and Party members will replace us, and that we will be moved to St. Avold or, according to some, northern France. I do not believe in this next parole, but I continue to hope for a release at the beginning of 1946.

I have completed fifty-one shifts. I could not, however, work since last Wednesday, when I was admitted to the sick bay with a festering wound on my back. This had developed gradually. First I hit my tail bone against a pole while I was crawling, and as is always the case when you have a sore spot, you keep on bumping it wherever you go. This is especially so when you have to crawl uphill and shovel, particularly when the place is crammed to the ceiling with coal. My injury became more painful and swollen until, finally, it burst, and the pus started running. By now it has begun to heal, so that I can lie on my back again. There are about sixty-one of us on the sick list, with another thirty in their own rooms (out of 1,400 men), nearly all with festering wounds. Hopefully, the doctor will keep us in bed a bit longer. Initially he discharged the sick back into the pits while they still had big open wounds.

I had to shave off my beard before I was admitted – it must have been quite impressive, as not a day passed without someone admiring it. I reminded the doctor that I had only a few razor blades and no soap.

"That is what the barber is for," was his reply. So I went to the barber, who removed the beard with a machine and then said that he had no soap either. Thus in the end I was not given a good shave and had to use my own last razor blade. I hope the release will come soon, otherwise I will just have to grow another beard.

December 4, 1945

I have been back at work since last Wednesday. This strange doctor discharged me too soon. The wound was still open, and because in this narrow space I am apt to bump it repeatedly, it has opened further and is festering again. I was discharged because we had to vacate the sick bay as it was needed for infectious disease cases. At first the upheaval upset us, but now we are happy because we have more space, and this larger place is not as easily overheated as the previous one.

Last week we had no water – a real disaster. The first day, coffee was unavailable, but the cook had sufficient water for soup. On the second day there was not even soup, and we had to be content with half a loaf of bread and some cheese. Beer was the only available liquid, but in insufficient quantity, and many went without. On the third day, everyone took containers to collect water from the pit, but the supply at camp was running again by the time we returned, and we were given a good noodle soup. Our food generally has improved. For the last few days we have received soup in the morning as well as in the evening, with an additional 50 grams of margarine, and usually marmalade, cheese, and sometimes even sausage. When we have soup servings twice daily, the half-loaf of bread is almost adequate.

Those people in the sick bay, who had not suffered an injury were unfairly given only one-fifth of a loaf of bread, 17 grams of fat, and 7 grams of meat, along with a drinkable soup. As a special reward, everybody who does not miss a day's work during the week is given a whole loaf of bread. Due to my five days of sick leave, I was not rewarded.

Today is a holiday – Barbara's day. Many complain about these holidays, as they do not know what to do with themselves. They are bored, and are hungry all day long. The holidays are always much too short for me, what with washing clothes, mending socks, and patching pants. Only a very short time is left for any reading. A camp library has been established under the auspices of a clergyman. At the moment there are only thirty-five books – what is that for 1,400 men? Some still have their own books, and the owners are offered a reward of a loaf of bread in return for donating them to the library. I gave mine in exchange for a half-loaf and 50 grams of fat. Now I have nothing left for private bartering and must rely on the library, which usually has no spare books.

The day before yesterday was the first of Advent. My dear ones were surely sitting together and lighting the first candle on the Advent wreath. I should not think about this because my heart grows too heavy.

December 24, 1945

Today is Christmas Eve – hard to believe, and I do not feel Christmas in my heart at all. I am in the sick bay in St. Avold, and my thoughts are with my love. My greatest wish of a letter from her was not granted. I hope that she has a letter from me and knows that I am all right. I have been here since last Tuesday. Before that I was lying with flu in the sick bay at "Klein Rosseln," and then they inexplicably moved me here, even though my illness was not serious. It all happened so suddenly that my garments from the pit were left behind. There they still hang. I did not welcome the move for other reasons either, and I wish they had left me where I was. I am afraid that my anticipated letter will get lost, and I am waiting so eagerly for some news. In any event, for the time being I am out of the pit. Lately I have not liked it anymore, especially changing my clothes. This was an ordeal, as our washroom was cut in half, and everybody was herded into one side. After you had removed your clothes it was hardly possible to budge under the trickling shower. Two or three people were crammed in, and after more or less cleaning yourself, you were smeared by those blackened individuals who pushed past you. By the time you finally found your way through the crowd to your garments, you were dirty again. In the camp itself, life improved steadily. We could smuggle enough coal from the mine to keep the room warm, and the food had improved too: twice a day a thick soup, one kilogram of bread, 51 grams of fat, and often one piece of cheese and sausage (mainly bitter blood sausage).

The closer to Christmas we approached, the higher mounted the number of escapees, they probably were all yearning to get home for the Christmas feast. One day there were eight escapes. Now I too have concluded that this is the only path to liberation. It looks as if we are the last of the dupes and all the rest are at home.

In the camp I came upon a big Christmas tree ornamented with electric candles on our roll call ground. The tree was nearly the size of the one in Reval (Tallinn) on Freedom Place, only this one was not so beautiful and was rather ragged.

Here we have nothing to remind us of Christmas and that is good – I want to be undisturbed in my thoughts of my love.

However, we were each given Christmas presents: half a packet of tobacco, five American biscuits, ten apples, and eleven dried prunes.

We lie here in a stone-walled barracks building, eight to a room with double windows, and despite the poor heating we are not cold. It is much cleaner and roomier than in the camp.

For the last three weeks the minds of the men, especially the *Unteroffiziere*, have been agitated by a manuscript reminding them of the terms of the Geneva Convention, whereby only the lower military ranks have to work and all the officers can work voluntarily. However, a decree accompanied it, indicating that they must still work above ground. The senior officers were removed after a few days and came to St. Avold. The *Unteroffiziere* had to sign a paper whereby they either agreed to work above ground or below, or refused all work. Rumour has it that anyone rejecting work will be sent to the south of France to a hunger camp.[4] Still, in "Klein Rosseln" only five signed up to work above ground, only two underground, and 300 rejected work. For the time being they are still in the mine, but after the holidays they may be taken out. Everybody is in suspense about what is going to happen. About 100 men have not signed anything. Here in St. Avold the whole business was handled in a different fashion. They had to sign a note whereby they agreed to work, except underground or in the searching of mines. But a refusal to sign meant a rejection of work, and about fifty percent have signed here.

January 1, 1946

Right after the holidays, on the 27th of December, I was released from the sick bay, and am now in the 6th division. We lie on straw in a big stable and are fairly warm. Roll call is fortunately held only once a day, at 0700 hrs. In the evening, after 1900 hrs nobody is allowed to go out, and at 2100 hrs the light has to be extinguished. Food is certainly scantier than in the command area, but still much better than in Saaralb. The soup for lunch and in the evening is thick with vegetables. In the morning there is coffee and 450 grams of bread.

---

4 Hunger camps are mentioned in Bacque (1989a). They were subjected to shortages of food, and the prisoners complained of unremitting hunger during their incarceration.

Now we have sailed into the New Year, and everybody hopes that it will soon bring our release. Last night there was a joint Evangelical and Catholic service. What the Pastor said was really good and the otherwise unadorned tree shone with genuine candles. At one end was the pulpit, and, on the opposite side, the bar, equipped with an impressive battery of beer barrels. It was announced that a New Year's party was to be held there. The altar and the Christmas tree were placed at one end of the hall, whereas the podium for the band was positioned at the other. The New Year's celebration was cancelled at the last minute, and after the service everybody had to return to their quarters immediately because two men had been caught attempting to escape. They were two orderlies who had dug a tunnel under the wall from the cellar of the sick bay, and they had planned to make their escape during New Year's night. Somebody must have reported them as they were caught shortly before they were through.

We withdrew quietly to our barn where I brewed delicious coffee from the real beans that I had saved since Italy and read my love's old letters. How glad I am that I still have them! Before now I had hesitated to take them out as I had been afraid they would distress me too much. However, rereading them now gave me much strength and trust in God. It is all too apparent that God has held his protecting hand over my loved ones and guided them during their flight. And then there was the reunion with Else. All this gave me confidence that He will continue to lead and protect my love and give her strength, so that we can be together again in the coming year.

Later, at 2030 hrs, the New Year's celebration was finally allowed. I went there, but did not expect much. Beer was consumed, the band played well, and music was made with great gusto. At 2400 hrs the camp leader said a few words for the occasion and everybody retired to bed. We had expected the ringing of bells and fireworks, but everything was calm and quiet, apart from the occasional shot from the guards. Then it was as still as can be, and a frigid, star-clear night, with frost, heralded the coming cold. Until now it had been quite unseasonably warm, a blessing for those who had no shelter. Hopefully it will not get too cold.

The accomplished camp ensemble put on an opera concert this afternoon. I do not know much about music, but I really enjoyed it. In earlier days I would not have known how to appreciate it. It is very different from the sickeningly superficial variety programs in Rimini.

Sunday, January 20, 1946

The New Year has started very cold and fuel is scarce. It is hard to believe that here, in the centre of the coal district, it is apparently impossible to get enough fuel. They are felling the last trees in the barracks yard for kitchen use, and you have to move quickly to snatch a few branches. From time to time a horse-cart load is brought in from the woods, but this is only a drop in the bucket. Those who go out to some kind of daily work, and return at night, have a chance to fetch a few old boards, and that saves us. Sometimes the guards at the gates confiscate the boards, for they are cold too.

It was still tolerable in the horse stable, as long as it was fully occupied. On the 3rd of January we were again redivided, those of us from the 6th division transferring to the 5th division, which is located in the big, dilapidated barracks building. The doors and windows are broken, with the wind blowing through the walls. Some rooms have been repaired superficially, and the windows have been covered with cardboard. Primitive stoves have also been set up. We are eight to a room.

The straw on the floor, never having been changed, is little more than dusty chaff. For a stove we had an old biscuit canister made of sheet metal, which used a lot of wood, yet gave off hardly any heat. On cold days it was effective only at a distance of one metre. Now we have obtained a real round stove, and even if it is only made from sheet metal, it does warm the whole room. We are not allowed to heat the room during the day, apparently to deter us from using the doors and window bars from the empty rooms. Even so, a washroom door disappears from time to time, or perhaps floor boards. The boards along the walls were the first to vanish. The only warm place is the canteen and everybody who is not working seeks refuge there from 0800 to 1100 hrs, and from 1400 to 1700 hrs. You can drink beer there (if you are lucky enough to have camp money) and from time to time other items are available (toothpaste, pipes, handbag mirrors, cigarette paper, and scribblers). In the canteen I always feel as if I am in the waiting room of some small railway station – everybody is waiting for a train that never arrives. Just about the only topic of conversation is the possibilities and prospects for escape. Those escapees who were recaptured earlier have to share their experiences. Many who had escaped from the interior of France made it to the border, only to be caught shortly before crossing.

It quite often happens that the canteen is closed to the public because the band has to practice. Then my alternative choice is the sick bay – the room where I lay while I was ill. The old pals with whom I shared the place are still there, and as they all have kidney problems they are given better heating.

I was concerned about how I would cope with working outside in that cold, without coat and gloves. However, the dear Lord came to my aid, right after New Year's Day, when, having acquired a boil on my left cheek, I was reassigned to the sick bay. After I had recovered, I got another one on the nape of my neck, and then one above my eye, and now I have been confined to my room until the 31st of January. In February it will be warmer, and then I will try to be allocated to farm work.

It was in January, when the discharge of the Saarlanders from the pits finally began. The only ones still to come are those from "Klein Rosseln." Moreover, as the long anticipated release did not occur, and they were, instead, all sent back to work, this became another great letdown for them. They were consoled by the fact that the release had not been cancelled, only postponed until replacements had arrived.

During these last few days 500 new people have arrived, 300 from a camp close to Paris, starved and full of lice, and 200 from Attichy, newly returned from the United States.

Of those 200 prisoners, only 140 came here. Sixty had disembarked earlier as a result of sickness and frostbite. In the United States, they were told that they would be released, but in Attichy they were informed that they first had to work ninety days in the pit. They felt just as much betrayed and misled as we did. Many men have worked 450 shifts and still there is no sign of release. They were treated very well in the United States, while the war lasted, but right after the capitulation, after the U.S. prisoners of war were released, the rations were cut by 80 per cent, and they were treated badly.

Strangely enough, they were first taken to Naples, and then driven to Attichy. The same camp regimen that we experienced in September prevails in Attichy. You may enter the cardboard tents only from 1100 to 1300 hrs, otherwise you have to stay outside all day, a bitter experience in winter. We are well off here and, judging by everything I hear, this is the best camp. Apparently the *Unteroffiziere*, working in the mine, not the Saarlanders, are going to be released first. The initial replacements for the first forty *Unteroffiziere* who arrived from "Klein Rosseln" yesterday were selected today.

The verdict now is that all *Unteroffiziere* will be pulled out, no matter whether they signed for work or not. We are puzzled about what is going to happen to them, and to the medics, who have apparently been forgotten.

Those disabled people declared unfit for work have been sent each month to Saaralb, where they will now be released for sure. Only those capable of work have no hope of being freed. The hated camp leader from "Klein Rosseln" had apparently realized this too. He who had talked so violently against running away and had personally whipped those caught fleeing has escaped himself now.

I am longing for news from my love. There has been mail from the American Zone – it amounted to six bags in volume. Maybe there is finally something for me!

Sunday, January 27, 1946

Last week we were again allowed to write a letter – is there ever going to be an answer? I do not give up hope.

According to rumour the "Klein Rosseln" camp leader Kindermann and the camp physician Manermann apparently fled the camp. They were guilty of so many malpractices and misdeeds that they no longer felt safe. Otherwise they would have experienced the same fate as the camp leader in Metz. There, the long-accumulated fury of the inmates apparently exploded, forcing him to leave the camp precipitately. One evening he was brought in here. There are many here who had suffered under him at Metz, and news of his arrival travelled like wildfire. Next morning he had to attend roll call, and when it was over the men from Metz pounced on him, beating him severely. He fled to the office were he was taken into safe custody by the French.

Now January is nearly over. Time seems to pass quickly. Most of the others complain that time never ends, but that is their own fault because they do not know what to do with themselves. As I have exchanged bread for an English dictionary with a man who had come from the United States, I can now learn English. Although, unfortunately, I cannot obtain any English newspapers here, I was, however, lucky in securing a detective novel from the library. German books are very scarce, especially with so many newcomers besieging the library – one is, understandably, happy to grab anything. The canteen is also crowded, such that no pin has room to drop. I do not visit there because of the lice, which the newcomers supposedly carry. I am amazed that we still have none in our room, as I am the only one from there who takes the opportunity to shower on Sunday. Some people never wash or change their underwear.

Thursday, January 31, 1946

January is almost over and it is no longer as freezing cold as it was at the beginning. It is now possible to endure the temperature of the room, provided that you are well wrapped in blankets. At the moment we have nothing to make a fire with as nobody from our room goes out to work, the only opportunity we have to obtain fuel. Subsequently I developed another boil on my forehead so that my room confinement has been extended to February 10th. That is very convenient as it gives me the chance to have my teeth attended to. A dentist here does good, conscientious work. As he had no tools in the beginning, he could only pull teeth. However, now he has a modest set of tools and an old-fashioned drill. Because this is worked by a foot pedal, it is periodically used by the dentist in town when he has no power. I lost two fillings, just when he started working, and I was able to go to him without delay and have one tooth very skillfully fixed. He cannot continue with the others as he has not the use of the drill at the moment. I hope he can do it before the 10th after which I will try to get work on a farm.

Thursday, February 7, 1946

Yesterday, the dentist finished his work, and it feels good to have one's teeth reasonably well in order. Next week I will try to get onto a farm detail. The food here is still generally inadequate, even when we do not work, especially since we have been given only 300 grams of bread since the 1st of February.

Another batch of 900 people arrived yesterday from Poitiers. They look well fed. Their provisions, having recently been greatly improved, were far better than ours. These people were given fat and sugar daily, altogether 2,000 calories, while we have only 1,150 calories daily. It is strange how differently these things are handled in the various camps.

Everything is full here at the moment. Supposedly, several details will be sent out to the pits during the next few days, to search for mines and undertake the necessary reconstruction work.

Moreover, the *Unteroffiziere*, who did not sign, will go to another camp, possibly Nancy. The disabled men will finally be removed as well, and hopefully released. Everything is performed so unbelievably slowly. Nothing further has been heard about the Saarlanders. It is rainy, the peak of the cold seems to be past, and it is more or less bearable in the room even without heating.

Thursday, February 14, 1946

On Saturday, when 800 of the newcomers went to the mines, the camp was largely emptied. In addition, another 200 fit men went out to work in Forbach, where high waters had broken a dam. Two men from our room, who had not counted on being removed, had to go as well. One of them was tutoring French in the camp and was thought to be indispensable. The other was very weak on his feet, but had to go as he was not considered to be sick. On Sunday my sick term ran out, and on Monday morning I went to the office to register for farm work. I had counted on waiting at least a week because there were numerous applicants, some of whom had to wait two or three weeks before a chance of placement arose. People with contacts in the office were the privileged ones. Thus I was really surprised when, after twenty minutes, I was told to bring my rucksack, called to the gates, and taken out right away. A possible reason is that all the able-bodied men had been called out for work on Saturday – that was my good fortune.

I was met by a young farmer, who spoke hardly any German, and we walked to the station. In town he took me to a bakery, where I had a good meal. What an experience to eat off a plate again! Then we rode by railway through the two stations to Falkenberg. Again we went to a restaurant, where he had bread, sausage, and bacon, and we revelled and drank beer. Finally we cycled for three kilometres to Landroff, a village with a predominantly French population. In the whole village, there are thirteen prisoners, and all except one sleep in a single room. I was given the choice of sleeping in a room at the farmer's place or with the others, and I chose the latter. It is quite cozy. Our beds include straw bags, we keep enough wood to stay warm, and I have become reasonably well used to living in a crowd. My farmer's family consists of an old mother with two sons and two daughters. For the moment we get along very well and we have enough to eat. The conditions are supposedly better on other farms.

It is a great feeling to move about freely, though my bones hurt, because I had forgotten how to work. We start at 0630 hrs and work until 1900 hrs, and at breakfast and lunch there is only enough time to eat.

✳ 4 ✳

RIED, UPPER BAVARIA

———⇒•⇐———

Tuesday, March 19, 1946

I came to Landroff intent on taking advantage of the first favourable opportunity to escape. I had obtained a sketch map of the border from the French teacher, whom I had planned to accompany.[1] At the very last moment he was taken to join the dam-building detail. That was good, for I am afraid he would not have been fit for such a strenuous undertaking (he owned a paper mill in Stuttgart). There was a rather mixed bunch of people in Landroff. We were rather cautious with each other. I was very distrustful. They were mostly old peasants who had been here half a year, and none had attempted escape. They all talked about escape, but none of them had any pluck, or was serious about it. I was asked right away if I had a map, but I denied it as I could not trust them. The first evening I considered not unpacking my rucksack, but rather, in fact, to start out the same night.

I decided not to set out too rashly, mainly because my map did not include Landroff and I had to establish how I could best get back near St. Avold. The man from Stuttgart had pointed out a definite spot north of that town which was a good border crossing, supposedly all forest and no mines. Elsewhere prison camps with adjacent minefields stretched along the border, and the area was heavily guarded. Besides, it was one week

---

1 See the following page.

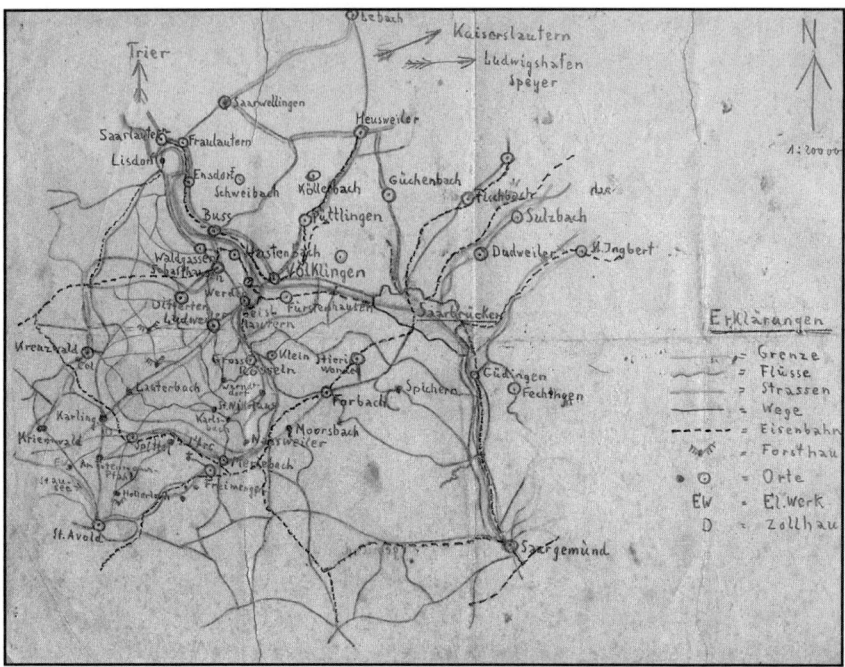

Map 4. The map carried by Jürgen von Rosen on his escape.

before full moon and the nights were too bright. So I decided to wait about two weeks, after which I planned to set out during the last quarter of the waning moon.

After a week I realized that some of the others were seriously contemplating running away – two enterprising youths from north Germany and a farm boy from Bavaria. Finally I showed them my map, which one of the north Germans then copied. The Bavarian wanted to join me, but did not want to leave before March, as he had agreed to flee on that date with another man in a neighbouring village. He was also expecting a parcel from home with butter and other provisions, that would help him during his flight. But I did not yield, as my timing was finalized and I was not going to abandon the date that I had set, for something as vague as a parcel, which very possibly would not even arrive. I had saved some of my small bread ration in the camp, and two little bags of rolled oats that had been sold on the last day in the canteen. I told him that he had had time and opportu-

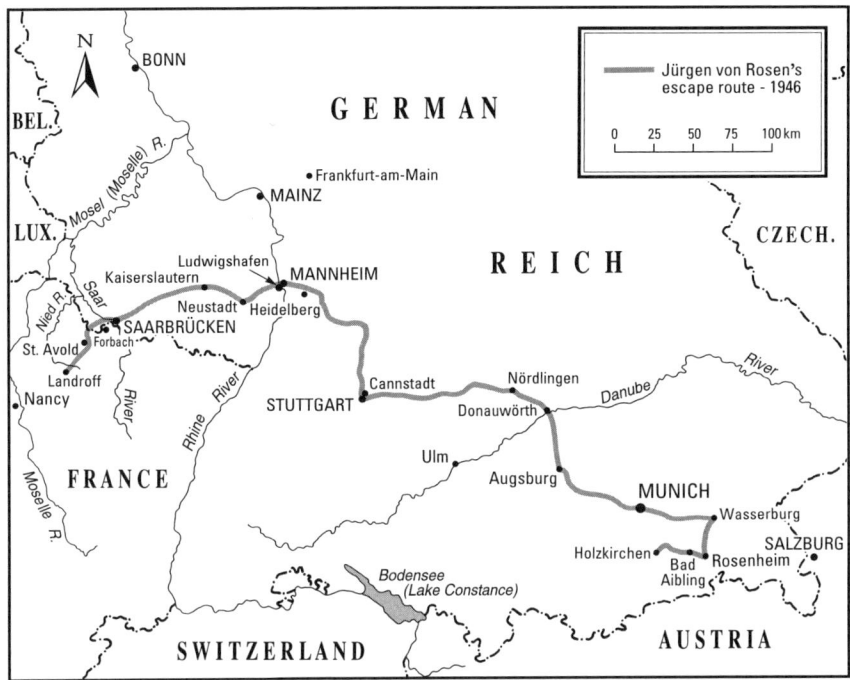

Map 5. The escape from prison (Lothringen-Saar district, France).

nity enough to put aside provisions during the half-year that he had been working on the farm, and if he had not been able to do that yet, I doubted that he would ever be able to do so. No, no, he definitely wanted to come with me, even without a parcel, but first he had to talk to his friend. So we decided that on Sunday he would go to the neighbouring village to tell his comrade that he was leaving. If he too felt like accompanying us, he had to walk over on Sunday night, arriving here, at the latest, before 0900 hrs.

The weather had, in the meantime, changed and become miserable. It snowed and it rained, and conditions were cold, wet, and muddy. Every night, when we returned from work, our Bavarian said you cannot leave in such weather, we have to wait for the waxing moon, and my answer was unwavering: "No, I am not going to wait for the waxing moon, the night is too bright and we cannot get out of the village in time. Besides, the weather will settle down by Sunday."

And again he said, "We have to wait until it dries out a bit, and besides in March, when the moon has waxed, we will have clear skies to see the stars. That will be crucial for orienting ourselves at the boundary." I would not agree, and said: "If we wait for dry and favourably warm weather, as so many others have, we will get among the big concentrations of fugitives, the guards will be alerted, and our hopes of succeeding will be very slim."

While I was still at the camp there had been an order that farmers should not permit prisoners to live on their own, and that there should always be a civilian and a guard with them where they slept. In Landroff this order had apparently not arrived, or the farmer had disregarded it because no one had escaped yet. In any event I did not want to wait for the farmer to place a guard here.

Two escapees were caught on Thursday in the neighbouring village, and at night we discussed this case exhaustively. Our Bavarian was very depressed, apparently having his doubts. The two refugees had worn unmistakable civilian clothes, fled in bright daylight, and had covered thirty kilometres. Furthermore, they had passed through the village without any difficulty. However, in the neighbouring village, which had only German-speaking inhabitants, they experienced bad luck, for when a dog started barking, one of the fugitives swore at him, in his native dialect, saying: *"Halt die Gosche, du Sauköter, du damisches Tier."* "Keep your mouth shut, damn dog, you stupid animal."

An old woman, passing by, heard him, and detected the unfamiliar dialect. She alerted two youths who had some kind of boar-hunting rifles, and they chased the two fugitives. At 300 metres distance they started shooting, wounding one in his ear and the other in the leg, and they were surrounded.

My feeling about the weather proved correct. An icy cold wind started on Sunday, blowing away the clouds. The sun came out, but it was really cold. In the morning, I went, with the Bavarian to a neighbouring village to visit the two refugees who had been captured on Thursday. One of the prisoners there was supposed to have a map. When we arrived, he was at church so we went to church as well, the first time in my life that I have attended a Catholic service. After the service, we met him in front of the church and established that his map showed no more than the boundary at St. Avold. Beyond St. Avold one had to take the main road past Falkenberg. More than this he could not tell us.

Now we were just as ignorant as before. I had no intention of going through Falkenberg, where there were coal mines and prison camps. The Bavarian mentioned that, half a year ago, when he was taken from the camp by truck, they had travelled on a small road, which was obviously shorter, and passed through some forests. This road ended exactly at our dwelling in the village. As this corner of territory was in ruins after the fighting, and uninhabited, it offered the best chance of undetected escape. Considering all the alternatives, we chose this route. According to the accounts of my Bavarian, the road led to the St. Avold railway station, which was two kilometres east of the city. By my calculations, we were about twenty-four kilometres to the southwest, and I surmised that the road made a big detour around the town. I decided to start out east along that road and then to leave St. Avold to the right, thereafter proceeding due north, aiming only at our border crossing, which was a bit to the northwest of St. Avold.

In the afternoon, my Bavarian visited his comrade in the neighbouring village, returning with the message that he too had decided to join us. He was not quite ready yet, as he had just obtained some dye to disguise his uniform. Even so, he decided to come immediately.

To our great satisfaction the two fellows from north Germany were going to leave on the same night as well. So we all started out together.

We packed silently, and I debated what to leave behind. Nonetheless, my rucksack was, and remained heavy, mainly because of the two blankets which I took. The two others had only a small satchel each, containing provisions (bread and many eggs which had been "organized" somehow), but at my urging they both took a blanket as well.

The door opened at 2045 hrs and the man from the neighbouring village entered with his knapsack. The four of us immediately jumped up and seized our packs, and only then did our room-mates descend from the clouds. They had not detected any of our preparations, which was good, as there were some you simply could not trust. With great satisfaction I noticed that our "child," a fifteen-year-old, was fast asleep. I did not expect any of the others to go to the neighbours to give us away. We switched the light out so that we could pass through the door unnoticed, and then slipped out in single file. I went first. The ground was frozen hard and every step was frightfully noisy, although I had nailed a patch of rubber to the heels of my boots. There was clear starlight and even without the moon it was quite bright. I felt greatly relieved after we had passed the last dilapidated house and turned behind the church yard.

Then I waited for the others, seemingly endlessly. Finally the Bavarian arrived with his friend. They needed to wait because a car had arrived just then, and of all things, had stopped at our door. Now we strode along and were soon in the forest. From the stars we ascertained, to our satisfaction, that the road was heading north. Because of the frost, the road was good to walk on and dry, but the pounding of our boots was extremely loud. This was especially true of Sepp, from the neighbouring village, whose nailed boots were extremely noisy. The Bavarian, Ferdl, had rubber soles and was perfectly quiet. Before entering the first village, we halted and tried to put strings around our shoes. Meanwhile the two men from north Germany had caught up with us. We whispered a good-bye to each other and they disappeared into the dark. We did not catch up with them – hopefully they made it.

Tying string around our boots did not help at all, for our steps remained distinctly audible, and at the first house in the village we were attacked by a fiercely barking dog. As we walked along we heard footsteps behind the home to the right, as well as approaching voices. We could not turn back so we hastened into the village. Once we were beyond the turn in the road we started to run at double quick pace through the length of the village, which seemed to be endless. House lights were still on everywhere and here and there dogs barked, but not a human being was to be seen. Furthermore, those behind us did not follow us. Once having passed the village, we rested briefly, then hurried on and relaxed only when we were back in the forest. We decided to be more careful and to take our boots off, proceeding in socks before entering the next village. The road forked just at the entrance to another village. To the right it went east through the village, and to the west, uphill away from the place. We were still deciding which route to take, our preference being to go right through the village, when suddenly we heard somebody walking nearby. Noiseless in our socks, we immediately rushed to the left, away from the village, and up a hill. Then we noticed that this road led into a sea of lights. That could only be Falkenberg camp. We would *have* to turn right, but decided to avoid the village by going around it. We donned our boots and stumbled through the frozen, ploughed fields.

A frightful noise resulted and I strove to go further left, away from the village, while the other two wanted to keep further right, close to the buildings. This village simply would not end. Every time you thought that this was it, we can get back onto the road, another light appeared and had to be bypassed. Finally we reached a small field path where the walking was slightly easier. As it led towards the east, we figured that the major road could not be too far away. If only we had known that this road ran far to the east and actually formed a huge crescent around St. Avold, we would not have tried to stick to it, but would rather have turned north across the railway tracks. Then we could have reached the frontier that night, since, in a beeline, it was hardly more than thirty kilometres away. Instead we kept going eastwards until, in the distance, we saw a streak of light, which we guessed to be the road. As our little path ran out in the sand, we stumbled on across freshly ploughed fields, aiming at the light which grew and widened. When finally we came closer, we discovered that it was no road, but water – simply flooded meadows.

Now what? Left or right around it? To the right was the street, but that meant going south. So we decided to go north, that meant left. We walked through wet meadows and we had to jump ditches, the width of which was hard to gauge in the dark, and we soon had sodden feet. Often we had to swerve west to avoid wider branches of the river, and were relieved when we eventually reached a rough dam that led right into the water. Without much hope we followed the dam, which appeared to end in the water itself. Yet when we reached the end, it afforded a narrow passage and we crossed to the other side. There we had to turn south as the dam formed a bend, and to the right were the flooded meadows, and to the left a little stream. We were obliged to walk back south again until we finally reached the main road. Now we crossed the river and, just beyond it, another village came into view, where we were met by barking dogs. Again we debated whether to take off our shoes and walk through the village, or to skirt it. Ferdl was for going around, I myself for going straight through, and Sepp was undecided. I did not feel like stumbling over furrows, so we decided to take off our shoes. We sneaked quietly into the village, where everything was in darkness. A dog started barking but calmed down as we continued on our way. This time we passed unnoticed and continued in our socks. I did not like the direction of the street, which was too far to the east. When we were on a bare flat, a car beam came towards us. We jumped into a ploughed field to the right and lay prone in a furrow. The car passed slowly, oh so slowly. As the beam swept over us, we felt exposed for an eternity, and then finally we were back in the dark. Two bicycles now passed. When their lights had vanished too, I instinctively remained motionless and was annoyed when Ferdl got up and moved towards me saying: "Well Jürgen, we figured that you had fallen asleep."

I signalled to him to lie down, which he finally did, just in time to have a third bicycle without lights glide past like a shadow. Then we strode on. This time the road turned north, only to bear eastwards after a short distance. All of a sudden we stood at a house from which a man approached whistling. We retreated rapidly and squatted in the shadow of a hedge. After a while, when everything was quiet, I declared that I was going to put my shoes on and walk across the fields due north. The road swerved too far to the east, and apparently there was another village there. The others agreed and we proceeded through the field. As the furrows ran south-north, we were able to walk with less effort. Fairly soon we met the road again. It had made a big bend and we had taken, so to speak, a short cut. The road apparently led into another village, and we heard footsteps from that direction, but we could not establish whether they were coming or going. Just then a car approached from behind, so we sprang back into the field and lay in a furrow. The car drove through the village and out again, swerving to the right, thus indicating that the road made a big bend. We decided to skirt the village on the right. There was still quite a bit of movement in the village. It was Sunday night and activity lasted until late.

We traversed the road, continuing through hedges and ditches, first northeast and then north. Subsequently, we encountered a wide, deep channel with steep loamy banks, freshly dug. Our first impression was that it was impassable. Then I detected something dark at one spot on the bottom. Carefully I slid down, and landed on a bundle of shrub. I had the two others follow me, and we tried to climb the opposite bank. We struggled for quite a while without success, because the loamy bank was slippery and partly frozen. It was steep, especially at the top, where there was an overhang. Finally Ferdl succeeded and pulled the two of us out.

Very muddy, wet, and dirty, we slugged onward. Soon we met the road, which had made another turn to the east. I decided to traverse the road and aim north. At first the other two dissented, yet finally agreed. Now our course continued up and down hill – at the top rough, newly ploughed fields, at the bottom squishy meadows and water. We reached a little river running from east to west, seemingly too deep to wade. To the left we heard gushing noises, so we turned that way and found a dyke with water pouring over its lip. As it was impossible to cross, we turned east. The worst that could happen was that we would meet the road again. We endlessly followed the winding river, encountering several dams but no crossing. The road was not in sight either. This was absolutely exasperating and my two comrades started to argue that we had made the wrong decision by not staying on the road. Finally, finally, we came to a spot where two long iron rails had been placed allowing us to cross.

What a relief! We teetered across the swaying, icy, slippery rails, but we managed. On the other side we turned again, in the direction that we imagined to be north. We could not make things out too well as the sky had clouded over and we could not see the stars. We climbed a little knoll, in the hope of seeing a gleam of light to the left, of Falkenberg, and to the right, of St. Avold. We walked and walked but never reached the top. It simply seemed to retreat. Then our course went downhill again, and at the bottom we met with wagonwheel tracks, which we decided to follow, even though they appeared to deviate rather too much to the left. The tracks led to a wooden bridge across a brook, on the other side of which they became a road, which in turn ran further uphill. We could smell cows, apparently because we were passing a farm. Other tracks now criss-crossed ours, so we followed the best worn ones and were led into a dense forest. The tracks grew muddy, and there was underbrush to the left and right of us. We squeezed along the edge of the bush to avoid sinking into the mud. The road ended. We were on the wrong scent. Yet we continued without any proper idea of direction, relying only on our senses, and met another little path that took us out of the woods. Again we went an endless distance uphill before we left this path, which was leading too far left. When we finally reached the top, the hill swept down again on the other side, and behind this hill was another higher hill. However, to our delight, a glow of light could be seen from behind it. Knowing that this was probably St. Avold, we held slightly to the left. We passed another small wooded section, where the young spruce made very inviting hiding places, especially as we all felt rather exhausted. Nevertheless, as it was only 0400 hrs, we decided to continue. Again we went uphill, and half-way up we unexpectedly found ourselves on a good wide tar road. We lifted our eyes desperately to heaven and, behold, the clouds allowed us a peek at the stars, and we determined that the road ran southeast to northwest. While we stood in thought, a light came into view from the right, so we tried to look inconspicuous by hiding behind a high tension electricity pole. It was an early bicycle rider, followed by another one from the other direction, and finally a car, which stopped not far from us. Apparently there was quite a bit of traffic, so we decided to avoid the street and rather move on to the north. The light, which we figured to be St. Avold, was to the northeast, so we guessed that we were on the right track. As the car had no intention of moving on, we crossed the highway and headed north. The moon now appeared, illuminating the landscape considerably. We decided to hide in the first dense wood affording the best opportunities. Except there was no forest here. When we finally did see something dark, we rushed towards it, but only found it to be a thin beech grove. We walked alongside it, constantly coming across piles of brush. We expected the workers to return, so we hastened on. Finally we turned down a rather steep hill into a grove of trees, the dry leaves rustling terribly under our feet.

Ferdl decided that we had experienced enough of this groping in the dark, so we sat down, hoping to find a hiding place in the early light. Our mood was rather despondent and I mentioned that the guards would hear us from miles away if there were more dry beech leaves at the boundary. While we sat, we noticed what was obviously a road, for we saw car lights shining to the left, then disappearing, only to reappear further to the right. There seemed to be a fair amount of traffic. It started to get brighter and we were able to make out the landscape. First it ran steeply downhill and then up again, to a knoll with a little dense wood. As the car lights were visible only to the left and right, I decided that the road led around the opposite height of land, and suggested that we cross the valley, as we might have more luck in finding a hiding place on the opposite hill. So we rustled downhill, until, to our great surprise, we stood on a railway embankment! Without any hesitation we climbed and then dropped down the other side, continuing through beech wood. Down below us was a white plain. First I took it to be a lake, and wondered if I should pass it on the left or the right. However, Ferdl ran down and shouted to us, "Here is the road, and further down is a frozen meadow," and started to walk across the meadow.

We both slid down onto the road, and just as I reached it, I noticed four civilians about 200 metres away marching towards us from the left. It was unbelievable that Ferdl had not noticed them, such a blunder. It was too late to retreat and Ferdl, who was already in the meadow, now saw them as well, and started to run. Both of us followed him. The four people on the road started shouting, but we disregarded them and hastened on. The meadow was about 300 m across, and beyond it was the enticing forest. Our shock was overwhelming when, at the end of the meadow, we came across a slowly flowing river, some six metres wide. This muddy water was all that separated us from the protective forest. Behind us we heard, "Just wait, we'll get you," and we were at the end of our wits. It was already fairly light but we could not see the people on the road, because the dark railway embankment was behind them.

They had not followed us into the meadow, but I concluded that they might have split up. If two of them continued on down the road and two then went the other way, we were liable to run into their arms if we followed the river in either direction. The forest reached down to the road on both sides and, as far as I could guess, the river as well. Just then a train arrived and halted near the highest point of the meadow. We immediately concluded that the civilians had stopped it, and envisioned a hundred people jumping out to chase us across the flats. Only later did we remember that we had seen a halt sign where we had crossed the tracks.

All three of us had stopped momentarily at the river in sheer disbelief. Then I ran a few steps to the left, like a chicken searching for the hole in the fence. Ferdl came running after me and shouted, "Where are you going? We will not be caught by them, and we have to get across!" With that he jumped into the water.

When we saw that the water reached only to his chest, we jumped in as well and waded through. The bottom was soft and muddy; however, we did not sink in very deep. Ferdl was already at the other side and out. I could not make it because my rucksack, having shipped water, had become much too heavy. I could just barely reach above the water with my arms; however, my hands could find nothing to hold onto except mud. After I had called Ferdl back, he grasped my hands and pulled me out, while he himself sank up to his knees in mire. We had about another eight metres of bog to cross before reaching the edge of the forest, and it was with our last strength that we climbed uphill. There we came across a trail leading slightly uphill to the right. A car stopped on the road at the exact point where we had seen the four; then it moved on. I thought, as these four probably know about a bridge, they will follow us here, so we chose to leave the road, starting up the fairly steep hill – slowly, ever so slowly. Our limbs were stiff and our knees especially refused to co-operate anymore, the same feeling that you have in a bad dream, when you are pursued yet cannot escape. Our desperate deed seemed rather hopeless to all of us, and I thought that it might be preferable to be handed over dry in St. Avold, than to be muddy, dirty, and wet.

Nevertheless, slowly and laboriously, we succeeded in getting up the hill. At the top, the forest continued, and we came across another street along which we were able to walk fast and undisturbed. We thus gained new assurance and courage. Probably there was no bridge nearby, the four people had gone to work, and the bounty of 1,500 francs a head had literally swum away. The only thing they could do was to alert the police. We had a comfortable head start and they would not comb the whole forest for us – there were not enough men for that. We walked for about an hour before arriving at a logging site. Now we needed to hide as soon as possible to avoid running into the arms of the loggers. But where? To the left it was too open, and from the right, where it was denser, we constantly heard railway noises. We guessed this to be St. Avold. Leaving the road, we decided to go half-way to the right. We slid into a deep gulley, and laboriously climbed out on the other side. At the summit, the forest obviously thinned out, as there was a fair amount of light to be seen. We decided to settle here, half-way up the hill. Then we located a spot with shrubs and loose brushwood, and searched for more of the latter so that we could build a nest. The brush was dry and translucent, but from a distance we would be reasonably hidden.

We took off our wet clothes and wrapped ourselves in the blankets, which fortunately had stayed dry on top of the rucksack. My second blanket came as a blessing, being big enough to cover all three of us. We could not hang up our wet clothes without betraying our presence. Anyway, this would have been pointless because it was foggy and the sun did not come out. We did not dare to start a fire. That was a wise precaution because we soon heard wood-cutters fairly nearby. We had discovered this hideout just in time.

At about 1700 hrs, towards evening, when everything was again quiet in the forest, we risked starting a small fire. It was impossible to put on our clothes, wet as they were. Because of my lack of clothes, I abandoned my plan to climb to the top of the hill to orient myself. When we were finally dry and ready to continue, it was pitch dark. Our clothes had been right in the flames – force dried. This worked, except that our boots hardened and became bone dry. It was torture to put them on, still more to walk in them. Previously I had worn two shirts and two pairs of underwear. Now I wore only one of each, in anticipation of a similar mishap in future. I would at least have a dry set.

We did not know what time it was after we had finally dressed and finished eating. As our two watches had gotten water into them during our swim, they had stopped. Before leaving, we made a brighter fire, spread out a map, and tried to establish where we were. Although we could not credit it at first, I concluded that we had been circling St. Avold.

The road that we crossed as the moon rose led northwest to St. Avold, and we had traversed the railway directly east of the city. Only in one place on the map was there a spot where railway, road, and river ran parallel. The light and the railway noises that we had thought indicated St. Avold, could quite possibly have come from Merlebach. That meant we had to keep heading northwest to reach our boundary crossing at Karling. But how to ascertain the direction without having stars to show the way? The sky was clouded over, and once we had put the fire out everything turned pitch dark. We scrambled and lurched uphill, entangling ourselves in blackberry creepers and stumbling over stumps. After we finally reached the crest, we saw that the forest broke, ran downhill again, and that there was a flood of light down below. No doubt that was a prison camp! We had spent all day in the vicinity of a prisoner of war camp keeping a fire going until fairly late at night! I conjectured that these lights came from the Spittel mine, and that the distant glow of lights further to the left marked the Kreuzwald mine. As a result, we decided that we had to proceed between the two. First we had to try to get back into the wooded area, and keep rough direction.

We gave up groping around, without a road. First of all it was too noisy, and secondly we could not make any headway, as we constantly got entangled in blackberries and brush. After we had located a path, we followed it, even though it bore too far to the left. Taking the first chance we could, we turned right along a simple woodcarter's trail. Before long we got back to the first path in a great circle. Thereafter we continued directly towards what I held to be St. Avold, and indeed we soon saw, down in the valley, the lights which could have only come from that place. Then we found another path going downhill to the right. We passed yet another one, apparently coming from town, and soon we crossed a highway. It was not quite as wide as I figured a highway should be, but nevertheless I took it to be the connection between St. Avold and Karling. That was a great mistake, as we discovered later. It was the highway to Spittel, marked on our map as a road.

After crossing the road, we did not continue in the same direction – where we soon would have met the right highway – but kept on half-way to the right. This tract of country was very favourable – sand, heather, and broom.

Our walking was noiseless and we made satisfactory progress. We reached a grove of trees, this time agreeable pine trees with no rustling leaves. Onward, we hiked through a long stretch of meadow dotted with individual trees, and passed under the power line that I had seen on the map. This strengthened my conviction that we were on the right track. However, we were taken aback when lights came into view at the end of the meadow. Had we gone too far to the left? Between Karling and Kreuzwald everything was supposed to be uninhabited, so it was impossible that those lights came from Kreuzwald. At any rate, we tracked a little farther to the right meeting a road in the woods that bore too far to the right. So we again turned left and continuing, suddenly discerned lights shimmering through the trees. In addition there were noises and train hoots to both left and right. When we finally emerged from the woods along a submerged road, we stood directly in front of a big workshop bustling with fuming activity. We retreated rapidly, crawled under Ferdl's coat, and tried to study the map by match light.

Finally, after burning up half the matches, my eyes were suddenly opened, yes, I finally understood. The first lights we had seen had not been Spittel, but St. Fontain. Spittel had been the lights to the left and that was where we now were. We had not crossed the road to Karling at all. Now we had to return all the way to the wooded meadow, there bear left into the forest, and take a circuitous route through this flood of light. At least we could be guided by the noise – the racket had to stay on our right – and finally we reached the proper road to Karling. Although it was late at night, the traffic was lively. A car approached from the left, and then two bicycles. As we rushed across, another car came from the right. We just had time to run through the meadow and reach the wood. The car stopped at the place where we had crossed. We were rather apprehensive, but to our relief it soon carried on. We found another path, which we followed, although the direction was not quite right, since the noise now came from behind. Then we took a road to the right, but that led us directly towards the noise. So left again we turned, along a narrow path into a dark, dense forest of firs, as dark and dense as only a fir forest can be. Relying solely on our sense of touch, we could just make out furrows under our feet. It was an endlessly long time, endless, endless, before we emerged from the woods, where a meadow stretched before us. To the right lay houses. That had to be Karling at last, a village stretching over several kilometres. The forest receded near the village, and past the village, according to the map, there had to be a section of field. We could have carried on along the edge of the forest, but decided to take a shortcut by crossing the fields next to the village. On the other side we anticipated finding more forest, then crossing a road and the railway tracks to Kreuzwald, yet another street, and then we should be at the boundary. Yet the village seemed to have no end, besides, as we walked and walked, the village began to awaken. We then decided to stay closer to the forest's edge. Fortunately the ground was not frozen so that our footsteps were less audible, except where the field was softer, when we splashed loudly at every step. We approached a house to the left, just as a man stepped outside. At the very last moment we thrust ourselves down into the mud, and he passed by on the street. Was that the first of the roads we had to cross? We moved on a bit further and soon met with the railway tracks. Yes, we were right. Now only the other road remained, and just beyond that the boundary. The church bell rang out 0600 hrs. We had only one hour before daylight, so we decided to hide in the forest and to venture further the following night, when we would be refreshed for the border crossing. These last twelve hours we certainly had not got very far, had made endless errors, and were now tired and footsore from the chafing of our bone-dry boots. We hugged the woods on our walk back, recrossed the first road and, after stumbling through the mud, entered the forest, where we sat down to await the first light of dawn so that we could locate a hideout.

A soft drizzle started, and we slept. It was fairly light when I awoke, and I immediately started out searching for a hiding place. The dense forest of firs that we had envisaged proved illusory. There were only tall trees. Yet, at one spot there were small firs with an understory of ferns. There we crawled under two firs, pulled out a few smaller ones by their roots, and strewed them all around us to make a real hideout. Then we wrapped ourselves in our blankets and were thankful to sleep, this time in our clothes. However, our feet and shoes were soaking wet. As we removed our boots, we already foresaw the struggle we would have putting them on again that night. We ate a little food and went right off to sleep. I could not tell how long I had been sleeping, before I was awakened by Ferdl's unbearable snoring. As I debated whether or not to wake him, I heard voices close by. I shook him and whispered in his ear to be quiet. Then we lay still, hardly breathing. Branches cracked, and voices approached and then receded. It was quiet for a while, then they returned. This continued for about two hours. Our nest was really dense and hard to detect, but our situation was nevertheless unnerving. After everything had finally calmed down, I went back to sleep and woke only when Ferdl pulled off the blankets and called, "Well, is it evening already?" Yes, it was nearly dark, although it felt like midday to us.

We had a quick snack in the last light, before lying down to sleep again. We were still very tired and thought it wiser to cross the frontier, now so close, a little later that night. After another snooze, it was pitch dark.

Relying on touch again, we folded our blankets and tormented our feet into our hard boots. After leaving our excellent hideout, we joyfully noticed that the stars were out – it could not have been better for the boundary crossing. We set out confidently and soon traversed the first road and the railway tracks at right angles. Past the railway track we had to keep slightly to the right, but all the glades ran in the wrong direction, either too far to the right or the left. So we began to zigzag, but could not find the second road. I decided to bear further right, my main fear being that we would go too far to the left. The boundary line hereabouts made a bend northwards, even northeast, and it would be easy to travel parallel to it, or possibly to cross back and forth, as had happened to so many fugitives, who had arrived from the remoter parts of France. Here the boundary has the most unbelievable and unexpected curves and blind alleys. Thus we walked straight east for a while, and finally, met the road, but in the open, as the forest had ended. Quite likely the fields still belonged to Karling, and we saw the bright pool of light from Spittel, and heard noises. We had not gone too far west after all. Next, after going straight across the road, we had to keep to a northeasterly direction and would then cross the boundary at right angles after walking a few hundred metres. Our map, not being too exact, did not show us if the distance was one or more kilometres. In any event, we marched on resolutely, and took our bearings from the Big Dipper which was more or less to the northeast. Our route ran diagonally across the furrows of a newly ploughed field, and it was therefore hard to keep direction.

All the time I believed that I could see the trees through the fog on the left of the highway, and tended to keep to the right as a result. The others, contrary to my inclination, kept too much to the right. Maybe I had told them too emphatically to bear right, which was where the highway from Karling to Ludweiler and Völklingen, running due northeast, lay. That was our rightward limit, while on the left the unseen boundary snaked along. It was strange that we were stumbling on through the rough field without the forest coming into view. All of a sudden a bicycle hushed by to the right. We squatted down, but the light came back and stopped. Apparently there was a house – you could see the shine of a window through the fog. We decided to bear further left, where there was something dark, which we took to be the forest. But no, when we got a clearer view, it turned out to be a house. We decided to pass it on the right, but there we found another house. We could not bear any farther to the right, where the bicycle's light was still visible. We sneaked through between the houses and again saw something dark like a forest. On approaching it, we encountered another house, and soon we were right in the middle of a big village. In front were houses, behind us houses, left and right houses. Wherever we turned there was a house. Fortunately there were no dogs and all was quiet, with everybody presumably asleep.

Nowhere was there a light to be seen. At first we could not make out what village this could be. According to our map there was no village between Karling and Kreuzwald, only forest. We had been climbing fences and sneaking between close-standing houses when, out of the dark, loomed a tall wire-netting fence, on the other side of which was a wide paved highway. That was no ordinary village road – that was a main highway and could only be the road from Karling to Völklingen. The direction was correct – it led exactly to the northeast. Very possibly we had already been walking along it for quite a while, and the bicycles had been moving along it. Those certainly belonged to the French border guards who were patrolling between Karling and Lauterbach. The village we were now in must be Lauterbach, so we were already in Germany and a good way past the frontier.

We had to keep to the left of the highway, so we went a little way back again, continuing quite a bit northwest to get out of the village. But we came across yet more houses all the time, and these we had to bypass. This village was endless, even if the houses were no longer so densely arranged. As the field became swampy once more, we sank up to our ankles in mud, every step emitting a noisy smack, and we could be heard from afar. However, nobody stirred in the houses, and we finally left them all behind, reaching the edge of the forest. Now we felt that we could breathe again, and rest a little.

It was such a blessing to have firm ground under our feet. We found a good path into the forest. As this led in the right direction, we could now stride out. After a while, since our road joined the highway, I decided to stay on it. The French bicycle guards did not patrol beyond Lauterbach? I hoped my memory served me right.

We had to be on constant lookout for approaching lights, but as the street was dead quiet and deserted, we made good progress. We marched about six kilometres to Ludweiler, which we decided to bypass when we again saw light. After climbing a knoll, we again started traversing ploughed fields. The forest had apparently disappeared. Occasionally we came across a road, which we tried to walk along, however it always led downhill towards the lights of the valley, Ludweiler's we guessed. As there were lights everywhere, we assumed that morning was dawning, which meant that we needed to search for a hideout. I was exhausted, with my blankets I was carrying the heaviest rucksack. Eventually Ferdl offered to exchange my rucksack for his, which weighed nothing at all, and we were able to continue without further trouble.

Finally we entered a wooded section on a slope above a village. One after the other we fell into a deep trench, and then got entangled in brambles. We decided to wait for more light before exploring further for a hiding place. With the coming of dawn we saw that the whole forest was crisscrossed with trenches. The trees, broken by shells, dangled in every direction. There was little undergrowth, but gathering branches and broken fir tops, we, once again, built a secluded nest. Then we decided that Ferdl should venture into the village to get some civilian clothes. He already had pants, but these were rather torn and I had to mend them first. After he put on Sepp's fur vest, he looked more or less *unsoldatisch*.[2]

Somewhat hesitantly, he started out. We gave him ceaseless good advice and warnings, telling him that we would wait until dark. If he was not back by that time, we would continue on our own.

But he was back in no time. At the edge of the forest he had met two workers spreading manure on a small field. They had promised to exchange our clothes, and had showed him their small settler home, the first one at the edge of the forest. All three of us set out and were met with great kindness. We were able to wash and clean ourselves thoroughly. The men brought their last items of clothing, which soon made us look like civilians. At first there were no caps, but later even these were found. A woman cooked a big kettle of soup, and lamented how scarce potatoes were, how difficult it was to obtain food, and how many of their belongings they had lost. During the war they had been evacuated, even though the neighbouring villages had been able to stay. And while they were away, these neighbours had stolen nearly everything. On their return they found the house stripped of almost all their possessions, but at least the house itself was still there. Some blankets and mattresses had been recovered from the trenches in the forest.

In the end, they did not do badly in their exchange with us. Our uniforms were much better than what we got in return. Moreover, we left all our blankets and my rolled oats, which we had hardly touched. Our military rucksacks were exchanged for ordinary satchels, and I took only the most important washing necessities with me. We now had to decide how to continue next.

---

2 *Unsoldatisch* = not like a soldier.

Originally we had planned to cross the Saar at Völklingen and then to head on northeast to Heusweiler, whence the railway could take us to Kaiserslautern. We believed that Saarbrücken should definitely be avoided. However, our hosts advised us that it was simplest to use the train to Saarbrücken, and to go on from there to Kaiserslautern. The crossings over the Saar were no longer guarded, and there were generally fewer occupying troops. There was no checkpoint at Saarbrücken station any longer, except when *D Zug* trains[3] arrived, at which time it was best to stay out of the way.

Thus we started for Saarbrücken. By now it was afternoon and the train was due to leave at 1800 hrs.

We were given a loaf of bread and 20 German marks, which we gratefully accepted, as our only money was Ferdl's 50 German marks and my meagre two German marks. Now all we possessed in total was 72 marks, and we hoped that this would get us to Munich. We walked down the chosen road to Ludweiler-Werden, the intended tramway station, and rode to the Geislautern railway station, where we saw the train leaving. The next train was scheduled for the evening. We had our doubts about being able to catch the connecting train to Saarbrücken on the same evening, and we had to avoid an overnight stay there. Finally we decided to walk. We wandered for a long stretch along the Saar, one village after the other, all industry, and went quite unnoticed in our workmen's clothes. Finally, we saw a streetcar on the other side of the river. We crossed over on a ferry, without any trouble or questions being asked. (According to the stories told in camp, crossing the Saar was the most difficult obstacle.) Then we took the streetcar to Saarbrücken, where we unwittingly overshot the station, having to retrace our steps for some distance. Arriving at the station at 1900 hrs, we learned that we had not missed anything, as the train to Kaiserslautern only left after 2200 hrs. Where should we stay the three hours? It started to rain and the station itself was only a skeleton. We sought out a restaurant, but all were closed, except for those reserved for the garrison. Finally we met a civilian, who shared our fate and took us down a small side lane to a tiny restaurant. There was still light, but the place was locked already. We knocked and knocked before the door was finally opened, and we enjoyed a beer, ate half our bread, and got warm. At 2030 hrs they threw us out, as they wanted

---

3 *D Zug* = express train.

to close. We sauntered to the station where there was a covered waiting room on the platform, just as we had been told. We bought tickets to Kaiserslautern, without any difficulty. Nobody asked for documents or passports as we passed through the gate. Just as we prepared to climb the stairs to the train, a French patrolman appeared, blocking the way at the top. We turned away quickly and, on the bulletin board, noticed that an express train was scheduled for Paris. That was the probable reason for the scrutiny, so we rushed back through the gate. Ferdl and Sepp hid in a quiet side lane, where they sat among the ruins of a bombed house. I was too cold to sit, and paced up and down the street.

Shortly before the train's departure we returned to the station. It was cold in the freight car, but we enjoyed the convenience of a railway ride after our nightly stumbling and wading across wet, newly ploughed fields. Once we were aboard, we had to make further payment, because the train took a circuitous route. It went against the grain to see our money shrink away.

We were worried about Kaiserslautern, where we had to wait for two hours, and we did not know where to hide during the curfew. Again, the station had been left in a shambles by the bombs, but we followed the crowd and were borne along beyond the gate to a small barracks, where we crammed in with the others. A black French soldier squeezed through the masses and with a searching gaze at the crowd asked repeatedly, "Nix Soldier? Nix soldier?" We did not look conspicuous. However, the civilians commented that the German police were much worse and quite often checked documents.

We were quite relieved to get back to our cargo wagon and resume our ride towards Ludwigshafen. I had the 'Neustadt/Wimstrasse' address of an old camp room-mate of long standing, whose wife I had intended to look up. He had also told me that he had contacts among the forwarding agents, who often crossed the Rhine, and who could certainly help us. At the time, he had been listed as unable to work and had every hope of being discharged. Anyhow, it was unlikely that he would be back home yet. As it was night when we passed Neustadt, we decided to go on to Rheingentheim (a suburb of Ludwigshafen). I had been given the address of a trusty innkeeper living there, by this same comrade. When we arrived at 0600 hrs, our innkeeper was still asleep and everything was locked. A blizzard had started and we stood rather depressed, wet, and frozen on the street, finishing our last bread. We tried to gain entry at another inn, but everything was closed. The only open one was reserved for the military. Finally, at 0830 hrs, a sullen maid opened up and indicated that no one was there and that everything was closed. This extra detour had been futile.

Right in front of the house stood the streetcar terminal, so before long we caught a streetcar and rode on to Ludwigshafen. There we stood at the Rhine, and could see the close and alluring houses of Mannheim on the opposite bank. What we could not see was a way of getting across. Walking along the river bank, we reached the only wooden bridge, where we watched as the pedestrians processed through a little hut. Vehicles were also checked, though not very thoroughly. Perhaps we could get across by hiding under the load on a truck, but where to find a willing truck driver? Or we could ask a civilian for a bridge permit – but who to ask? All the passers-by looked rather untrustworthy. Finally I suggested that we go to the railway station.

There was a group of cart pushers who conveyed passengers' luggage from Ludwigshafen station to Mannheim station, and vice versa, the railway bridge being impassable. I suggested that we make a deal with one of the cart drivers, because, as far as we could see, the carts were not invariably scrutinized. The man we finally approached proved to be rather unfriendly, and not even the watch offered by Sepp made any impression. He replied, "Even if you would offer me 1,000 marks, I would not help you." We could only be thankful that he did not expose us.

Thereafter we approached some other civilians who uniformly advised us to drive to Mainz, where the railway bridge across the Rhine was in use, and the scrutiny less searching. This meant an enormous detour and we had insufficient money. We grew downhearted for we were hungry and at the end of our wits. I suggested that we ride back to Neustadt and visit the wife of my room-mate. The others were against the idea because it would entail another drain on our slender means. But, agonized by hunger, they finally agreed, and we rode back. My room-mate had not yet returned home and his wife was exceedingly happy to receive my fairly up-to-date news of him. The invasion of three starved strangers initially startled her, but our hunger was soon satisfied, and we were able to wash properly, before retiring to sleep with a roof over our heads for the first time since we had set out. She advised us to take the route by way of Bingen, where a ferry operated across the Rhine, which was not so stringently checked. Beyond this, she had no other advice.

Reinvigorated, we decided next morning to make another attempt at Ludwigshafen, and if we still had no luck, to continue to Mainz.

On the train Ferdl started talking to a workman. He had been working at the bridge, and suggested that we approach the surveyor, who was to be found in a small wooden shed. In Ludwigshafen we immediately hastened to the bridge, where Ferdl went to the shed and talked openly to the man, offering Sepp's watch as a gift. After I had offered a packet of cigarettes as well, he agreed to take us across. Ferdl was given a screwdriver to carry and a rope, which was draped over his satchel. I became a welder with a hose hiding my bag. The surveyor himself took a tape measure in his hand, and we boldly marched across the middle of the bridge. Here and there the surveyor measured something, just for appearance. We left our equipment behind a shed, and the surveyor went back, bringing Sepp over in the same fashion.

Everything had happened so quickly, and we laughed when we thought how hopelessly we had stood the day before on the other bank. We would therefore have to return to Neustadt so that Ferdl could thank the worker who had given us the great tip.

In Mannheim we caught the midday train that took us all the way to Ulm. We bought tickets only as far as Stuttgart, where I intended visiting the home of my comrade who had given me the map, to see if he was back. We only arrived in Stuttgart late at night, and the train left in the morning at six, so I had to abandon my planned visit. Here we travelled in style on a passenger train. It was only in the French Zone that you had to ride in freight cars. We felt safe now that we were in Germany, and talked quite openly to our co-passengers. A wedding ring merchant from Pforzheim kindly gave us money, as he had not found what he needed on his current business trip. Now we did not need to worry about running out of money. We were advised to avoid Ulm, a small portion of which fell within the French Zone. At first we were incredulous, but after the conductor had confirmed this information, we decided to skirt the danger zone by travelling via Nördlingen, Donauwörth, and Augsburg. A freight train was expected from Cannstadt at six in the morning. So we left our train in Stuttgart, taking the tram to Cannstadt, where we looked for a place to stay overnight. We walked in vain from one inn to another, as there were no vacancies. During each visit we had a beer and a piece of bread. Finally, directed to a Christian hostel, we were met with great kindness. We were served cold potatoes and, even though every room was occupied, we were able to stay, because the other guests simply huddled closer together to make space for us. We had one wide mattress on the floor, a pile of blankets, and a wonderful sleep. Next morning at 0600 hrs we started out. A youth on the train gave us coupons for 1,000 grams of bread, and in Nördlingen, where we had a two-hour wait, we bought three pounds of bread, and ate three plates of unrationed potato soup.

We arrived in Munich at night, in the dark. My intention had been to first go to *Vohburger Strasse*, to the house of my sister-in-law, Nita. I changed my mind, however, because nobody could tell me how to get there. So I decided to accompany Ferdl, as no sleeping quarters were vacant. At 2000 hours we boarded the train connection to Rosenheim. We got out at Gräfelfing and, to our dismay, learned that the train did not leave until the next morning. The inn opposite the station had no overnight vacancies and we were sent back to the train we had just left. This would only return to Munich the next morning and would stay put all night. Still we were first given some bread and even some sausage, before spending a freezing night in the cold train. We had not been so cold during our whole escape.

Next morning we travelled to Erling near Wasserburg, where Ferdl was met by his siblings with much cheering and joy. It was Sunday, and we had spent a whole week in flight.

We were generously fed, and I spent the night there before travelling on Monday morning, the 4th of March 1946, from Wasserburg via Rosenheim to Holzkirchen. I had to pass through hateful Bad Aibling, which I had hoped never to see again. To my great satisfaction conditions were foggy and grey, and I could not see the place at all.

In Holzkirchen I asked for directions and walked through the beautiful, snow-covered countryside. My heart was filled with suspense – would I find my loved ones in Ried? On arriving there, I met neither my dear ones nor Nita, but a complete stranger – Helga. I am afraid my face looked foolish as I gazed at her, my unknown niece. However, she had received good news from my loved ones, and as everything had first to go wrong during our flight before changing for the best, I am confident that everything will come right in the end.

LIFE IN CANADA:

THE OPEN WORLD
by
Martha von Rosen

✳ LIFE IN CANADA ✳

THE OPEN WORLD
by
Martha von Rosen

Throughout all these tough refugee years my dear American friend Lee sent us care parcels. She packed them in person, all one hundred of them, with clothing, food, shoes – you name it. Then through Lee's connections we got a sponsor for us to emigrate to Canada. Our benefactress was a Mrs. Emma White of Philadelphia, whom I later met and who continued to lavish gifts on us throughout her life. Our happiness at becoming prospective immigrants was overwhelming. We were no longer refugees. My mother would have to stay behind, but we would apply for her to join us once we were in Canada and had work.

In the spring of 1951, we boarded the old ship *Beaverbrae*, in Bremen, on the first leg of our venture into the future. It proved a rough crossing and Jörn and I helped out by dispensing seasickness pills and interpreting for the doctor on his rounds, while Else assisted in the galley.

The conditions on the ship were poor, and the train taking all of us to our various destinations across Canada was not much better. Our family was lucky, for we were only going as far as Knowlton, Québec, a mere twenty-four-hour trip. Some of our friends were headed for British Columbia, on wooden benches and with nowhere to stretch out.

At the station, we were met by our new employer, an amiable French marquis. Our new home greeted us with icy coldness – there was no fire and the piles of wood for burning were covered in wet snow. In our correspondence with the new boss, there had been no mention of the members of the family having to work. We were in for a few surprises; Else was put to

The three-ton dump truck that transported the von Rosen family from Québec to British Columbia.

work sandpapering eggs in unventilated work conditions, while I had to help out with the laundry and housecleaning. After Jörn's proposals to improve the badly designed chicken coops was turned down flat, we decided to quit.

Our sponsor agreed, and we next found ourselves in St. Augustine, Québec, at the farm of a Mr. Schoen who was recovering from a serious tractor accident. It was a biodynamic farm run on principles advocated by Dr. Rudolph Steiner, namely the improvement of the soil without recourse to chemicals. Jörn was very keen to learn more about the subject. We were all involved in picking the horsetail weed, boiling it up in huge vats, straining it, and spraying it on badly infested wheat. In no time, the crop looked healthy again and the blackened ears had disappeared.

Our house was roomy enough for my mother to join us, but we lacked furniture. Here too, Lee came to our rescue. She was leaving New York to settle in California and had some surplus items from the boarding house she had run in New York. She wrote: "I have a bed for each of you and other furniture. Come and get it!" But how to get it? We borrowed a half-ton pickup and a small pig trailer – that would have to do. The next hurdle to overcome was a permit. Recent immigrants were not allowed to leave the country, and we had only been in Canada a few months. Luckily a permit was granted and, very proud of our admittedly humble conveyance, we set out.

Once we arrived in New York, Jörn's accumulated packing skills were sorely tested. I still have snapshots of this load. Lee wanted to give us everything she could. The truck and trailer were dragging on the ground by the time we left.

That winter, Mr. Schoen and his wife headed for California to escape the cold. Enduring my first Quebec winter, I did not blame them. For a change, I now had a chance to read a newspaper, which the Schoen's had not cancelled. "Where is British Columbia?" I asked my husband. "Is it possible that it is spring there while we still drown in snow?" This was the moment to choose our ultimate destination in this vast country, and we had no doubt that it would be British Columbia. Our friends had already written to us to come and join them. We would not be strangers to each other. We had all gone through similar hardships, and could be reunited as immigrants in this huge land of endless opportunity. But our contract with the Schoen's did not expire until June, so we would have to bide our time.

Meanwhile, my mother had started to paint icons again, and we soon made contact with people in Montreal who showed a real appreciation of her art. Before long, she had found buyers for several of her works.

At long last, June arrived, and we set out on our three-week-long trek across Canada to our proposed new home. Our newly acquired second-hand three-ton truck was just big enough to carry all our recently acquired furniture. Jörn filled every nook and cranny, and all our pots and pans were stored along the vehicle's sides. It was early afternoon when we left, and by evening we had passed Ottawa and were headed along the northern route. In the ensuing days, our journey took us even further to the north, past lovely inviting lakes. They were inviting, however, only from within the confines of the cab. As soon as you set foot outside, you were assailed by black flies by day and mosquitoes by night. Together they were a lethal combination.

Jörn was the only driver and stayed at the wheel throughout, with the old truck laden high, swaying like a boat on a choppy sea. The Trans-Canada Highway was still a planner's dream. Sometimes we had to take construction roads and would edge forward at a mere snail's pace. On such occasions, the eyes of the construction workers opened wide in disbelief. No Canadians took this route, preferring to detour via the United States. Being new immigrants, this option was denied us.

We always managed to find a good spot to pitch our tent, collect water, to light a fire, and, the main problem, park our big truck. In every province, we had contact with the police, who were unfailingly kind and help-

The von Rosens' first house, a picker's cabin in Oliver, British Columbia. Left to right: Lilly von Weymarn (Anna von Kügelgen's first cousin), Martha von Rosen, Anna von Kügelgen, Gerhard and Else.

ful. On one occasion, we were stopped because children were not permitted to ride on the back of the truck. The policeman, however, recognized that we had no option. On another occasion, we were found to be overloaded. Again we could not change the situation. Another time, when we came close to losing a wheel, a kind policeman noticed and waved us to a halt. For long stretches, there were no gas stations. We were invariably given a filled gas container to tide us over, and asked to leave the can at the next station. It was heartwarming to encounter so much kindness and trust. The Rockies were like paradise, magnificent in themselves and showing abundant evidence of man and beast in harmony.

Finally we reached the arduous road down the Kicking Horse Pass and through to Golden, British Columbia. We had no illusions about the state of the road, but the other, through the Crowsnest Pass, was even steeper and we still could not venture south of the border. The road that we took hardly warranted the name. Either half of it had already cascaded into the foaming river far below, or it was half-smothered with fallen rock from above. Every bend offered new surprises. I preceded our ark to warn oncoming vehicles. Sometimes they had to press against the hillside while we teetered past on the precarious outer edge. We all held our breath. The bridge across the Columbia River was sound enough, but several others were dilapidated and lacked railings.

The Okanagan Valley, where we were to settle, presented a wondrous picture – the intense blue of the sky was equalled by that of the lake, and all around the mountains were dotted with clusters of brilliant yellow flowers. Finally, on 2 July 1952, we reached Oliver. There we were greeted by Mother, who had preceded us by train, and by our anxious friends. We had taken our time, for we knew that this unrepeatable odyssey would end all too soon.

A home had been rented for us at $15 a month. It was small and primitive, but at that price you could not expect too much. At least we were all reunited under one roof.

Our first setback was immediate. The spring had been severe, so there was little money to be earned from fruit-picking. Moreover, Jörn's schemes to earn money with the truck misfired. A sum of $3,000 was needed to get into that business. Instead, he went north to work on a bridge across the Fraser. I did occasional work in the packing houses, and the children picked whatever fruit was available.

That Christmas, we had a stroke of luck. We had made friends with a local couple, the Claytons, who were interested in art, especially Mother's icons. We had invited them over for Christmas, and that evening Mr. Clayton, who worked for Cominco, offered Jörn a job in the silica mine right there in Oliver, to start immediately after the holidays. What a gift that was!

So began a year of contentment and a return to normality in our lives. We moved into a more comfortable picker's cabin on a fruit farm. Mother recreated the garden she had nurtured in Estonia and continued her painting. Jörn loved his job, and we could begin to repay our debts. We even traded in our old truck for a second-hand car, a Studebaker, which we used frequently to make outings into the country. A year of contentment – what a blessing we could not see into the darkening future.

In 1953, the silica mine in Oliver was closed down for a year. Miners who opted to stay with Cominco could either transfer to the Kootenays to work under the lake, or to Tulsequah in the far north. Jörn, always interested in the north, chose Tulsequah.

He left on 22 January 1954 and his letters were ecstatic. Tulsequah, fifty kilometres east of Juneau, Alaska, is bounded by two rivers, the Taku and the Tulsequah, and is surrounded by high mountains in a valley only a few kilometres long. On his days off, Jörn did some hiking, enjoying the beauty and the solitude, which he described in his many letters to us. I planned to go there in the summer with the children if I could find a companion to stay with Mother.

Then on the second of July, like a bolt of lightning, I received a telegram. Jörn had gone missing on Sunday, 27 June. Missing? A ground search had been mounted, as had a helicopter search. After six days, there was hardly any hope and absolutely no clue. Frantically we made plans. The bank was closed for it was a Saturday when we heard the news. The manager, however, loaned me enough to buy an airline ticket for Else, who was to fly from Seattle to Juneau, despite her lack of an American visa, as there were no direct flights from Vancouver.

Several of the miners started a new search of their own. Down in the valley, the undergrowth was all but impenetrable, huge devil's claw mixed with thick growth of thorny and wiry plants – only the grizzly felt at home down there. Else was unable to glean any further information, and to add to our troubles had experienced difficulty in re-entering Canada without the necessary visas.

Some of my husband's former colleagues did carry on the search and I encouraged them in every way. It was such a hopeless quest. A year later, I consulted a clairvoyant in Seattle in order to get some clue. He was very impersonal and said off-handedly, "What do you want? He is dead, drowned in quicksand." Then he gave me a description of the location. Later, my mother and I flew to Tulsequah. The land between the two swiftly flowing and foaming rivers was very treacherous, and the clairvoyant's description of the place proved all too convincing. After years, I gave up the search, but in spite of everything I never did give up hope.

Meanwhile, I had been left destitute with a family to support. Friends and even strangers in Oliver rallied round to help me find work. I did everything possible, and sometimes the impossible, to keep our heads above water. Not once did I accept welfare, although it was offered. After taking on various odd jobs, I eventually settled down into regular work as the assistant to the local dentist.

My mother helped out by painting and selling the occasional icon. Later, too, she became eligible for a German pension. Else, who had already completed her first year of study at the University of British Columbia when her father disappeared, managed, despite all hardships, to finish her studies by winning scholarships and by working to support herself. Besides that, the money she earned from checking coats was sent to me. I was thankful for my family, for it was they who kept me going.

In 1957, after Gerhard had completed his schooling, I decided to move to Vancouver to be closer to both of my children. There followed a period of great anxiety as I struggled through a succession of jobs, first as a dental assistant, then as a school matron, and later as a laboratory assistant at the University of British Columbia. Then, in 1960, Else graduated, completed her internship, and married a fellow doctor. She started her own practice and I became her receptionist. What a change in my everyday life! To work for my daughter was a happy time. I felt I had reached safe ground at last.

My mother joined us in Vancouver. Her icons were her life and she lectured and exhibited until her strength began to fail. In the last year of her life, her sight dimmed and she could paint no longer. Then she suffered a stroke, and in 1966, at the age of ninety-one, she left us for good. She left a great emptiness in her wake.

Gerhard graduated as a geologist and married Xenia von Lieven. Else's practice prospered. I was nearing retirement, and began to search in the rural areas so that my growing grandchildren could experience the natural environment of a farm. I remember well Sunday expeditions in my small Volkswagen Beetle, accompanied by Xenia's energetic grandmother, armed only with a map and some newspaper clippings. Despite several misadventures, we soon located and purchased a small property in the Fraser Valley near Mission.

A landowner once more, a new era of fulfillment was dawning in my life. When you acquire a property you sign a commitment. It is like an avalanche – the ball becomes bigger as it rolls. I could hardly wait for my retirement to start building on the property. Of course, there were many failures to begin with – empty promises and helpful people whose good intentions exceeded their skills. We had to learn as we went along. Helpful friends lost patience with the project – I did not blame them, for they did not have the vision that led me. Finally, in 1970, on a hot day in May, the last task was completed.

The house was not the end of it. The whole venture was like a fairy-tale. As soon as I had achieved one objective, I had a bucketful of new plans. First a pony, then a stable, and what was a farm without chickens, ducks, pigs, and even a cow? Where do you draw the line? The soil was rocky, not easy to tend, and very difficult to turn into pasture. But whatever I did, I don't regret. The harvest was not in terms of apples or plums, but in the happiness the grandchildren derived from it.

For eight years, the farm served as a haven to the families of both of my children. Then my son-in-law died. He had been living separated from his family in an apartment overlooking English Bay. This apartment could not be rented out. My daughter suggested that I move in. The moment was right, as I was no longer strong enough for the work the farm demanded. My son took over the property, and I returned to Vancouver.

In 1982, I married a widower, Albert Olds. Again I was happy, but it was not meant to last. Two-and-a-half years later, he died of cancer. Three months later, my daughter Else followed him, also a victim of this merciless disease. She left two children.

Looking at my long and varied life, I am thankful for many of the experiences that I have had. Often I ask myself whether and how I have been altered by all of this. I remind myself of the old adage of counting. I try to be worthy of my heritage. I think of goals, challenges and purposes. In one sense, I am grateful for all that I was given to overcome – hard, easy, and sometimes too demanding. I am amazed at the strength I have been able to muster. Certainly I have had much need of it.

THE END

EDITOR'S AFTERWORD

SOME ANTHROPOLOGICAL REFLECTIONS
ON ETHNOGRAPHY, WAR, ETHNICITY AND OTHER
MATTERS
by
Elvi Whittaker

✷ EDITOR'S AFTERWORD ✷

SOME ANTHROPOLOGICAL REFLECTIONS ON ETHNOGRAPHY, WAR, ETHNICITY AND OTHER MATTERS

by

Elvi Whittaker

> There are no truths ... only stories.
> Thomas King, *Green Grass, Running Water*

The von Rosen stories carry their own vivid authority. With undeniable force, these narratives make the consequences of war come to life. This tone of authenticity offers one solution to the most demanding problems that academic writing, especially that of social science, has encountered in the last two decades: a viable moral ground in the struggles over representation and appropriation. It is now widely acknowledged that those who lived historical events should play a part in how these matters come to be interpreted, remembered and, finally, written into texts. The question seems to be, "Who has the right to decide on the proper version?" Both in ethnography and in history, the von Rosen stories are discourses whose time has come. Yet is there nothing further to be added? No explanations or analyses to be offered? No theorizing to be created?

In the postmodern world, it is an academic's duty to note that all narratives point to innumerable sub-texts, other stories demanding to be told. Not only are these stories parallel and parenthetic versions, but they also contextualize events broadly and point to unities of experience or disunities of opinion. It is the goal of the Afterword to engage the reader in these alternate discourses and thereby recognize the readers' inclinations to generalize and to make the connections which enhance meaning.

The first of these sub-texts considers the position of autobiographical writings in ethnography and history. The von Rosen writings describe war, imprisonment and the life of a refugee. These are areas in which anthropological fieldwork has not been done. In particular, the narratives draw a dramatic ethnographic portrait of women in war, men in forced labour camps – particular circumstances in the human condition not directly available to anthropologists. Viewing the von Rosen diary and reminiscences as ethnographic records brings attention to the connections between autobiography and fieldwork.

The second major sub-text is that of the history of a particular group of refugees, the Baltic Germans, who moved through various parts of Europe after the Second World War – stateless and homeless. In this fate they resemble other refugees and immigrants, who have become part of an ethnic mélange in the countries in which they settled, and where they seem to be losing their ethnic identity. Thus Baltic Germans are becoming incorporated into larger nations, the only vestiges of their presence being in the insular histories of particular families. The existence of Baltic Germans, like the cultures of all peoples of the Baltic area, is not well documented. While it is probable that Estonian, Latvian, and Lithuanian cultures will become much better known outside of their own boundaries in the years to come, it is unlikely that this will happen to the German-speaking population who lived within those same boundaries for hundreds of years prior to the Second World War. While a full history of this ethnic entity is beyond this particular Afterword, the histories of the von Rosen and von Kügelgen families provide one account of how wars and nationalism have affected the fate of a whole ethnic group. In this case, biography parallels history and lends it depth.

Given these intentions to retrieve the sub-texts, the Afterword has an agenda of its own. It is very clear in what the Rosens have written that some stories have not yet been told. The Afterword draws the reader's attention to these forgotten lives, and suggests that the original documents could be seen as forms of resistance writing, claiming their part in rightful authoritative texts.

Storyteller as Ethnographer: Life as Fieldwork

The storyteller is, essentially, a skilled fieldworker. Two truisms support this assertion. The first is that ethnography has never been possible without the co-operation and the astute observations of those prsumably being studied. The stories they tell are transformed, in conventional methodology, by the observations, experiences and analyses of the ethnographer. Together, the stories told by people studied and the stories created by anthropologists support the assertion that "the autobiography of fieldwork is about lived interactions, participant experience and embodied knowledge; whose aspects ethnographers have not fully theorized" (Okely 1992:3). These experiences and stories constitute the bulk of all ethnographic writing. The role of anthropology, therefore, has been that of facilitator, scribe, explainer, interpreter, and, all too often, bureaucrat. It is no wonder then that the notion of collaborative research is emerging and is duly emphasized. This perspective recognizes that no ethnography, and indeed, no anthropology, is produced without the goodwill and the contributions of "those studied."

The second truism is that life itself is a kind of fieldwork. The very processes by which this act called fieldwork is performed are the same processes by which we learn to live a life. Thus, the skills we refer to as fieldwork skills are largely identical to the skills used in becoming a member of a culture. The individual who interacts with anthropologists in the field, who enriches our ethnographic and life experiences, who carefully teaches us the proper way to behave, was not born with her culture. She has resolved, or is always in the process of resolving, uncertainties about it. It is accepted without question that she is a competent spokesperson about the way things are. However, not surprisingly, each individual is not a static depository of culture, but is continually emerging within her own culture – creating, reifying, interpreting and modifying it. This means she is doing fieldwork daily – observing, participating, intuiting, interviewing, making sense, constructing mental notes. When she responds to our hesitant questions, she is reporting her own ethnographic observations, her own field experiences, her own tentative impressions. She reifies her own culture even as she communicates it. It is as important for her to know how to behave and be culturally competent, as it is for the anxious anthropologist. Her interpretations, like those of the alien ethnographer, are also being judged daily for their viability.

Eyewitnessing and living through events is awarded a special status in our culture, a status accorded no other type of experience. "Seeing is believing" is imbued with immediacy and truth.[1] It is central to the realist

---

1 Dundes (1975) gives a convincing account of the importance of eyewitnessing in North American culture. The very premises of fieldwork, as opposed to the productions of armchair anthropology, seem to be directed by cultural commitments to powerful visual metaphors.

ethnography that constitutes the body of anthropological work. Yet, even so, eyewitness accounts are too often merged into, and subjugated to, other kinds of knowledge, not only in the ethnographer's ongoing analysis, but in the textual record as well. It is the derived nature of ethnographic accounts that leads Oring to suggest that monographs are metaphors *about* fieldwork, not descriptions *of* fieldwork (1987:258). In these monographs "human subjects ... lurk behind ethnological objects" (Mandelbaum 1973:177), and their experiences do not become mere "'evidence' about the past but as the window on ways the past is culturally constituted" (Cruikshank 1990:14).

The von Rosens chose their own events and objects and controlled the interpretation of them. Such self-composed stories show how knowledge is managed, in that they proclaim "the facts of the case." In addition, diaries and autobiographies are rich in self-reflections and provide pointed critiques of the events at issue. They usually reveal matters beyond the reach of ordinary ethnography and tell us "less about events as such than about their meaning" (Barman 1988:11; Caplan 1992). They show what is important in their lives, and construct these indubitably as facts. The stories thus reveal much that eludes outsiders, such as "cultural ideals and norms, lifelong and newly emerging personal interest, the historical setting, factors in the immediate social milieu.... How they frame, dramatize, and organize such accounts reveal variations in conceptual orientation" (Luborsky 1987:368). In doing this, they very quickly solve the problem that frequently puzzles anthropologists as they attempt to find an appropriate ethnological or historical frame. This book, however, does not abandon conventional histories. It recognizes the suggestions of military historians and ethnohistorians that perspective lies in comparison with established conventions and familiar texts. Thus a sub-text of military history appears in footnotes and casts time into a broader focus and encourages the kind of contextualization that curiosity sometimes demands. Ultimately, however, the narratives speak with an authority that cannot be accorded to secondary texts.

The Ethnography of War, Survival and Homelessness

Some cultures have long been part of a *terra incognitae* on the ethnographic landscape. In particular, the culture of refugees, of prisoners of war in labour camps, and of women and children in conditions of war have not been subjected to fieldwork. There are no ethnographies of such survival strategies, of homelessness or of statelessness. These cultures have visibility only between the covers of novels. Among such forgotten cultures, and living only as minor footnotes in other texts, are the lives of slaves, of domestic servants, of survivors of various disasters, of children. "We are of course amazed when we discover that there exists no autobiography by a servant in the nineteenth century, whereas the servants, numbering one million, represented one-fourteenth of the active population of France. Practically no autobiography in peasant society either, which represented even more than one-half of the French population" (Lejeune 1989:164).[2]

The emerging compendium of Second World War writing includes innumerable official histories produced by professional historians and journalists, the reminiscences of generals and political leaders, the coffee table books of war photographs, the volumes that highlight individual battles, the reports about the Front formulated at news desks, and the scripts deemed proper for Hollywood. Each seeks to produce the definitive explanation, the truth of the matter, the real story. These texts about the war *are* the war. As Fussell has shown, the available texts *are* the memory, the convention, and the mythology. He refers to such texts as "the dynamics and iconography" of events and has suggested that, in that form, they have proved "crucial political, rhetorical and artistic determinants on subsequent life. At the same time the war was relying on inherited myth, it was generating new myth, and that myth is part of the fiber of our own lives" (1975:ix).

Even as the established images and icons continue to dominate what we think of as the war, alternate scripts do appear. Like those of the von Rosens, these alternate stories both defy and correct official scriptures. They seem to say that historians have legitimized individual experience, but it has been the experience of the political, economic and cultural elite (Tamke 1977:273). The presumption is that these privileged groups have special insights into "what really happened."

Within the intellectual climate that values narratives, the Second World War is emerging as a recognized experience. Barry Broadfoot has accumulated oral histories about the war in Canada (1974; 1985) and Studs Terkel has added an American collection, focusing on what has come to be called

---

2 One contemporary attempt to redress such perverse omissions is the recent emergence of publications devoted to the autobiographies of nineteenth-century slaves. They seem to hold a mirror up to the countless versions produced *about* them and, indeed, to the countless autobiographies and biographies of other sectors of the population. For recent work on slave narratives, see Hurmence (1984); Jacobs (1986); Perdue et al. (1976); Etter-Lewis (1991).

"the good war" (1984). More specifically, some narrative accounts parallel the imprisonment and survival stories produced by the von Rosens. For example, Sonia Games writes of how she survived the Second World War (1990); and Natalie Crouter (1980) records a detailed account of her internment by the Japanese in the Philippines between 1941 and 1945; Helmut Horner (1991), a German soldier describes his fate from the time of the German surrender, when he was placed in a prisoner-of-war camp in France, moved to seven different camps in the United States, then to England, and, finally, three full years after the end of the war, home to Germany.[3]

Among the narratives we call novels, there are many which concern military combat itself. These ethnographies of war include Charles Yale Harrison (1930), George Orwell (1938), and Norman Mailer (1948), writing about the First World War, the Spanish Civil War, and the Second World War, respectively. Recently, Hansen, Owen, and Madden have compiled the recollections of the veterans of contemporary warfare in Vietnam and Afghanistan (1992). Others have been fascinated by the genre of war writing itself (Aichinger 1975; Aldridge 1951; Beidler 1982; Cobley 1993; Hanley 1991; Jones 1976), thereby creating narratives about narratives.

Unfortunately, most governments have vested interests in supporting conventional accounts – histories that remove war from its pain and its human toll. In so doing, they permit it to be abstracted, sterilized, and removed from those who experienced it. Thus, strangely, this canonized knowledge, presented as both true and real, is, in some sense, neither. It is merely official. It is a text "composed of reported statements that are incorporated into the metanarrative of a subject that guarantees their legitimacy" (Lyotard 1984:35). The historian or journalist does the writing, asserts the analysis, and connects the events to each other with the help of some already accepted and therefore useful "fictions." The result is curiously non-human.

Individual narratives impose a correction on conventional histories. The immediacy of their first-hand experience reduces arm's-length accounts to the status of "fiction" and subordinate stories. As ethnographic writing, the von Rosen stories offer something about isolation, terror and loss, that

---

3   The experiences of children in war are rarely recorded. One extraordinary exception, now immortalized as world literature, is Ann Frank, *Anne Frank: The Diary of a Young Girl* (1952). Another is the reconstructed experiences of her childhood written by Karla Poewe, *Childhood in Germany during World War II: The Story of a Little Girl* (1988). The experience of child evacuees is discussed in Ben Wicks, *No Time to Wave Goodbye* (1989).

anthropology and history cannot. They are survival narratives. Yet interestingly, while they are forms of resistance to the canon of historical writing, perhaps, in one area, they comply with the very thing they criticize. As Cobley argues convincingly, narratives of war are complicit with the wars they so strenuously oppose. Lamentably, she suggests, realist accounts cannot help but romanticize war (1993).

There are procedures and formulae for coding memory into texts. These are what Hayden White calls "tellable stories," that is, familiar scripts to which we have accorded recognition for centuries. Each is a morality tale, for, where "narrativity is present, we can be sure that morality or a moralizing impulse is present too" (White 1980:26). The von Rosen narratives belong to this genre of heroic stories. That is, they tell of courage against all odds, of hapless innocence confronting massive evil. Like other heroic odysseys, the mythic trials of classic times, they wend their way through alien worlds to closure. Dangers are confronted, journeys taken, obstacles overcome, escapes dared, and grand conspiracies unmasked. Equally classic virtues of self-sufficiency and courage make it possible. Their story is one of paradise lost and regained. They tread a classic philosophical tightrope between determinism and free will – the evil out there, the determination within. The wide familiarity of readers with these "cognitive templates" and "guiding metaphors" (Luborsky 1987:364) provides the background knowledge that enables us to make the sense we need to make of the stories.

In the landscape in which the stories are told, all recognizable elements of social order have been either eroded or destroyed. Within the reigning atmosphere of unpredictability and loss, the von Rosens attempt to maintain tradition. They describe a state of tormented suspension between safety and mayhem, between the civilized and the brutish. They find themselves positioned between reliance on trusted social rules and their seemingly complete obliteration, between a continual search for material comforts and the complete destruction of property around them. They write of the strength of individuality against a backdrop of powerlessness. They praise family unity and inscribe memories of home.

They are separated not only from home, however temporary this may have been, but also from the possibility of reproducing a semblance of home. They must always move, or be moved, on. The attention given by both to the continual invention and reinvention of some of the trappings associated with home make up a large part of their writings. Consideration is given to the arrangements for sleeping and maintaining an adequate food supply. Coping is a daily undertaking. What can be accomplished with the resources at hand? How much risk should one take? Where is the most secure spot? Such strategizing is integral to the refugee experience.

Dragging their precious possessions with them, worrying about food, the unpredictability of transportation, and the scarcity of money, Martha von Rosen and her small, weary band tried to survive. Evading the enemy became a daily occurrence. Consequently, there is an extraordinary preoccupation with a steadfast horse, and a relentless anxiety about its health and welfare. Great value is placed on a small pot of potatoes, and jubilation follows the finding of enough straw to make beds. In this state of chronic homelessness, Martha von Rosen occasionally found the unexpected gift of shelter in the mansions of aristocratic friends.

At the same time, Jürgen von Rosen, always hopeful of repatriation, was forced from one prisoner-of-war camp to another, from one Allied prison authority to another. His diary also documents the preoccupation with survival, with the small comforts within the narrow parameters of his world. He writes of his water canteen, of the penknife so precious to his well-being, of sleeping space that might permit lying horizontally, of finding straw for bedding, of the chess set he was carving, of the daily condition of his feet and shoes, of the hoarding of food against the possibility of even greater deprivations, and, on rare occasions, of meeting a fellow prisoner with whom he could share a few common experiences. These preoccupations became more poignant as the hope of release slowly disappeared.

The complicated flow of refugees has been documented by historians. Back and forth across various borders they moved, escaping Nazism, escaping the Russian advance, and, in some cases, escaping the British, the French, and the Americans. It has often been noted that the Second World War was the most destructive war of all time. This extended agony produced, following the formal end of hostilities, millions of displaced persons from many countries, all attempting to reach home. The extent of homelessness at this time can be gleaned from the fact that, in September 1945, the Western Allies were responsible for about seven million displaced persons.

> Among these were every possible kind of individual – Nazi collaborators and resistance sympathizers, hardened criminals and teenage innocents, entire family groups, clusters of political dissidents, shell-shocked wanderers, ex-Storm Troopers on the run, Communists, concentration camp guards, farm labourers, citizens of destroyed countries, and gangs of marauders. Every European nationality was present in both East and West. (Marrus 1985:299)

Undoubtedly there were serious pressures on the military administration.

Upon this mass of unclassified humanity, the military, in its own peculiar, bureaucratic wisdom, inflicted what it considered to be workable classifications. One major category was that of displaced persons outside of their own countries; another was that of displaced persons inside their own countries. A more problematic category was that of German prisoners of war – a category made up of political prisoners, evacuees, civilians who were expelled or who escaped from the East, inmates of slave labour and concentration camps, and enemy soldiers (Marrus 1985:300). In this situation, the von Rosens found themselves each belonging to a different category – she was a displaced person from the Baltic; he was an enemy soldier who, upon the German surrender, became a prisoner of war.

Silent Victims: Women in War

Despite the long intellectual history that has been produced about war, very little of it has focused on the plight of women and children. Women's voices have been silent in this male domain and have been subsumed within the records constructed by men. Women's writings do, however, pointedly refer to the meaninglessness of collective violence and to the perverse excitement it seems to create (Vickers 1993). This male preoccupation with violence impinges forcibly on the lives of women, and, under such imperatives, a familiar cultural identity has become women's lot. In the iconic notion, they keep the home fires burning. Like Penelope, they sit and wait. As protectors of the status quo, namely traditional male positions at work and in the family, they stand in for men until these privileges can be reclaimed. They are seen as faithful and resourceful, uncomplaining and supportive. And they are rarely, if ever, heard.

Some women's writings point to the paradox of women as life-givers, being forced to co-operate with life-takers or even forced, in many circumstances, to take lives themselves. Much has been written about women's devotion to peace, during both the First World War (Florence, Marshall and Ogden 1915 [1987]) and the Second World War II (Isaksson 1988), as well as about women's work *vis-à-vis* the politics and ethics of peace (Elshtain and Tobias 1990). Other writings, adhering to the dominant discourses about heroism, depict women as soldiers, as resistance fighters, and as nurses (Saywell 1985). Of particular interest is an account of German women recalling life in the Third Reich (Owings 1993). It also seems particularly appropriate that women have been interested in the analysis of literature on the war (Hanley 1991; Cobley 1993). There has been, however, no women's history of any war, nor a women's ethnography about a war.

Martha von Rosen's writing captures some of the many faces of women during war. Her narrative reminds us that women's culture in war, whether in the zone of actual combat (as in her case) or on the home front, is generally under-documented. The actual power of women, too often ignored, emerges, as does their resourcefulness, in dealing with the extraordinary hardships imposed upon them. Women's writings have frequently pointed out that women see little heroism and little romance in the fighting of war. It is difficult, however, to view the accomplishments of Martha von Rosen as anything other than heroic.

The Baltic German Identity

In telling their stories and revealing their traditions, the von Rosens write a cultural portrait of Germanness.[4] "When people tell their life stories, culture speaks through their mouths" (Bertaux-Wiame 1981:260). They emerge as aristocratic Baltic Germans with cherished notions of propriety and purpose. Even under the excessive stress in which they find themselves, they cling to inner and outer markers of identity. In the face of poverty and degradation, they persevere with quiet dignity. If they have anxieties, doubts, angers, they relegate these to private worlds. If there are private wounds, the reader is seldom privileged to learn of them. It almost seems as if, for them, the public world of war and politics slides away, becoming merely an inferred oppression within which a private world is enacted.

The stories centre on family and tradition. Martha von Rosen's begins and ends with family unity. Jürgen von Rosen periodically refers to absent kin, his plans for being reunited with them, his fears about what has befallen them. In what is probably one of the most memorable incidents in the stories, Jürgen writes of hoarding biscuits from his meagre rations to have presents for when he will see his children again.

The restoration and maintenance of identity is also reflected in the family possessions that Martha struggles to protect. She faces many dangers to protect these valuable markers. The pull of the past, the nostalgia for the lost, is evident in every page. Yet, such longings aside, she is a strong matri-

---

4 I am indebted to Karla Poewe for insightful comments about the German identity as projected in the text – the quiet pietism, the almost spiritual link to nature, the small gradations of social rank, the deep commitment to family.

arch, always in charge, defending and nurturing the small group of refugees with almost mythic resolve.

Both husband and wife have a quiet, spiritual connection to nature and a keen awareness of natural life changing and evolving around them. They write approvingly and gratefully of the silent cover of darkness, the beckoning of friendly forests, the light given by the appearance of the moon. Nature is protective and supportive. It breathes with a presence of its own.

Ethnicity remains a supreme moral problem at the end of the twentieth century. Its place in human affairs has been initiated by, and complicated through, the great wars and innumerable numbers of smaller ones. As a demanding issue facing policy-makers of all kinds, ethnicity dominates all kinds of agendas, formal and informal, especially in the West. The subtexts of ethnicity, nationalism and class in the von Rosen stories is perhaps the most important. The history of the Baltic Germans, as seen in their life stories, is one of a closely knit ethnic group now dispersed to many parts of the world. Even as Martha and Jürgen von Rosen thought that the war was transforming their lives, their experiences were becoming a paradigm case for the whole of their ethnic kind. Their odyssey is the wider odyssey of all Baltic Germans.

The history of Germans in the Baltic region stretches from medieval times to the present. The early history of the German presence was tainted with bloodshed as the region was invaded first by the Crusaders intent on converting the indigenous population and later by the Teutonic Knights. This Christian militancy was followed by the arrival of traders and by the Germans claiming possession of Baltic lands. Seeing themselves as bearers of German civilization and culture, the Baltic Germans became a strong economic and cultural influence in the Baltic nations. This state of affairs was to endure through Danish, Swedish and Russian domination and into Estonian independence.

For centuries, the Germans maintained a powerful control over Estonia, where they constituted an integrated, educated and privileged minority, maintaining the German language and marrying other Baltic Germans, despite the passing of centuries. They were a landed upper class, so powerfully ensconced that their privilege continued unchanged throughout various kinds of foreign dominance until 1939.[5] Since then, they have been

---

5   For a scholarly, yet succinct, history of Estonia, see Raun (1987); Haltzel (1981); Parming and Javesco (1978); Lieven (1993).

dispersed throughout the world, in particular to Germany. Some scholars have predicated a diminishing existence for them, in that "they are shrinking fast, and will probably continue to do so, while to some extent held together by family tradition ... and by continued intermarriage among the Baltic German nobility" (Lieven 1993:138).

Beginning in 1939, and continuing in the ensuing years of the war, the Estonia that the von Rosens and other Baltic Germans knew was altered forever and finally incorporated unwillingly into the Union of Soviet Socialist Republics. As Baltic Germans and aristocrats, however, their fate was sealed first by the Bolsehevik Revolution, and later by the ascendancy of the Communists. Both events marked the end of their elite existence. The prelude to the Second World War and the agreement between the Russians and the Germans, the Molotov-Ribbentrop Pact, recalled the German population from the Baltic countries almost completely. The result was that, while in 1881 the ethnic Germans constituted 5.3 percent of the total population of Estonia, in 1922 their numbers had declined to 1.7 percent, and in 1934 to 1.5 percent. By 1945, no Germans were recorded as living in Soviet Estonia.[6] In present-day Estonia, fraught as it is with the complex problems of privatization and the return of property, word of mouth has it that only a few Baltic Germans are returning to the land where they were born. This contrasts with a much higher number of Estonian nationals returning home. By far the largest majority of expatriate Estonians and Baltic Germans appear to have decided to remain elsewhere.

---

6 They were essentially an urban population, constituting, in 1881, 29.3 percent of the urban population. They were the major landholders, holding more than half the land in the country before 1920. As the population of native Estonians in the urban centres grew, this high percentage diminished (Raun 1987:228-31). See also Kirby (1986:274). Apparently about 65,000 Baltic Germans were repatriated in 1939 from Estonia and Latvia (see Misiunas and Taagepera 1983:16). Many Germans welcomed the *Umsiedlung* (repatriation) which occurred from 1939 to 1941, seeing it as a solution to their problems with land in Estonia. When the nation of Estonia had been recreated again in 1919, the government began agrarian reform measures. Large estates were divided into several farms and returned to indigenous Estonians. What remained in the hands of the Germans was core property, such as the main house and farm buildings. The land that was given over to the cultivation of cash crops, however, became Estonian land. Many German landholders, now deprived of the revenue from the crops, fell upon hard times. Thus, in the supposed move to Germany, their *Heimat* (homeland), Baltic Germans hoped to be settled on arable lands commensurate with what they had left behind.

The History of the von Rosens

When the von Rosens and their children drove from Québec to British Columbia in the summer of 1951, they drew curious glances from the inhabitants of the small towns along the way. Instead of the usual motorized family vacationers Canadians were used to seeing, these travellers drove and lived in a dump-truck, carrying all their worldly possessions with them – like vagabonds from another time and place. The fate of many Baltic Germans was epitomized in this journey – from the comforts of pre-war Estonia, to uncertainty in the Canadian West. The von Rosen odyssey had begun in Estonia, and wound its way through the Russian heartland, Siberia, Japan, and, later, through continental Europe. Like many immigrants dispossessed both politically and materially by the Second World War, the von Rosens were determined to make a new life in Canada, where they were destined to become part of that country's diverse population. They settled quite happily in Oliver, a small town in British Columbia's Okanagan Valley. In these particulars, the Baltic German story was similar to that of the wider Canadian immigrant population. Yet the history of the von Kügelgen and von Rosen families reveals the turmoils and migrations which constitute the unique character of the Baltic German portrait.

While Martha von Rosen's family settled in Estonia in the nineteenth century, Jürgen von Rosen's first appeared in Estonia with the Swedish incursion of the sixteenth century. Such historical facts underscore the autobiographical drama of both the von Rosens, as they do the lives of all Baltic Germans. On more than one occasion during the first half of this century, homelessness and flight were forced on the von Rosens and other Baltic German families.

Martha von Rosen was born on June 10, 1904 to Ernst von Kügelgen and his wife Anna Petrovna Tcheremissinof. She was the third daughter, joining Nita and Else, to be followed seven years later by a brother, Werner. Her father was the chief psychiatrist and hospital administrator at Seewald, the only psychiatric institution in Estonia. Although they were not large landowners, the family had many of the privileges enjoyed by other Baltic Germans – a large house, servants, a well-tended garden and grounds, horses, and the kind of prospects and opportunities that could be derived from access to education, from a select social status, and from powerful connections.

On her father's side, Martha was descended from a family of German intellectuals whose connections to Estonia stretched back over two hundred years. Family records date from the fifteenth century, but the family is known to the modern world mainly through the accomplishments of the von Kügelgen artists, the twins Gerhard and Karl, born in Bacharach in 1772.[7]

On her mother's side, Martha von Rosen is descended from the old aristocracy of Russia. The family of her mother, Anna Petrovna Tcheremissinof, was mentioned in records of the year 1613 as being among the Boyars who elected the first Romanov Tsar. Indeed, Anna Petrovna's own father was an adviser to Tsar Nicholas II. Her grandfather, an English architect named William Trewheeler (1798-1860), was equally eminent in creating some of the beautiful buildings and fountains of the small town of Peterhof, about twenty kilometres west of St. Petersburg. Anna Petrovna who plays a large part in her daughter's flight, was herself a gifted woman as both a biographer and essayist. She was most renowned, however, as an icon painter, doing some of her best work in the latter part of her life in Canada.[8]

Jürgen von Rosen's family can be traced to Bogislaus Rosen (1572-1658), who was in the service of both Erik XIV and Gustaf Adolf, succeeding kings of Sweden.[9] In 1561, Sweden, under Erik, began the occupation of parts of Estonia, while other parts of that country were occupied by Russia, Denmark, and Poland. The Swedish occupation was completed by 1625, and the whole of the Estonian mainland came under Swedish control. It

---

7 For a recent publication about the painters Gerhard and Karl von Kügelgen, see Schöner (1982). Both were painters with a wide reputation during their lifetimes, one that has endured into the present century. Gerhard von Kügelgen was a portrait painter whose subjects included German intellectual figures, as well as many European aristocrats: Goethe, Schiller, Herder, Wieland, August von Kotzebue, Caspar David Friedrich, Tsar Paul I, Tsar Alexander I, and Tsarina Maria Feodrovna. He also painted biblical figures: Moses, Saul, David, and Christ and subjects from Greek and Roman mythology. Karl von Kügelgen was a landscape artist, who painted Estonia, Finland, Germany, Russia, the Crimea, Greece, and Italy. The works of both brothers hang in some of the leading galleries of Europe – the Hamburg Art Gallery, the Leipzig Museum of Art, the National Gallery in Berlin, the Goethe Museum, the Tallinn City Art Museum, the Finnish Art Museum, and the Hermitage. It was the son of Gerhard who established the von Kügelgens as a Baltic German lineage. His grandson, Ernst, was Martha's father. In Germany, Wilhelm von Kügelgen (1802-1867), son of Karl, distinguished himself as the author of a renowned work of nineteenth-century German literature – *Jugenderinnerungen eines Alten Mannes (Reminiscences of his Youth by an Old Man)*. It was issued in more than 250 editions and translated into many languages, including Japanese.

8 Anna von Kügelgen has, among other things, produced a biography of Zoege von Manteuffel, see Anna von Kügelgen (1931). Many of the icons she painted are in the collection of the Museum of Anthropology, University of British Columbia.

9 The major reference to the life of Bogislaus von Rosen is Elisabet von Rosen (1938). For Sweden's involvement in the Baltic, see Roberts (1973).

was during this time that Bogislaus Rosen apparently settled on an estate in Estonia, where Jürgen von Rosen's father, Gerhard, was born. In his adult years, he moved to Riga, Latvia, where, as a professor of art, he accepted a position at the Politechnicum. It was there that Jürgen, the third son, was born on 27 November 1907.

In 1919, the Bolsheviks gained control of Latvia. Gerhard von Rosen and his wife, being of German aristocratic backgrounds, were arrested. Because Gerhard was already of advanced years, and deemed socially valuable as a professor of art, he was released. His young wife, however, remained imprisoned by the Bolsheviks. On 22 May 1919, she was executed. With about thirty other Baltic German aristocrats, she was put to death on that infamous day – *Gedächtnistag* – a day still commemorated every year by Baltic Germans everywhere.[10] This event and others like it, marked the Bolshevik intention to create a classless society by force. It filled all Baltic Germans with a sense of great peril. They were determined to avoid Bolshevik domination at all costs.

In the aftermath of this tragedy, the widower von Rosen removed his three sons to safety in Germany. He took Jürgen with him to Berlin, and the other two sons remained with relatives in Lübeck. The old professor had to survive the uncertainties of inflation-ravaged Berlin without steady employment. Jürgen was often shoeless and frequently famished. For long periods, father and son supplemented their meagre meals with mushrooms picked in Berlin's *Grünewald*. In 1927, Gerhard von Rosen died. After nine years of hand-to-mouth existence, Jürgen was rescued from further deprivations by an uncle, Alexander von Rosen, who lived in Estonia and offered him financial support and an education. Alexander was financially comfortable and had interests in a liquor distilling plant, the *Spritfabrik Rosen & Co.* in Tallinn. It was now financially possible for Jürgen to attend the *Kolonialhochschule* in Witzenhausen, Germany. This agricultural college had a good reputation for educating young men in the agricultural sciences and in technology, as well as preparing them for employment as agricultural experts in the pre-Second World War German colonies (particularly in Africa). Jürgen had a great interest in emigrating from Europe

---

10 For an account of this event, as well as other Baltic German experiences, see von Stackelberg-Sutlem (1964). For other works about Baltic Germans, see Küster (1985), Thomson (1976) and Haltzel (1981).

and seeking his fortune far away from the problems which had accumulated for Baltic Germans over the centuries. Despite such early plans, however, Jürgen changed his mind after completing his education, and moved to Estonia, where he had relatives. In 1930, he applied for Estonian citizenship, and consequently, in 1931, along with Estonian males of a certain age, he was conscripted into the anti-aircraft division of the Estonian army. The stage was now set for the meeting with his future wife.

He first met his future wife, Martha von Kügelgen, in 1932. She recalls the occasion of that meeting for many reasons: for the young man's intent silent observation of her, for the excitement she experienced, for her self-conscious pride in the fashionable London hat she was wearing, and for the sense of something momentous happening. This first meeting ended, in keeping with the formalities typical of the time, by her inviting the young man to call on her family. This visit was made at the earliest that propriety permitted – he arrived at the door of her home a mere three days later. This was the beginning of their courtship.

Uncertainty Between Wars: The Exile to Siberia

At the time of this meeting, Martha was already a veteran of the wider fate of Baltic Germans. She had experienced the first of the many enforced expatriations that she was to encounter in her lifetime. These forced changes were to impress themselves indelibly on her character and philosophy. After the beginning of the First World War, the situation of Baltic Germans was drastically altered. Ensconced in the Baltic, Tsarist Russia was pointedly conscious of all Baltic Germans and of their possible collaboration with the enemy, Germany. The von Kügelgens, who had been attending closely to the progress of the war, soon heard news of the intolerable conditions under which young German and Austrian prisoners of war were being transported to remote locations in Siberia – in cattle trains in the dead of winter, wounded, frozen, hungry, and even naked. Anna von Kügelgen, a cultural leader in Estonia's German community, rose to the occasion. Using several rooms of their large house in Seewald, she collected and stored clothing from Baltic Germans, hoping to transfer these items to the prisoners. This was hardly a condoned activity, and when the planned transfer fell through, Anna von Kügelgen decided to take the goods to Moscow herself. She set out by train, alone, for St. Petersburg on the way to Moscow. She had five steamer trunks deposited in the freight car. She was detained by police in St. Petersburg, under suspicion of aiding prisoners. In an excruciatingly tense search, in which she was stripped naked of all her clothing, the police failed to link her to the freight and she was released. The clothing proceeded unhampered to its destination. Her perfect command of Russian and quick-wittedness had saved her from inevitable arrest and from the worst fate of all – disappearing forever.

These acts of charity by Baltic Germans soon came to an end. The Tsarist government decided that those suspected of aiding the enemy, especially the Baltic Germans, were enemy aliens and were to receive the classic Russian punishment, deportation to Siberia for the duration of the war. They were expected to depart within twenty-four hours, leaving their homes and properties unattended. Ernst von Kügelgen, however, as administrator of a hospital, was given preferential treatment and three days in which to find a replacement and to take his leave. The family boarded the train in the full knowledge that they might never return. They took with them all the necessities of life, including two Estonian servants. Their journey ended at the small Siberian town of Yeniseysk, to which many Baltic Germans had already been deported. This included five such families from Estonia.[11] Overcoming the homelessness that faced them, they created the comforts of life for themselves. Ernst von Kügelgen built furniture for his family and provided occasional medical help in lieu of the frequently inebriated village doctor. The pastors and professors developed a schooling system for the children, who went from household to household for their lessons, and Martha recalls this period for its educational richness and sense of community. She also remembers the attention her household attracted from the town, especially when her mother planted a flower and vegetable garden in the desolate landscape. Amidst the deprivations, however, there were exceptional meals of sturgeon and caviar, available, not by the teaspoonful, but by the kilogram.

Life in Siberia was proving to be relatively congenial. But it was not to last. Anna von Kügelgen became seriously ill. Kidney cancer was suspected. The small town was not equipped for surgery and the family requested permission to return to Estonia. The request was denied. The Tsar, however, did give his consent for a journey to Japan. Anna von Kügelgen was imme-

---

11 Among those in the community were the following Baltic Germans from Estonia: Baron and Baroness Girard, Baron and Baroness Stackelberg, Erich von Samson, Pastor Mühlen, and the von Kügelgen family. Other Baltic Germans were Pastor Hahn and his daughter-in-law Frau Sielman, Professor Seraphim, Pastor Stavenhagen, Baron Dellingshausen, Pastor Wuhner, and Lotte von der Vogt. See the photograph on the following page, which depicts some of the Baltic Germans from Estonia together with others from Latvia and Lithuania.

Group portrait of Baltic German exiles at Yeniseysk in Siberia, 1915.
Back row, left to right: *Dr. Ernst von Kügelgen, Pastor Konrad von zur Mühlen, Erich von Samson, Baron Eduard von Stackelberg, Pastor Sielman, Pastor Fritz Stavenhagen.*
Front row, left to right: *Baronin Else von Stackelberg, Baronin Lotte Dellingshausen, Anna von Kügelgen with daughter Martha, Pastor Traugot Hann, his daughter Pastorin Sielman. In the background, to the right, are Anna von Kügelgen's paintings of two scenes in Tallinn, St. Olav's Church, and Fat Margaret.*

diately taken to Tokyo where a highly qualified surgeon pronounced a new diagnosis and to everyone's relief, the dreaded malignancy was not found. The family remained there for a year, and schooling was resumed in an institution in Yokohama run by the small German community.

Meanwhile, political events were moving fast. The Tsar had abdicated, a provisional government had been instituted, and Estonians began to agitate for self-government. The Bolshevik revolution of 1917 replaced the provisional government, and the new powers attempted to establish control in Estonia. With the fall of the Tsar, Baltic Germans were no longer subject to exile. The von Kügelgens decided to return to Estonia and departed from Kamakura on 19 February 1918 on a journey that was to be even more eventful than their trip to Siberia and Japan.[12]

---

12 For a fuller description of these dramatic events, see Martha von Rosen, "Across Siberia: from Reval to Japan and Back," unpublished manuscript, (n.d.).

In trying to board the Trans-Siberian Express in Fusan, Korea, Ernst von Kügelgen was detained by authorities under suspicion of having committed some unspecified crime. Despite the terrifying stress of detention in a foreign country, this event proved to be one of the many acts of providence which seem to characterize Martha's life. The original train, from which they had been removed, was attacked by unidentified marauders and all its passengers simply disappeared.

Von Kügelgen's arrest was eventually declared an error and the small group departed this time on a Mongolian train – fourth class, unbelievably slow, crowded, and lacking in basic sanitary amenities. Charbin, the next major centre and the known southern boundary of Bolshevik influence, was the destination of the von Kügelgens, and also the refuge for those fleeing the Bolsheviks from the north. All trains were stopped there, the town was overcrowded, and some three hundred rail cars were crammed with refugees escaping from the turmoil in Siberia. Fortunately, however, Ernst von Kügelgen obtained a temporary position in a psychiatric hospital, and equally quickly, he took immediate possession of a rail car as the town was overflowing with refugees from the parts of Russia and Siberia occupied by the Communists. Rail car number 2512 was to be home for the von Kügelgens for the next seven weeks.

As soon as the trains began to move again, the family was travelling once more, this time accompanied by another Baltic German, Baron Bodo von Schilling. They carried their own provisions, which they cooked on a primus stove. The journey was painfully demanding. Ernst von Kügelgen and von Schilling were detained and interrogated at the small town of Chabarovsk. They were pressed hard by suspicious officials, but they used their wits to conceal the one serious fact that would have robbed them all of their liberty, namely, that von Schilling was on a mission to rescue Baltic German aristocrats awaiting execution at the hands of the Bolsheviks. To this was added the equally damning fact that he had been a marine officer in the Tsarist navy during the war. Both men were in serious danger but managed somehow to extricate themselves.

Searches of papers and of luggage became regular occurrences. The travellers hid food, kerosene, and medicine. Such necessities were eagerly sought by the thousands who crowded railway stations and small towns along the railway line. One of these early searches was particularly memorable, in that chocolate, the epitome of bourgeois luxury, was discovered among the von Kügelgen possessions. An explanation was immediately demanded.

Sharing this rare luxury with the inspector, and offering him medication to relieve his acute headache, moved the man to issue a document which spared the family future searches until they reached St. Petersburg. This precious document, humble by today's officious standards, folded and unfolded countless times, diverted fifty-six possible searches and enabled the family to proceed unmolested and with some dignity. It stated simply: "These people should not be searched. They are honest people."

After many delays and misadventures, the von Kügelgens and their small party reached St. Petersburg on Easter Sunday, 1918. Immediately they had to contend with the prospect of a search, from which they knew that their small but valuable document could no longer protect them. As rumours of a desperate hunger in St. Petersburg had reached them, the travellers were aware that officials would confiscate any food, however small the quantity. They were also in continual danger from other refugees claiming a share. Upon arrival in St. Petersburg, Ernst von Kügelgen firmly reminded officials of the impropriety of conducting a search, or indeed any official business on Easter Sunday. Before the guards could decide, the family quickly unloaded fifty-two pieces of luggage belonging to them and departed. As they did so, they watched a woman overcome by a large crowd and forcibly separated from the precious packet of butter that she had jealously guarded during a long journey.

A week later the family again boarded a train, this time for Estonia. A lengthy detour was forced upon the train because of the barricades set up by the Germans who now occupied the country. This occupation lasted from February to November, 1918, ending with the close of the World War. This short German occupation had apparently been prompted by, on the one hand, the fact that Moscow had declared Baltic Germans to be traitors, encouraging Germany to move into the country to protect its nationals. On the other hand, the occupation was occasioned by the presumption that there were many conspiratorial efforts by Baltic Germans, as well as by some Estonian leaders, to solicit German help in their attempts to evade a Bolshevik occupation.[13]

The von Kügelgens arrived in the Estonian capital on 19 May 1918. With their usual skill, they avoided the quarantine and delousing that the Germans wanted to impose upon them. They had now been travelling for three months since leaving Japan.

---

13 Quite expeditiously, the German invasion ousted the Bolsheviks and permitted the eventual independence of Estonia to take place without direct Bolshevik interference, as the sources of immediate control were now outside borders of the country. See Raun (1987:104-11).

Estonia was in the throes of considerable political and social strife. The German occupation soon ended. Deftly and judiciously, on 2 February 1920, before the Bolsheviks could establish a permanent stronghold, Estonian leaders managed to bring about the Tartu Peace Treaty with Soviet Russia – a treaty in which the latter recognized Estonian independence. The odds for this happening had been very low indeed. Estonia's geographical position, its alluring natural resources, and its invaluable seaports made it very vulnerable and appealing to the Soviets. Yet despite such great odds, Estonia claimed its much desired independence.[14] This freedom, however, was not to last. Barely twenty years later, the Tartu Peace Treaty was reversed by the Soviets entering the country at the beginning of the Second World War.

Despite the turmoil in the country, the life of the von Kügelgens once more assumed normality. Schooling started again for the children, and the two elder daughters left to attend school in Germany. Nita had decided on nursing and was destined to remain in Germany for the rest of her life. Else went to Marburg to matriculate in preparation for attending the university. As there was no alternative, both had to sign *part pour toujours* (departure for all time) documents, making return impossible. Thus, they agreed to forsake Estonia forever. Meanwhile, Martha, who for most of her life had been tutored privately, now went to school. During the next two years, she attended two different German schools, where, in addition to the usual curriculum, she studied English, French, and German. In her final year, Estonian was added to the curriculum, a late addition, one might argue, for people who were citizens of Estonia. She went on to study book-binding in Tallinn at the *Riigi Kunst-tööstuskool* (National School of Arts and Crafts), and later she continued with the same subject at the Leipzig Academy. On her return to Estonia, she practised this craft in a workshop which her father had outfitted for her at Seewald. Thus she earned her first salary. During the summers, she took over the management of the family *dacha*, Bentota, which she transformed into a retreat for vacationers from Tallinn and overseas.[15]

---

14 Latvia and Lithuania were equally successful in their independence bids.

15 During one of the summers at Bentota, Martha formed a life-long friendship with a vacationing American, Leila Sherman, the daughter of a cotton manufacturer. It was Leila Sherman who made it possible for Martha to visit England in the early 1930s and was instrumental in organizing the von Rosen immigration to Canada. For further references to her, see pp. 89, 273-5.

In 1927, Martha accepted, rashly and to her later chagrin, a teaching position as a one-term replacement at a finishing school near Berchtesgaden in Bavaria. She replaced a relative who was unable to assume the position, and she took upon herself the task of teaching German to English students and English to German students. Like many Baltic Germans, she had ample opportunities to return to Germany, for education and for employment.

This brings Martha von Kügelgen to the meeting with Jürgen von Rosen and their subsequent marriage. Their courtship continued for more than a year. Because both lacked financial resources, their marriage seemed untenable. Coming to the rescue, Anna von Kügelgen suggested the sale of the *dacha* so that the proceeds could be invested in a small farm for the young couple.

A small Estonian farm in the depression years entailed a seven-day work week with no luxuries or conveniences. Many friends and relatives thought that this would be too heavy a price for Martha to pay. Nevertheless, the young couple were married in 1934 and moved to a newly purchased farm, Lepiko, about fifty kilometres from Tallinn. This began their first five years together. The work was indeed more difficult and demanding than Martha could have ever envisioned. Both she and her husband, however, were eager to succeed. In October 1935, a daughter, Else, was born, and in March 1939, a son, Gerhard. By the late thirties, however, it was clear to all that another war was imminent. In September 1939, Germany's invasion of Poland precipitated this event, the beginning of the Second World War.

Repatriation – To Poland

The backdrop to the von Rosen's stories, the conglomeration of events which controlled the lives of millions and decided the fate of all Baltic Germans, was the Second World War. Heralding events to come, the first severe blow fell on them in October 1939. The Baltic Germans learned that the agreement between Hitler and Stalin, concluded in August 1939 and known as the Molotov-Ribbentrop Pact, called for the repatriation of all Baltic Germans to Germany.[16] Once again they were permitted only a few days to

---

16 The Russo-German Non-Aggression Pact was signed on 23 August by Vlacheslav Mikhailovitsch Molotov, the foreign minister of the Soviet Union, and Joachim von Ribbentrop, the foreign minister of Germany. The Pact gave control of the Baltic States to the Soviets. It also freed the Baltic German population from the consequences of this political decision and from subsequent control by the Soviet Union through what was termed *Umsiedlung* (resettlement). This was understood by the people to be a repatriation to Germany. Instead, having dispossessed the Polish people of their lands, Hitler offered the dispossessed Baltic Germans leaseholds in the Warthegau in western Poland.

prepare to leave their homes. Estonians, like colonized people everywhere, looked on the departure of the German upper class with mixed emotions. While released from their demeaning status as subordinates, the Baltic people did not know what further calamities this change might herald. They were to learn very soon that the Pact permitted the Soviets to militarize their interests in Estonia, Latvia, and Finland. Estonia's newly won independence was quickly eroded, first by a mutual assistance pact which had permitted Soviet use of Estonian sea bases, and, later by a pact which cleared the way for the full-scale advance of Soviet troops in June 1940.

For the von Rosens, however, the few days of grace prior to departure mercifully turned into weeks, and the work on the von Rosen farm continued as if nothing was happening. A harvest of potatoes was taken from the ground. Meanwhile, preparations for departure were made in a desperate hurry and belongings were packed and transported to the station in anticipation of transfer to the docks. A resettlement committee appointed an overseer to attend to the affairs of the farm. By the end of October, therefore, the von Rosens and the von Kügelgens, along with other Baltic Germans, were on their way to what they thought would be Germany. They were never to see Estonia again. Nor were they to go to Germany.

Without any information or any explanation, they found their lives had radically departed from their expectations. After a voyage to the German port of Stettin, they were surprised to be travelling eastward by train through a landscape many recognized as Poland. Deprived of both food and information, hunger and fear were soon upon them. The train finally stopped at Posen (Poznań) in central west Poland. Baltic Germans, it appeared, were intended to replace Polish farmers as supervisors in this long-contested land. The von Rosens were quickly settled on a dilapidated estate near Hohensalza, and the von Kügelgens in the neighbouring city of Posen. The Nazis offered Ernst von Kügelgen a leading position at a psychiatric hospital. He refused, arguing that he was now too old for such a demanding undertaking.

The supervision of the Polish farm went well, the von Rosens seemed to be escaping much of the war. Then, the dreaded event happened. Jürgen von Rosen was drafted in 1941 into the anti-aircraft arm of the *Afrika Korps* and ordered to Italy. He was replaced on the farm by a German who showed himself to be both officious and inhumane, and who in quick order destroyed whatever trust and loyalty the von Rosens had instilled in the farmhands. Martha and her young children moved in with her parents in Posen until she was able to arrange another position for herself. Eventually, she was placed at a Geppertsfeld estate near Jarotschin in western Poland, in a district that the Germans called the Warthegau. She moved there with her children to take upon herself the management of the estate. To make her existence more bearable, she was successful on several occasions in prevailing upon the German authorities to grant leave to Jürgen, arguing that he was an agricultural expert and could give instructions and assistance in managing the estate. Then came the threats of the oncoming Soviet advance, the family's isolation, and the terror of occupation that preceded the end of the war. The von Rosen and von Kügelgen experiences reflect the universal turmoil war inflicted on countless numbers. The odyssey from Estonia to Poland and finally to Canada completed a family and ethnic saga. It is a formidable example of the struggles of many displaced persons who eventually became Canadians.

Bibliography

Aichinger, Peter. 1975. *The American Soldier in Fiction, 1880-1963: A History of Attitudes toward Warfare and the Military Establishment.* Ames: Iowa State University Press.

Aldridge, John W. 1951. *After the Lost Generation: A Critical Study of the Writers of Two Wars.* New York: Farrar, Straus and Giroux.

Bacque, James. 1989a. *Other Losses.* Don Mills, Ontario: Stoddart.

———. 1989b. "The Last Dirty Secret of World War Two." *Saturday Night* 104:31-8.

Barman, Jean. 1988. "Accounting for Gender and Class in Retrieving the History of Canadian Childhood." *Canadian History of Education Association Bulletin* 5:5-27.

Beidler, Philip D. 1982. *American Literature and the Experience of Vietnam.* Athens: University of Georgia Press.

Bertaux-Wiame, Isabelle. 1981. "The Life History Approach to the Study of Internal Migration." In *Biography and Society: The Life History Approach in the Social Sciences,* edited by Daniel Bertaux, 249-65. Beverley Hills, CA: Sage.

Broadfoot, Barry. 1974. *Six War Years: Memories of Canadians at Home and Abroad.* Toronto: Doubleday.

———. 1985. *The Veterans' Years: Coming Home from the War.* Vancouver: Douglas and McIntyre.

Caplan, Pat. 1992. "Spirits and sex: a Swahili informant and his diary." In *Anthropology and Autobiography,* edited by Judith Okely and Helen Callaway, 64-81. London: Routledge.

Cobley, Evelyn. 1993. *Representing War: Form and Ideology in First World War Narratives.* Toronto: University of Toronto Press.

Crouter, Natalie. 1980. *Forbidden Diary: A Record of Wartime Internment, 1941-1945.* New York: Burt Franklin.

Cruikshank, Julie. 1990. *Life Lived Like a Story*. Vancouver: University of British Columbia Press.

Dundes, Alan. 1975. "Seeing is Believing." In *The Nacirema: Readings in American Culture*, edited by James P. Spradley and Michael A. Rynkiewich, 14-9. Boston: Little Brown.

Elshtain, Jean Bethke and Sheila Tobias. 1990. *Women, Militarism, and War: Essays in History, Politics, and Social Theory*. Savage, Maryland: Rowan & Littlefield.

Etter-Lewis, Gwendolyn. 1991. "Black Women's Life Stories: Reclaiming Self in Narrative Texts." In *Women's Words: The Feminist Practice of Oral History*, edited by Sherna Berger Gluck and Daphne Patai, 43-58. New York: Routledge.

Florence, Mary Sargant, Catherine Marshall and C.K. Ogden. 1915 [1987]. *Militarism versus Feminism: Writings on Women and War*. London: Virago.

Frank, Anne. 1952. *Anne Frank: The Diary of a Young Girl*. Garden City, NY: Doubleday.

Fraser, John. 1989. "Slow-Death Camps." *Saturday Night* 104:13-14.

Fussell, Paul. 1975. *The Great War and Modern Memory*. London: Oxford.

Games, Sonia. 1990. *Escape into Darkness: the Story of a Young Woman's Extraordinary Survival during World War II*. New York: Shapolsky.

Gault, John. 1989. "A Story He Didn't Want to Know." *Saturday Night* 104:43-6, September.

Haltzel, Michael H. 1981. "The Baltic Germans." In *Russification in the Baltic Provinces and Finland, 1855-1914*, edited by Edward C. Thaden *et al.*, 111-204, Princeton, NJ: Princeton University Press.

Hanley, Lynne. 1991. *Writing War: Fiction, Gender and Memory*. Amherst: University of Massachusetts Press.

Hansen, J.T., A. Susan Owen, and Michael Patrick Madden. 1992. *Parallels: The Soldiers' Knowledge and Oral History of Contemporary Warfare*. Chicago: Aldine.

Harrison, Charles Yale. 1930. *Generals Die in Bed*. New York: Morrow.

Horner, Helmut. 1991. *A German Odyssey: The Journal of a German Prisoner of War*. Golden, CO: Fulcrum.

Hurmence, Belinda, ed. 1984. *My Folks Don't Want Me to Talk About Slavery: Twenty-One Oral Histories of Former North Carolina Slaves*. Winston-Salem, NC: J. F. Blair.

Isaksson, Eva, ed. 1988. *Women and the Military System*. New York: Harvester-Wheatsheaf.

Jacobs, Harriet A. 1986. *Incidents in the Life of a Slave Girl Written by Herself*, edited by Maria Child and Jean Fagan Yellin. Cambridge, MA: Harvard University Press.

Jones, Peter G. 1976. *War and the Novelists: Appraising the American War Novel*. Columbia, MO: University of Missouri Press.

King, Thomas. 1993. *Green Grass, Running Water*. Boston: Houghton Mifflin.

Kirby, David. 1986. The Baltic Germans. In *The Soviet Union and Eastern Europe*, edited by George Schopflin, 272-9. New York: Praeger.

Küster, M.F. 1985. *The Baltic-Germans: Reminiscences.* Edmonton: Central and East European Studies Society of Alberta, Ethno-cultural Groups in Alberta Study Project.

Lejeune, Philippe. 1989. *On Autobiography.* Minneapolis: University of Minnesota Press.

Lieven, Anatol. 1993. *The Baltic Revolution: Estonia, Latvia, Lithuania and the Path to Independence.* New Haven, CT: Yale University Press.

Luborsky, Mark R. 1987. "Analysis of Multiple Life History Narratives." *Ethos* 15:366-81.

Lyotard, Jean-François. 1984. *The Postmodern Condition: A Report on Knowledge.* Minneapolis: University of Minnesota.

Mailer, Norman. 1948. *The Naked and the Dead.* New York: Rinehart.

Mandelbaum, David G. 1973. "The Study of Life History: Gandhi." *Current Anthropology* 14:177-96.

Marrus, Michael R. 1985. *The Unwanted: European Refugees in the Twentieth Century.* New York: Oxford.

Misiunas, Romuald J. and Rein Taagepera. 1983. *The Baltic States: Years of Dependence 1940-1980.* Berkeley: University of California Press.

Okely, Judith. 1992. "Anthropology and Autobiography: Participatory Experience and Embodied Knowledge." In *Anthropology and Autobiography,* edited by Judith Okely and Helen Callaway, 1-28. London: Routledge.

Oring, Elliott. 1987. "Generating Lives: The Construction of an Autobiography." *Journal of Folklore Research* 24:241-67.

Orwell, George. 1938. *Homage to Catalonia.* London: Secker and Warburg.

Owings, Alison. 1993. *Frauen: German Women Recall the Third Reich.* New Brunswick, NJ: Rutgers University Press.

Parming, Tonu and Elmar Javesco, ed. 1978. *A Case Study of a Soviet Republic: The Estonian SSR.* Boulder, CO: Westview Press.

Perdue, Charles L. Jr, Thomas E. Barden, Robert K. Phillis, Federal Writers Project, ed. 1976. *Weevils in the Wheat: Interviews with Virginia Ex-Slaves.* Charlottesville: University Press of Virginia.

Poewe, Karla. 1988. *Childhood in Germany During World War II: The Story of a Little Girl.* Lewiston, NY: Edwin Mellen.

Raun, Toivo U. 1987. *Estonia and the Estonians.* Stanford: Hoover Institution Press.

Roberts, Michael, ed. 1973. *Sweden's Age of Greatness 1632-1718.* London: Macmillan.

Saywell, Shelley. 1985. *Women in War.* New York: Viking.

Schöner, Hans. 1982. *Gerhard v. Kügelgen: Leben und Werk.* Carius, Kiel: Satz und Druck.

Tamke, Susan S. 1977. "Oral History and Popular Culture: A Method for the Study of the Experience of Culture." *Journal of Popular Culture* 11:267-79.

Terkel, Studs. 1984. *"The Good War": An Oral History of World War Two.* New York: Ballentine.

Thomson, Erik. 1976. *Who are the Baltic-Germans? A Short History.* Edmonton: Canadian Baltic Immigrant Aid Society.

Vickers, Jeanne. 1993. *Women and War.* London: Zed.

von Kügelgen, Anna. 1931. *Werner Zoege von Manteuffel: Professor der Chirurgie in Dorpat 1857-1926: Lebensbild in Briefen, Erinnerungen und Worten seiner Freunde und Schüler.* Stuttgart: Ausland und Heimat Verlags-Aktiengesellschaft.

von Rosen, Elisabet. 1938. *Bogislaus Rosen aus Pommern 1572-1658: Stammvater des Estländischen Geschlechts der "Weissen" Rosen.* Tartu: Herausgegeben von Familienverband der "Weissen" Rosen.

von Stackelberg-Sutlem, Eduard Freiherr. 1964. *Aus meinem Leben: Die Kriegsjahre 1914-1918 Verschickung nach Sibirien.* Hannover-Dohren: Verlag Harri von Hirschheydt.

White, Hayden. 1980. "The Value of Narrativity in the Representation of Reality." *Critical Inquiry* 7:5-27.

Wicks, Ben. 1989. *No Time to Wave Goodbye.* Toronto: Stoddart.

INDEX

Adelheim, Herr and Frau, 105
Adige Line, 152n
Adriatic Sea, 170, 182, 196
AE1 *(Alarmeinheit 1)*, 141n, 142
Aerial bombardments, xix, 33, 37-8, 38n, 39n, 42, 43, 46-9, 53-5, 67, 84, 106, 125, 126, 139n, 141n, 146-7, 152, 266
Afrika Korps, xviii, 133, 168-69
Aibling, Germany, 201, 214, 215, 217, 219, 229, 231
Aichinger, Peter, 288, 306
Aken, Germany, 83
Aldridge, John W., 288, 306
Allie(d) Forces, xvi-xvii, xix, 47, 53, 55-6, 58, 59, 77n, 79, 135, 140n, 143n, 147n; D-Day, xix; liberation of Paris, xix; occupation, 93n; and refugees, 58, 290 *See also* American, British, French, Russian
Alps, Mountains, 147, 157
Alsace, workers from, 232
Altenbeken, Germany, 119
American(s), attitudes towards, 79, 105, 210, 231; as captors, 135, 210, 220, 231; citizen, 114-15; culture, 285; "death camps," 136n; Eighth Army, 135; Fifth Army, 135; forces (troops), 47, 49, 56n, 79, 105, 122, 139n, 191, 196, 287; guards, 207, 210, 213; Ninth Army, 47n; officers, 204; POWs (prisoners) of, xi, 136n, 191, 194, 196, 200, 204, 205, 207, 209, 210, 213, 215, 216, 220, 228, 231, 239n; and refugees, 105, 120-21; relations with Russia, 231; soldiers, 122, 133n; visa, 278; Zone, 56n, 72n, 79, 82, 105, 119, 120, 121, 193-94, 197, 232, 243 *See also* United States
Ami(s), 120, 121
Ancona, Italy, 160, 169-70, 178, 179, 180, 188
Anglo-American: drive into Germany, 139n; Zone, 193 *See also* American, British
anti-air craft, 139n, 141n; Afrika Korps, xviii, 133, 305
Arenshausen, Germany, 118
aristocracy, Baltic German, xvii-xviii, 290, 294
Arkade, Italy, 141, 143, 144, 145, 146, 151, 152n, 160

Arronet, Dora, 11 (illustration)
Attichy, France, 211, 213, 214, 215, 216, 218, 229, 242
Augsburg, Germany, 190, 249, 268
Austria(ns) 106, 169, 170, 172, 176, 192, 193, 210, 218, 232, 234, 236, 298
Autobahn, 35; Breslau-Berlin, 50n
autobiography, as forgotten culture, 287
avanti, 142, 143
Axis *See* German

Bacque, James, 136n, 306
Bad Aibling, Germany, 269
Bad Liebenswerda, Germany, 13, 40
Baltic States, xvii-xix, 45, 78, 284, 293-94, 298; annexing of, xviii, 294, 294n, nationalism, xvii-xviii *See also* Estonia
Baltic Germans, xvii-xix, 5n, 32n, 78, 98, 114, 170, 171, 192, 284, 292-94, 295, 297, 298-302, 304, 304n, 305; perceived by Russians, 298-99
Baltic Sea, xix, 7
Barden, Thomas E., 287n, 308 *See* Perdue
Barman, Jean, 286, 306
Baumann, Frau, 5, 14, 15, 20
Bavaria(n), xvi, 7, 118, 123, 130, 140n, 196, 218, 248, 250-52, 304
Beaverbrae, 273
Beidler, Philip D., 288, 306
Belgium, xix, 204
Bellaria, Camp 14, Italy, 139-192, 210; German HQ, 179, 181, 191
Belluno, Italy, 12, 141, 157, 158, 160
Berchtesgaden, Germany, 304
Berlin, 7, 20, 35, 36, 47, 48, 50, 53, 66, 67, 81, 88, 142, 293; bombing, 49
Bernburg, Germany, 13, 93, 95, 96, 98, 101, 105, 108, 109, 111, 116, 119, 121, 128, 217
Bertaux-Wiame, Isabelle, 292, 306
Beuthen (Bytom), Poland, 24
Bingen, Germany, 267
Bischofstein, Schloss, 117
Bitterfeld, Germany, 96
Black Sea Germans, 42

Blainville, France, 214
Blitz Mädel, 204
blue railway workers, 186, 204
Bober (Bóbr) River, Poland, 13, 33
Bohemia, 171n
Bologna, Italy, 13, 140n
Bolshevik, 16, 20, 33, 42, 50, 52, 56, 57, 78, 84, 106, 297, 301-02; and classless society, 297; occupation of Baltic, 297, 302; revolution, xviii, 294
Bolshi, 40
bombing *See* aerial bombardment
Borch, Count and Countess von der, 5, 11, 14-16, 23, 25-28
Borowiak, 15, 19, 30, 32-34, 37, 39, 51, 56
Boyars, 296
Bozen, Austria, 200
Braunschweig, Germany, 53
Bremen, Germany, 12, 273
Bremke registration station, 105
Brenner Line (Pass), Austria-Italy, 197, 199, 200
Breslau, Poland, 13, 35, 36n, 50n
British, attitudes towards, 105, 118, 166, 172, 231; camp, 55, 165, 187, 288; documents, 105n, 108; forces (troops), 56n, 127, 141n, 145, 157, 158-59, 166, 287; guards, 166, 191; looting (pilfering), 159, 163, 164, 172-73; occupation, 105, 145; officers, 162, 166, 179, 189; official documents, 105; as POWs (prisoners), 40-41; POWs (prisoners) of, 135, 146, 159, 165, 167-68, 171-73, 177, 180, 182, 184, 188-90, 193, 200, 215, 231; and refugees, 105, 130; Royal Air Force, 38n, 39, 166; soldier(s), 120, 164; Zone, 79, 80, 82, 104, 105, 108n, 118, 120, 189, 196-98, 202 *See also* English
British Columbia, Canada, 273, 275, 276, 295
Broadfoot, Barry, 287, 306
Buda, 11, 15, 19, 26, 32, 33, 37, 38, 55, 56
Bulgaria, xix
Burg, Germany, 48, 80
burshui, 57
Byelorussia, xix, 36

California, 274, 275
camp(s); administration, 178, 180, 183, 227, 242; army 58; authorities, 180, 181; choir, 189, 240; civilian, 233; command, 173, 180, 182, 187, 189, 191; concentration, 57, 59, 71, 76, 190, 288, 290; "death camps," 136n; German commanders, 173, 180; Falkenberg, 252; French, 214; German, 75, 87, 221, 227, 233; guard(s), 191; international, 170; Kölleda, 115, 116; labour, 204, 212, 282, 284; leader, 172, 175, 221, 227, 229, 235, 240, 243; library, 237; main, 168, 169, 172, 175, 176, 218; officers, 171; physician, 173, 227, 233, 243; police, 213, 229; prisoner of war, 75, 87, 116, 135, 136, 169, 173, 178, 179, 180, 182, 183, 186, 190, 194, 195, 196, 198, 204, 209, 212, 219, 244, 247, 250, 282, 284, 285; provision, 55; rations, 187; Russian, 176; transit, 168, 169, 172, 176, 179, 183; Camp 5, 190, 212, 213; Camp 5a, 213; Camp 5d, 190; Camp 11, 179, 184, 185, 186, 190, 192, 193, 196, 198, 205; Camp 11a, 192, 193; Camp 13, 204; Camp 14, 185, 187, 190, 196, 212; Camp 14a, 190; Camp 17, 183, 185, 187, 192, 194, 195, 201, 202, 216
Canada, xvii, 23, 55, 138, 273-75, 278, 287, 295, 296, 306
Cannstadt, Germany, 268
Caplan, Pat, 286, 306
Carpathian(s) Mountains, xix
Caserta, Italy, 135
Castelfranco, Italy, 141, 160
Catherine the Great, decree by, 42n
Chabarovsk, Siberia, 301
Châlon-sur-Marne, France, 209
Champagne, France, 107, 206
Charbin, Siberia, 301
chess, 174, 175, 176, 177, 186, 187, 189, 206, 287
Chiaravalle (Chiasavalle), 160, 170
Clayton, Gerry, 277
Cobley, Evelyn, 288, 289, 292, 306
Columbia River, Canada, 277
Comacchio Lake, Italy, 141, 160
Cominco (Consolidated Mining and Smelting Company), 277
Communist(s), xviii, 88, 93, 232, 290, 294, 301; German, 78, 94
Compiègne, France, 213
Conegliano, Italy, 141, 144, 147, 155, 156, 157, 158, 159, 160, 167
Cosswig, Germany, 13, 43
Crouter, Natalie, 288, 306
Crowsnest Pass, British Columbia, 276
Cruikshank, Julie, 286, 307
Czechoslovakia(ns), xix, 7, 12, 13, 171, 172, 176

D-day, xix
"death camps," American, 136n
Denmark, 293
Dessau, Germany, 43, 53
diary, and experience, 135; of Jürgen von Rosen, xv, 133-38, 139ff, 284, 290
Disarmed Enemy Forces (DEF), 136n
displaced persons, xix, 290, 291 *See also* refugees
documents, 33, 105, 106, 107, 113, 118, 128, 153; *part pour toujours*, 303
Donauwörth, Germany, 268
Dora (battery), 11, 139, 147
Dorna, Germany, 42
Dresden, Germany, 12, 13, 38, 39, 53; bombing of, 38, 125
Dümelin, Frau, 64, 69, 71, 72
Dundes, Alan, 285n, 307

East Prussia, 11, 12
Eastern Front, 38n, 42; railway, 7; Zone, 94, 105, 108, 114
East/West division of Germany, 93
Eichwald, Poland, 13, 16
Eighth Army, United States, 135
Eighth Army Air Force, United States, 38n
Eisenhower, General Dwight D., 67n, 136n
Elbe River, Germany, 9, 13, 41-43, 46, 47, 49, 53, 54, 56-59, 60, 63, 65, 69, 72, 75-77, 79, 80, 83, 85, 92, 126
Elshtain, Jean Bethke, 291, 307
Elsner, Herr and Frau, 60, 64, 66, 68
Engelbrechten, Baron, 81
English, captivity, 177, 198, 230, 231; dictionary, 97, 175, 243; forces (troops), 47, 49, 72, 79, 159, 161, 162, 168; guards, 162, 196; language, 101, 105, 138, 175, 190, 243; newspaper, 166, 175, 243; POWs (prisoners), 40-41; Zone, 194 *See also* British
English Channel, 12
Epinal, France, 213
Erik XIV of Sweden, 296
Erling, Germany, 269
escape(s) *See* prisoners of war
Estonia(ns), xvii, xviii, 4, 5, 11, 21, 32, 46, 48, 65, 93, 96, 98, 106, 112, 223, 277, 290, 291, 292, 293, 294, 295, 296, 297, 298, 299; anti-aircraft, 293; army, xviii, 293; citizenship, 293; culture, 282; expatriate, 291; German community, xviii, 32n, 292-98; independence, 293, 300, 302n, 303; property, 294; psychiatric institute, xviii; sea ports, 303

ethnography, analysis, 284; and autobiography, 284-85, 287; collaborative, 285; of forced labour camps, 284; of homelessness, 286-87; realist accounts, 289; of women in war, 284
Etter-Lewis, Gwendolyn, 287n, 307
Ettal, Bavarian Monastery, 130
Euskirchen, Germany, 82

Falkenberg, France, 245, 250, 252, 255; camp, 252
Feltre, Italy, 160, 161
Ferdl, 252, 253, 254, 256, 257, 260, 261, 263, 264, 265, 266, 268, 269
Ferrara, Italy, 160, 168
fieldwork(er), collaborative, 285; and ethnography, 286; eyewitnessing, 285-86; life as, 285; storyteller as, 284-85
Fifth Army, United States, 135
Finland, 305
Florence, Italy, 160, 288
Florence, Mary Sargent, 291, 307
FMG, 139, 140, 141, 143, 144, 145, 146, 163
Foggia, Italy, 170
Forbach, France, 228, 233, 245, 249
forced labour, 135, 177, 179, 187, 204, 207, 209, 210, 213, 217, 219, 220, 226, 229, 233, 236, 245, 282; brick factory, 209; farms, 209, 245; work quotas, 219, 225, 230, 232, 236, 242 *See also* prisoners of war
Forces *See* Allied, American, British, French, German, Russian
Foreign Legion, 216
Forli, Italy, 160, 168, 171, 175
France (French), attitudes towards, 228, 231; campaigns, xix; camps, 214, 233, 236, 239, 241, 288; civilians, 224, 235, 245, 247, 273, 287; forces (troops), 290; front, 189; guards, 263; hunger camps, 239; Nazis, 180-81, 235; newspapers, 231; POWs (prisoners) of, 107, 135, 214ff, 288; reconstruction of, 228; refugees, 262; soldiers, 266; Zone, 197, 202, 232, 268
Frank, Anne, 288n, 307
Frankfurt, Germany, 13, 87, 123
Frankfurt-am-Main, Germany, 12, 204
Fraser, John, 136n, 307
Fraser River, British Columbia, 277, 279
Frauenstein, Herr, 96-97
Freedom Place, Estonia, 238
Freystadt (Kożuchów), Poland, 13, 26
Friedland, Germany, 105, 118

Front(s), Eastern, xix, 7n, 38, 42, 47; First Byelorussian, 36; home front, xvii; in Italy, 5; news from, 3; Southern, 139, 140, 166, 194; Western, 47 *See also* American, British, French, Russian fronts, Zones
Fusan, Korea, 301
Fussell, Paul, 287, 307

Games, Sonia, 288, 307
Gammel, Frau, 42
Garmisch, Austria, 201, 203
Gault, John, 136n
Gedächtnistag, 297
Geneva Convention, 135, 239
Genoa, Italy, 135
Geppertsfeld, Poland, xviii-xix, 3, 5, 6, 8, 9, 10, 13, 35, 36, 39, 50, 68, 115, 306
Germany (Germans), aircraft, 48; appropriation of property, 53; attitude towards, 14, 184, 198, 207, 215; Black Sea, 42; camp commander, 173, 180, 221; camp physician, 233; camp police, 213, 229, 266; captured, 55, 135, 220-21; civilians, 200, 206, 288n, 297; colonies, 297; communists, 78n, 88, 93-94; defeat, 135, 139-59, 166; defences, xix, 8, 47, 55, 57, 50n, 135, 139n 166; dismantling base, 139ff; as enemy, xvii; forces (troops), 8, 27, 36n, 50n, 133, 135, 139n, 166, 171n; guards, 40; identity, xvii, 42, 169, 170, 171, 176, 192, 194, 292; interest in Baltic, xviii, 293; invasion of Poland, 304; Italian alliance, 143; looters, 180; military, 43, 47, 133; Molotov-Ribbentrop Pact, xviii, 78, 294, 304; nationals, 171, 242; occupation of Estonia, xvii, xviii, 292-94, 302; occupied, 105n; officer(s), 17, 19-21, 32, 64, 173; Polish, 192; POWs (prisoners), xvii, 135, 136n, 141, 161, 171, 177, 189, 193, 198, 207, 215, 216, 248, 251-52, 263, 265, 268, 288, 291, 298; reputation, 207, 215; retreat, 10, 18, 26; Russian threat to, 14; from Schwaben, 42; soldier(s), 19, 26, 32, 43, 53, 55, 56, 135, 141, 148, 153, 167, 180, 200, 288; SS, 142, 177, 180, 202; Sudeten, 169, 170, 176, 192; surrender, 55, 93n, 105n, 135, 231, 232, 288, 291; unconditional surrender, 67; women, 291 *See also* Baltic Germans, Nazi(s)
Gestapo, 173
Ghengis Khan Line, 140
Glogau (Głogów), Poland, 36n, 50n

Golden, British Columbia, 276
Gommern, Germany, 13, 56, 61, 64, 70, 71, 72
Gorgast, estate, Poland, 7, 9, 48
Görlitz, Germany, 13, 36
Gostingen (Gostyn), Poland, 13, 18
Göttingen, Germany, 105, 119
Gräfelfing, Germany, 269
Grünbaum, Jan, 5, 11, 15, 19, 27, 28, 29, 30, 31, 32, 33, 34, 37, 39, 40, 41, 47, 50, 51, 52, 56, 58, 59, 93
Grünberg (Zielona Góra), Poland, 26
Gustaf Adolf of Sweden, 296
Güsten, Germany, 103, 116

Hahn, Baron Alexis, 17; Werner, 18 *See also* von Hahn
Halle, Germany, 43
Haltzel, Michael H., 297n, 307
Hanley, Lynne, 288, 307
Hanover, Germany, 47, 53, 119
Hanseatic League, xvii
Hansen, J.T., 288, 307
Harrison, Charles Yale, 288, 307
Harz Mountains, Germany, 81, 93, 103, 126
Heideberg, Germany, 37
Heidekrug, Germany, 13, 24
Heiligenstadt, Germany, 117
Hermitage Museum, St. Petersburg, 32n, 296n
Heusweiler, Germany, 265
history, Allied, 135; alternate, 287; and appropriation, 283; biography and 284; as experience, xv-xvii; eyewitnessing and, 285; of forgotten lives, 284; nature of xv, xvii, 286, 288, 289; World War II, 287
Hitler, Adolf, xviii, 73, 74, 76, 78, 144, 171, 304
Hohenlochau, Germany, 42, 43, 45, 47, 55, 57, 79, 80, 82, 110
Hohensalza, Poland, 5, 13, 48
Holzkirchen, Germany, 107, 269
homelessness, 286-87, 289-90, 295
Horner, Helmut, 136n, 288, 307
Hoyerswerda, Germany, 13, 37
hunger, xv, 19, 87, 97, 123, 130, 181, 232, 239, 242, 267, 297, 298, 302 *See also* prisoners of war, refugees
Hurmence, Belina, 287n, 307

icons, 130, 275, 277, 278, 279, 296
Inglesi, 158
Inn River, Switzerland, 130
Innsbruck, Austria, 200

Iron Cross, 133, 134, 210
Isaksson, Eva 291, 307
Italy (Italian), xvii, 107; Afrika Korps in, xviii, xix; 133, 305; civilians, 141, 148, 154, 162, 173; front, 5; Germans in, 133, 135, 141, 142, 143, 154-58, 202, 206, 216, 219, 233; guards, 191; liberation, 135; looters, 142, 149; partisans, 133, 135, 141, 142, 143n; POWs (prisoners) in, 135, 170, 231, 240; soldiers, 157, 200

jabo, 134, 183
Jacobs, Harriet A., 287n, 307
Jan *See* Grünbaum
Japan, 21, 191, 288, 299-300, 302
Jarotschin (Jarocin), Poland, xviii, 8, 13, 14, 16, 50, 115, 306
Javesco, Elmar, 293n, 308 *See* Parming
Jodl, General Alfred, 67n
Jones, Peter G., 288, 307
Jörn *See* von Rosen, Jürgen

Kaiserslautern, Germany, 265, 266
Kalmucker, 63
Kamakura, Japan, 300
Kames, Herr, 56, 59, 72, 126
Karling, Germany, 258, 259, 260, 262, 263
Karlsruhe, Germany, 207
Kassel, Germany, 105, 119, 122
Kehl, Germany, 207
Keitel, General Wilhelm, 67n
Kesselring, Field Marshal Albrecht, 139
Keyserling, Graf, 114
Kicking Horse Pass, British Columbia, 276
Kienast, Fritz and Cora, 111-12, 116
Kienast, Dr. Herman, 96, 111
King, Thomas, 283, 307
Kirby, David, 294n, 307
Kirchhain, Germany, 51-52
Kirgiser, 63
Klein Rosseln, 218, 219, 238, 239, 242, 243
knowledge, nature of, 286, 288, 289
Knowlton, Québec, 273
Kölleda, Germany 115, 116
Köln (Cologne), Germany, 143
Kolonialhochschule, 297
Költsch, Germany, 25, 26
Konev, Marshal Ivan, 36n, 47n
Kootenays, British Columbia, 277
Kortnitz (Kórnik), Poland, 13, 27
Koskull, Baroness Elisabeth, 18
Kottbus, Germany, 13, 36, 37, 39, 50, 51, 52

Krauschwitz, Germany, 36
Krause, Frau and Herr, 68-69, 70, 74, 86, 88, 98
Kreuzwald (Creutzwald), France, 259, 260, 263
Krohla, Poland, 35
Krummacher, Pastor, 95
Kuster, M.F., 297n, 308
Küstrin, Poland, 7, 36, 50

Laim, Germany, 105, 106, 107
Landroff, Germany, 245, 247, 249, 250
Landsberg, Germany, 48
Latvia, xvii, 284, 297, 299n, 303n
Lauterbach, Germany, 263
Leine River, Germany, 119
Leinefelde, Germany, 116
Leipzig, Germany, 28, 43, 297
Leipzig Academy, 303
Leitzkau, Germany, 9, 13, 35, 39, 42, 43, 45, 48, 53, 54, 55, 56, 64, 82
Lejeune, Philippe, 287, 308
Lenin, Vladimir Ilyich Ulyanov, 118
Lepiko, farm, Estonia, 223, 304
Lieven, Anatol, 293n, 308
Lindenberg, Christoph, 107
Lindenberg, Dr. Horst, 114
Lindenberg, Nita (née; Nita von Kügelgen), 42, 72, 105, 107, 108, 111, 113, 114, 116, 123, 125, 140, 269, 295, 303
Lipie, estate, Poland 5, 7, 48
Lissa (Leszno), Poland, 13, 19, 20, 21, 42, 50
Lithuania, xvii, 284, 299n, 303n
Litzmannstadt, Poland, 9, 10, 13, 21
Livonia, 32
Livorno, Italy, 200
London, England, 298
Lönewitz, Germany, 13, 41
Lorraine, France, 224, 232
Lothringen, Germany, 218, 249
Luborsky, Mark K. 289, 308
Ludweiler, Germany, 262, 263, 265
Ludwigshafen, Germany, 266, 267, 268
Luftwaffe, 133, 134
Lüneburg, Germany, 67n
Lutheran Church, 111
Lyotard, Jean-François, 288, 308

Madden, Michael Patrick, 288, 307 *See* Hansen
Magdeburg, Germany, 9, 43, 46, 47, 53, 64, 67, 72, 79, 83, 86, 91
Magdeburg-Altkönigsborn road, 84
Mailer, Norman, 288, 308

Index

Mainz, Germany, 267
Mandelbaum, David G., 286, 308
Mannheim, Germany, 181, 267, 268
Mantua, Italy, 135
map, 21, 22, 37, 103, 162, 247, 248, 250, 258, 259, 260, 262, 263, 268, 279
Marrus, Michael R., 290, 291, 308
Marseilles, France, 216
Marshall, Catherine, 291, 307 *See* Florence
Martha *See* von Kügelgen, Martha; von Rosen, Martha
Massdorf, Poland, 34
Memel, Lithuania, 7, 12
Merlebach, France, 258
Mestre, Italy, 160, 168
Metz, France, 214, 218, 243
Misiunas, Romuald J., 294n, 308
Mission, British Columbia, 279
Molotov-von Ribbentrop Non-Aggression Treaty, xviii, 78, 294, 304
Mongolia(n), 63, 301
Montebellino (Montebelluna), Italy, 153, 160
Moscow, Russia, 298, 302
Mückeberg, Germany, 13, 40
Münchausen, Baron, 9, 45, 46, 47, 50, 55, 57, 80; Baroness Lotte, 47, 55
Munich, Germany, 7, 42, 72, 73, 80, 82, 97, 103, 105, 106, 107, 113, 116, 122, 123, 125, 130, 140, 142, 196, 197, 199, 201, 206, 216, 217, 265, 269
Muskau, Germany, 13, 36
Mussolini, Benito, 142, 143

Nahrstädt, Germany, 48
Nancy, France, 207, 213, 214, 244
Naples, Italy, 200, 242
narratives, authenticity of, 283; authority, 286; as culture, 292; heroic, 289; sub-texts, 283; survival, 289; of war, 289 *See also* Stories
National Safety Service, 39, 41
National School of Arts and Crafts, Tallinn, Estonia, 303
National Socialist Peoples' Welfare (N.S.V.), 29, 62
Nazi (Party), 56, 69, 78n, 115, 125, 143, 149, 202, 235, 287, 305
Neff, Timoleon, 32, 39
Neiden, Germany, 41, 42
Neisse River, Germany, 13, 36, 47
Neisse-Oder line, 36
Nervesa, Italy, 143, 144, 145, 152, 160
Neusalz (Nowa Sól), Poland, 13, 25, 26

Neustadt, Germany, 266, 267, 268
New York, U.S.A., 274, 275
Nielitsch, Poland, 13, 22
Nordhausen, Germany, 103, 116
Nordheim, Germany, 119
Nördlingen, Germany, 268
Norway, 219

Obergefreiter, 133, 134
occupation, Allied, 93; British, 105; laws, 95; Russian, 63, 93; Swedish, 293; terror of, 306; troops, 76, 265; Western, 101
Odenwald, Germany, 197
Oder-Neisse line, 50, 93
Oder River, Germany, 13, 23, 24, 25, 26, 36, 47, 50, 87, 93
officer(s), military, 17, 19-21, 30, 32, 35, 46, 61, 64, 65, 67, 68, 74, 85, 97, 128, 146, 147, 149, 153, 155, 157, 158, 159, 162, 165, 166, 167, 171, 173, 177, 178, 179, 180, 185, 191, 203, 204, 239, 301
Ogden, C.K., 291, 307 *See* Florence
Okanagan Valley, British Columbia, 277, 291
Okely, Judith, 285, 308
Olds, Albert, 280
Oliver, British Columbia, 276, 277, 278, 295
Oring, Elliott, 286, 308
Orwell, George, 288
Ösel (Saaremaa), Estonia, 98
Ostrów, Poland, 14
OT (*Operation Todt*), 143, 181
Other Losses, 136n
Ottawa, Canada, 275
Ottersleben, Germany, 46, 73, 93
Owen, Susan, 288, 307 *See* Hansen
Owings, Alison, 291, 308

Paderborn, Germany, 119
Padua, Italy, 152, 160
Panzer, 17, 142, 143
Paris, France, xix, 216, 227, 242, 266; liberation of, xix
Parma, Italy, 135
partisan(s), 133, 135, 141, 142, 143, 144, 145, 146, 147, 149, 151, 152, 153, 154, 155, 156, 157, 158, 159, 161, 162, 166, 167, 176, 180, 181, 197, 198 *See also* Italian
Parming, Tonu, 293n, 308
Pasing, Germany, 206
Paulshuben, estate, Poland, 13, 19
Perdue, Charles L. Jr., 287, 308
Petacci, Clara, 143n

Peterhof, Russia, 296
Petrovna Tcheremissinof, Anna, 111, 295, 296 *See also* von Kügelgen, Anna
Pforzheim, Germany, 268
PG (*prisonnier de guerre*), 220, 232
Philadelphia, U.S.A., 273
Philippines, 288
Phillis, Robert K., 287n, 308 *See* Perdue
physician, 32, 173, 227, 233, 243, 295
Piave River, Italy, 149, 152, 153, 160, 161, 162, 163
Pleschen (Pleszew), Poland, 14
Po River, Italy, 141, 144, 147, 160, 168, 202, 207, 213, 235
Poewe, Karla, 288n, 308
Poitiers, France, 244
Poland (Polish), xvii, xviii, xix, 4, 5, 6, 9n, 10, 11, 14, 15, 49, 78, 93, 133, 169, 170, 175, 191, 192, 304, 305, 306
  police, 128, 178, 180, 181, 182, 183, 213, 229, 257, 266, 275, 298
Ponte Priula, Italy, 152, 167
Posen (Poznań), Poland, xviii, 4, 5, 7, 9, 12, 13, 14, 27, 28, 87, 305
Potsdam Conference, 93
POWs *See* prisoners of war
Pretsch, Germany, 13, 41
prisoners of war (POWs), xv, xvii, 40-41, 93, 113, 135, 136, 138, 142, 143, 146, 153, 157, 159, 163, 171, 174, 180, 189, 191, 194, 214, 216, 242, 259, 284, 285, 287; camps, xvi, xvii, 135, 136, 153, 172, 174, 178, 179, 189, 209, 211, 214, 219, 242, 247, 250, 259, 286, 288, 290, 292; Christmas, 238-39; classification of, 169, 170, 171, 172, 175-76, 181, 182, 185-86, 192, 203, 290-91; clothing, 229, 230, 232; coal mines, 218, 219, 221-24, 234; deaths, 181, 186, 207, 232, 235; English, 40-41; entertainment, 176, 185, 189-90, 204, 221; escape(s), 161, 177, 180, 184, 216-17, 220, 224, 229, 231, 232, 233, 234, 235, 238, 240, 241, 243, 247, 250; experience, 135; food, 165-66, 172, 177, 179, 184, 185, 195, 202, 204, 205, 206, 213, 216, 218, 220, 221, 225, 227, 232, 235, 236, 237, 238, 239, 244, 245; French, 135; and Geneva Convention, 135; German, 135, 167, 288, 298; gossip, 228, 231; guards, 40, 165, 166, 169, 178-79, 213, 214, 218, 221, 224, 233, 250, 263; labour, 135, 177, 179, 187, 204, 207, 209, 210, 213, 217, 219, 220, 226, 229, 245; lectures, 185, 190; letters, 167, 171, 189, 191, 232, 234, 240, 243; lice, 168, 170, 176, 181, 197, 201, 210; looting by, 59; luxuries, 212, 215; marches, 136, 137, 159ff, 177, 191; New Year's Day, 240; news, 167, 181, 188, 231; police, 180, 213; punishment, 180-81, 187, 190, 215, 217, 220-21, 224, 243; reading, 175, 188-89, 197, 219, 243; registration of, 176, 195, 196, 197, 202, 205, 215, 231; release of, 176, 182, 190, 193, 200, 203, 204, 212, 240, 242; rumours, 190, 191, 197, 225, 231; Russian, 86-88, 176; shelter, 164-65, 168, 178, 182, 183, 186, 187, 188, 212, 214, 226, 245; sick and wounded, 173, 193, 201, 203, 213, 217, 232, 233, 235, 236, 241-42, 243; sport, 173, 182, 184, 186, 187, 188, 196; thievery, 165, 170, 172, 173, 180, 181, 187, 215, 220, 224, 228; trade among, 169. 172, 175, 220, 229, 233, 238; trains, 177, 199-200, 213-14; washing, 175, 181, 216, 219
Pretzien, Germany, 13, 57, 58, 62, 64, 65, 70, 71, 72, 73, 75, 77, 78, 79, 81, 88, 89, 91, 96, 116
Prosna River, Poland, 10, 13
Prussia, East, 11, 12
Putschversuch, 142

Québec, Canada 273, 274, 295

radio, 9, 29, 60, 64, 145, 166, 204; English, 9;
railway, 7, 16, 48, 51, 58, 69, 94, 107, 117, 119, 127, 159, 170, 171, 177, 182, 183, 185, 193, 194, 198, 199, 200, 204, 206, 207, 214, 219, 222, 241, 245, 251, 252, 256, 258, 260, 261, 265, 266, 267, 298, 301-303; people (blue), 204
ration(s), 28, 69, 94, 97, 99, 100, 125, 172, 173, 182, 185, 187, 194, 195, 199, 201, 206, 210, 212, 213, 217, 227, 232, 248; cards, 28, 94, 125, 199, 201, 217
Raun, Toivo U., 293n, 294n, 308
Red Cross, 41, 114, 227, 228, 232
reform, agrarian, 94, 96
refugee(s), xv, xvii, xix, 10, 16, 17, 18, 21, 22, 28, 29, 30, 38, 39, 41, 42, 46, 49, 50, 55, 58, 59, 66, 68, 74, 78, 81, 88, 94, 115, 116-17, 121, 122, 125, 130, 250, 273, 290-92, 297, 298-302, 306; armed, 16, 64; Baltic Germans as, 284, 294, 299-302, 306; camps, 40, 116, 118, 120-21, 130; culture

of, 286; dead, 19, 38; delousing, 302; escaping Russians, 8, 10, 17; flow of, 290; outwitting Russians, 82, 101, 103-105, 110, 113, 129, 301; and permits, 83, 114, 115, 116, 118, 120, 122, 125, 128, 301, 302; shelter, 120, 123; thievery, 302; trains, 117, 119-20, 121-23, 128, 130, 301-302, 305
Reich Minister of Armaments and Munitions, 143
Reims, France, 67n, 209
Reminiscences of his Youth by an Old Man, 95, 296n
resettlement, 5, 300, 304-305
resistance, 135, 146, 282, 290; German, 135; writing, 288, 289
Rhine River, Germany, 56, 207, 214, 266, 267
Rhineland, Germany, 59, 73, 119, 187, 192
Ried, Bavaria, 107, 115, 123, 140, 196, 206, 269
Riga, Latvia, 50, 292
Rimini, Italy, 160, 177-87, 188, 193-94, 197-99, 201-04, 212, 214, 215, 221, 240
Roberts, Michael, 296n, 308
Rosenheim, Germany, 201, 269
Rosenstein, 187, 188, 189, 193
Rosslau, Germany, 13, 51
Royal Air Force, 38
Rubicon River, Italy, 187
Ruhr, Germany, 126
Rumania, xix, 12, 171, 192
Russia(n), 63, advance, xix, 7-9, 14, 16-17, 20, 26, 29-30, 32-36, 47-49, 58, 80, 133, 287, 290, 305-306; agrarian reform, 94, 96; attitudes towards, 29, 30, 60, 62, 63, 67, 69, 73-74, 228, 231; and Baltic, xviii, 303; border, 82, 103, 121, 126; camp, 176; defeat, 21, 29; forces (troops), 9, 10, 20, 21, 36, 56, 68, 79, 105, 235; guard, 82, 103, 111, 129; "hunters of women," 85; language, 97, 111, 112, 127, 299; looters, 60, 61, 62, 64, 66, 67, 78, 80; occupation, 63-65, 56-57, 61, 66, 69-71, 76-78, 82-86, 93n, 96-97, 101, 104-105, 109, 116, 118, ; officer(s), 65, 67, 68, 73, 74, 97, 128; officials, 73, 86-88, 97, 108, 110, 111, 301-302; old aristocracy, 296; pact with Germany, 294, 304; POWs (prisoners), 59, 74-75, 89, 176; and refugees, 74, 97, 127; release of prisoners, 86-88, 231, 232; Siberia, 20, 61, 63, 87, 298-301; soldiers, 56, 59, 61, 62, 63, 66, 71-72, 74, 80, 85, 86, 95, 96, 127, 176, 198; tanks, 20, 29, 35, 58, 59; Treaty with Estonia, 303; Tsarist, 298; Zone, 79, 82, 94, 104-105, 108n, 121, 125, 126, 128, 193, 194, 197, 200, 217, 231

S.S., German, 10, 49, 52, 53, 77, 89, 142, 177, 178, 180, 181, 182, 185, 202, 204, 211, 212, 236
Saale River, Germany, 100
Saar River (district), Germany, 218, 228, 249, 265
Saaralb, Germany, 214, 218, 219, 220, 221, 229, 230, 239, 243
Saarbrücken, Germany, 12, 214, 217, 265
Saarburg, Germany, 214
Saaremaa, Estonia, 98
Saarlander(s), 234, 236, 242, 244
Sagan (Żagań), Poland, 13, 34, 35
Salnikoff, 66, 67, 68, 76
Saxony, Germany, 184
Saywell, Shelley, 291, 308
Schalkau, estate, Germany, 16
Schatzdorf, estate, Germany, 18, 46
Schauer, Dr., 109
Schleife, Germany, 36
Schlesiersee, Poland, 13, 23, 24
Schloss Leitzkau, Germany, 64
Schoen, Mr., 274, 275
Scholefield, Sergeant Major, 141, 144, 151
Schöner, Hans, 296n, 308
Schröder, Dr., 125
Schröter, Pastor, 95, 99, 103, 109, 110; Renate, 99, 103
Schwerin (Skwierzyna), Poland, 111
Sczyfter, Herr, 5, 10, 14, 15
Seewald, Estonia, xviii, 5, 295, 298
Senftenberg, Germany, 13, 38, 39
Sepp, 252, 253, 264, 266, 267, 268
Sherman, Leila (Lee), 89, 273-75, 303n
Siberia, 20, 61, 63, 87, 298-301
Silesia, Poland, 7, 16, 26, 198, 216, 217
Social Democrat, 73, 181
social science, and representation, 283
Soissons, France, 213
soldier(s), 16-17, 26, 27, 28, 31, 32, 38, 39, 51, 54, 55, 56, 59, 60, 61, 62, 63, 64, 65, 66, 67, 69, 70, 71, 72, 73, 74, 75, 76, 77, 78, 79, 80, 81, 84, 85, 86, 89, 95, 96, 106, 107, 110, 115, 120, 122, 127, 128, 135, 141, 142, 148, 153, 157, 163, 164, 166, 168, 172, 176, 179, 180, 181, 189, 195, 200, 231, 232, 266, 285, 288, 291, 305 *See also*

American, British, French, Italian, German, Russian soldiers
Solveigh Company, Germany, 97, 110, 112
Sorau (Żary), Poland, 13, 35
Sörchen, Poland, 36
Soviet (Union), xviii, 9, 50, 303; advance, 306; army, 36; incorporation of Estonia, 294, 305; military, 50, 305; offensive, 9; troops, 10 *See also* Russia(ns)
Spanish Civil War, 285
Spittel mine, 259-60, 262
Spreewitz, Germany, 37
Spremberg, Germany, 13, 36, 37
Spresiano, Italy, 142, 144, 145, 146, 147, 160, 164
Spritfabrik Rosen & Co., Tallinn, 297
Sprottau (Szprotawa), Poland, 7, 13, 27, 29, 34, 35, 39
St. Augustine, Québec, 274
St. Avold, France, 214, 236, 238, 239, 247, 250, 251, 252, 255, 257, 258, 259
St. Charles, France, 227, 229
St. Fontain, France, 260
St. Nikolas Church, Estonia, 4
St. Petersburg, Russia, 32, 296, 298
Stalin, Josef, 78, 118, 304
Steiner, Dr. Rudolph, 274
Stendal, Germany, 46, 48, 49
Stettin, Germany, 88, 305
Stollberg, Count (Graf), 29, 84
stories *See* Narratives
Strasbourg, France, 214, 215
Stromberg, Baroness Thea, 106, 125
Stuttgart, Germany, 12, 107, 108, 247, 268
Sudeten, 169, 170, 171, 176, 192
surrender, German, 67, 135, 136n, 139n, 147n, 153, 154, 158, 288, 291
Susegana, Italy, 152, 153, 160, 163, 164, 167, 169
Swabia, 42
Sweden, 106, 293, 296
Switzerland (Swiss), 106, 108, 109

Taagepera, Rein, 294n, 308 *See* Misiunas
Taku River, British Columbia, 278
Tallinn (Reval), Estonia, 4, 238, 297, 303, 304
Tamke, Susan S., 287, 308
Tarent (Taranta), Italy, 176
Tartar, 63, 65
Tartu Peace Treaty, 303
Tcheremissinof, Anna Petrovna *See also* Petrovna, Anna; von Kügelgen, Anna

Terkel, Studs, 287-88, 308
"Terror without End," 67
Teutonic Knights, xvii, 293
Third Reich, 291
Thomson, Erik, 297n, 309
Tito, Marshal Josip Broz, 157, 166
Tobias, Sheila, 291 *See* Elshtain, 307
Tokyo, Japan, 300
Tommy (British), 145, 152, 157, 158, 164
Torgau, Germany, 40, 42, 47
Toul, France, 207
Trakehner, Prussia, 11
Trans-Canada Highway, 275
Trans-Siberian Express, 301
Treuenbrietzen, Germany, 55, 75, 87
Treviso, Italy, 142, 144, 147, 149, 152, 153, 154, 160, 164
Trewheeler, William, 82, 296
Trieste, Italy, 160, 176
Tsar(ist), government, 298, 300
Tsar Nicholas II, 32, 296, 299, 300
Tucholsky, Dr., 50, 52
Tulsequah , British Columbia, 277, 278
Tungusers, 63
typhoid and typhus, 27, 83, 101
Tyrol, Italy, 200

Uckro, Germany, 51
Ulm, Germany, 268
Umsiedlung (resettlement), 5n, 294n, 304-305
Ungern-Sternberg, Baron Herman, 18
Union of Soviet Socialist Republics (U.S.S.R.), 294 *See also* Soviet
United States (U.S.), 121, 243, 275, 288; Eighth Army, 135; Eighth Army Air Force, 38n, 39n; Ninth Army, 47n; POWs in, 242 *See also* American
University of British Columbia, 279, 296n

Valdobbiadene, Italy, 160, 162
Vancouver, Canada, 278, 279, 280
Venice, Italy, 135, 160
Verona, Italy, 135, 141, 160, 193, 195, 196, 199
Verschlüsse, 153, 154
Vickers, Jeanne, 291, 309
Vietinghoff, Field Marshal, S. von, 139
Vietnam, 288
Vistula River, Poland, 9, 13
Vittichy, France, 209
Vittorio Veneto, Italy, 156, 158, 160
Vohburger Strasse, Munich, Germany, 105, 107, 269

Völklingen, Germany, 262, 263, 265
Volksdeutsche, 171
Volkssturm, 143, 144
von Brevern, Herr, 64, 65
von Grünewald, Frau, 55, 56, 80
von Hahn, Baron Werner, 18 See also Hahn
von Harpe, 46, 48
von Hentig, Helga, 269
von Horn, family, 3, 15, 22, 29
von Kügelgen(s), xviii, 93, 295-96, 298, 300-302, 305; ancestral house, 95-96
von Kügelgen, Alexander (Sandy), 45
von Kügelgen, Allo, 43, 82
von Kügelgen, Andrea, 82
von Kügelgen, Anna (née Anna Petrovna Tcheremissinof), 6, 111, 276, 295, 296, 296n, 298-300, 304, 309; in Canada, 274-79; death, 279; icons, 130, 275, 277, 278, 279; illness, 299-300; as translator, 63, 73, 97, 110, 111, 116, 127, 128
von Kügelgen, Else, 295, 303
von Kügelgen, Ernst, xviii, 5, 6, 295-96, 299, 302, 303, 305; arrest, 301; death, 130; heart attack, 94, 130; as translator, 73, 97, 110, 116, 127, 128
von Kügelgen, Fritzi, 9, 42, 43, 45, 55-56, 58-59, 72, 106, 114
von Kügelgen, Gerhard, 82, 296
von Kügelgen, Karl, 296
von Kügelgen, Martha, 4, 295, 298, 299, 303-304 See also von Rosen, Martha
von Kügelgen, Nita, 42, 72, 105, 107, 108, 111, 113, 114, 116, 123, 125, 140, 269, 295, 303 See also Lindenberg, Nita
von Kügelgen, Werner, 18, 29, 81, 82, 83, 106-107, 111, 117, 291
von Kügelgen, Wilhelm, 32n, 95
von Lieven, Xenia, 279
von Lilienfeld, Christa, 47
von Oppeln, Fräulein, 98, 109
von Rosen(s), xvii-xix, 5, 8, 9, 11, 18, 33, 46, 48, 77, 284, 286, 287, 288, 289, 290, 291, 292, 293, 295-98, 304-306
von Rosen, Alexander, 297
von Rosen, Bengt, 108
von Rosen, Bogislaus, 80, 296-97
von Rosen, Elisabet, 296n, 309
von Rosen, Elizabeth, Baroness, 5, 7, 14-16
von Rosen, Else, 4-10, 18, 33, 43, 46-49, 57-58, 60, 68, 73, 75, 83, 88, 89, 94, 96, 98, 99, 100, 103, 115-17, 119, 120, 123, 130, 226, 240, 273, 276, 278, 279, 280, 304

von Rosen, Eva, 115
von Rosen, Gerhard, 4-6, 14-17, 20, 26-28, 30, 36-40, 45, 54, 57, 58, 68, 73, 75, 82-83, 100-101, 103, 110, 116, 117, 119, 121-23, 276, 279, 304
von Rosen, Hillo, 106
von Rosen, Jürgen, xv-xix, 4, 5, 14, 20, 45, 106-108, 113-15, 122, 123, 125, 130, 133-38, 278, 290, 292, 295-98, 304-306; arrival in Canada, 273; attitudes towards other prisoners, 180, 181, 184, 186, 187, 188, 198, 199, 207, 215, 216, 224, 229, 233, 235, 243; capture by British, 158; carving, 177, 187, 206; clothing, 156, 220, 221, 227, 237; cold, 241-42, 250; conscription, xviii, 133, 305; as diarist, xv-xvi, 137-38, 290; disappearance, 278; escape, 114, 161, 216-17, 238, 247ff; and family, 292; farm work, 125, 130, 133, 134, 206, 244, 245, 274-75; and German retreat, 139-59; letters to wife, 107, 140, 167, 193, 196, 203, 206, 218, 226, 232, 234, 238, 243; meeting with Martha, 298; mine(s), 218, 221ff, 233, 235-36, 277; news, 141-43, 166, 175, 204, 232, 236, 243, 269; penknife, 164, 171, 175, 210, 287; permits, 125, 153, 232; possessions, 150, 161, 177, 206, 209, 211, 251; presents for children, 184, 205, 206, 210, 215; as prisoner, xv-xvi; prisoner of Americans, 207ff; prisoner of British, 158ff; prisoner of French, 214ff; reading, 219, 231, 237, 243; registration, 215; schooling, 297; shoes, 178, 192, 210, 290; sickness, 231, 236, 237, 238, 239, 242, 244, 245; wedding of, 4, 304 See also Diary, prisoners of war
von Rosen, Martha (née Martha von Kügelgen), xv-xviii, 4, 5, 6, 14, 43, 59, 72, 73, 107, 108, 133, 138, 140, 276, 290, 292-93, 295-96, 298-306; arrival in B.C., 275-77; birth, 295; to Canada, 273, 303n, 306; escaping Russians, 76-77, 81, 299; exile to Siberia, 298, 299-300; and family, 292; farm work, 273-75; horses, 11, 15, 17-18, 26, 27, 29, 35, 36, 40, 49, 50, 53, 57, 59, 60, 62, 65, 76, 81, 82, 84, 85, 86, 89, 92, 94, 95, 96, 97, 126, 290; in Japan, 299-300; letters, 111, 113-15; marriage, 4, 304; marriage to Albert Olds, 280; meeting with brother, 81-82, 106-107; meeting Jürgen, 304; meeting with sister, 105-106, news from husband, 106-107, 113-15; permits, 115, 129, 274,

302; possessions, 50-52, 56, 59, 60, 61, 64, 66, 69, 78, 80, 116, 119, 128, 274; relations with Russians, 66, 68-69, 73, 74, 75, reunion with husband, 123; as translator, 61-62, 273; schooling of, 303; search for husband, 278; supervision of farm, 305; *Umsiedlung*, 304-305 *See also* Reminiscences
von Rosen, Paula, 109
von Rosen, Tatjana, 108
von Rosenstiel, family, 5, 18, 33, 46, 48
von Rundstedt, Field Marshal Gerd, 139n
von Schilling, Bodo, Baron, 7, 301-302
von Stackelberg-Sutlem, Eduard Freiherr, 297n, 309
von Stritzky, Irmgard, 3, 8, 15, 22, 28, 29, 56, 80

Wanzleben, Germany, 46, 47
Warburg, Germany, 120
Warsaw, Poland, xix, 7-9, 12, 13
Warthegau district, Poland 5, 6, 12, 13, 53, 56, 65, 306
Wasserburg, Germany, 130, 269
Wehrmachtbericht, 142
Weisswasser, Germany, 13, 36
Wendel mine, 221, 227-28
Western Zone, 128, 200
Westerwald, Germany, 192
White, Hayden, 289, 309
White, Emma, 273
Wicks, Ben, 288n, 309
Wittenberg, Germany, 13, 42, 43

Witzenhausen, Germany, 297
women in war, xvii, 26, 35, 55, 65, 66, 67, 69, 70-71, 72, 74, 75, 85, 89, 121, 127, 141, 144n, 155, 156, 202, 207, 264, 284, 286, 288, 291-92; and peace, 291; and rape, 84-85; writings of, 291-92
World War, First, xviii, 228, 288, 291, 301, 302
World War, Second, xv, xvii-xix, 284, 287, 288, 290, 291, 294, 297, 298, 303, 304-306; ethnography of, 288; experience of, xv, xvi; mythology of, xv; official histories, xv, xvi, 287; oral histories of, 287; survival stories, 288; texts, 287; women and peace, 291

Yalta Agreement, 79
Yeniseysk, Russia, 299
Yokohama, Japan, 300
Yugoslavia(n) partisan, 166

Zerbst, Germany, 13, 43
Zhukov, Marshal Georgi, 36, 47, 67
Zoege von Manteuffel, Heinrich, 32n, 296n
Zone, 225, 234, 236; American, 72, 105, 119, 120, 193, 194, 197, 232, 243; Anglo-American, 193; British, 80, 104, 105, 197; combat, 289; danger, 268; divisions, 205; Eastern, 93n, 94, 105, 108, 114; fighting, 51; French, 197, 202, 232, 268; neutral, 108, 115; occupied, 194, 196, 202; Russian, 82, 104, 105, 108, 125, 126, 128, 193, 194, 197, 200, 217, 231; sorting by, 211; Western, 128, 200
Zörbig, Germany, 65